HERBS

Acknowledgements

It would not have been possible to complete this book without the help of many people. We are particularly grateful to Duncan Donald, curator of the Chelsea Physic Garden, for checking the text so thoroughly and to Martyn Rix for checking the identifications and answering many questions. We would also like to thank the following gardens and herb suppliers for allowing us to visit them frequently and photograph their plants: Bateman's, Barnsley House Garden, The Chelsea Physic Garden, Eccleston Square Garden, Hollington Nursery and Garden, Iden Croft Herbs, The Royal Botanic Garden Kew, Michelham Priory, Hardwicke House, The Royal Horticultural Society Garden at Wisley, The Savill Gardens in Windsor Great Park, The Stephen Pearce Pottery, Suffolk Herbs, The Westonbirt Arboretum and the Herb Society.

Among others who have helped in one way or another we would like to thank: James Compton, Ros Forster, Harry Hay, Judith Hopkinson, Jacqui Hurst, Christopher Lloyd, Stephen Pearce and Kim Mai Mooney, Rosemary Verey, Phillippa Voss, Anne Thatcher, Phillippa Staniland.

The authors and publishers believe the information contained in this book to be correct and accurate at the time of going to press. The book is not intended to be a guide to medical self-treatment with herbs. If you think a plant might be useful in helping with a particular ailment, consult a doctor or other medical expert. It is essential to be sure of the identification of any herb or plant before cooking or using it medicinally. If in any doubt, don't. Neither the authors nor the publishers can accept any legal responsibility or liability for errors or omissions that are made.

First published 1990 by Pan Books Ltd
This paperback edition published 1992 by Pan Books Ltd,
a division of Pan Macmillan Limited,
Cavaye Place, London, SW10 9PG
9 8 7 6 5 4 3 2
Text © Roger Phillips & Nicky Foy 1990
Illustrations © Roger Phillips 1990
ISBN 0 330 32600 7
Photoset by Parker Typesetting Service, Leicester
Printed by Toppan Printing Co. (Singapore) Pty. Ltd

HERBS

ROGER PHILLIPS & NICKY FOY

Layout by Jill Bryan

A Pan Original

For Sam, Phoebe and Amy

Contents

Introduction 6
Glossary 11
Culinary herbs 12
Salad herbs.. 46
Vegetables 56
Berries 61
Herb teas 66
Scented herbs 68
Strewing herbs 82
Dye plants 84
Medicinal herbs....................................... 90
Useful Addresses 186
Bibliography... 187
Index.. 188

A tunnel of scented sensations at Suffolk Herbs

Introduction

The use of herbs for medicine and cooking probably dates back over 60,000 years. Of the eight species of flowering plants' pollen which were found in the grave of Neanderthal man in Iraq, seven were from plants still found in the area in the twentieth century and which are still used for medicine.

Herbal medicine has been practised for thousands of centuries by tribes all over the world and the knowledge that was first gleaned by observation and trial and error was passed on orally from one generation to another. Eventually this knowledge was recorded in lists, one of the earliest being that of a Chinese herbalist Shen Nung who, in 2800 BC, made a list of 366 plant drugs. In the first century AD Dioscorides wrote his authoritative herbal, *De Materia Medica*, which was the prototype for all future works on the subject.

In ancient Greece herb suppliers, known as *rhizotomoki* (root gatherers) provided physicians with herbs, presumably gathered from the wild, but in Britain the earliest records of herbs being grown specifically for medicine was in the seventh century. With the advent of Christianity monks, whose duty it was to care for the sick, established physic gardens in their monasteries for growing the most commonly used medicinal plants.

From the earliest times until the end of the nineteenth century plants have been the most common source of medical treatment yet, during the twentieth century, this vast body of knowledge has been swept aside in favour of the mass produced chemical medicines, which, while saving countless lives in certain fields, have not proved to be the universal panacea that researchers had hoped for. Now, again, the pendulum is swinging back to research into medicinal plants and their chemistry.

There are somewhere in the region of 25,000 plant species recorded for the whole world of which about 2,500 have traditionally been used for medicinal purposes. To date, about 250

plants have been thoroughly investigated to discover whether there is a scientific explanation for their reputed effects. As a result, many new complex chemicals have been discovered; some easily reproduced in the laboratory, others extremely difficult to reproduce and thus much more easily obtained from the plants themselves. Furthermore, plants have been developing ways of protecting themselves against diseases and viruses for millions of years and it is highly probable that scientists will find hundreds, perhaps thousands, of new medicines from plants during the next century. It is imperative therefore, that we do not eliminate sections of this enormous, virtually untapped and as yet unknown, bank of plant knowledge. We must accept that man is but a part of the total world ecology; if he becomes too dominant the whole structure will be in danger of collapse. Man must resist destroying plants which have managed to survive in the wild for millions of years and thus, through selection, produced chemicals of enormous complexity that can provide knowledge for mankind on which the health of the world and its future survival may depend.

The pendulum has swung back; medical scientists are again investigating plant sources for our health.

The Aim of this Book

The aim of this book is to provide a comprehensive illustrated guide to over four hundred plants that are loosely termed 'herbs'. For many people herbs immediately conjure up the idea of food and, indeed, many are primarily used in cooking. For others, herbs are mainly associated with medicine and, until the present century, they were the principal ingredients in medicines that were used to cure every conceivable ill, for kings and paupers alike. Although over the last hundred years chemical medicines have largely replaced herbal medicines, there has been much interesting modern research into a number of traditional herbal

A view of the historic Chelsea Physic Garden founded in 1673

medicines. This research has scientifically analysed the plants' constituents and helped to explain and verify the beneficial effects that they have long been credited with. The science of using herbal medicines to treat the sick is known as phytotherapy.

Apart from the herbs or plants most commonly used for cooking or medicine or both, the term 'herb' in this book also refers to plants that can be used to make teas, salads and dyes, and also includes scented plants and those used for strewing. The book is arranged into these categories and although numerous herbs could be put into more than one section (for instance for making teas and also, in the past, for strewing) basically the plants are put into the category with which they are most commonly associated. For example, there are several different camomiles each of which is used for a different purpose so the different species will be found in different sections of the book. It should also be noted that while leaves are the most frequently used part of the plant, in many instances the flowers, stems, seeds, berries or roots are also used.

Planting a Herb Garden

When faced with planting between fifty and two hundred plants, the majority of which are rather small, you must first devise a system which will keep the groups and types well separated so that you will be able to go quickly and easily from plant to plant.

The solution is to have a series of small beds, not more than an arm's length from edge to centre, so that picking and cutting can be carried out with ease. The divisions to the beds can be made a feature of the garden in themselves. Perhaps the most satisfactory solution is to plant Box hedges and keep them clipped to about 30 cm (12 in) high. The hedges can be laid in complex or graphic designs to provide a year-round feature in the garden. Planting a knot garden with Box hedges and filling the centre area with herbs of different foliage and flower colours and heights serves to augment the original shapes of the knot patterns and also makes an interesting addition to a garden. There are lots of other ways of solving this problem: small brick or stone walls, paths laid with stone, brick or gravel paths, or even narrow grass paths can be decorative and functional. A series of raised beds perhaps 75 cm (30 in) high is one way of also doing away with much of the backache of weeding at the same time. If you have a small back garden or a patio garden, the best idea may be to plant the whole herb garden in pots. Many herbs, especially those from the Mediterranean area, are used to fairly dry conditions: thymes, sages, bay trees, nasturtiums and lavenders will all certainly do well, but remember that even these plants from hot, dry areas will benefit from watering so the pots should be as large as possible. I use quite a bit of peat and leaf-mould in my mixture to ensure reasonable water retention but I am also rather lucky in that my soil is totally free of clay.

The herb garden at the Royal Horticultural Society, Wisley

A tub garden in Eccleston Square

Tubs on a brick terrace

The lovely knot garden, Barnsley House

A series of beds divided by brick walls

Hollington's herb garden

Narrow paths amongst the culinary herbs

Whichever way you decide to plant your herb garden, it is worth putting a lot of thought into both the design and planning of the beds' surrounds. Choosing which herbs to plant in your garden is one of the great pleasures of gardening.

How to Use the Book

The plants are organized in nine sections, covering the main areas for which herbs are used. These are culinary herbs, salad herbs, vegetables, berries, teas, scented herbs, strewing herbs, dyeing herbs and medicinal herbs. The photographs show the plants, either individually or in groups, that appear at similar times of year – some are studio shots with the plants laid out on a plain background; others show the herbs growing in their natural habitat or in a herb garden. Occasionally a variety is shown as well as the main species. The plants are arranged as far as possible, chronologically in order of flowering, within their sections.

The first part of the text for each plant covers distribution and habitat and gives a brief description of the plant. The main body of the text deals with the history of the plant and summarizes its traditional uses in cooking, medicine, cosmetics or whatever. If a plant is still used by modern herbalists a recipe for an infusion or ointment may be given and, where appropriate, information about modern research and scientific confirmation of empirically held beliefs and uses for plants, is also given. Finally, where appropriate, there is a brief paragraph on how to grow the herb in a garden or window box. Sometimes we have included related species, in addition to the main plants in the book, either because they are well-known for their use in cooking or medicine or because, although their medicinal value has not been thoroughly investigated, they are frequently grown in herb gardens or by herb suppliers and they are, therefore, included for the sake of comparison and thoroughness.

The book is not intended to be a guide to medical self-treatment with herbs. If you think a plant might be helpful in curing a particular ailment consult a specific book on the topic (see the bibliography, p. 187) or seek the advice of a qualified medical herbalist (see Useful Addresses, p. 186).

Protection of Wild Plants

Please remember that all plants are protected by law and it is illegal to uproot plants without the landowner's specific permission. Where it says 'collect' or 'gather' in the text it means harvesting the top section of the plant, not uprooting the whole thing. However, it is a fact that the greatest threat to wild plants is loss of habitat due to building, road-making, draining and farming. Careful collection of wild plants is not in itself an ecological menace. For further information about the conservation of wild plants write to: The Nature Conservancy Council, Northminster House, Peterborough, PE1 1UA. In the US, the Center for Plant Conservation, 125 Arborways, Jamaica Plain, Massachusetts 02130.

The Photographs

The studio shots were taken with a Hasselblad 500 cm and a 80 cm Planar lens. The light source was a Strobe Fish Fryer light using around 3,000 jewels of flash power.

The field shots were taken with a Nikon FM in the main using a normal (50 mm) lens. The film in both cases was Ektachrome 64 ASA professional, which is now only available in bulk from Kodak. I use it because the colour saturation is better on these slower films.

Glossary

abortifacient causes abortion

achene a small, dry, single-seeded fruit, which does not split to release the seed

alternate leaves arranged successively on alternate sides of the stem or branch

antidote a remedy that counteracts a poison

antiscorbutic prevents scurvy, a disease caused by lack of vitamin C in the diet

antispasmodic prevents or cures spasms

aperient produces a natural bowel movement

aphrodisiac excites the sexual organs

astringent has a binding quality; causes contraction and firming of the skin, mucous membrane or tissue

axil angle formed by bract or leaf with branch or stem

basal leaves those at the stem base

biennial a plant that completes its life cycle within two years, usually flowering in the second year

biternate a leaf that divides into three and then into three again

bitter principles various bitter-tasting substances, such as aloin, tannin, lupulin, which are extracted from plants and stimulate the appetite

bract a small modified leaf at the base of the flowerstalk or sometimes beneath the flowerhead; also refers to the parts of cones

cardiotonic has a beneficial effect on the heart

carminative eases griping pains and relieves flatulence

casual an introduced plant which grows wild but does not become permanently established

corm an underground storage organ formed by a swollen stem, lasting only one year, the next year's one arising from the old one

crenate leaves which have scalloped edges

cryptogram the group of plants which have no stamens, pistils or flowers e.g. ferns, mosses, fungi etc.

decoction an extract of a substance which is obtained by boiling

decumbent lying on the ground and tending to rise up at the end

diaphoretic a medicinal herb that induces perspiration

diuretic a medicinal plant that promotes the flow of urine

dyscrasy a disordered condition of the body

dyspepsia indigestion

emetic a medicinal plant that causes vomiting

emmenagogue a medicinal plant that promotes menstrual discharge

escape a plant growing outside a garden, but not well naturalized, derived from cultivated specimens

flatulence wind; gases that build up in the stomach, and alimentary canal, causing discomfort

glume an outer, sterile bract which, alone or with others, encloses the spikelet in grasses

haemostatic herbs or drugs used to control bleeding

infusion a diluted liquid obtained from steeping herbs in water

involucre a ring of bracts forming a calyx-like structure around and below a flowerhead

lactogogue promotes the flow of breast milk

laxative gently stimulates bowel movements

leucorrhoea a mucous discharge from the vagina; 'the whites'

mucilaginous sticky and glutinous

nervine relieves pain and nervous irritation; restores nerves to their natural state

obovate oblong, egg-shaped

ovate egg-shaped

oxytocic accelerating parturition (childbirth)

perennial a plant lasting more than two years

pinnate referring to a compound leaf having two rows of leaflets on either side of a central axis

pinnatifid a leaf divided halfway to the midrib, like a feather

purgative to cleanse or purify; to clear waste matter from the body

raceme flowers with stalks of equal length growing from a central stem

rhizome an underground organ formed from a swollen stem, which lasts for more than one year

sedative a medicine which calms nervous excitement

sorus (plural **sori**) a cluster of sporangia or soredia

subsp. subspecies

sternutatory produces sneezing by irritation of the mucous membrane

stimulant increases energy or produces activity in some organ or vital bodily process

stoloniferous having a short creeping stem produced by a plant with a central rosette or an erect stem

striate marked with long, narrow depressions or ridges

sudorific produces copious perspiration

taproot a straight root, of circular section, thick at the top and tapering to a point, growing downwards from the stem

tincture a solution, usually in alcohol, of a medicinal substance

tonic an invigorating substance which tones up the system and produces a feeling of well-being

var. variety

vermifuge substance which expels worms from the body

vulnerary a plant or ointment used for healing wounds

whorls leaves or flowers arranged at the same level around the branch or stem

Wisley herb garden with its central area and diverging path system

Rosmarinus officinalis 'Sissinghurst'

Rosemary *Rosmarinus officinalis*

Rosmarinus officinalis 'Tuscan Blue'

Rosmarinus officinalis 'Fota Blue'

Rosemary *Rosmarinus officinalis* is an aromatic, evergreen shrub native to the Mediterranean, but introduced into many other parts of Europe. It is found growing wild on dry scrub near the sea and cultivated extensively for ornament and culinary purposes. Rosemary has a tap-root and a twisted stem with slender brown branches, and reaches a height of 2 m (6½ feet). The stalkless, linear leaves are bright green, slightly glossy above, silvery below and somewhat curled back at the margin. The pretty, mauvish/blue or occasionally white flowers grow in spikes at the tops of the branches and bloom from June to July in colder climates, longer in warmer ones.

The generic and common names are derived from the Latin *ros-marinus*, 'dew of the sea', in reference to its favourite habitat near salty sea spray. Its specific name refers to its inclusion in the early pharmacopoeias because of its medicinal properties.

Traditionally, rosemary was a symbol of friendship, love and fidelity. A rosemary wreath would be worn by a bride to denote love and loyalty. It was also carried at religious ceremonies and funerals, in the belief that it warded off evil spirits, or that its pungent scent would provide protection from disease and infection; and it was burnt as incense when that was unavailable. Rosemary was thought to strengthen the brain and memory and Greek scholars wore garlands of it while sitting examinations. In some countries rosemary has traditionally been burned in sick chambers and hospitals to purify the air and one old herbal recommends putting the flowers among clothes and books to protect them against moths. It also recommends various concoctions from the leaves to preserve the skin, cure a cough, preserve the teeth and generally preserve youth.

The use of rosemary as a culinary, cosmetic and medicinal herb goes back to ancient times. The Romans first introduced it into Britain, probably because they loved, as they still do, to flavour their food with it. Today it is frequently put on grilled meat, particularly lamb, and shellfish. It is also added to soups, stews and vegetables, often with wine and garlic. Rosemary can also be used to flavour sweet dishes – jellies, jams, biscuits and cakes. Bees love rosemary and the honey produced from those that have fed on it is extremely delicious. Cosmetically, rosemary is most famously associated with Hungary Water. In the fourteenth century the gouty invalid, Queen Isabella of Hungary, claimed she had regained her youth as a result of using Hungary Water made from a recipe given to her by a hermit. Several claims have been made for the 'original' recipe but basically it consists of rosemary flowers and flowering tips, macerated for a month in alcohol, then strained through a fine muslin. The resulting mixture can be taken internally in tiny doses of about ½–1 tsp for rheumatism and similar aches and pains. In some recipes it is combined with other herbs such as thyme, marjoram and lavender.

Rosemary is also recognized as a stimulant, cardio-tonic, *digestif*, anti-spasmodic and diuretic. Thus an infusion is useful as a tonic for invalids, depressives, those suffering from anaemia, asthma, insomnia, anxiety and nervous migraine. Used externally it can help heal wounds and mouth infections and soothe bruises, falls and sprains.

To make an infusion, put 30 g/1 oz of flowering tops into 1 1/2 pt of boiling water and leave for five to ten minutes. Strain and drink three cupfuls a day.

Rosemary can either be collected from the wild if available or cultivated in the garden. It can be grown from seed but germination only takes place in very warm conditions. However, it is easily propagated from cuttings taken in August. Protect young plants from winter frost by keeping them indoors until spring, then place them in a sunny position in light, dry, sandy soil. Gather the flowering tips in spring and summer and hang up in small bunches to dry, for use all year round.

Rosmarinus officinalis 'Tuscan Blue' is an excellent garden variety with broader, bright green leaves and blue flowers.

Bay or **Sweet Laurel** *Laurus nobilis* is a perennial shrub or small tree, native to the Mediterranean region but naturalized all over the world, which is sometimes found growing wild but is more commonly cultivated in gardens. Sweet bay is an evergreen shrub that can reach a height of 20 m (66½ ft). It has smooth, thin twigs and glossy, leathery, veined, lance-shaped leaves that are dark green above and opaque, yellowish green below. The little yellowish-green flowers grow in small clusters and bloom in June succeeded by black, one-seeded berries.

The specific name of *nobilis*, 'noble', is an indication of the esteem in which the plant has been held since ancient times. It was dedicated to Apollo, the god of light, and was also a symbol of peace and victory and hence used to make wreaths for emperors, generals and poets. In medieval times learned men and successful graduates were crowned with wreaths of laurel berries or *bacca laurea*, hence the French term

Bay or **Sweet Laurel** *Laurus nobilis*

baccalaureat for those who successfully complete their secondary education; the term Bachelor, awarded for passing a degree, is also probably a corruption of the phrase. For centuries sweet laurel has been considered a symbol of good fortune and a protection against evil. It has also been used as a strewing herb because of its aromatic smell and antiseptic properties.

Bay leaves always have been used in cooking – their spicy, aromatic qualities are an important constituent in soups, sauces, pickles, *bouquet garni*, meat and fish dishes – and they have been used medicinally in a variety of ways. An infusion of the leaves 30 g/1 oz, steeped in 1 1/2 pt of boiling water for ten minutes then strained, is recommended as an aid to digestion, reducing dyspepsia and flatulence, and is also

said to be good for treating influenza and bronchitis. An infusion of the pitted crushed berries (same amounts as above) is prescribed as a diuretic and anti-rheumatic. A specific remedy for alopecia (baldness) has also been made from them.

Bay trees are frequently grown in gardens, and small plants can be propagated by planting cuttings of half-ripened shoots. Generally bay will grow in virtually any soil but, if it is being grown in a pot, moderately rich soil in a sunny, warm position is needed for it to thrive. The leaves can be picked from the tree as and when they are needed, or picked in the summer and dried and stored in a dark place for use throughout the year. The flavour becomes stronger when the leaves are dried, crushed or shredded.

Coriander
Coriandrum sativum

Flat Parsley

Curled Parsley
Petroselinum crispum

Photographed May 7

Parsley and **Curled Parsley** *Petroselinum crispum* is a stout, erect biennial. Probably native to southern Europe, it is now naturalized in almost all temperate regions, and found growing in grassy places, walls, rocks, waste places and along roadsides, escaped from cultivation. Parsley has a white, spindle-shaped tap-root and a solid, striate stem with ascending branches that grow to a height of 30–75 cm (12–20 in). The shiny, three pinnate, lobed leaves are flat or curly and the yellowish flowers which grow in dense, flat-topped clusters bloom in June or July.

For centuries parsley has been one of man's favourite herbs. The ancient Greeks believed it sprang from the blood of Archemorus, the forerunner of death, and so they did not eat the herb but used it for making wreaths to adorn the dead and their tombs. The Romans wore garlands of parsley at feasts to prevent intoxication but kept it away from nursing mothers, believing that it would cause epilepsy in their infants. Numerous rites and superstitions grew around the plant because of its slowness to germinate. It was said that the seed had to go to the Devil several times and then, only if the woman was the master of the household, would it start to grow.

The medicinal claims for parsley are numerous and go back centuries. Early on it was thought to destroy poison, probably because of its ability to counteract strong smells such as garlic. It is used in a lotion or fresh as a first-aid treatment for insect bites and parsley juice is an effective mosquito-repellent. Parsley is a mild laxative useful for treating anaemics and convalescents. It is a diuretic, a stimulant used for bringing down fevers, and also helps to regulate the menstrual cycle. Culpeper says, 'The seed provides urine, and women's courses . . . and applied to women's breasts that are hard through the curding of their milk it abates the hardness.' He also says, 'The distilled water is a familiar medicine with nurses to give children when troubled with wind in the stomach or belly.' It aids digestion and relieves flatulence. Large doses can cause congestion of the membrane lining the uterus and result in abortion so it should not be taken by pregnant women. Applied externally, parsley soothes bruises. It is said to heal eye infections, and a wad of cotton soaked in parsley juice will relieve earache or toothache. It is also reputed to prevent hair loss and make freckles disappear.

Despite these numerous medicinal claims most people probably value parsley most highly for its culinary uses. Rich in vitamin C, iron, iodine, magnesium and other vitamins and

Curled Parsley *Petroselinum crispum*

Flat Parsley *Petroselinum crispum*

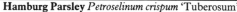

Hamburg Parsley *Petroselinum crispum* 'Tuberosum'

Coriander *Coriandrum sativum*

minerals, it is an excellent addition to the diet. Although commonly used as a garnish, it can be used much more liberally in the cooking process itself. On the continent it is included in most herb mixtures and *bouquets garnis*; it is added to salads, soups, casseroles and fish dishes and made into parsley sauce for cold lamb.

Parsley can sometimes be collected from the wild but great care must be taken not to confuse it with Fool's Parsley *Aethusa cynapium* which is similar in appearance but poisonous. Alternatively it can be grown easily in a herb garden or window box but remember the seeds do take a long time to germinate. You can reduce the germination period by soaking the seeds in lukewarm water before planting them in rich, moist soil in the shade. Sow the seeds all through the spring and summer, keep well watered and under glass to shade and encourage humidity in the soil. Transplant before the seedlings get too leggy and when fully grown constantly cut the leaves to encourage new growth.

French Parsley is a form with plain, flat uncurled leaves slightly more strongly flavoured than Curled Parsley.

Hamburg Parsley *Petroselinum crispum* 'Tuberosum' is grown for its edible root which can either be cooked or grated raw into salads.

It is not mentioned in the literature of the Middle Ages but during the eighteenth century Miller wrote of it in his *Gardener's Dictionary* (1768) 'This is now pretty commonly sold in the London markets, the roots being six times as large as the common Parsley. This sort was many years cultivated in Holland before the English gardeners could be prevailed upon to sow it.'

The roots of Hamburg Parsley should be harvested during the second year. To store for use in the winter, dry in a cool oven with the door ajar, then put in an airtight container in a cool, dark cupboard.

Coriander *Coriandrum sativum* is an erect, aromatic annual, native to southern Europe, now found widely distributed in central and southern Europe, Asia, India and parts of North and South America. It is extensively cultivated and also grows wild in waste places as a weed and an escape. Coriander has slender, branched stems that grow to a height of 35–90 cm (14–36 in). The lower leaves are stalked and pinnate with oval, slightly toothed leaflets, the upper leaves are linear and more divided: all are bright green and shiny. The very pale mauve or pinky white flower clusters bloom from June to August. The seeds are small, round and ridged, and fall as soon as they are ripe.

The generic name is derived from the Greek *koros*, an 'insect', referring to the strong bed bug-like smell of the leaves. As an aromatic stimulant and spice, coriander seed has been used since ancient times. It was a favourite with the Egyptians and the Romans who introduced it into Britain where it was mixed with cumin and vinegar and used as a preservative for meat. In the Middle Ages coriander was added to love potions, presumably because it was held to have aphrodisiac qualities. The Chinese believe that coriander seeds confer immortality on those who consume them.

Coriander is included in the British Pharmacopoeia of medicines but is chiefly used to flavour or disguise the taste of unpleasant

purgatives or as an antidote to griping tendencies caused by some of the stronger ones. Coriander water was formerly used to ease flatulence and windy colic. Externally it is used in ointments for rheumatism and arthritis.

Coriander is now most frequently used as a culinary herb or spice. It is an important ingredient in curry powders and spice mixtures, very popular in Indian cookery, and in the German sausage industry for flavouring frankfurters. Both the ground spice and the fresh leaves are common ingredients in Egyptian and Peruvian dishes and pork cooked with coriander is a popular Greek dish. Coriander is used to flavour bread, cakes, pastries, milk puddings, fruit, sweets, cocoa, chocolate, liqueurs and other alcoholic drinks as well as in meat and vegetable dishes.

To grow coriander in a herb garden sow the seeds in early spring in light, fertile soil, in a sunny position. The seeds should be ready for harvesting in August when they have turned from green to grey and the disagreeable odour has given place to a pleasant, aromatic smell. Leave them on the plant for a few days, then thresh and dry thoroughly before storing in an airtight glass jar. The smell actually improves with time. Coriander is one of India's favourite herbs, so to store fresh coriander Madhur Jaffrey recommends putting the whole fresh plant, roots and all, in to a jar with water – like flowers in a vase – then cover the whole plant and jar with a plastic bag and put into the fridge. Discard the yellowing leaves each day and the fresh coriander should last for weeks and can be used to garnish and flavour dishes as needed.

Sweet Cicely *Myrrhis odorata*

Chervil *Anthriscus cerefolium* is a small, erect, slightly aromatic, branched annual, native to south-eastern Europe and introduced into Britain by the Romans. It is now widely cultivated in most parts of Europe, North Africa, North and South America, East Asia and New Zealand. Chervil is occasionally naturalized and found along hedgerows and in waste places as an escape. Chervil has a thin, whitish root, smelling a little like aniseed, and hollow, lined, somewhat hairy stems that grow to a height of 30–50 cm (21–20 in). The delicate, pale green, lacy leaves are deeply indented and the small, white flowers bloom in May or June.

In the Middle Ages chervil was a valued medicinal plant, prescribed as a diuretic and for cleaning the liver and kidneys, for jaundice, green-sickness (a form of anaemia prevalent in adolescent girls), colic and dissolving blood clots. Women in labour were bathed in it. Chervil is still used by herbalists today for treating circulatory disorders, liver complaints, urinary disorders, haemorrhoids, skin complaints and painful joints. The ancients also used it to soothe sore or inflamed eyes – a treatment still used by modern-day herbalists. Make an infusion by putting 40–60 g/1 oz–2 oz of fresh leaves in 1 1/2 pt of water; bring to the boil and continue boiling for half an hour, then strain. Use as an eyewash or compress three times a day for inflamed eyelids or as a facial beauty treatment to delay the onset of wrinkles.

Apart from its medicinal properties, chervil has long been valued as a great culinary herb. The French value it as a flavouring herb and it is one of the essential ingredients in '*Fines Herbes*' and *bouquets garnis*. Chervil has such a delicate taste that it should always be used fresh. Fresh leaves are excellent for flavouring or decorating salads, soups or sauces and for egg and chicken dishes.

Be wary of picking chervil in the wild unless you are certain of your identification as there are some similar looking species that are poisonous. Young hemlock, for instance, could be mistaken for Chervil. Buy seeds from a reputable herb grower and allow them plenty of space in your herb garden or window box. Sow them in the top of light soil, lightly press down then keep them regularly watered and in partial shade. Seeds can be sown in early spring or late summer and as they germinate quickly it is soon possible to have fresh leaves almost all the year round.

Sweet Cicely *Myrrhis odorata* is an aromatic, perennial herb, native to Europe and widely cultivated there as well as in Asia, so it is often naturalised as an escape. It is found growing wild in grassy places, woods and hedges in hills or mountainous areas. Sweet Cicely has a thick root and furrowed, hollow stems that reach a height of 60–100 cm (24–40 in). The large, somewhat downy leaves are feathery and light green, turning purple in the autumn. The white flowers grow in compound clusters and bloom from May to June.

The generic name is derived from the Greek word meaning 'smelling of myrrh' and together with the specific name from the Latin *odorus*, 'fragrant', refers to the plant's lovely perfume. Sweet Cicely has been grown in Europe for centuries, primarily as a culinary herb. It has a delicious sweet flavour reminiscent of anise and can be used to remove the tartness from food, particularly fruit, so that less sugar is necessary to sweeten it. This makes it a particularly useful herb for diabetics and slimmers. The leaves are an important ingredient in *bouquets garnis* or they can be added to soups, stews or salads. The boiled roots can also be added to salads and, according to Grieve, were reputed to be particularly good for 'old people that are dull

and without courage'. The seeds were used by sixteenth and seventeenth-century housewives to polish furniture as they gave it a lovely glossy finish and an aromatic smell.

Medicinally, Grieve says, Sweet Cicely was described by old herbalists as 'so harmless, you cannot use it amiss'. It was recommended as a gentle stimulant for digestive upsets and useful for coughs and consumption and was said to be particularly good as a tonic for girls between 15 and 18! A decoction of the antiseptic roots was used for snake-and dog-bites and an ointment was used to ease gout and soothe wounds and ulcers.

Sweet Cicely is a very attractive plant to grow in a herb garden and it will adjust fairly easily to any kind of soil. Sow seeds in March or April in well-weeded ground, allowing room for the roots to spread, or propagate by dividing and transplanting roots in spring or autumn. The leaves can be picked from February when they appear, until November when they die down. The flowerheads should be cut back promptly otherwise there is little goodness left in the leaves. Use fresh all year but dry a few extra leaves during the growing season and store in airtight jars for use during the winter months.

Fenugreek *Trigonella foenum-graecum* is a hardy, erect annual, native to the Mediterranean, cultivated and widely naturalized in central and southern Europe and also grown in India, Africa and North America. It is rarely found growing wild but extensively cultivated for cattle fodder and culinary and medicinal use. Fenugreek has a tap-root and erect, hollow stems, with few branches, that reach a height of 10–50 cm (4–20 in). Each leaf has three distinct, oval leaflets, finely toothed at the margin and downy on the upper surface. The scented, creamy-coloured flowers grow singly or in pairs and bloom from June to August, succeeded by the long compressed fruit pods, each containing about sixteen seeds.

The generic name is derived from the Greek, meaning 'three-angled', in reference to its flower, while the specific name means 'Greek hay' from its use by the Romans as cattle fodder; the common name is derived from this. The Egyptians used fenugreek for food, as an embalming agent and for cosmetics. The Romans also cultivated it for food although some believed it to be fit only for cattle fodder. In medieval times it was grown in monastery gardens to treat liver and kidney complaints, fevers and palpitations.

The seeds are used for culinary purposes in many countries. They are an important ingredient in mango chutney and, ground, are used in curry powder. The Jewish sweetmeat, Halva, is flavoured with fenugreek and the fresh chopped herb is added to salads and vegetable dishes, just before serving, in many Mediterranean, Middle Eastern and Eastern dishes. It is also used as a substitute for maple syrup in flavouring confectionery. Cosmetically, the crushed seed, mixed with oil and rubbed into the scalp, is recommended for glossy hair, while an infusion used as a skin lotion is reputedly good for the complexion.

Fenugreek contains many essential elements – iron, phosphorus and sulphur as well as mucilage, protein, oil and enzymes. It is very nourishing, body-building and an excellent tonic for invalids or those debilitated by nervous or infectious diseases or anaemia. It is used to soothe sore throats, mouth ulcers, coughs and inflamed intestines. Externally poultices are applied to heal abscesses, boils and corns.

To make a decoction, put 30 g/1 oz of coarsely crushed seeds into 1 1/2 pt of boiling water and simmer for fifteen minutes. Strain and drink three cups a day for digestive problems and add lemon and honey to soothe a sore throat. Fenugreek is one of several traditional medicinal herbs that have been exciting the attention of modern scientists. In the past fenugreek was recommended for increasing milk flow and women in the harems of North Africa took fenugreek to round out their breasts. Modern experiments have shown that the seeds contain diosgenin, an important substance in the synthesis of oral contraceptives and sex hormones.

Fenugreek can easily be grown from seed in a herb garden providing it is given a mild, sheltered spot and put into well-drained soil. The seeds take about four months from flowering to mature sufficiently for threshing and drying. Some seeds can be used to sprout green shoots for use fresh, in salads. (See page 55).

Cumin *Cuminum cyminum* is a low-growing annual probably native to upper Egypt, Arabia and Turkey, but introduced into India, China and Mediterranean Europe in ancient times and now also grown in North and South America. It is widely cultivated and sometimes found naturalized or as an escape. Cumin is a slender plant with a branching stem that reaches a height of 10–50 cm (4–20 in). Its small, deep green leaves are long and narrow and the little clusters of white or rose-coloured flowers bloom in June or July followed by the fruits which are ½ cm (¼ in) long, oblong, finely ridged, yellowish-brown and covered in minute hairs.

Since biblical times, cumin seeds have been taken in wine, water or bread for their carminative and digestive properties, or used as a condiment: the common name is derived from the Hebrew *kammon*. According to Pliny, the followers of the learned rhetorician, Porcius Latro, smoked cumin seeds to give their complexions an unhealthy pallor suggesting excessive hours of study – giving rise to Horace's expression *exsangue cuminum*, the bloodless pallor from cumin. Cumin was considered a symbol of cupidity by the Greeks and misers were jokingly asked if they had used cumin. Although cumin was a popular spice during the Middle Ages in Britain, it has been largely replaced by caraway since the

seventeenth century because the latter has a less bitter taste. However, cumin is still an important ingredient in curry powder and is widely used in India, Mexican and eastern European countries in a variety of dishes. Cumin is also used commercially to flavour cheese, meat, pickle, chutney, breads, rolls, biscuits and cakes. The volatile oil distilled from the seeds is used in perfumery.

Cumin was once used externally as a poultice to relieve stitches and pains in the side. Nowadays cumin is rarely used medicinally except in veterinary medicine because of its rather sharp, bitter flavour.

Cumin can be cultivated in a herb garden if the weather remains fair and equable. Sow the seeds in pots in a hot bed and later transfer to a warm bed of rich, loamy soil in a sunny position. They will take three or four months of warm pleasant weather to mature. Thresh the seeds when ripe. Dry and store in airtight jars.

Anise *Pimpinella anisum* is a strongly aromatic annual, native to the Middle East but cultivated in Europe for centuries and also grown in North Africa, South America and India. It is found widely cultivated and sometimes found naturalized on old rubbish dumps and in waste places. Anise is finely hairy with a striate stem, branched above, and grows to a height of 10–50 cm (4–20 in). The light green leaves are different shapes: rounded and toothed at the base, heart-shaped and toothed in the middle, and at the top are three or five narrow sections. The creamy white or pink flowers are grouped in loose clusters and bloom in July and August. The aromatic fruits contain two little hairy seeds in each capsule.

Anise has a very long history of culinary and medicinal use (cf. Matt. xxiii, 23). The Romans, recognizing its aromatic and digestive properties, incorporated it into a special spiced cake that they ate at the end of their meals to ease flatulence and aid the digestion of the rich food they had consumed. Anise is still a very popular ingredient in cooking, particularly on the Continent, where it is used to flavour cakes, rolls, bread and Christmas fare. It is also an important constituent in many popular liqueurs and cordials – the most famous being Pernod, Ouzo and Anisette. It can also be used to flavour soups, stews and pies. Medicinally, anise is taken internally for gastric disorders – it reduces flatulence, eases diarrhoea in children and stimulates the appetite. It also relieves coughs and asthma, induces sleep, stops hiccups and stimulates the mammary glands of nursing mothers. Taken in lozenge form, it sweetens the breath and eases dry coughs. Anise oil is a good antiseptic and is sometimes used to flavour toothpaste.

It is very rare to find anise growing wild but it can be cultivated in a herb garden. Sow the seeds in April in light, well-drained soil, with plenty of lime, in a sunny but sheltered position. The fruits will ripen in August only if it has been a very hot summer. When the tips of the fruits are greenish grey, cut the stems at ground level and tie in bunches. Hang over a large bowl, heads down, in a dry place and leave for a week to complete the ripening process. Gently thresh out the seeds and store in a dry, airtight container in a dark cupboard. To make an infusion, put 10 gr/⅓ oz of seed into 1 l (2 pt) of boiling water, leave for five to ten minutes, strain and sweeten. Drink one or two cupfuls a day to aid digestion and ease painful periods. Make a decoction twice as strong to use externally on swollen breasts and to stimulate the flow of milk.

Chervil *Anthriscus cerefolium*

Cumin *Cuminum cyminum*

Fenugreek *Trigonella foenum-graecum*

Chives
Allium schoenoprasum

Three-cornered Leek
Allium triquetrum

Photographed May 2

Three-cornered Leek *Allium triquetrum*

Garlic Mustard or **Jack-by-the-Hedge**
Alliaria petiolata

Garlic Mustard or **Jack-by-the-Hedge** *Alliaria petiolata* is a perennial herb, native to Europe, North Africa and Asia to the Himalayas and also found in Australia. It grows in damp hedgerows, wood edges, shady roadsides and gardens. Garlic mustard has a tap-root that smells strongly of garlic and an erect, cylindrical, usually unbranched stem that reaches a height of 20–100 cm (8–40 in). The kidney- to heart-shaped basal leaves have long stalks, wavy or distantly toothed margins and form a rosette; the stem leaves are more triangular-ovate, short-stalked with more deeply wavy or toothed margins: both are thin, pale green and smell of garlic when crushed. The white flowers form in a flat-topped cluster and bloom from April to June.

The generic name derives from the Latin *allium*, 'garlic', because of the unmistakable garlic smell the plant emits when crushed; hence, too, one of its common names.

The plant has been long used in cooking as well as for medicine. It can be eaten boiled as a vegetable, and raw in salads: not only does it impart a delicious garlic flavour but it is also thought to strengthen the digestive system. Country people used it frequently to flavour sauces, stews and salted meat.

Medicinally, the plant was taken internally as a sudorific – to produce sweat. It was also said to be beneficial in cases of dropsy. Applied externally, its antiseptic properties can relieve itching from bites and stings.

Collect from the wild and use fresh leaves for salads in the spring and summer. Dry the leaves or seeds for use throughout the year.

Chives *Allium schoenoprasum* is a hardy perennial plant, native to northern Europe and north-eastern North America. It is found growing wild in dry, rocky places. Chives has small, flat bulbs and grows in tufts with thin, hollow, flowering stems arising from them that reach a height of 15 cm (6 in). The long, thin leaves are grass-like and the delicate purple or pink flowers grow in a round, pompom-like cluster at the top of the stem, blooming from June to July.

The specific name comes from the Latin

Schoenus, 'a rush or sedge', and means rush-like; the French name *Petit poureau* also refers to its rush-like appearance. The common name derives from Latin *cepa*, 'onion'. Chives was used in China nearly five thousand years ago and the Romans introduced it into Britain, presumably for culinary purposes.

Chives has a milder, more delicate flavour than its near relative, the onion, and is frequently used in cooking. Its leaves are generally added raw, finely chopped, to soups, salads, eggs, cream cheese and cooked vegetables – their bright green colour making them an attractive garnish.

Chives can be easily grown in a herb garden or a window box or pot. It is happy in any kind of soil though needs extra moisture in dry weather and the soil should be enriched occasionally to ensure strong, new growth.

Giant Chives *Allium mortanum* synonym *Allium schoenoprasum* var. *sibiricum* grows to 30 cm (12 in) and has a thicker, stronger growth. It can be used like chives and the flowers used as a decorative feature for salads.

Three-cornered Leek *Allium triquetrum* is a native of the western Mediterranean region found naturalized in hedgebanks and waste places in other parts of Europe.

Ramsons, Bear's Garlic or **Wood Garlic** *Allium ursinum* is a perennial herb, native to Europe and Asia Minor, which is often found growing in damp woods, shady places and along stream banks up to 420 m (1400 ft). Ramsons has a white bulb from which the flowering stems grow to a height of 10–45 cm (4–18 in) and two or three elliptical, spear-shaped, dark green, glossy basal leaves arise 10–25 cm (4–10 in). The six-petalled, white flowers grow in a cluster at the top of the stem and bloom from April to June. The small black seeds are contained in a three-chambered capsule and are dispersed by black ants.

A relative of cultivated garlic, (the common name derives from Old English, *hramson*, 'wild garlic'), ramsons can be used in many of the same ways for medicinal and culinary purposes. The fresh young leaves can be gathered in spring and used in salads. The freshly pressed juice is commonly used in slimming diets and can be made into a syrup, tincture or decoction and used for coughs, colds, sore throats and bronchitis. Although little is known about its constituents, the main action seems to be on the intestine. It is recognized as having a good effect on fermentative dyspepsia.

Lemon Grass *Cymbopogon citratus* synonym *Andropogon schoenanthus* is an aromatic grass, native to India but also widely cultivated in Sri Lanka, the Seychelles and Uganda, and grown in herb gardens.

The specific and common names of the plant are an allusion to its strong lemon scent, derived from its constituent citral. The aromatic oil distilled from the plant is very important in the manufacture of tonene, the artificial violet perfume. It is also commonly used to adulterate lemon oil. In recent years lemon grass has been highly prized as a culinary herb, used for its tangy lemon flavour. Easily grown but difficult to get hold of the plants.

Ramsons, Bear's Garlic or **Wood Garlic** *Allium ursinum*

Lemon Grass *Cymbopogon citratus* synonym *Andropogon schoenanthus*

Welsh Onion *Allium fistulosum* Photographed June 4

Garlic *Allium sativum* (bulbs)

Garlic *Allium sativum* (flowers)

Garlic *Allium sativum* is a strong-smelling, bulbous perennial, native to central Asia but cultivated all over the world for its bulbs and sometimes found growing as an escape. Garlic has a bulb consisting of 8–10 distinct segments or 'cloves' and an erect, hollow stem that reaches a height of 30–120 cm (12–48 in). The flat, linear leaves sheath the lower stem and the pink or whitish flowering clusters bloom from June to July.

The generic name is said to derive from the Celtic *al*, 'caustic', in reference to its strong taste, while the common name originates from the Anglo-Saxon *gar*, 'a spear', and *leak*, 'a leek', a reference to the shape of its leaves.

Garlic has been known as a culinary and medicinal plant for centuries. Thought to impart strength, it was given to Egyptian labourers building the pyramids. According to Homer's *Odyssey*, Ulysses ate it to protect himself from being turned into a pig by Circe. Galen and Dioscorides thought it the great panacea for the common man and recommended it for a wide variety of ailments. Though highly regarded by many, garlic was detested by others for its strong smell and considered as a sign of vulgarity. In medieval times cocks and horses fed on garlic were believed to be stronger than those fed solely on corn. Poultry fed on garlic mixed with grain will lay more eggs than those fed on grain alone. Modern research has confirmed that garlic is very beneficial in keeping amoebic dysentery at bay.

Throughout Europe but particularly in Mediterranean countries, garlic is an essential ingredient in cooking and the basis of many dishes. It is used in large quantities to flavour soups, stews, vegetables, sauces, oil, mayonnaise, meat and fish dishes. Its strong odour and taste adds a characteristic smell to cooking and the breath. Some people find it unpleasant and it can be disguised by peppermint or parsley. Others find it attractive, according to Mességué in *Health Secrets of Plants and Herbs*. He said the breath of a Cavalry officer of his acquaintance could be smelled ten yards away, yet he was renowned for being totally irresistible to women.

Garlic has also been used for centuries for medicinal purposes. It has long been recognized as having antiseptic and antibiotic properties and was the main ingredient of the Four Thieves' Vinegar. This was consumed by robbers who plundered the bodies of plague victims, yet did not catch the deadly disease. Also French priests working in the poor quarters of London during the nineteenth century, who ate garlic regularly in their diet remained healthy, while the English clergy, who did not, frequently died from the infectious diseases they caught. The antiseptic properties of expressed garlic juice applied to their wounds saved the lives of thousands of soldiers in the First World War. Garlic is good for regulating man's intestinal flora, according to Mességué, and he prescribes it for diarrhoea, stomach cramps, flatulence and sluggish bowels. It is also a vermifuge and a general tonic for regulating all the vital functions. Taken in infusion, garlic may lower high blood pressure and regulate the blood glucose level, thus making it useful for diabetes. To make a decoction for hypertension put a head of garlic in 1 1/2 pt of boiling water or stock and simmer for ten to fifteen minutes. Drink three cupfuls of the resulting liquid a day. Soaked in honey, garlic cloves relieve bronchitis and coughs by expelling catarrh. This is particularly recommended for children with chesty colds. To make a syrup for relieving

Tree Onion *Allium cepa* var. *proliferum*

Garlic Chives *Allium tuberosum*

coughs, put 5 fat, sliced cloves in 100 g/4 oz of honey and marinate for several hours. Give two to three teaspoonfuls every three hours. Numerous modern studies confirm the antibacterial and tonic properties of garlic and it is considered useful for treating intestinal disorders, arteriosclerosis, consumptive diseases and retinitis. However, it must be noted that the most effective results have been achieved with fresh bulbs – extended storage reduces the anti-bacterial action. A Bulgarian scientist, Petkov, has discovered that garlic aids detoxification of chronic lead poisoning. Regular consumption of garlic is thought to be a great aid to general health. If you find the smell offensive chew either chervil, parsley or coffee beans, or sprinkle yourself with Angelica water.

Garlic bread – French bread smothered with butter into which a clove or two of garlic has been crushed, then heated for ten minutes in a hot oven – is a tasty way of eating your weekly ration.

Easily grown by breaking up a head of garlic into individual cloves and planting them out in the spring.

Onion *Allium cepa* is a strong-smelling, bulbous biennial plant, probably native to the Middle East but now grown all over the world. It commonly grows in vegetable gardens and is cultivated commercially. Onion has a bulbous root with layers of flesh covered by white, yellow or violet coloured tunics from which erect, hollow stems grow, sometimes reaching a height of 100 cm (40 in). The smooth, hollow leaves are slightly channelled and the clusters of

numerous greenish white flowers form a round head at the top of the stem. They bloom from June to September.

Onions have been used since ancient times and were one of the earliest plants to be cultivated for use in cooking and medicine. Over the centuries numerous varieties have been developed but all with similar culinary and medicinal properties. Onions are an essential ingredient in soups, stews, meat, fish and vegetable dishes and sauces. Fresh, finely chopped onion gives a distinctive tang to salads, cheese and egg dishes and they are also popular baked, boiled or pickled.

Very similar in its medicinal virtues to garlic, regular consumption of onion (particularly raw) is claimed to increase longevity and general health.

Onions, like garlic, are antiseptic, antibiotic, antisclerotic, diuretic and expectorant. They reduce blood pressure, aid digestion, heal wounds, clear the system and relieve coughs and colds. High in vitamin C and other vitamins and minerals, they were eaten to ward off scurvy, and they will help keep coughs, colds and other minor infectious diseases at bay. High in phosphorus, onions are reputed to aid memory, concentration and creative thought. They are considerably more potent if consumed raw than cooked, but they don't always agree with everyone, especially those who suffer from wind, and some people dislike the taste and smell left on the breath. Jean Palaiseul in *Grandmother's Secrets* suggests taking onion wine if you find eating it raw disagreeable. Put 300 g/12 oz chopped onion and 100 g/4 oz honey

in to a bottle of white wine. Leave to macerate for at least two days, shaking every few hours. Strain and take two to four tbsps a day. This can be taken for anaemia, as a tonic, for bronchial complaints, diabetes, stomach or urinary infections. Certain American Indians used the crushed juice to relieve insect stings. Grated raw onion applied externally may relieve rheumatic joints, burns and migraine. Soaked into cotton wool it is thought to relieve some earaches and toothaches.

Easily cultivated in a vegetable garden, onions are propagated by seed or small bulbs known as 'sets'. They like a sheltered, sunny position and quite rich, well-drained soil. Harvest the bulbs about the end of July. Tie them in bundles and hang then, bulbs down, in a cool, well-ventilated place to dry.

Tree Onion *Allium cepa* var. *proliferum* forms little onions that are good for pickling.

Welsh Onion *Allium fistulosum* is a hardy, perennial bulb grown as a vegetable. It has long tapering roots, round hollow leaves and yellowish white flowers. It is similar in flavour to onion but milder and used for more delicate seasonings.

Garlic Chives *Allium tuberosum* has a mild garlic flavour and flat white flower heads. It is delicious added to salads or cream cheese.

French or **Buckler-leaved Sorrel** *Rumex scutatus*

Red-veined Dock *Rumex sanguineus* var. *sanguineus*

Sheep's Sorrel *Rumex acetosella*

Curled Dock *Rumex crispus*

Common Sorrel or **Garden Sorrel** *Rumex acetosa* (foreground) Photographed June 1

Common Sorrel or **Garden Sorrel** *Rumex acetosa* is an erect perennial, native to Europe, temperate Asia, North America and Greenland, which commonly grows wild in grassland, meadows and open woods. Sorrel has deep roots and erect, juicy, branched stems that reach a height of 100 cm (40 in). The broad, oblong leaves are arrow-shaped at the base, green becoming crimson, and the reddish green flowers grow in lax spikes, blooming from June to July. The male and female flowers are usually on different plants.

Common Sorrel has been used since ancient times as a culinary and medicinal herb. The Egyptians and the Romans ate it to counteract discomfort caused from overindulgence in rich food and it was a very popular pot herb and salad plant in medieval times. Common Sorrel can be made into sauces and eaten with roast meat or cold meat. It can be added to salads, omelettes, vegetables and stews, or the young leaves can be collected and eaten as a vegetable, like spinach. The juice from the leaves and stems will curdle milk and Laplanders used it as a substitute for rennet for this purpose. Always use stainless steel knives and non-stick pans when cooking as the plant's chemicals react badly with iron.

High in oxalic acid, Common Sorrel should not be taken continuously as this can lead to the formation of small stones of calcium oxalate. It should be avoided particularly by those suffering from bladder stones, rheumatism, gout, asthma and pulmonary complaints. Medicinally, Common Sorrel has been valued since Greek and Roman times for its diuretic and cooling properties. It was used to make a cooling drink for those with fevers and, because of its high vitamin C content, was thought to be excellent for preventing scurvy; its astringent

properties made it useful for stemming haemorrhage. Externally it was prescribed for scabbing, ringworm, itchy skin, festering sores and wounds, mouth ulcers and boils.

Common Sorrel tea is useful as a laxative or diuretic. Infuse 30 g/1 oz dried leaves in 1 1/2 pt of boiling water for ten minutes. Strain and drink three cupfuls a day. Mességué in *Health Secrets of Plants and Herbs* recommends an infusion made from the roots and seeds for stomach ache, colic and diarrhoea. Put a small chunk of root and 10 g/⅓ oz of seeds in 1 1/2 pt of water and boil for ten minutes. Strain and drink one cupful a day.

Common Sorrel can either be picked from an unpolluted spot in the wild or easily cultivated in the garden by root division in the spring or autumn. Plant it out, well-spaced, in rich soil in a sheltered spot. Harvest four months after planting and continue throughout the year if put under glass during winter. Replace old plants after four years, otherwise they become too woody.

French or **Buckler-leaved Sorrel** *Rumex scutatus* is a smooth perennial, native to central and southern Europe, western Asia and north Africa, which grows on old walls and in mountain pastures. It is distinguished from Common Sorrel by its smaller size and shield-shaped leaves which are succulent and brittle. French sorrel is less bitter than common sorrel and is generally more favoured for culinary use. It can be used as the main ingredient in the delicious dish of Sorrel Soup and the young leaves give a lovely, slightly lemon tang to spring salads.

Sheep's Sorrel *Rumex acetosella* is native to central and south-eastern Europe and widely

distributed throughout most of the world except the tropics. It commonly grows in pastures and dry, gravelly areas. Much smaller than either common sorrel or French sorrel, it is nevertheless used in similar ways, although less active in its medicinal properties.

Curled Dock *Rumex crispus* is an erect perennial, native to Europe and naturalized in most other parts of the world. It commonly grows wild in grassy places, waste ground, cultivated land, roadsides and near sand dunes. Curled dock has long, fleshy roots, reddish-brown outside, white inside, and a branched stem that reaches a height of 50–100 cm (20–40 in). The largish leaves are oval and pointed, with strongly crisped or wavy edges. The green flowers, in dense whorls on a terminal spike, bloom from June to October.

High in iron, curled dock is recognized medicinally as a tonic and prescribed for anaemia and general debility or for those convalescing. It also has diuretic and laxative properties and is recommended for rheumatism, digestive upsets and chronic skin conditions. In homoeopathy a cough tincture is prescribed for tickly coughs and throats. Some people have claimed that it arrests the continuing onset of cancer.

Red-veined Dock *Rumex sanguineus* var. *sanguinus* is grown as a decorative addition to many herb gardens.

Salvia
'Icterina'

Salvia
'Tricolor'

Salvia
'Purpurascens'

Salvia
hians

Garden Sage or
Common Sage
Salvia officinalis

Photographed June 10

general tonic for mind and body and also recommended it for snake bites. In the Middle Ages it was still a very popular medicinal herb prescribed for colds, fevers, epilepsy, cholera and constipation. One medieval tradition said that the growth of sage in the garden indicated the prosperity of the household: business would thrive if the sage bush was flourishing, business was bad if the bush withered. Another tradition held that a strong woman ruled the household in the garden of which a sage bush grew vigorously.

Over the centuries sage has become increasingly valued as a culinary herb and nowadays it is principally used in the kitchen to flavour meat, fish, stews and soups. Because of its digestive properties it is frequently cooked with rich, fatty meat like pork or duck, or oily fish like eel. Sage and onion stuffing is a well-known accompaniment for poultry, and Sage Derby is a traditional English cheese flavoured with the herb. Bees that have fed on sage make a delicious, highly sought-after honey. Medicinally it has many valuable uses. Its digestive properties have already been mentioned. It is also astringent and still included in the United States Pharmacopoeia for use as a mouthwash and gargle to clear ulcers, bleeding gums and sore throats. Often added to toothpaste, it helps whiten the teeth and it is also said to be a good hair tonic.

Sage tea is said to be an excellent tonic for nerves and a stimulant to the circulation. It has been recommended for convalescents, depressives, anaemics and also for students and academics suffering the stress of examinations. It is reputed to be good for regulating menstruation, reducing fever, soothing rheumatic pain and migraine and warding off disease. Smoking dried sage leaves can relieve asthma; burning sage in an invalid's room will fumigate it; a cold infusion of sage can be given to babies with diarrhoea. Externally it is used for wounds, scabs, eczema and spots. To make an infusion put 15 g/½ oz of dried sage into 1 1/2 pt of cold water, boil for five minutes and infuse for five more. Drink three cupfuls a day. Use sage liberally in cooking to help keep in general good health.

Sage is easy to grow in the garden and likes ordinary, dryish soil and plenty of sun. Propagation is best from cuttings taken off well-established plants in April or May. Woody stems should be cut back in early spring to encourage a bushy growth and even though it is quite hardy it should be mulched in winter. Plants should be replaced every four or five years, otherwise they become very woody. Harvest the herb for drying in early summer before the flower spikes appear, otherwise cut all year. Dry sage slowly to prevent it going mouldy, then crumble and store in airtight jars.

Garden Sage or **Common Sage** *Salvia officinalis* is an aromatic evergreen shrub native to the Mediterranean and widely naturalized in other parts of southern and central Europe. It occasionally grows wild on dry sunny slopes or limestone rocks but is commonly cultivated as a pot herb, in kitchen or herb gardens. Garden Sage has a woody, branched tap-root from which arise square, erect stems with many whitish, woolly branches, that reach a height of 60–200 cm (24–40 in). The stalked, oblong-elliptical leaves are grey-green above and woolly white below, with a distinct network of veins. The violet, purple, pink or white flowers grow in whorls and bloom from June to August.

The generic name is derived from the Latin *salvere*, 'to save or cure', and alludes to the ancients' belief in the plant's healing properties. The common name also comes from Latin *salvia* 'the healing plant'. The specific name recognizes its inclusion in the list of plants officially used for medicinal purposes. The Romans considered sage to be a sacred herb that not only had the ability to save life but also to create it. Women who had difficulty in conceiving were advised to drink sage juice for four days, abstaining from conjugal relations while they did so. After four days conjugal relations would recommence and conception would take place forthwith. An old proverb goes: 'Why should a man die who has sage in his garden?' The Greeks and Romans used it as a

Purple or **Red Sage** *Salvia officinalis* 'Purpurascens' has red leaves and bright blue flowers and, although it can be used in cooking, it is particularly good for use as a gargle.

White Sage *Salvia officinalis* 'Albiflora' is a narrow-leaved sage with white flowers, best used for culinary purposes.

Golden Sage *Salvia officinalis* 'Icterina' is a smaller plant with green and gold variegated leaves. It can be used in cooking.

Spanish Sage *Salvia lavandulifolia* is a small, narrow-leaved species with blue flowers that bloom in early summer. It can be used in cooking like garden sage.

Golden Sage *Salvia officinalis* 'Icterina' (left) and **Purple Sage** *Salvia officinalis* 'Purpurascens'

White Sage *Salvia officinalis* 'Albiflora'

Garden Sage or **Common Sage** *Salvia officinalis*

Clary Sage *Salvia sclarea*

Salvia patens

Salvia patens 'Cambridge Blue'

Clary Sage *Salvia sclarea* is an aromatic biennial or perennial plant native to Syria and southern Europe and now naturalized in many other parts of Europe. It grows wild in waste places and is cultivated in gardens. Clary sage has erect, numerously-branched stems that reach a height of 100 cm (40 in). The large, ovate to heart-shaped leaves are arranged in pairs, wrinkled, velvety and toothed at the edges. The whorls of lilac or pale blue flowers grow in long, loose spikes and bloom from June to September.

The specific name and the common English name that is a corruption of it, derive from the Latin *clarus*, 'to clear', an allusion to its use as an eyewash.

Because of its strong, warm, aromatic taste and odour, this plant was commonly used in Germany to adulterate wine and give it a muscatel flavour. In Britain it was used as a substitute for hops with the result that beer made with Clary sage was powerfully intoxicating and made those who drank it either dead drunk or insanely exhilarated. The leaves can be dipped in batter and fried to make delicious fritters.

In medicine it is generally used as an aid to digestion. Culpeper also recommends it as a compress for swellings, ulcers, boils and to draw out splinters and says that 'the juice of the herb put into ale or beer, and then drunk, bringeth down woman's courses and expelleth the after-birth.' In Jamaica it is a popular eye lotion and frequently added to the bath for a soothing, aromatic effect. Oil of Clary sage is used in the cosmetics industry as a fixative in perfume. Easily grown from seeds or young plants, it makes a striking perennial in any part of the garden.

Salvia glutinosa has pale yellow flowers that bloom in August and it yields an aromatic gum.

Salvia neurepia synonym *Salvia grahamii* is best grown as a pot plant in a cool conservatory. It has bright crimson flowers that bloom all summer and last into the winter if the temperature is kept at about 10°C/50°F.

Salvia patens has lovely bright blue flowers.

Salvia patens 'Cambridge Blue' is a beautiful light blue variety.

Salvia hians, and *Salvia mertaurea* are also often grown in herb gardens, although little used in medicine or liquor-making as far as I know.

Painted Sage or **Salvia 'Bluebeard'** *Salvia horminum* with attractive pink or purple flower bracts grows well on sunny borders and is good as a gargle when made into an infusion. Adding leaves or seeds to fermenting liquors makes them more intoxicating.

Pineapple Sage *Salvia rutilans* should be treated as a conservatory plant and only put outside in the summer. It has pineapple-scented leaves which can be used in fruit salads or added to plain cakes or put on roast pork.

Salvia verticillata is a hairy, foetid perennial, native to the mountains of southern Europe but also naturalized in many other areas including North America, which grows in waste places.

Pineapple Sage *Salvia rutilans*

Salvia verticillata

Salvia glutinosa

Painted Sage *Salvia horminum*

Salvia hians

Salvia neurepia

Salvia mertaurea

Angelica *Angelica archangelica* Photographed at Barnsley House June 18

White-flowered Borage

Borage *Borago officinalis*

Angelica *Angelica archangelica* synonym *Archangelica officinalis* is a tall, sweet-scented perennial herb, probably native to Syria and now widely cultivated and found naturalized in Europe at high altitudes as far north as Norway, in the Austrian and Swiss Alps and the Pyrenees, especially near rivers and in waste places. Angelica, a handsome umbelliferous plant that can grow to a height of 2 m (6 ft), has thick, fleshy, spindle-shaped roots and stout, hollow, fluted stems. The large, broad, pointed leaves have serrated edges and are indented into three sections. The numerous, small, whitish or pale yellowish or greenish flowers form large, dense, round clusters at the top of the stem and blossom in July, followed by pale yellow, oblong or egg-shaped fruits.

Throughout the centuries the virtues of Angelica have been extolled by numerous writers. According to one legend its name refers to an angel that revealed in a dream that it would cure the plague and Paracelsus called it a 'marvellous medicine' during the plague epidemic in Milan in 1510; the common name derived from medieval Latin *herba angelica*, 'angelic plant', reflects this. Another legend says that its name derived from the fact that it blooms on the feast day of Michael the Archangel, 8 May in the old Julian Calendar. Known to Renaissance doctors as the 'root of the Holy Ghost' because of its purported ability to cure any malady, angelica was also thought to offer protection against witches, spells and evil spirits.

Medicinally, angelica is nowadays recommended as a stimulant, diaphoretic, tonic, stomachic and expectorant. It is frequently used on the Continent to ease flatulence, indigestion, chronic bronchitis and typhus. Culpeper agrees that a syrup of the stalks 'helps digestion and is a remedy for surfeit', also that it 'procureth women's courses and expelleth the after birth'. Mességué recommends angelica to ease painful periods, stomach ache and migraine but he warns that if the potent juice is not used carefully it can cause unpleasant skin irritations and it must never come in contact with the eyes. In modern herbalism angelica oil or Spirits of Angelica are sometimes used as a rub for rheumatic conditions. As well as its medicinal use angelica has long been renowned for its use in confectionery, though few people realize that crystallized angelica stems can be used for purposes other than decorating cakes and sweets. The seeds are used by distillers to flavour liqueurs such as Chartreuse and it is also

used to some extent in perfumery. The stems are used in jam-making. A little of the root or stem added to rhubarb helps to reduce its tartness. An infusion can be made with 22 g/¾ oz of grated root or 15 g/½ oz of seeds steeped in 1 1/2 pt boiling water. Drink one cupful a day. Do not exceed the dose as it can be overstimulating.

Angelica is sometimes hard to find in the wild but is easily cultivated in a herb garden. Propagation can be either by root division followed by transplantation of young plants or by seeds sown as soon as they are ripe, in August or early September, since their germinating capacity deteriorates rapidly. Angelica likes good soil and shade. The stems should be harvested in April or May and the leaves in May or June before flowering. The roots should be gathered at the end of the autumn. Dried and stored, the roots will retain their medicinal properties for years and the leaves can be used to make tisanes, infusions and decorations.

Wild Angelica or **Wood Angelica** *Angelica sylvestris* is a related species found in shady woods, damp meadows or moist hedgerows. It is less rich in active principles and is not normally used in herbal medicine.

Borage *Borago officinalis* is a stout, erect annual, probably native to North Africa, the Middle East, Mediterranean and central Europe and now naturalized in Britain and North America. It is frequently found on waste ground and growing as a garden escape near dwellings as well as being cultivated in kitchen gardens. Borage is a sturdy plant, rough all over with stiff, prickly, white hairs. The round, hollow stems are branched and grow to a height of 30–60 cm (1–2 ft). The large oval, pointed, dark green leaves, 10–20 cm (4–8 in), are wrinkled and alternate, the lower ones stalked, the upper opens stalkless. The bright blue, occasionally white, star-shaped flowers bloom from June to September. The fruit consists of four brownish black nutlets containing black seeds.

The generic name is thought to be derived either from the Latin *borra*, 'rough hair', referring to its hairy stems and leaves, or to a corruption of the Latin, *corago*, 'I bring courage

to the heart'. The specific name refers to its inclusion in official lists of medicinal plants. Since ancient times borage has been regarded as having a wonderful effect on mind and body, for dispelling melancholy and inducing euphoria. According to Dioscorides and Pliny, borage was the nepenth of Homer which, when steeped in wine, brought absolute forgetfulness. Gerard said that syrup made from borage flowers 'quietest the phrenticke and lunaticke person'.

Young borage leaves used to be boiled and eaten as a pot-herb and also, finely shredded, were eaten in spring salads. The fresh leaves have a taste like cucumber and can be used to make a refreshing drink combined with lemon and sugar or honey. Borage is frequently grown near hives as bees love its plentiful, sweet nectar and make delicious honey from it. Since ancient times borage leaves have been used to flavour and garnish wine cups. The flowers are also edible and were frequently candied and eaten as sweetmeats or used to decorate cakes. The flowers look very pretty added to salads.

Medicinally, borage has diuretic, anti-inflammatory and soothing properties because of its high mucilage content. It can be used internally to soothe bronchitis, catarrh, congested membranes, pleurisy and rheumatism. In France it is used for some fevers and pulmonary complaints: Mességué says his father used it as a 'soothe all' and he claims it is efficacious for colds when used in foot- and hand-baths.

To make a decoction, infuse 30 g/1 oz of dried plant in ½ l/1 pt of boiling water. Strain and drink three to four wineglassfuls a day.

To make a refreshing summer drink, add two to three borage leaves and two to three flowers to a pint of homemade lemonade (juice of 1 lemon, 2 tablespoons of sugar or honey dissolved in ½ l/1 pt of boiling water, then chilled).

Borage can either be found in the wild or grown in a window box or herb garden, from seed. Sow the seeds in March, covering them well with soil. Borage germinates quickly and easily reseeds itself so you will find it coming up year after year on the same spot. It grows in moist soils but favours loose, stony soil with some chalk and sand in it.

Borage should always be used fresh as it loses its flavour and colour if dried.

Fennel *Foeniculum vulgare* (in flower)

Fennel *Foeniculum vulgare*

Fennel *Foeniculum vulgare* synonym *Foeniculum officinale* is a stout perennial, native to Mediterranean Europe and probably other parts but now naturalized in most temperate countries and cultivated almost worldwide. It is found growing wild on sea cliffs and in waste places and cultivated extensively.

Fennel has a large, spindle-shaped root and an erect, solid, striate stem that grows to a height of 60–125 cm (24–50 in). The bright green, feathery leaves have a thick, fleshy sheath that is edible and the clusters of yellow flowers bloom in July and August. The fruit or seeds are ovoid and prominently ribbed and the whole plant has a faint smell of anise. Fennel has been cultivated as a culinary herb and for medicine since ancient times and several different varieties have been developed as a result of this.

The Romans ate fennel shoots as a vegetable and in modern times the Italians are particularly fond of 'Carosella', the young stems of **Sweet Fennel** *Foeniculum vulgare* var. *dulce*. Pliny also wrote of the medicinal properties of fennel,

recommending it for improving the eyesight, while Hippocrates suggested that wet-nurses used it to increase their milk supply. In medieval times fennel was one of the herbs hung over the doors on Midsummer's Eve to ward off evil spirits and seeds inserted into keyholes were believed to bar the way to ghosts. Fennel was an important ingredient in sack, a popular beverage in Elizabethan England and Culpeper recommended it as an antidote to poisonous mushrooms and snake bites. Fennel is still a very popular culinary herb. Its sweet aniseed flavour is delicious in a sauce or stuffing and it counteracts the oily indigestibility of some fish. It is used in marinades for pork or veal, in soups and salads and to flavour cakes. The seeds are also used to flavour liqueurs as well as to scent soaps and perfumes.

Medicinally fennel has numerous uses. Firstly it is a marvellous aid to the digestion and the dried seeds are prescribed for stomach pains, sluggishness, loss of appetite, flatulence, anaemia and general debility. It is often added

to babies' gripe water to ease painful wind. Fennel is also said to be useful in the treatment of earache, toothache, coughs, asthma, headaches and sore eyes, and a decoction of fennel root is an excellent diuretic recommended for kidney and bladder disorders. It is also said to aid slimmers by speeding up the digestion of fatty foods.

To make fennel tea, bruise 30 g/1 oz fennel seeds and pour on ½ l/1 pt of boiling water. Infuse for five minutes then strain. Drink in small cupfuls to relieve flatulence. Fennel can easily be grown in the garden or in a window box. It likes well-drained loamy soil and a sunny position. Either sow seeds in early spring or propagate by root division in March. Cut the green leaves when the plant begins flowering and collect the seeds in September or October when they are grey-green in colour.

Bronze Fennel *Foeniculum vulgare* 'Purpurascens' is a popular form with bronze-purplish tinged foliage that looks very pretty in a herb garden or a herbaceous border. Plant and use in the same way as ordinary fennel.

Florence Fennel *Foeniculum vulgare* var. *dulce* has thick, basal stalks which, when young, can be eaten like celery or boiled, braised or baked as a delicious vegetable.

Lovage *Levisticum officinale* is a perennial plant, probably native to Continental Europe and naturalized in some areas. It has also been introduced into North America. It is found growing wild in mountainous pastures and in hedgerows near streams and sometimes also cultivated as a crop for distillation and in herb gardens. Lovage is a herbaceous plant with a long, fleshy tap-root and a cylindrical, hollow, channelled stem that reaches a height of 100 cm (40 in). The large, dark-green leaves are divided into narrow, wedge-like segments and when crushed have a strong, aromatic, somewhat yeasty odour. The clusters of small, yellow flowers bloom in June and July followed by the small, aromatic fruits.

Lovage was a popular herb with the Greeks and Romans and commonly grown in monastery gardens in medieval times for both culinary and medicinal uses. The leafstalks and stem-bases can be blanched and eaten like celery, the young leaves added to soups, stews and salads, and the young stems candied like angelica. The popular, old-fashioned lovage cordial also used to contain yarrow and tansy which probably gave it more flavour than the lovage itself. Nowadays, the essence distilled from lovage is used in perfumery and liquor distillation for its distinctive, aromatic flavour and an infusion made from the dried leaves is recommended as a digestif.

In olden times an infusion of the root was recommended for gravel, jaundice and urinary problems and the bruised leaves fried in hog's lard were said to break a blotch or boil. Nowadays, some aromatherapists use lovage oil for removing spots and freckles from the face. The root and seeds do have diuretic and carminative properties and in herbal medicine they are used for colic and flatulence in children as well as being considered a good emmenagogue.

Lovage is easy to grow in a herb garden either from seed or by root division. Sow seeds in rich, moist, well-drained soil, preferably in a sunny position, in late summer when they have just ripened. Transplant seedlings in late autumn or early spring to their permanent position, and the plants should last for several years if the ground is well cultivated. Propagation by root division should be performed in early spring.

Bronze Fennel *Foeniculum vulgare* 'Purpurascens' at Eden Croft herb garden

Florence Fennel *Foeniculum vulgare* var. *dulce*

Lovage *Levisticum officinale*

Red Raripila
Mentha × smithiana 'Rubra'

Apple Mint
Mentha × rotundifolia
(text page 35)

Curly Mint
Mentha spicata 'Crispa'

Mentha × villosa

Pineapple Mint
Mentha suaveolens 'Variegata'

Spearmint *Mentha spicata*

Ginger Mint *Mentha × gentilis*

Mints There are many varieties of this popular, aromatic herb which are used all over the world both in cooking and medicine. All the varieties listed here have similar properties in a greater or lesser degree and they can be used interchangeably.

The generic and common names are supposedly derived from the nymph Menthe, who was turned into the plant we now call mint by the jealous goddess Proserpina when she discovered Pluto's passion for her.

Mints have been extremely popular culinary and medicinal herbs for centuries. The ancient Greeks, recognizing its antiseptic qualities, used mint to scour their banqueting tables and added it to the bath to invigorate their bodies. The Romans used it in sauces (mint sauce is mentioned in records dating back to the third century), as an aid to digestion, and as a mouth freshener. Pliny advised scholars to wear a crown of mint to aid concentration but warned lovers that it was 'contrary to procreation'. However, the Greeks, in line with modern opinion, believed the opposite and warned soldiers to eschew it for fear their courage in battle would be diminished by their increased love-making. From ancient times to the present Arabs have drunk mint tea and carried sprigs of fresh mint to ward off disease-carrying insects and to increase virility.

Spearmint was introduced into Britain by the Romans and remained very popular. As all the early medieval plant lists testify, it was commonly grown in convent and monastery gardens. The Pilgrim Fathers probably introduced mints into North America and they were popular flavouring herbs for sauces and teas. Mints, usually spearmint, are used to make jams, jellies and sauces to accompany meat, fish or vegetable dishes. Fresh, they are also used to make teas and added to fruit drinks, cocktails or punches. Peppermint oil is used as a flavouring for liqueurs, cordials, confectionery, medicine, soaps and toothpastes.

The medicinal properties of various mints are numerous and well-tested. They provide a general tonic that is particularly good for children who are off-colour, old people and convalescents. They are anti-spasmodic and recommended for calming the nerves, insomnia and anxiety, also for soothing coughs, bronchial trouble and asthma. They are excellent for the digestion – easing wind, calming the stomach after sickness, stimulating a poor appetite and soothing nauseous headaches. Mints have antiseptic and anaesthetic properties so can be used as a gargle for sore throats, toothache, mouth ulcers and externally for wounds, cuts and bruises; peppermint is particularly good for this.

Rats and mice intensely dislike mint which is why it was put near cheeses or in sacks of grain and used as a strewing herb in medieval times.

To make mint tea infuse 15–30 g/½ oz fresh or dried leaves in ½ l/1 pt of boiling water for a few minutes. Drink two cups a day after meals to aid sluggish bowels and ease flatulence. In some people it can cause sleeplessness so make a weaker infusion and only drink it in the morning and at lunchtime. Generally, a mild infusion acts as a sedative, a stronger infusion acts as a tonic and stimulant.

Mességué recommends the following infusion, which he prescribes for participants in the Tour de France to put them in top form: 15 g/½ oz mint and 5 g/⅙ oz rosemary infused in 1 1/2 pt of boiling water. To ward off frigidity and promote sexual harmony Mességué prescribes 2 pinches/ 4 g mint to 1 pinch/2 g of savory infused in a cup of boiling water.

Mints are easily grown in a herb garden and make a pretty aromatic border or look and smell good in a rockery or large pot. They thrive so

Spearmint *Mentha spicata*

Pineapple Mint *Mentha suaveolens* 'Variegata'

well they can sometimes become a nuisance. Loewenfeld and Back recommend pushing bits of slate vertically in to the soil to control their spread. Propagate by root cuttings in spring and autumn. They like damp, light soil with shade at the roots and sun on the foliage. Keep different varieties apart to prevent mingling of flavours and watch out for rust fungus on the leaves. If this occurs dig up the affected mint immediately and burn it, replacing with new stock elsewhere, and burn off the topsoil where the blight occurred to kill the spores. Generally rust should not occur if beds are renewed every few years.

Pick fresh mint throughout the summer and dry some in the shade for winter use.

Curly Mint *Mentha spicata* 'Crispa' has curly, bright green leaves and is a decorative form of spearmint. It is good for making mint sauce, jelly and tea.

Ginger Mint *Mentha × gentilis* has golden variegated leaves and a slight ginger scent that makes it an interesting addition to fresh salads.

Red Raripila *Mentha × Smithiana* 'Rubra' has red-tinged leaves and stems and is a good culinary mint.

Mentha × villosa is a hybrid between apple mint and spearmint with lilac or pale pink flowers. It is good in salads and vegetable dishes.

Pineapple Mint *Mentha suaveolens* 'Variegata' is so decorative that it is often grown as a border plant. Use to decorate salads.

Spearmint *Mentha spicata* is a pungent, perennial herb, native to the Mediterranean area and now found naturalized in many other parts of Europe and America. It is most commonly cultivated as a pot herb and naturalized in many damp, waste places and along roadsides. Spearmint has a smooth erect stem, generally branched, that reaches a height of 30–90 cm (12–36 in). The green, oblong to lance-shaped leaves are toothed at the margin and usually smooth on both sides with no stalk. The whorls of lilac flowers form a cylindrical spike at the top of the stem and bloom from July to October.

33

Apple Mint *Mentha rotundifolia* (rear)

Peppermint *Mentha × piperita*

Peppermint *Mentha × piperita* is a pungent perennial herb, a hybrid of spearmint and watermint whose origin is unknown but which is widely cultivated in Europe, southern and eastern Asia, North and South America and Australia. It is occasionally found wild in ditches and damp roadsides and very commonly cultivated. Peppermint has a rhizome and stolons from the nodes of which erect, quadrangular, slightly hairy stems grow that reach a height of 30–80 cm (12–32 in). The short-stalked, lance-shaped leaves which grow in opposite pairs are dark green, deeply veined and rough-textured. The small, reddish-lilac flowers grow in an oblong spiral at the end of the stem and bloom from June to August.

Eau de Cologne Mint *Mentha × piperita citrata* has small green leaves and a strong lemony scent.

Water Mint *Mentha aquatica* grows in very wet places and was formerly used as a strewing herb because of its pleasant, fresh scent. It has green leaves, tinted with purple. It is often used for herbal baths and herb pillows but it is too pungent to be used in cooking.

Pennyroyal *Mentha pulegium* has bright green leaves and purple flowers. Ideal for planting among paving stones, this plant should not be used medicinally as, according to Weiss, pulegon, the main constituent of the volatile oil, is very toxic and can cause abortion.

Eau de Cologne Mint *Mentha × piperita citrata*

Horse Mint *Mentha longifolia*

Water Mint *Mentha aquatica*

Pennyroyal *Mentha pulegium*

Mentha × verticillata

Corsican Mint *Mentha requienii*

Mentha × verticillata is a hybrid between water mint and corn mint and is very variable but robust with a mild scent.

Corsican Mint *Mentha requienii* has tiny leaves and minute purple flowers and a peppermint smell. It makes good ground cover and easily self seeds.

Horse Mint *Mentha longifolia* has grey leaves with purple flower-heads which makes it popular for flower arranging. It is also used in herb pillows but is not used in cooking.

Apple Mint *Mentha rotundifolia* has large, round, hairy leaves and is excellent for use in cooking and for flavouring summer drinks.

French Tarragon *Artemisia dracunculus*
'Sativa' is a perennial herb, native to European Russia, Siberia, Mongolia, northern China (where it is found along rivers and streams) and western and central North America. It is rarely found in the wild but cultivated in kitchen gardens in the drier, warmer areas of Europe or occasionally found as an escape along roadsides near gardens. This aromatic, fragrant plant has long fibrous roots which spread by runners and stems which reach a height of 1 m (3 ft). It has long, smooth, shiny leaves and tiny yellow flowers clustered in a spike, which bloom from June to August.

The generic name is derived from the Greek goddess Artemis, (the Roman Diana), who was said to have given this group of plants to Chiron the centaur. The specific name is taken from the Latin *dracunculus*, 'a little dragon', and similarly its common name is a corruption of the Arabic *tarkhun*, 'a little dragon'. Across the Continent the use of such similar names reflects the belief that tarragon was efficacious in curing the bites of venomous beasts and mad dogs.

Tarragon is chiefly known as a culinary herb. It is an important ingredient in tarragon vinegar, Béarnaise, Hollandaise and sauce tartare, tarragon butter, and it is used in a great variety of chicken dishes, with steaks, chops and fish sauces, in herb mixtures and stuffings and particularly with grilled lobster. However, its value and popularity in cooking doubtless stems from its medicinal value as an aid to digestion. Like the other wormwoods, to which it is related, it has a stimulating effect on the whole digestive system. As an infusion or a *digestif* it can be taken for poor digestion, intestinal distension, nausea, flatulence, hiccups; also for rheumatism, gout, arthritis, as a vermifuge and to soothe the pain of toothache. To make a poultice for rheumatism or toothache, take a wad of leaves, heat gently for a minute or two with a hot iron, allow to cool then place on the affected area.

To make a *digestif*, put 30 g/1 oz of fresh leaves, 1 stick of vanilla, 300 g/12 oz sugar in 1 1/2 pt of 40° or 50° alcohol; macerate for a month, shaking periodically; strain and drink in small glassfuls after meals (from *Grandmother's Secrets*, Jean Palaiseul).

To make tarragon vinegar, fill a glass bottle with fresh leaves, cover with good quality white wine vinegar, leave to stand for two months, then use in salads or mayonnaise.

For tarragon dressing, heat 1 egg yolk, 1 tbs sugar, ½ tsp arrowroot. Add 2 tbs tarragon vinegar and ½ tsp fresh dried tarragon. Stir over boiling water in a bain-marie until thick. Cool and stir in 2 tbs double cream (from *The Complete Book of Herbs and Spices*, Claire Loewenfeld and Philippa Back).

French tarragon can be grown from cuttings or by root division. Plant during spring in well-drained soil, in a warm, sunny position about 45 cm (18 in) apart. Cut plants down in winter and cover with straw to protect against frost. Renew the beds every four years. Tarragon can also be grown indoors and should be watered once or twice a week.

Pick fresh green leaves during the summer flowering period and cut and dry in early autumn for use during the winter.

Russian Tarragon *Artemisia dracunculus*
'Inodora' is a more vigorous, almost weedy, form of the same species, also in cultivation and often sold in error as French Tarragon, but it has a much inferior flavour.

Russian Tarragon
Artemisia dracunculus
'Inodora'

French Tarragon
Artemisia dracunculus
'Sativa'

Tarragons (only distinguishable by taste and scent) Photographed August 4

Caraway *Carum carvi* is an erect biennial, native to Europe, Siberia, Turkey, Asia, India and North Africa and also growing wild in many parts of North America as well as being cultivated commercially in the Netherlands, USSR, Hungary, Germany and Czechoslovakia. It is found growing wild in grassy fields, meadows, roadsides and waste ground from lowland to mountain elevations. Caraway has a spindle-shaped root and smooth, branched, furrowed stems that reach a height of 25–75 cm (10–30 in). The deeply lobed leaves have a pretty feathery appearance and the small white flowers grow in terminal clusters and blossom in June or July. The ripe fruits consist of two, slightly curved, dark brown seeds marked with five distinct, pale brown ridges. They emit a strong, sharp, spicy smell when crushed.

The common name is thought to be derived from the Arabic *al-karwiya*, 'seeds', also presumably the origin of the Latin *carvi*. Caraway has been used by man for thousands of years both in medicine and cooking and numerous superstitions have grown up around it. In German folklore a dish of caraway was put under a child's cot to protect it from witches and it was also believed that any object containing caraway could not be stolen. Thought to prevent lovers from being fickle, it was a common ingredient in love potions. In Elizabethan times it was valued as a condiment. In Shakespeare's *Henry IV Part Two*, Justice Shallow invites Falstaff to partake of 'a pippin and a dish of carrawayes', and farmers traditionally served caraway seed cake at Harvest Suppers.

Caraway is related to dill, fennel and anise and it has similar medicinal properties and uses.

It is a digestive, a carminative, antispasmodic and antiseptic. It was used to stimulate the mammary glands, aiding lactation for nursing mothers. Nowadays it is generally used with other medicines as a corrective or flavouring agent. Distilled caraway water is considered good for infant colic and, sweetened, it is excellent for flavouring children's medicine.

First and foremost however, caraway is cultivated for its culinary uses. It is thought to have been used as far back as the Stone Age. A characteristic flavouring in German and Austrian cooking, it is a seasoning for cheese, dumplings, port, goose and sausages. It is also used to flavour vegetable dishes such as sauerkraut, as well as cakes, bread and sweetmeats. The seeds yield an essential oil which is used to flavour the liqueur kümmel. Young caraway shoots can be added to salads for an aromatic tang and the boiled root makes a delicious vegetable. An infusion made from the seeds has a soothing effect on the digestion and the seeds can be chewed to sweeten the breath and relieve heartburn after a rich, highly spiced meal.

If unobtainable from the wild, caraway can be grown from seed. Plant in almost any kind of soil in a sunny position either in April or in August for use the next summer. If the ground is weeded and hoed well the seeds should freely self-sow and the plants should be cut when the seeds are ripe. Dry thoroughly, then thresh and store in a cool, dry place out of the sunlight.

Dill *Anethum graveolens* is an aromatic upright annual, native to Iran, India, southern Europe and Russia. It was probably introduced into

Dill *Anethum graveolens*

Dill *Anethum graveolens* (flowers) Photographed July 15

English Mace *Achillea decolorans*

Caraway *Carum carvi*

northern Europe at an early date and is now commonly cultivated there and in many parts of the world and often found naturalized in North America. It grows wild along roadsides and in waste places in the warm areas of southern Europe. Dill has a long, thin, spindle-shaped root and a smooth, hollow, finely striped dark-green stem, 60–100 cm (24–40 in) in height. The feathery, blue-green leaves are similar to those of fennel but more luxuriant, and the stem bears flat clusters of numerous yellow flowers with small, inrolled petals. They blossom from June to August. The flat, brown fruits or seeds have prominent ribs, divide into two and have a pungent, bitter taste.

Dill is one of the herbs mentioned in the Egyptian papyri and is thought to be the anethon described by Dioscorides. The name dill is perhaps derived from the Old Norse word *dylla*, 'to soothe', an allusion to the carminative properties of the plant.

Used in the Middle Ages as both a medicinal and culinary herb, dill is nowadays mostly cultivated for its culinary value. However, the two uses are interlinked. The essential oil, of which the seeds contain up to 4 per cent, has stimulant, carminative and stomachic properties, and promotes lactation. Infant gripe water is made from dill seeds and is used to soothe babies with indigestion, flatulence or colic and to induce sleep. An infusion of the herb has also been recommended for treating piles.

Dill is considered of premier importance in the preparation of fish dishes and it is a common ingredient in pickling. It is the essential ingredient in the famous Scandinavian dish Gravalax as well as being a favourite herb in many of their other dishes.

As the leaves lose their flavour when cooked for any length of time, it is best to use them raw or add to a cooked sauce only minutes before serving.

To relieve indigestion soak about 50 g (approx. 2 tbsps) of crushed dill leaves in a cup of water overnight then strain and sweeten with a little honey. A tablespoon of this mixture taken after a heavy meal is an excellent way to calm the stomach. Smaller doses can be given to young children.

Dill is not found in the wild in Britain, but can be cultivated in your herb garden. Seeds should be sown from April to June in any kind of soil as long as it is kept moist and well-weeded. The leaves can be cut at any time but are best just before flowering. The seeds should ripen on the plant, then be shaken out and dried in the sun or over a moderate heat indoors.

English Mace *Achillea decolorans* is a perennial herb of uncertain taxonomic status (probably a hybrid of sneezewort, *Achillea ptarmica*) which is thought to have been introduced into cultivation from Switzerland in 1798. English mace grows to a height of 50 cm (20 in). It has narrow, bright green leaves with a toothed margin, and cream-coloured, daisy-like flowers that bloom from July to September. The aromatic leaves can be chopped finely and sprinkled on potato salad or used to flavour soups and stews.

It is an excellent plant to grow in a large pot: the long stems will tend to arch out and down and continue to flower for a long time.

Thymus serpyllum 'Coccineus Majus'

Thymus hirsutus

Thymus herba-barona

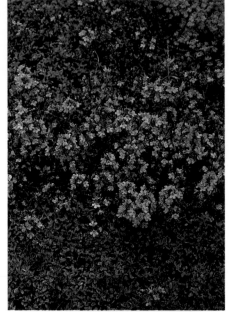

Wild Thyme *Thymus serpyllum*

Thymus cilicicus

Thymus pseudolanuginosus

Thymus 'Broad Leaf'

Thymus praecox subsp. *arcticus*

Golden Lemon Thyme *Thymus* × *citriodorus* 'Bertram Anderson'

Thymus serpyllum 'Lemon Curd' has grey-green leaves and a lemon scent

Wild Thyme *Thymus serpyllum* is a shrubby perennial plant, native to central and northern Europe, which grows wild on dry stony ground, green heaths and grasslands and often along hilly sheep tracks. Wild thyme has a woody, fibrous root and long, creeping stems from which arise flowering branchlets, covered in short, white hairs, that reach a height of 10 cm (4 in). The opposite leaves are broadly elliptical to ovate and the pinkish-mauve flowers, growing in a dense spike at the end of the branches, bloom from May to September.

The generic name is derived either from the Greek *thymon*, 'to fumigate', because it was used as a sweet-smelling incense, or from the Greek '*thumus*', 'courage', alluding to the belief that it invigorated warriors. The common name is from Greek *thymus*, 'to burn a sacrifice'. Roman soldiers used to bathe in thyme water to imbibe energy. The antiseptic properties of thyme were recognized in ancient times and the Egyptians incorporated it into their embalming ointments. During the Middle Ages members of the nobility carried posies of aromatic herbs, including thyme, to ward off the odours and germs of the populace. Modern research has shown that thyme essence is so strong it can kill bacilli in forty seconds. What need is there to take courses of antibiotics for minor infections when regular use of thyme keeps one germ-free?

Thyme is used extensively in the manufacture of cosmetics, perfumes and liquors. It is often an ingredient in mouthwashes, gargles, toothpastes and powders. It is used to scent soaps and powders and added to pot pourris. Thyme is an essential ingredient in bouquet garni and is used to flavour a wide variety of dishes – soups, stews, meat, fish and vegetables. Bees are particularly fond of thyme and the honey they make after feeding on thyme has a delicious flavour. Oil of thyme is used in aromatherapy and is a comforting rub for rheumatism, sciatica and similar aches and pains.

Thyme is a stimulant and a tonic and is recommended for respiratory, digestive and circulatory disorders. It is reputed to be good for coughs, colds, flu, whooping cough, bronchial problems and asthma; it is excellent for poor digestion, over-eating, flatulence, loss of appetite and sickness; it soothes migraine, depression and nervousness and it is said to regularize women's periods.

Taken regularly in food or drunk as a herbal tea, it helps to keep one in good health. To make an infusion, put 30 g/1 oz of fresh or dried thyme in ½ l/1 pt of boiling water. Steep for five minutes, strain and drink three to four cupfuls a day after meals. Double the quantity of thyme to make a stronger decoction for external use as either a gargle, or a lotion to add to the bath to relieve pain, or to put in a compress to soothe cuts, sores and wounds.

Wild thyme should be collected from an unpolluted spot or is easy to grow in dry, chalky or stony soil, in the sun, protected from the wind. Gather fresh leaves to use as needed and dry some bunches in a dark place for winter use. When dry store in dark, airtight jars and it will retain most of its flavour.

Thymus serpyllum 'Coccineus Majus' has rich red flowers and dark green leaves.

Thymus herba-barona has pink flowers and strongly lemon-scented leaves.

Garden Thyme *Thymus vulgaris* is a low, spreading evergreen shrub native to the western Mediterranean as far east as south-eastern Italy, and cultivated in many other parts of Europe. It grows wild in dry, gravelly soil on rocky ground and in maquis and is also cultivated as a herb. Garden thyme is an aromatic plant with quite strong roots and woody, branched stems that reach a height of 30 cm (12 in). The tiny, linear to elliptical leaves are slightly hairy, and the numerous pale mauve flowers growing in spikes at the top of the branches bloom from May to October.

Thymus × citriodorus
'Nyewoods'

Thymus × citriodorus
'Aureus'

Thymus
× citriodorus
'Silver Queen'

Thymus doerfleri

Thymus 'Porlock'

Thymus praecox
subsp. *arcticus* 'Albus'

Thymus comosus

Thymus
vulgaris

Thymus
pallasianus
synonym *odoratissimus*

Thymus × citriodorous
'Variegatus'

Thymus richardii 'Peter Davis'

Thymus doerfleri
'Bressingham Pink'

Thymus
herba-barona

Thymus × citriodorus 'Silver Queen'

Garden Thyme *Thymus vulgaris*

Lemon Thyme *Thymus × citriodorus*

Thymus × citriodorus 'Variegatus'

Garden Thyme and Wild Thyme are very similar in their medicinal and culinary properties although garden thyme is generally a bit stronger and more active than wild thyme.

Many related species and garden varieties are grown to add ornamental value to gardens and to add varying flavours to cooking. We mention some and illustrate many others.

Thymus pseudo lanuginosus has pale mauve flowers and grey woolly leaves (See page 38).

Thymus praecox subsp. *arcticus* has white flowers and small green leaves.

Thymus cilicicus synonym *azoricas* has pink flowers and spiky, bright green leaves. (See page 38).

Thymus 'Porlock' has mauve flowers and dark green leaves. It grows into a robust bush and is a good alternative for cooking.

Thymus doerfleri has pink flowers and long, grey, woolly leaves.

Thymus doerfleri 'Bressingham Pink' has pink flowers and long, grey-green leaves.

Thymus 'Doone Valley' has purple flowers, golden variegated leaves and a lemon scent.

Thymus × citriodorus 'Variegatus' synonym 'Silver Posie' has pink flowers and silver variegated leaves.

Lemon Thyme *Thymus × citriodorus* has pink flowers and a strong lemon scent.

Golden Lemon Thyme *Thymus × citriodorus* 'Bertram Anderson' forms a small mound of golden green leaves. (See page 39).

Thymus serpyllum 'Snow Drift'

Thymus praecox subsp. *arcticus* 'Albus'

Thymus 'Doone Valley'

Thymus pulegioides synonym *montanus*

41

Origanum vulgare 'Golden Tip'

Origanum vulgare 'Curly Gold'

Pot Marjoram Origanum onites

'Purple Ruffles'

'Green Ruffles'

Purple Basil Ocimum basilicum var. purpureum

Sacred Basil Ocimum sanctum

Anise Scented Basil

Sweet Basil Ocimum basilicum

Lemon Basil Ocimum citriodorum

Photographed August 10

Photographed August 20

Wild Marjoram or **Oregano** *Origanum vulgare* is an aromatic perennial, native to Europe and north and western Asia and also found cultivated in North America. It grows in dry pastures, along hedgebanks and in scrub, favouring dry chalky soil. Wild marjoram has creeping roots from which grow erect, quadrangular stems that are reddish and finely haired and reach a height of 30–80 cm (12–32 in). The aromatic, dark-green leaves are ovate with minute stalks and scattered hairs. The rose-lilac flowers grow in clusters at the tops of the branches and bloom from July to September.

Three main species – wild marjoram; sweet marjoram (*Origanum majorana*) and pot marjoram (*Origanum onites*) – and numerous other varieties are cultivated, but they all have similar properties and uses although historically specific uses have often been associated with particular kinds.

The generic name derives from two Greek words, *oros*, 'a mountain', and *ganos*, 'joy', alluding to their delightful appearance on the mountain sides. Marjoram has a very long history of medicinal and culinary use. The Greeks believed it brought joy to the dead and planted it on graves and both they and the Romans considered it a symbol of happiness and used it to crown young couples. Because of its strong, aromatic odour and antiseptic properties, from the thymol which Wild Marjoram contains (although the cultivated variety does not), it was used in medieval times as a strewing herb and to sweeten water and powder and make aromatic bags, like lavender bags.

Both sweet marjoram and wild marjoram are used for cooking though the former has the

sweeter, more delicately spicy flavour, while the latter has the spicier flavour, particularly if grown in a warm climate. Pot marjoram is slightly bitter and not nearly so sweet and delicate as the other two, although its flavour lasts longer in cooked dishes. The Italians and Germans are particularly fond of using marjoram in their cooking. It blends well with thyme and basil and is used to flavour sausages, salamis, pizza, spaghetti, stuffings and tomato dishes. The essence obtained from sweet marjoram is used in making liquor and perfume while that of wild marjoram is used to make toothpastes.

Medicinally, marjoram has strong sedative properties and care must be taken not to take large doses, but mild teas have a soothing effect on the nerves and aid sleep. It also has a soothing effect on the digestive system, acting as a tonic and diuretic and relieving colic and dyspepsia and it has been considered useful for regularizing menstruation. Its antiseptic properties make it a good remedy for coughs, colds, tonsillitis and respiratory problems when inhaled, while external gargles help to cure thrush and mouth infections. Compresses or lotions ease external wounds and swellings and a pad of cotton wool soaked in marjoram infusion will relieve hay fever; inhaling the fresh juice is said to cure headaches. Marjoram is particularly good for herbal baths and pillows.

To make an infusion, put 15–30 g/½ oz–1 of the dried herb in 1 1/2 pt of boiling water and leave for five to ten minutes.

Jean Palaiseul recommends making an unguent from 100 g/4 oz of fresh marjoram simmered for one hour in ½ l/1 pt of olive oil or 500 g/1 lb of butter or lard in a bain-marie, then

strained and bottled. Use this to rub into areas of muscular or rheumatic pain and apply in a compress to relieve headaches and around the nose to clear a cold.

Wild marjoram can either be picked in the wild or grown in a herb garden. Marjorams are easy to grow from seed in any kind of soil but they may need to be protected from the cold. When putting the seedlings out, make sure to choose the driest, sunniest spot you can find.

Gather the whole plant (except the roots) in August or September and hang it up in little bunches to dry and store for winter use.

Compact Marjoram *Origanum vulgare* 'Compactum' is a low-growing variety that can be used like oregano.

Golden Marjoram *Origanum onites* 'Aureum' is a very pretty variety with golden leaves, though they scorch easily in the sun.

Pot Marjoram *Origanum onites* is a perennial, dwarf shrub native to Mediterranean Europe. It grows in dryish soil and is commonly grown as a pot or house plant.

Pot marjoram has creeping roots and erect, hairy reddish stems that reach a height of 40–60 cm (16–24 in). The soft, green, ovate to roundish leaves have raised veins on the under surface and the white flowers which grow in a dense cluster at the end of the branches bloom in August.

Sweet Basil *Ocimum basilicum* is a low-growing, aromatic, annual herb probably native to Iran and India but now grown all over the world. It is rarely found in the wild except as an escape but frequently cultivated in gardens. Sweet Basil has a tap-root and a square stem, branched at the top, that reaches a height of 50 cm (20 in). The fragrant, alternate leaves are oval to lanceolate and bright shiny green with distinctive veining. The small, creamy flowers grow in whorls in the leaf axils and bloom from June to September.

The specific name is the medieval Latin form of the Greek word from which the common name derives, *basileus*, 'King', indicating the esteem with which this herb was regarded. Its history dates back many centuries and it is said to have come to Europe from India via the Middle East. In Iran, Malaysia and Egypt, it is planted on graves and in Crete it denoted sorrowful love, while in parts of Italy it was used as a love token. By contrast, in ancient Greece and Rome it was believed that basil would only prosper where there was abuse and it was associated with poverty, hate and misfortune.

In medieval times there seemed to be considerable controversy about the medicinal value of basil. Some old medics considered it poisonous because it would not grow near Rue, others thought it good for cheering the spirit and clearing the brain.

Basil is a very popular culinary herb, particularly on the Continent. In France it is the basic ingredient of the famous Provençal *soupe au pistou* and in Italy, of *pesto*, the wonderful sauce, originated in Genoa, used to flavour pasta. Fresh basil is delicious added to salads and particularly good sprinkled on tomatoes. It is used in all kinds of soups, stews, vegetable dishes and with eggs, poultry and mushrooms. Use sparingly if cooking the herb as heat develops the flavour. Basil oil is also used in the perfumery and liquor industries.

Although most famous for its gastronomic uses basil also has a history of medicinal use. It has sedative and antispasmodic properties that make it an excellent aid to digestion and beneficial for nervous disorders, headaches, migraine, vertigo and colic in children. In the Far East it has been employed as a cough medicine and in parts of Africa it is used to expel worms. Fresh juice from the leaves dropped into the ear is said to ease inflammation and according to Mességué, it stimulates milk in breast-feeding mothers and, as a gargle, cures thrush. To make an infusion put 30–45 g/1–1½ oz of dried leaves in 1 1/2 pt of boiling water and infuse for five minutes. Drink two to three cups a day for bad nerves, digestive upsets and headaches.

To make a decoction to increase lactation put 30 g/1 oz of fresh leaves into 1 1/2 pt of water and drink twice a day.

Basil is easily grown from seed in a herb garden, window box or pot but it likes plenty of light, sun and warmth so if growing it in a temperate climate keep it under glass. It hates frost so sow seeds in May and once the plant is 15 cm (6 in). high, keep using the top leaves to encourage bushy growth.

Purple Basil *Ocimum basilicum* var. *purpureum* has a strong, aromatic scent but it also very decorative with its purple leaves and pale pink flowers.

Lemon Basil *Ocimum citriodorum* is a smaller compact variety with a wonderful lemon scent.

Bush Basil *Ocimum minimum* is an annual that grows to 15 cm (6 in). Traditionally the dried leaves were used as snuff and the fresh leaves taken to relieve flatulence. They are mildly sedative. The leaves can also be used in salads and sauces.

Wild Marjoram or **Oregano** *Origanum vulgare*

Golden Marjoram *Origanum onites* 'Aureum'

Compact Marjoram *Origanum vulgare* 'Compactum'

Sweet Basil *Ocimum basilicum*

Bush Basil *Ocimum minimum*

Wild Basil *Clinopodium vulgare*

Basil Thyme *Acinos arvensis*

Saffron Crocus *Crocus sativus*

Sacred Basil *Ocimum sanctum* has a spicy scent and is grown in Thailand around Buddhist temples. It is used in stir fries.

Wild Basil *Clinopodium vulgare* is a perennial herb, native to Europe, central and western Asia, Siberia, North Africa and North America. It is found growing wild in hedges, wood margins and scrub, and in dry grassland. Wild Basil has a shortly creeping rhizome and erect, simple or sparsely branching stems that reach a height of 30–80 cm (12–32 in). The ovate to round, furry leaves have a thyme-like smell and the clusters of rose-purple or pink flowers bloom in July.

The leaves have been used medicinally to make an infusion that helps to overcome weak digestion.

Collect leaves from the wild.

Basil Thyme *Acinos arvensis* is usually an annual, occasionally a short-lived perennial herb, native to most parts of Europe (except the extreme north and parts of the south), Asia Minor and the Caucasus. It is found in dry, sunny habitats such as arable fields, open grassland or rocks. Basil Thyme has erect, ascending, hairy stems, branching from the base, that reach a height of 10–20 cm (4–8 in). The leaves are ovate to lance-shaped, with conspicuous veins underneath. The violet flowers form loose terminal clusters and bloom from June to August.

Basil Thyme can be cultivated in a herb garden by planting in any well-drained soil. It makes good ground cover and the flowerheads are used for seasoning and to decorate salads.

Saffron Crocus *Crocus sativus* is a small, perennial plant, native to Asia Minor but extensively cultivated in southern Europe since ancient times, and now found as far east as India and China; sometimes naturalized. Saffron Crocus has a flattened, underground corm from which arises a short stem encased in sheaths. The narrow, deep-ribbed leaves have a longitudinal white line on the upper surface and the individual, pale-lilac coloured flowers consist of a long tube that broadens out at the top and in the centre bears the reddish-orange, tripartite stigma which yields the saffron spice. The flowers bloom in September.

The generic name is derived from the Greek *krokos*, 'a thread', alluding to the stigmas. Also known as *karkom* by the Hebrews, it is mentioned in the Song of Solomon. Greek myths and poetry often refer to the beauty of saffron – both the colour and smell were greatly admired and it was highly prized as a dye. The ancients recognized its medicinal properties – it is antispasmodic, carminative and an emmenagogue. Saffron tea was drunk to refresh the spirit and was also said to be useful in the treatment of hysteria.

To make an infusion, put a pinch of saffron (4 g) into ½ l/1 pt of boiling water and infuse for three minutes. Drink warm and sweetened if necessary.

Nowadays it is rarely used for medicine but highly prized in cooking. Unfortunately it is very expensive because at least sixty thousand flowers have to be gathered and the stigmas picked out and kiln-dried to make one pound of

Creeping Savory *Satureja spicigera*

Winter Savory *Satureja montana*

Summer Savory *Satureja hortensis*

Summer Savory *Satureja hortensis*

saffron spice. Fortunately, however, only a tiny amount is needed to colour and flavour such dishes as *paella*, *bouillabaisse*, *risotto milanese* and numerous Indian dishes with its spicy, aromatic and pungent taste.

At one time saffron crocus was extensively cultivated around Saffron Walden in Essex but nowadays the best saffron is imported from south-eastern Spain. Cheaper saffron is also being extensively cultivated in Iran but it has not the depth of colour of the European variety. Because of its cost, Saffron is frequently adulterated with similar-coloured raw materials such as safflower or marigold.

Saffron crocus can be grown from seed but it takes three years for the plant to flower. Alternatively bulbs can be planted in August in rich, sandy, well-drained soil in a sheltered spot. The flowers will bloom in September; the stigmas should be picked out by hand as soon as these open, and immediately dried in the sun or in a low oven, before being stored in a dark place in an airtight container.

Winter Savory *Satureja montana* is an aromatic, perennial undershrub, native to southern Europe and introduced to many other parts, which is found growing wild on rocky mountain slopes and in dry places and much cultivated as a pot herb. Winter savory has erect ascending stems, with stiff branches that reach a height of 15–40 cm (6–16 in). The narrow, oblong leaves are pointed and the pale purple or bluish-purple flowers bloom in June. Winter savory has a sharper, spicier taste than Summer savory but is used for medicinal and culinary purposes in much the same way as Summer savory.

Winter savory is woody, unlike the annual summer savory but it too is easy to grow from seed; alternatively it can be grown from root division or cuttings. It prefers a light, well-drained soil and will grow into a decent-sized shrub if the conditions are right.

Creeping Savory *Satureja spicigera* is a much smaller creeping species with white flowers. It looks charming on rockeries or borders and has a good strong flavour for culinary use.

Summer Savory *Satureja hortensis* is an aromatic, hardy annual herb, native to the Mediterranean region and now cultivated all over the world, which is sometimes found growing wild on moors and mountain slopes but extensively grown as a pot herb and found as an escape. Summer savory has a small,

fibrous, spindle-shaped root and a branched, striate stem that reaches a height of 10–35 cm (4–14 in). The narrow, pointed leaves are mid-green to red and glossy with glandular dots. The clusters of small white, pink or lilac flowers bloom in July.

The generic name comes from the Latin *satyrus*, 'a satyr', alluding to its ancient reputation as an aphrodisiac. Mességué claims it is an essential ingredient in the love potions he made for frigid or impotent couples, having been told by his father when he was a boy that it was the 'herb of happiness'.

It is also known as the 'bean herb' because, when added to all kinds of bean dishes, it brings out their flavour without dominating it; it also aids the digestion of beans, which give many people wind.

For centuries the aromatic, slightly peppery taste of Summer savory has been relished in cooking. In Roman times it was used to make a sauce similar to mint sauce, as well as being added to stuffings for poultry and as a flavouring for pies, sausages, eggs, meat or fish. Because of the strong volatile oil it contains, which aids digestion, it is particularly recommended for flavouring foods that are difficult to digest such as pork and cucumber.

Although chiefly used as a culinary herb, Summer savory was recognized in the Middle Ages for its stimulant and soothing properties. It was most highly regarded for its ability to regulate the digestive system – it calms stomach cramps, relieves wind, has an antiseptic effect on fermenting intestinal flora, is diuretic and mildly purgative. It was also considered useful as an expectorant and for asthma and as a wash for throat or mouth ulcers.

Nowadays it is used extensively in the perfume industry and also in the distillation of wines and spirits.

Bees are extremely fond of it and if it is planted near beehives they produce excellent honey from it. Interestingly, many gardeners will testify that the crushed leaves of Summer savory will bring instant relief to a bee or wasp sting.

To make an infusion, put 45–60 g/1½–2oz of leaves in 1 1/2 pt of boiling water and infuse for five to ten minutes. Drink three cupfuls a day after meals to aid digestion.

Summer savory is easy to grow from seed in a herb garden. It likes rich, light soil and plenty of sun. Sow seeds in April: they should be ready for use in June and, once they have flowered, can be pulled up and dried – in bunches, in the shade – for winter use.

Hairy Bittercress *Cardamine hirsuta*

Watercress *Nasturtium officinale*

Hairy Bittercress *Cardamine hirsuta* is an annual herb, native to Europe and most of the northern hemisphere. It is commonly found growing wild on rocks, screes, walls and bare ground. Hairy Bittercress has a slender tap-root and a smooth, erect stem that reaches a height of 8–30 cm (3–12 in). The numerous basal leaves grow in a compact rosette and are pinnate with three to seven pairs of roundish leaflets that are somewhat hairy on the upper surface and the margins. The small white flowers bloom throughout the year.

This very common weed grows on bare soil in the garden during winter and the sharp, hotly flavoured leaves can be eaten from October onwards. They are delicious in sandwiches and with cheese or added to soups and winter salads.

Watercress *Nasturtium officinale* is a perennial herb, native to Europe, North Africa and Asia and also introduced and abundant in many parts of the world. It is commonly found growing wild in shallow, slow-moving water in rivers, streams and ditches and also cultivated for culinary use. Watercress has many rootlets and smooth, hollow, angular shoots that grow to a length of 10–70 cm (4–28 in). The glossy, bright green leaves are stalked at the bottom, stalkless at the top, each leaf with five to ten leaflets, the terminal one being more heart-shaped than the ovate lateral leaflets. The small, whitish cream flowers grow in small, flat-topped clusters and bloom from April to October.

The generic name is derived, according to Pliny, from the Latin *nasus tortus*, 'writhing nose', and refers to the pungent odour of the plant. The specific name indicates that it was formerly included in official lists of medicinal plants, and it was listed in Dioscorides' *Materia medica* of AD 77. Rich in vitamin C and numerous minerals, watercress makes a very nutritious addition to the diet and it has been eaten for centuries not only for the culinary flavour but also for its tonic properties. Nowadays it is commonly used to make soups, salads and stir-fries and as a garnish for sandwiches.

Since Roman times it has been used in a wide variety of ways. Diocorides considered it an aphrodisiac. Hippocrates advocated it as an expectorant and stimulant. Because of its anti-scorbutic properties, it was recommended to be taken internally in a salad or soup as a general tonic, to promote the appetite, to help counteract anaemia, to lower the blood-sugar level in diabetes and as a diuretic.

Taken externally, it has a long-standing reputation as an effective hair tonic, helping to promote the growth of thick hair, and the expressed juice or bruised leaves are recommended by Culpeper for clearing the complexion of blemishes, spots and freckles. Watercress poultices are also said to be good for healing glandular tumours or lymphatic swellings.

Watercress can easily be found in the wild but great care must be taken when picking it because of the possibility of liver-fluke pollution, which can easily occur if cattle, or particularly sheep, graze anywhere near water that flows into the area in which watercress grows. Thorough washing of the freshly gathered plant is essential, though there is no danger if it is cooked, so watercress soup is an ideal way to consume it.

Chickweed *Stellaria media* is an annual or overwintering herb, native to Europe and naturalized almost throughout the world. One of the most common weeds, it is found growing along streams and roads and in fields, gardens and waste places. Chickweed has a slender tap-root and numerously branched, weakly ascending or procumbent stems that reach a length of 5–40 cm (2–16 in). The stems are smooth except for a single line of hairs growing down one side. The succulent, oval leaves grow in pairs and the numerous, small, white flowers are deeply lobed and bloom from March to September.

Although now generally considered to be a troublesome garden weed, chickweed has been used as a culinary plant since the Middle Ages. The whole plant can be eaten raw, in salads, or cooked as a vegetable that is very similar to spinach, or used to make a delicious soup. However, though it is highly recommended by wild food aficionados, some authorities warn against eating chickweed because of its high saponin content. Medicinally, it has soothing and cooling properties and has been used for centuries either as a poultice or as an ointment to soothe wounds, ulcers, chilblains, roseola and other skin irritations. The expressed juice of the plant was formerly used in eyewashes and an infusion of the fresh herb drunk to alleviate constipation. It was also thought to be good for kidney complaints.

Culpeper described some of its virtues as follows: 'The juice, or distilled water, is of much good use for all heats and redness in the eyes, to drop some thereof into them; and it is of good effect to ease pains from the heat and sharpness of the blood in the piles . . . it is used also in hot and virulent ulcers and sores in the privy parts of men and women, or on the legs or elsewhere.'

Chickweed is very easily found in the wild or will spread rapidly if introduced into bare ground in the garden.

Spring Beauty or **Miner's Lettuce** *Montia perfoliata* synonym *Claytonia perfoliata* is an annual herb, native to western North America and naturalized in western Europe. It is found growing wild on rather dry, sandy soils, along roadsides and on lower mountain slopes. Miner's Lettuce has erect or ascending stems which reach a height of 30 cm (12 in). The fleshy, elliptical to ovate basal leaves form a long-stalked rosette. The two connate stem leaves form a kind of saucer beneath the small, white flowers on the flowering stem. These bloom from April to July.

One of the common names of this plant goes back to the days of the American gold rush: Californian gold miners ate the plant to prevent scurvy when fresh fruit and vegetables were in short supply and, as recently as 1891, the members of the Health Expedition to California ate large quantities of the plant after they emerged from several months travelling in the desert during which time they had eaten no fruit or vegetables of any kind.

The blossoms and leaves make an attractive, cress-like addition to salads, or the leaves can be cooked and eaten like greens – apparently a favourite with the Mendocine Indians in California. Although small and labour-intensive to collect, the roots are recommended as similar to chestnuts if boiled and peeled.

Chickweed *Stellaria media*

Spring Beauty or **Miner's Lettuce** *Montia perfoliata* synonym *Claytonia perfoliata*

Shepherd's Purse *Capsella bursa- pastoris* is an annual or biennial plant, originally native to Europe, but now found all over the world. It grows abundantly in waste places, roadsides and cultivated land. Shepherd's Purse has a tap-root and a slender, erect stem which can reach a height of up to 60 cm (24 in). The long, hairy, basal leaves form a rosette and vary in shape from deeply pinnafid to entire; the stem leaves are also variable but generally small, arrow-shaped and clasping the stem. The many small, white flowers, arranged in a cluster, bloom all year. The triangular fruit pods which follow the flowers contain numerous yellow, oval seeds.

The generic name is derived from *capsella*, 'a pocket or purse', and the specific name *bursa-pastoris*, the French common name, *Bourse de pasteur*, the German name *Hirtentasche* and the English name Shepherd's Purse all allude to the resemblance of the flat seed-pouches to the old-fashioned leather purses commonly worn by shepherds on their belts.

The plant has been used medicinally since the Middle Ages, primarily as a blood herb because it is so effective in stopping bleeding. It was used for open wounds and injuries, nosebleeds, blood spitting, excessive menstruation and uterine haemorrhage. Modern research has tried to explain the nature and extent of the haemostatic properties the plant appears to have but the studies have been contradictory. It is now thought that batches of the plant are inconsistent. One theory has it that a white fungus, commonly, but not always, found on the plant, has the haemostatic properties; however, this has not been proved conclusively.

It has also been used as a substitute for quinine in treating malaria and poultices applied to the wrist are said to have helped reduce intermittent fevers.

An infusion can be drunk as an excellent spring tonic and a wad of cotton wool soaked in fresh juice or an infusion can be inserted into the nostrils to stop a nosebleed.

In olden days shepherd's purse was used commonly as a pot herb and, similar to cress in taste, it is delicious in sandwiches or added to salads. However, some authorities have recently suggested it may be somewhat toxic, so it should perhaps only be eaten in small quantities, if at all.

To cultivate, either collect it from the wild (make sure to find a good pollution-free site) or grow from seed in any kind of soil.

Shepherd's Purse *Capsella bursa-pastoris*

Dandelion *Taraxacum officinale* Photographed April 12

Chicory or **Wild Succory** *Cichorium intybus*

Winter Cress *Barbarea vulgaris*

Land Cress or **American Winter Cress**
Barbarea verna

Dandelion *Taraxacum officinale* is a hardy perennial herb, native throughout the northern hemisphere, which is commonly found growing wild in pastures, lawns, meadows, roadsides and waste places. Dandelion has a fleshy root, white inside and brown outside, and a simple, hollow stem that reaches a height of 10–20 cm (4–8 in). The lance-shaped leaves with a toothed margin form a rosette at the stem base and the bright yellow flowers bloom from April until October, succeeded by the familiar fluffy 'clock' of fruits – seeds bearing a feathery pappus. The whole plant contains a milky white juice.

The generic name is either derived from the two Greek words *taraxis*, 'eye disorders', and *akeomai*, 'to cure', alluding to one of the plant's traditional uses as a cure for eye disorders, or from the Greek *taraxo*, 'I have caused', and *achos*, 'pain', alluding to the medical effects of the plant. The common name comes from the Old French *dent de lion*, tooth of the lion, referring to the jagged edges of the leaves. In France it is also known as *pissenlit*, pissabed or wetabed, an allusion to its diuretic properties.

Used by Arab physicians in the eleventh and twelfth centuries, the numerous curative properties of dandelion are still recognized today. Rich in protein, sugar, vitamins, minerals and bitter principles, it is a wholesome food as well as an active medicinal herb.

The young leaves are delicious in soups or salads and the French manner of serving them with vinaigrette and bits of crunchy bacon is delicious. The root, roasted and ground, is a popular substitute for coffee, particularly among those who like their beverages caffeine-free. The leaves and flowers are made into the traditionally popular dandelion wine, and the young pickled buds make a very acceptable substitute for capers. Eating or drinking dandelion in any form or shape will have a beneficial effect on the body. It is a diuretic, a mild laxative, a tonic, a blood purifier and an aid to the digestion. It is recommended for liver complaints, jaundice, problems in the gall bladder and kidneys, loss of appetite, eczema and dropsy, and it has also been prescribed as a relief for rheumatism and arthritis.

Weiss reports that the latest research substantiates the empirical knowledge that has advocated dandelion for treating diseases of the liver, bile duct and particularly gallstones. Dandelion is also recognized by modern herbalists as being effective in treating chronic degenerative joint diseases. Courses of dandelion therapy help to increase mobility, reduce stiffness and decrease the tendency for further lesions to develop.

To make a decoction, put 30 g/1 oz of dried leaves and 30 g/1 oz of chopped root in 1 1/2 pt of cold water. Bring to the boil, simmer for two minutes and infuse for a further fifteen minutes, then strain and drink three cups a day before meals. To make a toilet water to whiten the skin, put a handful of flowers in 1 1/2 pt of water, boil for thirty minutes, strain, cool and dab on the face morning and evening.

Collect from the wild or your own garden and gather young leaves in spring for salad, older leaves in summer for making tea and wine, and pull out the roots in autumn.

Chicory or **Wild Succory** *Cichorium intybus* is a perennial herb, native to Europe and Asia, which has been introduced and is now naturalized in many parts of North and South America, South Africa, Australia and New Zealand. It is found growing wild in pastures, waste ground, roadsides and on limestone hills. Chicory has a long, stout tap-root, a short vertical stock and erect, grooved, branched, hairy stems, that reach a height of 30–125 cm (12–50 in). The basal leaves are broadly lance-shaped, toothed and form a rosette, while the stem leaves are stalkless and more lance-shaped. The beautiful, mauve-blue flowers grow in clusters in the axils of the upper leaves and bloom from May to September.

Chicory has been used medicinally since ancient times and the Romans also used it as a delicious vegetable. Dioscorides recommended it as a digestive and Galen used it for sore eyes. The ancient herbalists thought the leaves made a good poultice for swellings and inflammations and taken in a broth considered it effective against ague and for those needing a general cleaning tonic. Mességué says that he considers the main value of chicory to be as an antidote for liver troubles and also good for cleansing the digestive and urinary systems and treating skin problems such as boils and eczema. The boiled root taken in the form of a syrup of succory is a gentle and effective laxative for children.

However, chicory is probably more well-known as an adulterant to coffee. The roasted, ground roots are added to coffee giving it a dark colour and bitterish taste that is particularly popular on the Continent where it is generally believed that chicory counteracts the stimulating effect of the caffeine. In Europe chicory is also cultivated not only as animal fodder but extensively for human consumption: the fresh leaves give a sharp tang to winter salads or are delicious cooked as a vegetable, as are the white blanched leaves of the cultivated variety. In some countries the roots are also boiled and eaten as a vegetable and are considered particularly good for diabetics. The flowers can also be eaten and are a very attractive addition to a salad.

The cultivated varieties of chicory are easy to grow in a kitchen garden. Sow the seeds in May or June and remove the flowers as soon as they appear to encourage root growth. To force the white leaf crowns, dig up the roots in October, remove the leaves and replant in a warm greenhouse in boxes half-filled with sand. Cover to exclude the light and the new leaves that grow will be soft, creamy-white and much less bitter than those grown in the open air.

Winter Cress or **Yellow Rocket** *Barbarea vulgaris* is a biennial or perennial herb, native to Europe and North Africa, and also naturalized and quite abundant in northern North America, Australia and New Zealand. It is quite commonly found growing along damp hedgerows, waysides and streams. Winter cress has a stout, yellowish tap-root and a smooth, branching stem that reaches a height of 30–90 cm (12–36 in). The smooth, glossy, deep-green leaves have coarsely toothed or wavy margins, and the dense clusters of bright yellow flowers bloom from May to August.

The generic name is derived from the fact that this used to be the only green plant available to be gathered and eaten on St Barbara's Day, which falls on December 4th.

Similar in flavour to watercress, it has been eaten since early times as a salad or pot herb and was popular with early settlers who introduced it into North America. It makes a delicious vegetable when lightly boiled and served with butter and pepper.

To increase the plant's productivity, remove the flowering stems as they appear and pick the outer leaves as the plant regrows.

Land Cress or **American Winter Cress** *Barbarea verna* is a biennial herb, native to the western Mediterranean and now widely naturalized in western and central Europe, North America, South Africa, Japan and New Zealand. It is found growing in waste or cultivated ground. Land Cress has a yellow tap-root and erect, generally branching stems that reach a height of 20–70 cm (8–28 in). The rosette leaves are stalked, the stem leaves deeply divided with five to eight pairs of long, narrow lobes. The flowers are bright yellow and bloom from March to May.

Land cress has a really hot, spicy flavour that is delicious in salads.

Easy to grow from seed, it thrives in moist soils and matures very quickly.

Sweet Rocket or **Dame's Violet** *Hesperis matronalis* Photographed July 20

Sweet Rocket or **Dame's Violet** *Hesperis matronalis*

Sweet Rocket or **Dame's Violet** *Hesperis matronalis* is a biennial or perennial herb, native to Italy, found throughout most of central and Mediterranean Europe and naturalized in North America. It is found growing cultivated in gardens or as an escape and occasionally naturalized in meadows, hedgerows, plantations and grass verges. Sweet Rocket has a tap-root and branching stock, with one or more erect, leafy stems, often branching, that reach a height of 40–90 cm (16–36 in). The pointed, spear-shaped leaves are finely toothed with rough hairs. The showy heads of white, purple or variegated flowers are scented and bloom from June to August.

Sweet rocket is held to represent deceit, because it has a lovely smell in the evening but none during the day. The leaves have a rather bitter taste but many people, particularly in Germany, like to add it to their salads, rather like cress, to give an extra tang to the flavour.

Medicinally, sweet rocket is primarily valued as anti-scorbutic – useful in preventing or curing scurvy because of its high Vitamin C content.

In gardens, it prefers rich, moist soil and plenty of sun. For eating purposes, cut before flowering; for medicinal uses, gather when in flower.

Nasturtium *Tropaeolum majus* is an annual or short-lived perennial plant, native to Peru, which is now widely cultivated all over the world, in gardens and sometimes found naturalized as a garden escape. Nasturtium is a climbing herb with a tuberous root and a very branched stem which can reach a height of 4 m (13 ft). The opposite, alternate leaves are bright green and shaped like umbrellas, with distinct veins and a gently undulating margin. The bright red, yellow or orange flowers bloom from May to September.

Nasturtium is a very decorative plant and was introduced to Europe at the end of the sixteenth century. The flowers, leaves and seeds have a pungent peppery taste. The flowers in particular make a decorative, tangy addition to salads or they can be used, with the leaves, to make a tisane. The seeds, pickled, are a substitute for capers.

Nasturtiums are high in vitamin C and are thought to be effective against scurvy, for lung problems and blocked bronchial tubes. They contain bitter principles which have an antibiotic effect on infection. The crushed seeds are prescribed for urinary inflammation and influenza. Nasturtiums have also been recommended as a general tonic for the digestion, for relieving constipation and depression, and for clearing the skin and eyes. Mességué says a hip-bath of nasturtiums will regularize a woman's periods and a lotion will prevent baldness. To make his hair lotion for preventing baldness, take two handfuls of nasturtium flowers, leaves and seeds, add ten nettle leaves and three oak leaves and macerate in 1 1/2 pt of alcohol 90% proof for two weeks. Strain and rub into the scalp. (from Mességué's *Health Secrets of Plants and Herbs*).

Nasturtiums will grow from seed in the garden, or in a window box or on a balcony, and will self-seed prolifically once they have taken hold.

Pick buds for pickling in May or early June and flowers or leaves for salads at any time.

Marigold *Calendula officinalis* is an annual plant, native to central and southern Europe and Asia and also popularly cultivated as a garden plant all over the world. It is found growing wild in cultivated fields and vineyards or as a garden escape. Marigold is a pubescent

Nasturtium *Tropaeolum majus* 'Empress of India'

Marigold *Calendula officinalis*

Nasturtium *Tropaeolum majus* a compact variety

Double Marigold *Calendula officinalis*

plant with a contorted, spindle-shaped root and an erect, branched stem which grows to a height of 40–50 cm (16–20 in). The pale green, oval leaves are slightly indented and the golden to orange-red flowers have numerous, brightly coloured petals and bloom from June until the first frost appears.

The generic name is derived from the Latin *kalendae*, the 'kalends', or first day of the month in the Roman calendar, as marigold is said to bloom then. It may also come from its supposed efficacy in dealing with menstrual problems. The specific name refers to its inclusion in official lists of medicinal plants.

Marigold only opens its flowers during the day, which Shakespeare alludes to in *The Winter's Tale*: 'The marigold that goes to bed wi' the sun And with him rises, weeping.' In German folklore it is a sign of rain if the flowers remain closed after seven o'clock in the morning.

Marigold has a very long history of medicinal, culinary and cosmetic use. In the Middle Ages, marigold was used for intestinal problems, obstructions of the liver, jaundice, fevers, smallpox, measles, for insect bites and snake bites. Externally it has been used for conjunctivitis and inflammation of the eyes, wounds, bruises, burns, eczema, boils, corns, warts and acne. Marigold was cultivated in kitchen gardens and dried for use in broths and the flowers, which contain a colouring substance calendulin, were used to dye cheese and butter a yellow colour and they can be added to fresh salads. Marigold petals are also used as a saffron substitute, giving rice a similar colour to saffron but a different flavour. Soaked in warm milk before adding it to buns and cakes helps to give them an appetizing pale yellow colour.

Cosmetically, marigold is sometimes made into a skin lotion or added to shampoo to lighten hair.

To make a soothing ointment for cuts, wounds and ulcers, add 2 tbsps of marigold juice (pound leaves in a pestle and mortar) to 500 g/1 lb butter or lard. Blend thoroughly, store in a cool place, and use as necessary.

To make an infusion to be drunk two or three times a day for a week before menstruation to regulate bleeding and pain, add 1 flower to ¼ l/½ pt of boiling water and infuse for ten minutes.

Marigolds will grow in any soil in a sunny position. Sow seeds in March or April. Cut flowers about mid-morning before they have fully opened out and use them fresh where possible. Otherwise dry in a well-aired shady place and store for future use.

Rocket *Eruca vesicaria* subsp. *sativa* Photographed April 20

Rocket *Eruca vesicaria* subsp. *sativa*

Biting Stonecrop or **Wall-pepper** *Sedum acre*

Rocket *Eruca vesicaria* subsp. *sativa* is an annual or overwintering herb, native to the Mediterranean and eastern Asia, which has established itself as a casual in other parts of Europe and is naturalized in North America. It is found growing in waste places or cultivated in herb gardens. Rocket is a strong-smelling plant with a slender tap-root and an erect, hairy stem that reaches a height of 100 cm (40 in). The pinnatifid leaves are lyre-shaped and coarsely toothed or lobed. The pretty flowers are yellowish or cream with deep violet veins, and bloom from February to October.

The common name is derived from Latin *eruca*, 'downy stem [like a caterpillar]'. The young leaves are delicious in salad and are reputed to be a good tonic.

Rocket can be grown from seed in any kind of soil, in a sunny position. Cut the leaves in spring and summer as required.

Biting Stonecrop or **Wall-pepper** *Sedum acre* is a small, fleshy, evergreen perennial, native to Europe, northern and western Asia and North Africa and also naturalized in North America. It is found growing on walls, rocks, sandy places and dunes near the sea and very dry grassland. Biting stonecrop has a fibrous root with minute threads that penetrate the tiniest crevices. The numerous creeping stems form mats or cushions that reach a width of 10–25 cm (4–10 in) and the erect stems reach a height of 5 cm (2 in). The alternate, egg-shaped leaves are thick, fleshy and succulent and crowded densely together. The tiny, yellow, star-like flowers grow on short, erect stems and bloom in May or June for a brief season.

The generic name derives from the Latin *sedare*, 'to calm', because some of the numerous species of this genus are reputed to have soothing properties. The specific name, *acre* (from which the word acrid is derived), alludes to the pungent, bitter taste of the fresh plant, as does its common name Wall-pepper.

In medieval times biting stonecrop was used as a vermifuge and for scurvy and scrofulous ulcers. In large doses it is emetic and when applied externally it can sometimes cause blisters or skin irritation. Nowadays its main use, medicinally, is as an effective corn remover. In recent years it has aroused interest because of its edibility and use as a survival food particularly in harsh climatic areas. Because the leaves hold moisture which can enable the plant to survive in the driest conditions, it is a useful survival food in either desert or arctic conditions. The leaves can be eaten fresh but are very bitter. It is best to dry them (which takes some time as the moisture content is high) and then grind them to a fine powder and use to add a hot peppery taste to other wild foods.

White Stonecrop *Sedum album* is an evergreen perennial, native to southern Europe, north and western Asia and North Africa, which is occasionally found growing wild in walls and rocks but more often as a garden escape. White stonecrop has a fibrous root and numerous creeping stems that form large mats up to 15 cm (6 in) across. The smooth, succulent egg-shaped or oblong leaves are bright green and the numerous small, white, star-like flowers that grow in flat tufts at the top of the flowering stems bloom in July and August.

The generic name, derived from the Latin *sedare* 'to calm', is appropriate to this species

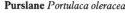

because the old herbalists used the leaves and stalks as a cooling poultice for all kinds of inflammations, including haemorrhoids. Culpeper called this plant Small Houseleek and it used to be pickled in the same way as marsh samphire. Nowadays it has gained popularity as a salad ingredient or it can be cooked as a green vegetable.

Salad Burnet *Sanguisorba minor* is a hardy, perennial herb, native to central and southern Europe as far north as southern Norway, and to Asia and also naturalized in North America. It is found growing wild in grassy meadows and by the roadside, favouring chalky soil. Salad Burnet is a small plant with a somewhat woody rootstock and erect stems that reach a height of 15–40 cm (6–16 in). The numerous pairs of oval leaflets have deeply toothed margins and the deep crimson flowerheads, which have female flowers at the top, hermaphrodite flowers in the middle and male flowers at the bottom, bloom from June to late August.

The generic name derives from the Latin *sanguis sorbere*, 'to absorb blood', and alludes to its traditional use as a wound herb for staunching bleeding. Its common name refers to the fact that it was always grown in medieval herb gardens and used in salads. It was particularly prized because it often lasted throughout the winter, providing greenery in the diet when not much else was available. Its nutty, cucumber-like taste also makes it a good addition to soups, stews and seasonings as well as adding a cool flavour to wine cups and cold drinks. Infused in wine or beer, it is recommended for gout and rheumatism; drunk as a tea, it is mildly diuretic, astringent, promotes perspiration and aids digestion.

Readily found in the wild, salad burnet can also be easily grown from seed in a herb garden or in an indoor pot. It likes chalky soil and thrives in sun or shade. Keep cutting the plant back once the flowers appear in order to get a constant supply of young leaves.

Salad Burnet *Sanguisorba minor*

Purslane *Portulaca oleracea*

Wild Celery or **Cutting Celery** *Apium graveolens*

Purslane *Portulaca oleracea* is a trailing, annual herb, native to many parts of Europe and Asia and introduced widely around the world. It is found growing wild in fields, roadsides, by the sea and cultivated in garden vegetable plots. Purslane has a tap-root and a trailing or ascending stem which can reach a height of 10–30 cm (4–12 in). The glossy, bright-green, obovate leaves are stalkless, opposite at first, then alternate and finally almost whorled. The yellow flowers growing on erect stems bloom from July, but they only open in full sunlight.

Purslane has been cultivated for centuries as a salad and pot herb. Its sharp, pleasant taste makes it an excellent addition to salads, dressed with oil and vinegar or, tied in bundles, it can be cooked as a vegetable.

Medicinally, it was said to bring relief to those suffering from dry coughs, shortness of breath and immoderate thirst. Mixed with oil of roses, the juice was recommended for sore mouths, swollen gums and loose teeth. Purslane tea was prescribed as a tonic for blood disorders. Culpeper said it allayed heat and cooled inflamed eyes.

Loewenfeld and Back in *The Complete Book of Herbs and Spices* suggest the following recipe from a seventeenth-century cookbook, for Summer Salad: mix together young, chopped purslane leaves with twice the amount of lettuce

leaves. Add chervil, borage flowers and marigold petals and serve with oil and lemon dressing.

Purslane can easily be grown in a herb garden. Propagate either by seed, by cuttings or by root division in about mid-April, then plant every month until August. It favours light, rich soil in a sunny position and needs to be watered if the weather is warm. It should be ready for picking in six weeks – then a new crop will grow. For winter use gather, dry and store in an airtight container to make a tisane.

Wild Celery or **Cutting Celery** *Apium graveolens* is an erect, strong-smelling biennial, native to Britain and many parts of Europe, Asia and Africa and also widely grown in North America. It is found growing wild in damp places near the sea or tidal areas and marshlands. Wild celery has a tap-root and a grooved, shiny, branched stem. The delicate, light green leaves are lobed and toothed, growing at the tip of the swollen stem. The greenish white flowers grow in clusters and bloom from June to September.

Cultivated Celery *Apium graveolens* var. *dulce* is sometimes found by roads, as an escape. It is less pungent than the wild variety and the swollen leaf stalks are commonly eaten.

Celeriac *Apium graveolens* var. *rapaceum*, the turnip-rooted variety, is a very popular vegetable on the Continent. The generic name is derived from the Latin *apium*, 'bee', because the plant is much visited by them. Wild celery was used in ancient times as a diuretic, a stimulant, a tonic for the stomach and for rheumatism, bronchitis, intermittent fevers and hysteria. Hippocrates said 'For shattering nerves, let celery be your food and your remedy'.

The cultivated variety of celery that we commonly use today was developed during the seventeenth century by the Italians. It contains many vitamins and minerals and is an excellent vegetable to eat when feeling off-colour.

According to Mességué, celery is also an excellent aphrodisiac and increases virility! He also claims that his grandmother Sophie used the water in which celery had been boiled to wash her hair and it is particularly good for those with dandruff.

Wild celery is rather pungent for culinary puposes. Growing it or any of the cultivated varieties from seed is quite difficult without a greenhouse. It may be better to buy small plants in late spring and plant them in well-dug and manured soil. The leaves of wild celery can be cut at any time, for use in salads, but celeriac should be harvested in the autumn when it has reached a good size.

Adzuki Beans *Phaseolus angularis*

Alfalfa or **Lucerne** *Medicago sativa*

Puy Lentils and **Large Green Lentils** *Lens culinaris*

Curled Cress *Lepidum sativum*

Salad Rape *Brassica napus*

Fenugreek *Trigonella foenum-graecum*

Mustard *Sinapis alba*

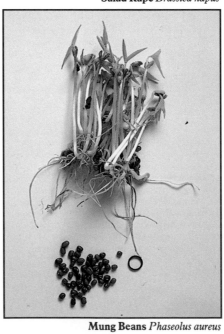

Mung Beans *Phaseolus aureus*

Bisai or **Japanese Radish** *Raphanus sativus*

Manna *Amaranthus hypochondiachus*

Joseph's Coat or **Tampala** *Amaranthus tricolor*

Green Amaranth *Amaranthus retroflexus*

Green Amaranth or **Pigweed** *Amaranthus retroflexus* is a hairy, annual herb, native to North America, which has been introduced into Europe and is usually found as an arable weed, growing wild on waste ground and roadsides. Green Amaranth is a stout plant with a rough hairy stem, erect or spreading, that reaches a height of 30–120 cm (12–48 in). The big, ovate to lanceolate leaves have long, hairy stalks and the dense clusters of tiny, greenish flowers bloom from August to October.

Green Amaranth – sometimes called Pigweed, although this name also applies to other species of Amaranth and to other plants – is considered by most to be a weed, but American Indians considered the young leaves and stems to be a good vegetable, similar to spinach, and the early colonists also ate it. The Indians also cultivated this group of plants for their small seeds which, when parched and ground into flour, made a nutritious addition to the diet. They are said to be a food of the gods and are especially good grown as a salad shoot.

Joseph's Coat or **Tampala** *Amaranthus tricolor* is often grown in gardens.

Alfalfa or **Lucerne** *Medicago sativa* is a deep-rooting perennial plant, probably native to the Mediterranean and western Asia but introduced into other parts of Europe and North and South America. It is either found growing naturalized on waste ground or cultivated in fields. Alfalfa has a deep root and erect stems that reach a height of 30–90 cm (12–36 in). The leaflets are narrowly egg-shaped and the pretty purple flowers bloom from June to October.

Alfalfa has long been a staple food in the diet of American Indians. The Utah Indians ground seeds into a flour which they used to make mush or bread and the leaves, which are an excellent source of vitamins A and D, were used to make Pablum, a popular infants' cereal. The young leaves can be collected in spring or early summer and used fresh in salads or infused to make a tea. Blended with fresh mint leaves, they make a particularly nutritious tisane. The young shoots are also good in salads or stir-fry. Excellent for putting nitrogen in the soil, farmers will often cultivate alfalfa for this purpose and also because it makes very good animal fodder.

Medicinally it has been claimed to be a valuable natural cure for jaundice.

Sprouted Seeds Sprouted seeds are highly nutritious because they are full of vitamins and minerals. They make an excellent addition to fresh salads all year round but are particularly beneficial in the winter months when green, leafy vegetables are harder to come by. Sprouts can be kept for up to four days in the refrigerator and are simple to grow – a special sprouting tray is easiest but a screw-top jar with tiny holes punched in the top will suffice. Remember to keep the sprouts warm and rinse thoroughly twice a day.

Alfalfa or **Lucerne** *Medicago sativa* are nutritious sweet tasting sprouts that take four to six days to grow.

Fenugreek *Trigonella foenum-graecum* These sprouts have a mild curry flavour and are delicious added to salads or served with curries. They take three to five days to grow.

Puy Lentils and **Large Green Lentils** *Lens culinaris* These crunchy fresh tasting sprouts take five days to grow.

Bisai or **Japanese Radish** *Raphanus sativus* These sprouts have a hot, radishy flavour and are delicious in salads. They take six days to grow.

Manna *Amaranthus hypochondiachus* These sprouts take eleven days to grow but they were considered worth waiting for by the Mexicans who referred to them as the 'Food of the Gods'.

Mung Beans *Phaseolus aureus* These sprouts are used in many Chinese dishes and are ready after four or five days.

Adzuki Beans *Phaseolus augularis* These sprouts are best eaten after five days; if left until the leaves appear after about nine days they are usually too tall and stringy.

Curled Cress *Lepidium sativum* This is the cress most commonly grown and it takes about seven days to sprout. It is sometimes referred to as cress or common cress.

Mustard *Sinapis alba* This grows faster than the cress so start the sprouts about three days earlier if growing them to eat at the same time.

Salad Rape *Brassica rapus* This takes about four to five days before it is ready for cutting.

55

Sunflower *Helianthus annuus* Photographed in Gascony August 11

Sunflower *Helianthus annuus* is a large, annual herb, native to North and Central America and now extensively grown in most parts of Europe. It is commonly found growing cultivated as a crop or for ornament and sometimes as an escape. The common sunflower has a tap-root with numerous rootlets and a stout, erect, spongy-textured stem that sometimes reaches a height in excess of 3 m (10 ft). The large, stalked leaves are broadly ovate, veined, toothed and hairy. The large, bright yellow flower-heads are composed of many, small tubular flowers arranged compactly on a flattish disk, and they bloom in July and August.

The generic name is derived from the Greek *helios*, 'the sun', and *anthos*, 'a flower', thus giving rise to the common name sunflower alluding both to their sun-like appearance and the fact that their flowers follow the sun during the course of the day. The sun-worshipping Aztecs of Peru decorated their temples with beautiful, wrought-gold sunflowers and crowned their priestesses with sunflowers.

Introduced into Europe by the Spanish explorers in the sixteenth century, the sunflower is now widely grown for its economic value as well as for ornament. Not only do the seeds yield a high-quality oil which is low in cholesterol and excellent for cooking or in salads, but the seeds can also be eaten raw or roasted or ground into a nutritious flour (sunflower bread is popular in Portugal and Russia) or used as a substitute for coffee. The second oil pressings are used to make soaps and candles and are incorporated into cattle and poultry fodder. Fowl fed on bruised sunflower seeds are known to increase their laying capacity. The stems yield a fibre extensively used in textile and paper-making and the burnt stems are an excellent source of potash. The leaves are used in herbal tobaccos and for cattle fodder and the growing plant is an excellent

soil-improver. Bees get large quantities of wax and nectar from the flowers which also yield a yellow dye. The young flower buds boiled and served like asparagus are said to make a pleasant vegetable.

Medicinally, the seeds are reputed to have diuretic and expectorant properties and have been used to treat coughs, colds, whooping cough and bronchitis. A tincture made from the seeds, used instead of quinine in Turkey and Iran, is said to relieve fevers and ague.

Sunflowers can easily be grown in the garden. Sow seeds in boxes in April and plant out in June, preferably in enriched soil, though any soil will do as long as there is plenty of sun and light. The flowers will bloom in July and August; the seeds are ripe when the flower heads droop. Cut off the heads, leave to dry and, when fully dried, the seeds will easily fall out. Store in a dry, cool place until needed.

Horseradish *Armoracia rusticana* is a stout perennial herb, probably native to south-eastern Europe and western Asia and now naturalized as an escape from cultivation throughout Europe, North America and New Zealand. It is found growing wild in fields, banks and along roadsides. Horseradish has long, fleshy, white cylindrical roots and erect, leafy stems that reach a height of 100–125 cm (40–50 in). The large, long, dark-green, ovate leaves 30–50 cm (12–20 in), have a toothed margin and long stalks up to 30 cm (12 in) long. The white aromatic flowers bloom from June to August.

In Britain, where it was known as 'red cole' it was not used as a condiment until the seventeenth century, unlike in Europe. The Germans and Danes sliced it thinly and mixed it with vinegar to eat as an accompaniment to fish and meat. The French adapted the custom and called it *moutarde des Allemands*.

The flavour of raw horseradish is hot, biting

and pungent; qualities it loses when cooked. The raw root, grated or cut into thin strips mixed with cream, a touch of white wine vinegar and a little sugar, makes a delicious sauce. Traditionally served with roast beef, it is also excellent with smoked mackerel or herring.

Both the roots and leaves of horseradish were used medicinally during the Middle Ages. It was used as an aid to digestion, which accounts for its traditional use with rich foods. It is also a strong diuretic and has been used for treating infections of the urinary tract. Modern research has shown that the plant has antibiotic properties which explain its usefulness for cystitis, problems in the respiratory tract and for treating wounds.

Applied to chilblains the root will relieve the pain. Horseradish juice mixed with water will help remove freckles, and horseradish syrup will relieve persistent coughs.

Despite its common name, several cases have been recorded in which farm animals have died after eating large amounts of horseradish, the volatile oils in the plant having apparently caused acute inflammation of the stomach walls.

You can gather horseradish from the wild or propagate in the garden by root division. Gather the roots in autumn and store in damp sand to replant the following spring in fairly rich, well-weeded soil, in trenches 60–90 cm (24–36 in) deep, with plenty of manure. Trim off the lateral roots in late spring so that you have a good, thick, strong root by autumn. Store roots for future use in a damp, dark place and use fresh as needed.

Common Oat *Avena sativa* is an annual plant, possibly introduced from southern North America and now extensively cultivated all over Europe. Common oat has a smooth hollow stem up to 1 m (3 ft) high and alternate, lance-shaped, veined leaves clasping the stem at the

Horseradish *Armoracia rusticana*

base. The flowers form a curved, branched panicle at the end, each spikelet consisting of 2 flowers with glumes. The seeds are gathered in summer.

The generic name comes from the Latin *avena*, 'nourishing' while *sativa*, 'sown' or 'cultivated' is in contrast to the wild oat *Avena fatua* whose specific name means 'insipid' or 'tasteless'. Oats contain starch, cellulose, mineral salts, vitamins and an indole alkaloid called gramine, and, eaten as porridge, are, of course, advocated by dieticians as a tonic and remineralizing food, excellent for children and convalescents. A decoction made from oats is also recommended as a mild diuretic and laxative for convalescents, and to cure insomnia in children. Weiss says that work done in India on opium addicts and subsequently repeated with nicotine addicts shows that claims made for the hypnotic, sedative properties of oats seem to be true. Addicts given a decoction of oats in place of nicotine smoked fewer cigarettes than those who were given a placebo and the effects were long lasting.

Oat straw in mattresses was formerly used for those suffering from rheumatic conditions and a handful of grains in the bath keeps the skin soft because of its emollient properties. Oats are, of course, also used in whisky making.

Buckwheat *Fagopyrum esculentum* synonym *Polygonum fagopyrum* is an annual, herbaceous plant, native to central Asia and largely cultivated in China, North America and parts of Europe, which is found growing as a casual in waste ground or cultivated as a crop. Buckwheat has an erect, knotted stem that grows to a height of 60 cm (24 in). Lateral branches grow from the joint and the heart-shaped or arrow-shaped leaves grow alternately from opposite sides. The numerous pink or white flowers bloom from July to September. The nut or seed, with its dark

Common Oat *Avena sativa*

brown rind enclosing the kernel, is three-sided and angular, resembling a beech nut.

Buckwheat is extensively cultivated in many parts of the world for its nuts which can be ground into a delicious flour that is particularly good for making cakes, crumpets and bread. In Japan buckwheat, called *soba*, is used in numerous ways to make dough, noodles and dumplings. Excellent beer can be brewed from the grain. In Britain buckwheat is chiefly cultivated as food for pheasants and poultry and used to fatten pigs.

Although not as nutritious as wheat, buckwheat is more nutritious than rice and has

Buckwheat *Fagopyrum esculentum*

the added advantage of growing rapidly and easily on poor, badly tilled land. If sown in April two green crops can be raised in one season.

Medicinally, an infusion of the leaves has been used for erysipelas (an acute infectious skin disease causing fever, vomiting and purplish raised lesions on the face) and as a poultice, mixed with buttermilk, to restore milk flow in nursing mothers. Because of its glutinous nature it can cause constipation but is also effective for those suffering from diarrhoea. Taken regularly over a long period it is said to relieve the symptoms of varicose veins.

Chenopodium bonus-henricus

Good King Henry, Mercury or **Fat Hen** *Chenopodium bonus-henricus*

American Wormseed or **Epazote**
Chenopodium ambrosioides

Japanese or **Common Perilla** *Perilla frutescens*

Red Garden Orach *Atriplex hortensis rubra*

Garden Orach or **Mountain Spinach** *Atriplex hortensis* is an erect annual, the exact origin of which is unknown, but it is now found widely distributed throughout most of Europe, particularly in central and southern regions. It is extensively cultivated and sometimes found wild as an escape. Garden orach is a tall, hardy plant growing to a height of 250 cm (100 in). It has large, succulent, heart-shaped or triangular leaves. 10 cm (4 in) long, slightly mealy when young but generally smooth in maturity. The greenish flowers bloom from June to October.

Red Garden Orach, *Atriplex hortensis rubra* has dark, reddish-purple leaves which can be shredded into salads or cooked like spinach. It is a very popular vegetable on the Continent. In times past Garden orach leaves, heated with vinegar, honey and salt, were considered a useful poultice to treat an attack of gout.

To grow Garden orach in a herb garden, plant the seeds in May, in rows 60 cm (2 ft) apart, and keep well watered to obtain speedy growth.

Red Valerian *Centranthus ruber* showing red, white and pink forms

Good King Henry, Mercury or **Fat Hen**
Chenopodium bonus-henricus is a perennial,
native to Europe, western Asia and North
America, which is found growing wild in
nitrogen-rich soil; in pastures, farm-yards,
roadsides and waste ground near habitation.
Good King Henry has a woody root and erect,
ribbed stems that reach a height of 50 cm
(20 in). The large, triangular, arrow-shaped
leaves are alternate with wavy edges and the
tiny, yellow-green flowers in numerous close
spikes grow both at the end of the stem and in
the leaf axils and bloom from May to August.
The whole plant is often covered with a sort of
yellowish powder.

The generic name derives from the Greek
words *chen*, 'a goose', and *podus*, 'a foot',
alluding to the supposed resemblance of the
leaves to the webbed foot of a goose. The
specific name is thought to refer to King Henry
IV of Navarre. The common name Fat Hen is a
translation of the German *Fette Henne*, arising
from the practice of fattening poultry on the
plant.

For centuries the young leaves of Good King
Henry have been eaten as a pot herb in place of
spinach. The taste is similar but milder and it is
excellent for those suffering from anaemia
because of its high iron content. The young
shoots, cut when 13 cm (5 in) high and the
thickness of a pencil, can be boiled and eaten
like asparagus.

In times past poultices were made from the
leaves and used to cleanse and heal chronic
sores, boils and abscesses. The seeds are gently
laxative and suitable for giving to slightly
constipated children.

Good King Henry can either be gathered in
the wild from an unpolluted area or grown in
the garden from seed. Plant in about April in
rich, well-drained soil and leave to establish

themselves during the first year. After that, pick
or cut shoots and leaves as desired but always
leave some young shoots for the plant to keep
healthy.

American Wormseed or **Epazote** *Chenopodium
ambrosioides* is an annual or short-lived
perennial, native to Mexico and South America,
which is now naturalized in many parts of North
America and central and southern Europe. It is
found growing wild in waste ground or along
roadsides or cultivated for medicinal use.
American wormseed is strongly aromatic and
has a numerously branched, downy stem that
reaches a height of about 100 cm (40 in). The
oblong to lance-shaped leaves are smaller at the
top of the stem. The numerous, small, yellow-
green flowers grow in small clusters in the axils
of the leafy branches and bloom from July to
September, followed by the small green fruits
which encase small, black seeds that are
collected in October.

North American Indians probably learnt
about the medicinal uses of wormseed – also
known as Mexican Tea and Herba Sancta Maria
– when Mexican Indians fled north to escape the
Spanish conquistadors. It is thought that the
Maya civilization used wormseed as a
vermifuge.

Oil of Chenopodium derived from the seeds
has long been considered effective against round
worms, hookworms and other intestinal
parasites, but care must be taken when using
this medicine internally as differing amounts of
the active principle are contained in the
commercial preparations of the oil and
poisonings have occurred. Use only under the
guidance of a qualified practitioner.

American Wormseed is easily grown from
seed in any kind of soil.

Japanese or **Common Perilla** *Perilla frutescens*

is an aromatic, annual plant, native to India and
China, which is cultivated for ornament and for
its aromatic oil in European gardens. Japanese
perilla is a somewhat hairy plant that grows to a
height of 100 cm (40 in). It has strongly scented
purple foliage with leaves broadly ovate and
deeply serrated at the edge. The white flowers
bloom from August to September.

Japanese perilla contains an aromatic oil and
is commonly used in Japan to flavour fish,
tempura, bean curd and pickles. The plant also
gives a scarlet colour to preserved ginger.

Easily grown from seed.

Red Valerian *Centranthus ruber* is an erect
perennial native to central and southern
Europe, North Africa and Asia Minor and now
well naturalized as far north as the British Isles.
It is found growing in old walls, cliffs, chalk-
pits and waste places especially near the sea and
is frequently cultivated in gardens. Red valerian
has a freely branching rootstock and stout,
hollow, smooth stems that reach a height of
75 cm (30 in). The long, pointed, rather fleshy
leaves are arranged opposite one another in
pairs. The numerous pink, crimson or
occasionally white flower clusters bloom from
June to September.

The generic name comes from the Greek
kentron, 'a spur', and *anthos*, 'a flower', alluding
to the spur at the base of the corolla which
distinguishes it from the related true valerian,
with which it might otherwise be confused.

Red valerian has none of the medicinal
properties of Valerian, *Valeriana officinalis*.
However, in some parts of Europe the leaves are
eaten either boiled as a vegetable or added,
freshly chopped, to salads. In France the roots
are also sold for soups.

Red valerian can either be gathered from the
wild or grown from seed in a herb garden.

Alexanders or **Black Lovage** *Smyrnium olusatrum*

Alexanders *Smyrnium olusatrum*

Biennial Alexanders *Smyrnium perfoliatum*

Skirret *Sium sisarum*

Alexanders or **Black Lovage** *Smyrnium olusatrum* is a stout biennial plant, native to south-western Europe and now widely naturalized in other parts. It is commonly found near the sea growing in hedgerows, waste places and on cliffs. Alexanders has a solid, furrowed stem, becoming hollow in age, that reaches a height of 50–150 cm (20–60 in). The large, dark green leaves are unequally divided into three, and toothed or lobed in the upper part. The roundish, terminal clusters of green-yellow flowers bloom from April to June, succeeded by the small, black fruit.

The generic name derives from the Greek word for myrrh and alludes to its myrrh-like flavour and the specific name from the Greek *olusatrum*, 'black pot herb', refers to its fruit.

Mentioned in 322BC, by Theophrastus, the ancient Greek botanist, as an official plant, alexanders has long been regarded as a delicious edible. It was introduced into Britain by the Romans to add to soups, stews and salads, and it remained a popular monastery garden plant throughout the Middle Ages. In the seventeenth century John Evelyn included it in his list of 'plants for the kitchen garden' and it remained a popular and widely cultivated pot herb until it was displaced by celery, carrots and onions. The shoots and leafstalks of alexanders should be picked in late spring just before flowering. Cut the stems low, trim into suitable pieces and peel with a knife as you would rhubarb. Boil for six to eight minutes until tender then serve with lots of butter and black pepper. The flavour is reminiscent of celery but more pungent. Leftovers are delicious in a salad. Although mainly cultivated as a culinary herb, alexanders is mildly diuretic and aids digestion.

Easy to cultivate in a kitchen or herb garden, plant alexanders seeds in autumn, then transplant in spring.

Biennial Alexanders *Smyrnium perfoliatum* from southern Europe has light green leaves which clasp the stem. It is often grown as a decorative garden plant.

Elder, Elderberry or **European Elder** *Sambucus nigra* is a shrub or small tree, native to Europe, western Asia and North Africa and sometimes cultivated as a garden plant in North America. It is found growing wild in woods, waste places and along roadsides, often near habitation, favouring nitrogen-rich soils. Elder is a sprawling shrub, with furrowed bark, that can reach a height of 10 m (33 ft). The light-brown branches with tentacles are pithy within and often arching, and the large lanceolate-ovate leaflets are clearly veined with serrate margins. The creamy-white, scented flowers grow in flat-topped clusters at the top of the branches and bloom from June to July, succeeded by round, purple-black berries which ripen in September.

The generic name is believed to have derived from the ancient Greek *sambuca*, 'the sackbut', (a stringed instrument), but it seems odd that elder should have been used for such a thing since it is now generally associated with wind instruments such as pipes and whistles. The specific name *nigra*, 'black', refers of course to its berries. One theory about the origin of the common name is that it is a corruption of the Anglo-Saxon word *aeld*, fire, because the hollow stems, with their pith removed, were used to blow up fires.

In medieval times elder was associated with magic and witchcraft. The Danes believed a dryad lived in its branches which would haunt anyone who had furniture made from elder wood. By one tradition, Judas was believed to have hanged himself from an elder tree, and another has it that the Calvary cross was made from it. Thus it became an emblem of sorrow and death and in some areas branches were buried with the dead to protect them from evil spirits and the hearse driver carried a whip of elder wood, presumably for the same purpose. But despite these traditions elder also has a long history of medicinal, cosmetic and culinary use dating back to ancient times and its numerous virtues have been extolled by herbalists and medical practitioners of old.

The wood of old elder trees is fine, white and smooth and was highly prized by carpenters for making a wide variety of objects such as butchers' skewers, shoemakers' pegs and small toys. The bark, as well as the root, yields a black dye, and the berries a violet dye which the Romans used for dyeing their hair and distillers

Colour forms of **Elderberry** *Sambucus* (l. to r.) 'Purpurea', 'Albovariegata', 'Laciniata' and 'Aurea' at Hollington's herb garden

used to colour and flavour wine and spirits – mainly port. An infusion of the leaves dabbed on the face is reputed to be a helpful insect repellent and a decoction is sometimes used by gardeners to sprinkle on delicate plants to rid them of minute pests.

For culinary purposes it is principally the berries and flowers that are used to make delicious jams, jellies, wines and beverages, as well as to flavour puddings, sweets and cakes. Elder-flower water is used cosmetically as a soothing, mildly astringent lotion for skin and eyes and is recommended for whitening the skin, clearing blemishes and making a very refreshing bath.

Medicinally, elder has been considered beneficial in many ways. The crushed leaves mixed with oil or lard and applied to piles soothes and relieves the pain, and taken in a decoction acts as a purgative, diuretic and blood purifier. The leaves are also frequently a component of soothing, cooling ointments used to ease various swellings, wounds and bruises. The flowers too are gently laxative, diuretic and anti-rheumatic and induce perspiration so an infusion was recommended for catarrh, bronchitis, rheumatic gout and also for eruptive fevers such as measles. To make an infusion that can also be drunk daily as a spring tonic, put 30 g/1 oz of blossom into 1 1/2 pt of boiling water and infuse for ten minutes. Strain and drink three cups a day. Take very hot if trying to induce a strong sweat.

The leaves are principally used to make wine or jams but also have purgative and anti-rheumatic properties which explains why some people have found that cheap port (port that has been heavily adulterated with elderberry wine)

Elder, Elderberry or **European Elder** *Sambucus nigra*

is good for rheumatic sufferers. Elderberry wine is also said to be good for asthma.

Elders can easily be grown in a garden. They like fertile, damp soil and can be propagated from seed, by root division or by cuttings. Gather the leaves at any time but harvest the flowers carefully when in full flower and dry quickly, discarding any that turn black. The berries should be collected when fully ripe, in September or October, and stripped from their stalks before either being used immediately or dried or bottled.

Skirret *Sium sisarum* is a perennial plant, probably native to central Europe, Russia and China, which has become naturalized in central Europe and northern Italy. It is found wild in damp places or cultivated in vegetable gardens.

Skirret has a white, aromatic tuberous root and a striate stem that reaches a height of 45 cm (18 in). The pinnate leaves have lobed leaflets and the small white flowers bloom in August.

The generic name is derived from the Celtic *siu*, 'water', referring to the watery kind of habitat that the species in this genus enjoy. Skirret has been cultivated in England for its edible roots since the sixteenth century and Culpeper says this of it: 'It is under Venus. The root is opening, diuretic, and cleansing . . . The young shoots are pleasant and wholesome food, of a cleansing nature and aid digestion, provoking urine.' Nowadays, as in the Middle Ages, the sweetish roots are boiled and served with butter, in the manner of salsify or parsnip.

Skirret can be grown in the garden in ordinary soil, in sun or shade.

Cape Gooseberry or **Chinese Lantern** *Physalis alkekengi*

Juniper *Juniperus communis* is an aromatic, evergreen shrub or tree, native to northern Europe, south-west Asia and North America, which is found growing wild on chalk downs, heaths, moors and pine woods and also cultivated for ornament in gardens. Juniper has creeping or erect branches (depending on habitat) with red-brown, shredding bark and it can reach a height of about 10 m (33 ft). The thin, narrow, pointed, blue-green leaves are leathery and pungent. The male and female flowers are borne on separate plants and bloom in May and June. The green berries take three years to ripen and become bluish, then black. The ripe berry contains one to six seeds and the whole plant has a strong pine-like smell.

Juniper is a well-known culinary and medicinal herb that has been used for centuries. Pliny says that Hannibal ordered the beams of the temple of Diana at Ephesus to be made of juniper because of its reputation as a very strong, durable wood. Branches of juniper were used as a strewing herb to sweeten the smell of rooms and they were burnt in the streets, squares and houses during epidemics in the belief that this would purify the air and cleanse it of infection.

Juniper berries and the oil obtained from them are widely used in the distilling industry to flavour gin and other spirits which, it is said, protect those living in damp, cold countries from gout and rheumatism. The crushed berries have also been used in cooking to flavour roast meat, particularly game, and to make sauces or conserves to eat with cold meat.

Medicinally, juniper has digestive, diuretic and antiseptic properties. It is prescribed for urinary complaints, bronchial catarrh, fevers, loss of appetite and digestive upset due to wind, and for skin complaints. It is also prescribed for arthritis and rheumatism and chewing juniper berries is recommended for those in contact with the sick or visiting swampy countries. One old doctor recommended breathing juniper smoke through the nose to cure a head cold, as well as disinfecting a room by throwing a handful of berries or a branch of juniper on the fire. However, juniper should not be eaten by pregnant women as some varieties have abortive properties. Externally, a decoction of the berries on a compress may soothe rheumatism, neuralgia and muscular pains and promote the healing of wounds and sores.

To make juniper berry tea, put about fifteen crushed berries in ¼ l/½ pt of water, bring to the boil and infuse for ten to fifteen minutes. Strain and drink three cupfuls a day. To make juniper wine, put 60 g/2 oz crushed berries in 1 l/2 pt of white wine and macerate for a fortnight, shaking every three or four days. Strain and sweeten if desired and drink one wineglassful a day.

Juniper bushes can be grown in the garden and they are quite hardy. In poor soil they will form a low, spreading tree; in rich soil they may become a good-sized tree. Propagation is either by seeds (which are very slow to germinate) or by cuttings planted in a cold frame in spring and put out once they are well established.

Collect the berries when they are black (after the third year) and dry on a metal tray in the open air, turning frequently. When shrivelled, store in an airtight jar.

Raspberry *Rubus idaeus* is a prickly shrub, native to Europe, Asia and North America, which is commonly found growing in woods,

Juniper *Juniperus communis*

Raspberry *Rubus idaeus*

heaths and on waste ground and often cultivated for its fruit. Raspberry has a creeping perennial root and erect, prickly, biennial stems that reach a height of 100–160 cm (40–64 in). The alternate, pinnate leaves have three to seven leaflets which are deeply veined and sharply toothed at the margin. They are green and somewhat hairy above and densely white and velvety below. The pretty white flowers bloom in May or June and the fragrant, round, red fruits ripen from the end of July.

The generic name comes from the Latin *rubus*, 'a bramble', and the specific name refers to Mount Ida in Greece where it apparently grew abundantly in ancient times.

The raspberry has been highly valued for centuries not only for its delicious, edible fruits but also for the medicinal properties contained in its fruit, leaves and flowers. The leaves are astringent and decongestant and a decoction of them has been recommended externally for cleansing wounds, ulcers and burns and also as a gargle for sore throats and mouths. Put in a compress, it soothes inflammation of the eyes. Taken internally, raspberry leaf tea is good for chills, colds, flu, tonsillitis and fevers and stomach complaints in children. It has a long history of use in the later stages of pregnancy. It helps to ease childbirth by toning and bracing all the reproductive muscles and continued use after the baby is born will help strengthen the tired muscles of the womb and vagina.

To make a decoction, put 45–60 g/1½–2 oz of raspberry leaves in 1 l/2 pt of boiling water. Infuse for several minutes, then strain and sweeten with a little honey. Jams, jellies, syrups

and vinegars made from the ripe fruits are not only delicious to eat but made into drinks are also very cooling and thirst-quenching, and particularly beneficial for those suffering from colds, sore throats or fevers.

Jean Palaiseul in *Grandmother's Secrets* gives the following old-fashioned apothecaries' recipe for raspberry syrup.

'Put together 500 g/1 lb of very ripe raspberries, 500 g/1 pt of wine vinegar and 500 g/1 lb of sugar; bring gently to the boil stirring continuously; press and strain through a fine cloth and store in a tightly corked bottle.'

One tablespoon of this syrup in a glass of water makes a deliciously cooling tonic drink for feverish patients.

Raspberry can either be found in the wild (choose an unpolluted spot to pick the fruits) or grown in a garden. It likes sun and dry, slightly acid soil but is a very fast growing plant and once it has taken root is inclined to spread all over the garden. Pick the leaves and flowers just before the flowers open and dry them in the shade before storing in an airtight jar. Pick the berries when they are very ripe.

Blackcurrant *Ribes nigrum* is a deciduous, aromatic shrub, native to Europe and northern and central Asia, which is found by streams and in woods either wild or as a garden escape and often cultivated for its fruit. Blackcurrant is quite a large shrub that reaches a height of about 1–2 m (3–6½ ft). The large, lobed leaves are toothed at the margin with small, brownish scent glands on the underside which diffuse an aromatic odour. The pretty, pale pink, five-petalled flowers bloom in April and May and the

Blackberry *Rubus fruticosus* (in autumn colour)

Blackberry *Rubus fruticosus*

Buffalo Currant *Ribes odoratum*

round, black fruit ripens in July and August.

The specific name, the Latin *nigrum*, means 'black', and refers, of course, like the common name, to the intensely black fruits of the plant. The plant is extremely rich in vitamin C and has been recognized by herbalists since the Middle Ages, and probably before, as having numerous medicinal properties. It has been successfully prescribed as a diuretic for kidney and liver problems and urinary infections, for chronic diarrhoea, stomach ache and colic, for arthritis, rheumatism, migraine, fever, mouth and throat infections, colds, flu and general fatigue. For centuries blackcurrants have been associated with longevity and good health and eaten to allay ageing.

The fruit can be eaten fresh when very ripe and made into delicious jams, jellies, syrups and liqueur. The leaves and flowers can be used to make a decoction or put into baths. To make a decoction, put 45–60 g/1 ½–2 oz of fresh or dried leaves and flowers in 1 l/2 pt of cold water (if dried, soak first for an hour in cold water and use the water to make the decoction). Bring to the boil, remove from the heat and infuse for ten minutes. Drink three to four cupfuls a day.

Blackcurrants are easily grown in the garden. The leaves and flowers should be picked in spring, before the flowers open, then dried and stored in an airtight jar.

Buffalo Currant *Ribes odoratum* is a deciduous spineless shrub, native to North America and introduced in Europe, which is found in woods and hedges. Buffalo currant has numerous branching, arching stems that reach heights of 2–2.5m (6½–8ft). The generally three-lobed,

often wedge-shaped leaves are pale green and coarsely toothed. The spicily fragrant leaves are bright yellow and bloom in April, succeeded by the smooth, round dark purple or purple-black fruits.

Blackberry *Rubus fruticosus* is a sprawling shrub, native to Europe and commonly found all over the world growing wild in woods, scrub, waste places and hedges. Blackberry has a woody root with numerous suckers and red-brown, woody, prickly stems (erect at first, then trailing as they get heavier) which often reach a length of several metres. The alternate, stalked leaves are palmate and composed of three to five oval leaflets with a toothed margin and rather downy under surface. The white or pink flowers grow in apical groups and bloom from May to September, followed by the fruits which are red at first, becoming black when ripe.

Blackberry has been used since ancient times not only for its delicious berries – which can either be eaten raw or made into numerous kinds of jams, jellies and sauces – but also for its astringent and tonic properties. The Greeks recommended blackberry for gout, the Romans for inflammation of the mouth and bowel. High in tannin and vitamin C, blackberry can be a valuable and effective treatment for diarrhoea and dysentery and has also been recommended for piles, cystitis and congestive problems in the uterus. It is used as a gargle and mouth wash for ulcers, sore gums (it is said to fasten loose teeth), sore throats and hoarseness. The young shoots can be eaten in salads and the roots, boiled, are sometimes eaten as a vegetable. The leaves, particularly if mixed with raspberry

leaves, make a delightful scented tea.

To make a decoction, put 30–45 g/1–1 ½ oz of dried leaves in 1 l/2 pt of water. Boil for five minutes, leave to infuse for a further ten minutes, then strain. Drink three to four cupfuls a day for the afflictions listed above, or use as a gargle.

Blackberry syrup (equal weights of juice, pressed from the not fully ripened berries, and sugar, boiled hard until a syrupy consistency is achieved) can be taken for bronchial catarrh or sore throats (2–3 tbsps a day) or watered down to make a refreshing drink for invalids.

Blackberry fruits can easily be gathered from the wild but try and find as unpolluted an area as possible.

Cape Gooseberry or **Chinese Lantern** *Physalis alkekengi* is a perennial plant, native from southern and central Europe east to China and Japan, and now found as an escape in North America. Cape gooseberry has a horizontal rhizome and an erect stem that reaches a height of 25–75 cm (10–30 in). It has broadly ovate, dark green leaves, and dirty white flowers that bloom in May and June, succeeded by the red to orange fruit which is the size of a cherry and contains many flat, kidney-shaped seeds.

The generic name is derived from the Greek *phusa*, 'a bladder', alluding to the way the calyx becomes inflated after the petals have fallen off and encloses the fruit in a large, leafy balloon.

In early times the berries, which are diuretic, were recommended for gout, to cure epilepsy and to assuage the after-effects of scarlet fever. The leaves, boiled in water, were said to make soothing poultices and compresses.

Sea Buckthorn or **Sallow Thorn** *Hippophae rhamnoides*

Sea Buckthorn or **Sallow Thorn** *Hippophae rhamnoides* is a thorny shrub, native to western and central Europe and temperate Asia. It can form thickets on sand dunes and chalky cliffs because its long suckers help to bind loose sand and therefore it makes a useful dune shelter barrier. Sea Buckthorn has long roots, numerous suckers and many branches which reach a height of 1–3 m (3½–10 ft). The pointed, lance-shaped leaves are alternate and silvery-green above, light brown below with a distinct vein. The very small, green flowers appear before the leaves in April or May, succeeded by the round, orange fruit that contains a seed in a woody case.

High in vitamin C, the edible fruit can be made into a sharp, but pleasant, jam or jelly, apparently used as an ingredient in a fish sauce in Sweden and Finland. The crushed berries put on open wounds may staunch bleeding.

Barberry *Berberis vulgaris* is a perennial shrub, generally distributed over most parts of Europe, North Africa and temperate Asia, which has become naturalized in North America. It is found growing wild in copses, hedgerows and waysides, and cultivated in gardens for ornament. Barberry has thick, creeping roots, a very branched, grey stem and reaches a height of 2.5 m (8 ft). The branches are grooved, thin and spiny, with a characteristic yellow inside tissue, and the elliptical, leathery, shiny leaves have finely-toothed margins with tiny spikes at the base of the stalk. The small, yellow flowers hang in drooping clusters and bloom from May to June. The wine-red berries, which contain two to three corneous seeds, are pleasantly acidulous when ripe.

The generic name may derive from the Phoenician *barbar*, 'glossy', referring to the sheen on the leaves. One of its common names, Pipperidge Bush, is a corruption of *pepou*, 'a pip', and *rouge*, 'red', describing the red fruit. In Italy barberry is known as Holy Thorn because it was thought to be one of the plants used to make Christ's crown of thorns.

Farmers consider it a harmful plant because the wheat rust fungus spends part of its life on the barberry bush and if it is near a wheat field red rust spores will be transmitted to the crop. The roots yield a marvellous yellow dye used for dyeing wool, cotton and linen and for staining wood and polishing leather to a tawny sheen.

Barberry berries have principally been used to make jams, jellies and syrups and as the berries contain citric, malic and tartaric acids they possess astringent and anti-scorbutic properties. The jelly is very refreshing for a sore throat and the syrup makes an excellent gargle. The berries are also used to cool inflammatory fevers, diarrhoea, dysentery and scurvy. A decoction of the inner rind of the stalk and bark used to be recommended for disorders of the liver, gall bladder, spleen and pancreas as well as dropsy and rheumatism but has now largely gone out of use. However, homoeopaths use barberry as a valuable remedy for liver and kidney insufficiency and recent research has shown that the plant contains an alkaloid, berberine, which is useful for treating hypersensitive eyes, inflamed lids and chronic conjunctivitis.

Barberry berries can be collected from the wild or grown in the garden. Grow your own bush by planting suckers in the autumn and, when they are well rooted, replant where you want the bush to grow. Alternatively, they can be propagated by cuttings or by seeds sown in spring, or even better in autumn, in a sheltered border, where they will germinate the following spring.

Collect the stem bark by shaving off bits and drying in a well-ventilated place. Store in an airtight container with similarly dried pieces of root bark.

Bearberry *Arctostaphylos uva-ursi* is a prostrate, evergreen shrub native to Europe, north Asia, north Japan and North America, whose distribution covers virtually the whole arctic and temperate zone of the northern hemisphere, south to the Mediterranean and California. It is found growing wild on moors, banks and rocks, generally in damp, shady, mountainous places. Bearberry has semi-trailing smooth stems and numerous branches with leathery, obovate leaves, dark green and glossy above, paler and conspicuously veined below. The dense, drooping clusters of flowers are white with a red tip and bloom in May or June before the young leaves. The glossy, thick-skinned, bright red berries ripen in the autumn.

The generic name is a corruption of the Greek *arktos*, 'a bear', and *staphyle*, 'grapes', and the Latin specific name means the same, probably alluding to the fact that bears eat the berries.

The medicinal properties of bearberry were recognized as far back as the thirteenth century by the Welsh physicians of Myddfai. It entered the London Pharmacopoeia in 1763 and the United States Pharmacopoeia in 1820 and was used for its astringent and diuretic properties. Infusions were used to treat diseases of the bladder and kidneys and inflammations in the urinary tract such as cystitis. It was used by Indians in British Columbia for similar disorders and they also mixed the dried leaves with tobacco to form the Indian smoking mixture known as *kinikinik* by the western tribes.

Bearberry produces an ash grey dye. The leaves contain an abundant amount of tannin so they are used for tanning leather in Sweden and Russia but, because of this abundance of tannin, bearberry should only be taken on the advice of a physician. Long-term use may impair the liver and cause constipation or vomiting in children.

Weiss says that, contrary to traditional belief, bearberry leaves have no diuretic action, though they have proved useful in the treatment of cystitis in paraplegics; modern herbalism has restricted bearberry to urinary problems. As it has oxytocic properties, it should never be taken during pregnancy.

Bearberry is not normally cultivated but collected in the wild.

Barberry *Berberis vulgaris*

Bilberry *Vaccinium myrtillus*

Bearberry *Arctostaphylos uva-ursi*

Bilberry, Blaeberry or **Whortleberry** *Vaccinium myrtillus* is a deciduous shrub, native throughout Europe, northern Asia and North America, which is found growing wild on heaths, moors and in woods. Bilberry has a creeping rhizome and numerous erect, branched stems that reach a height of 40–60 cm (16–24 in). The twigs are green and angled and the ovate, bright green leaves with a toothed margin are shiny above, strongly veined below, and they turn red in autumn. The white or pink flowers emerge from the leaf axils and bloom in May, succeeded by the round, blue-black edible berries with their greyish bloom that ripen in July and August.

The common name Bilberry is derived from the Danish *bollebar*, 'dark berry', while the Scottish name blaeberry is derived from an old Northern word *blae*, 'livid' or 'bluish', alluding to the grey bloom on the dark berries, and this in turn has become the blueberry of North America.

The culinary and medicinal qualities of bilberries have been recognized for centuries. Dioscorides recommended them for dysentery and their long use as a natural remedy for diarrhoea and intestinal infection has been supported by modern research which has shown that the disinfectant and astringent properties of the berries can kill typhoid and colon bacilli. Modern research has also supported the centuries-old belief that the berries improve night vision; a lotion from the leaves eases inflamed eyes. A decoction made from the leaves lowers the blood sugar level and is prescribed for diabetes, dropsy, gravel and scurvy. Used externally, a decoction made from the berries or bark is an effective mouthwash and gargle or it can be used as a lotion to soothe eczema and haemorrhoids. Fresh, ripe bilberries eaten in fairly large quantities will have a laxative effect and are beneficial for chronic constipation.

To make a decoction, put 30 g/1 oz of leaves in 1 1/2 pt of water, boil for ten minutes. Strain, sweeten and take three cups a day. To make a decoction of berries, use 60 g/2 oz of fruit.

Ripe bilberries are delicious eaten fresh or they can be made into jams, jellies, syrups and tarts and, if eaten soon after being made, they do not require as much sugar as many other wild fruits.

Gather from the wild: the leaves in spring, the berries from July to September. Use fresh, or dry some leaves and berries in the shade for winter use. They keep very well.

Wild Strawberry or **Wood Strawberry** *Fragaria vesca* is a perennial herb, native to Europe and

Wild Strawberry or **Wood Strawberry** *Fragaria vesca*

eastern North America and also introduced into other parts of the world. It is found growing wild in woodlands and damp undergrowth and grassland. Wild strawberry has a rather thick, woody, cylindrical rhizome producing very long, arching runners that root at the nodes and form fresh plants. The downy, elliptical, coarsely toothed leaves are bright green and emerge from the rhizome on long stalks. The five-petalled white flowers are on stalks that can reach a height of 20 cm (8 in) and bloom from April to July. The red, ovoid fruit is covered all over with tiny projecting achenes and appears in May.

The generic name is derived from the Latin *fragrans*, 'fragrant', alluding to the delicate fragrance of this beautiful plant. It was once thought that the common name of 'strawberry' came from the habit of putting straw under the cultivated plants to facilitate ripening, but it is perhaps more likely to be a corruption of the Old English word 'to strew' referring to the tangle of strawberry vines which cover the ground where they grow.

Fossilized wild strawberry seeds have been found in the settlements of the early lake dwellers and it is mentioned in the writings of the ancient Greeks and Romans. During the Middle Ages it was regarded as a magic plant and by the sixteenth century it was considered useful for the liver, kidneys, spleen and bladder as well as for curing wounds, ulcers, mouth

infections, colic and dysentery. Scientific research has confirmed some of its traditional uses. High in iron, potassium and salts, wild strawberries are excellent for those suffering from anaemia and their salicylic acid content means they are indeed beneficial for kidney and liver complaints as well as rheumatism and gout. The Swedish botanist Linnaeus swore that his gout was cured when he confined himself to a diet of wild strawberries, for a period of time. A decoction of the fresh leaves or roots is recommended for chronic dysentery or used externally as a lotion for chilblains or as a throat gargle (one handful of leaves and roots boiled for five minutes in 1 1/2 pt of water). The leaves (fresh or dried) make a delicious herbal tea, ideal for children, and the strawberries themselves are a wonderful beauty treatment and are used extensively in the cosmetic industry. They tone and whiten the skin, combat wrinkles, lighten freckles, soothe sunburn and whiten teeth. Some people may be sensitive to strawberries and come out in a blotchy rash after eating them; however, this is more frequent after eating commercially cultivated strawberries. Note, too, that the urine is often pink after drinking strawberry tea; do not be alarmed, it is perfectly harmless.

Best grown from young plants.
Alpine Strawberry *Fragaria vesca* 'Alexandria' is one form of wild strawberry often grown for its fruit.

Bergamots *Monarda:* 'Cambridge Scarlet' (top), *M. didyma* (left), *M. fistulosa* (right)

Linden or **Common Lime** *Tilia europaea*

Bee Balm or **Oswego Tea** *Monarda didyma*

Wild Bergamot *Monarda fistulosa*

Bergamot, Bee Balm or **Oswego Tea** *Monarda didyma* is a highly scented perennial herb, native to North America, which is found growing wild in rich woods, roadsides and streams, and often cultivated for ornament in gardens. Bergamot has square, grooved, hard stems that reach a height of 60–150 cm (24–60 in). The opposite pairs of leaves are ovate to lanceolate, coarsely toothed, dark green and rough-textured. The beautiful, bright red tubular flowers form a dense cluster at the top of the stem and bloom from June to August.

The generic name commemorates the Spanish physician, Nicholas Monardes, who discovered the plant's properties in the sixteenth century. The common name of bee balm alludes to its popularity with bees, which are attracted by the scent of its nectar-rich flowers, and the other common name alludes to its use among the Oswego Indians and later colonists as a substitute for tea. The name bergamot arose because the scent is similar to that of the Bergamot Orange (a Mediterranean plant).

Several Indian tribes extracted the oil from **Wild Bergamot** (*Monarda fistulosa*), also native to North America, and inhaled it to soothe bronchial complaints and ease colds. The thymol contained in these plants has been prescribed as a stimulant and to relieve digestive flatulence and nausea. The leaves and flowers can be added sparingly to salads.

To make bergamot tea, put 30 g/1 oz dried leaves into 1 1/2 pt of boiling water and infuse for five minutes. Strain and sweeten if desired.

Bergamot can be successfully grown in the garden in rich, moist soil. Dig up the roots every two years and replant the healthy stock, then the plant will spread rapidly.

Lemon Bergamot *Monarda citriodora* is a smaller plant with pink or purple flowers. It has strongly lemon-scented leaves which are also good for making teas and for flavouring salads or wild game.

Linden or **Common Lime** *Tilia europaea* is a large decorative tree, native to Europe, which is sometimes found growing wild in woods and extensively cultivated in parks, copses, gardens and along roadsides and urban streets. Linden is a large tree with smooth bark, often irregularly bossed, that can reach a height of about 25 m (83 ft) or more. The branches are fairly wide-spreading with small twigs and roundish, sharply-toothed leaves. The deliciously fragrant, whitish-yellow flowers grow in loose clusters on long, thin stalks and bloom in July.

The use of linden goes back many centuries. Pliny recommended its bark to make a vinegar that was good for clearing up skin blemishes. According to Jean Palaiseul and St Hildegard a fragment of linden, wrapped in a spider's web and set beneath a green stone in a ring, was reputed to ward off the plague.

Culpeper, like many other herbalists, said of linden that it was 'excellent for apoplexy, epilepsy, vertigo and palpitation of the heart'. Carpenters greatly value linden wood for carving small, delicate articles because it is smooth, white, close-grained and flexible. It is used in making pianos, organs, furniture veneers and artists' charcoal. Bees love its nectar and produce wonderfully fragrant honey from it which is highly prized not only at the breakfast table but also in liqueur-making.

Linden is most well-known for the lovely fragrant tisane that is made from its flowers. It is drunk particularly after dinner to aid digestion and sleep. The tea can also be drunk to aid bronchial problems, loosen catarrh in the lungs, induce perspiration and thus help dispel colds and flu. An infusion is prescribed for nervous complaints, migraine, insomnia and asthma. It also has a reputation for thinning the blood and is prescribed for arteriosclerosis and poor circulation. Taken externally, a decoction will remove freckles and wrinkles, cure mouth ulcers and burns, encourage hair growth and, added to the bath, aid relaxation and soothe rheumatic aches and pains.

To make tilleul tisane, put 30–45 g/1–1½ oz of flowers in 1 1/2 pt of boiling water and leave to infuse for five to ten minutes. Strain and sweeten with a little honey if you like. It is a particularly good drink to give to children with colds and flu. Mességué says if you drink this regularly it will prolong longevity and keep you in excellent health.

Harvest linden flowers (including bracts) from a tree that is as far away from pollution as possible. Gather them carefully without pressing them down at all and spread out in the shade to dry as quickly as possible. When dry, store in an airtight jar.

Camomile There are at least two plants known as camomile which are very similar to each other in appearance, habitat and medicinal properties. However, there are two important features that distinguish them botanically – Roman camomile or lawn camomile (see pages 80–1) has a solid receptacle at the base of the flowers and chaffy receptacular scales amongst the yellow disk-florets, while German camomile or scented mayweed has a hollow receptacle at the base of the flower-head and no receptacular scales.

German Camomile, or **Scented Mayweed**
Camomilla recutita, synonym *Matricaria recutita* is an aromatic annual herb, native to Britain, Europe, western Asia and India, and found also in North America and Australia. It grows wild in sandy or loamy soil in cornfields, along waysides or on waste ground. German camomile is a low growing plant with erect, smooth, branched stems that reach a height of 15–50 cm (6–20 in). The small, doubly pinnate leaves are feathery and the flowers are like small daisies with yellow centres and single white ray-florets that bend backwards. They bloom from May to August.

There seems to be considerable disagreement in some of the best-known herbals as to which camomile is the best medicinally. Claire Loewenfeld and Philippa Back in *The Complete Book of Herbs and Spices* say that Roman camomile has no other value than as a lawn herb while German camomile is of great medicinal value, while other writers like Jean Palaiseul in *Grandmother's Secrets*, say that medicinally they are equally efficacious. The modern herbalist Weiss says that they are both effective medicinally and some traditional claims made for camomile can now be scientifically explained.

Over the centuries camomile has been used to beat numerous ills. For digestive problems, flatulence and insomnia; for fever, influenza, premenstrual migraine and menstrual pain, conjunctivitis, inflammation of the eyelids and skin infections such as eczema, a decoction of 60 g/2 oz of dried flowers infused in 1 1/2 pt of boiling water can be very helpful. Grieve says that it is important to make the tea in a covered vessel so that the healing properties of the plant

German Camomile, Sweet False Camomile or **Scented Mayweed** *Camomilla recutita*

do not escape in the steam and to infuse the tea for at least ten minutes.

Camomile tea is marvellously soothing and sedative and can be given to children to ease stomach upsets and diarrhoea, to calm the nerves and to cure nightmares. Hence Mother Rabbit gave it to Peter Rabbit after his traumatic experience in Mr MacGregor's garden. 'His mother put him to bed and made some camomile tea; and she gave a dose of it to Peter! "One table-spoonful to be taken at bed-time"'.

Externally, camomile oil can be used to ease cramps, rheumatic pain and gout, or as hot compresses applied on wounds, burns, swellings or around the throat for loss of voice.

To make the oil, put 60 g/2 oz of flowers into

a glass jar with ½ l/1 pt of good olive oil. Cork and expose to the sun for several days. Macerate for two hours in a bain-marie, then strain, press and apply very hot. This oil can also be used as a scalp massage; rinsing the hair in a decoction of camomile is particularly good for lightening golden tints in blond hair.

German camomile is best sown in a plot of its own. It is happy with rich, sandy soil and if the easily germinated seeds are sown in rows it makes subsequent picking of the flowers easier. The flowers should be gathered in midsummer before they are in full bloom and dried rapidly in a well-ventilated place at a temperature of 35°C (95°F) then stored in cellophane bags or very large glass jars and kept in the dark. For Roman camomile see pp. 80–1.

The Apothecary's Rose *Rosa gallica* 'Officinalis'

Dog Rose *Rosa canina* (hips)

Rosa gallica 'Versicolor'

Dog Rose, Wild Briar or Wild Rose *Rosa canina*

The Apothecary's Rose *Rose gallica* 'Officinalis' is a deciduous shrub, native to southern and central Europe as far north as Belgium, which is commonly cultivated in gardens for ornament. The Apothecary's Rose has spreading, thorny stems that grow to a height of about 100 cm (40 in). The leathery, oval to elliptical leaflets are smooth, dullish-green above and paler and more hairy below. The strongly scented, semi-double flowers generally grow singly, or in groups of two to four, and bloom from May to July, followed by round, bright red hips.

The generic name is derived from the Greek *roden*, 'red', alluding to its deep crimson colour, while the specific name refers to the fact that this is probably the oldest form of rose in cultivation, reputed to have been brought from its native Damascus to Gaul (France) by Thibaut le Chansonnier in the thirteenth century.

From early times roses were used gastronomically, cosmetically and medicinally. Named 'Queen of the Flowers' by the Greek poetess Sappho in 600BC the beautiful deep crimson colour of the Apothecary's Rose led the ancients to believe that it sprang from the blood of Adonis. Traditionally associated with love and life, rose garlands were used to decorate statues of Cupid, Venus, Flora and Hymen. Bunches of roses were found in Tutankhamun's tomb, thought to have been laid there by his young wife as a symbol of love. The Romans used rose petals lavishly to strew the floors at banquets, decorate the tables and float in their wine. They were also used to adorn the prows of war vessels and roses were a political symbol during the Wars of the Roses in the fifteenth century. The rose has been an emblem of silence. Cupid is said to have given Harpocrates, the god of Silence, a rose to bribe him not to betray the amours of Venus, so for this reason, a rose was carved on the ceiling of banqueting rooms to remind the guests what was spoken *sub vino* was not to be repeated *sub dive*. From this comes *sub rosa*, under the rose, meaning in strict confidence.

Cakes, jams, wines and sweetmeats flavoured with crushed rose petals were popular as was rose powder, rose oil and rose petals to perfume the body and sweeten the breath. Medicinally, it seems to have been recommended by Arab doctors for tuberculosis and pulmonary complaints and it was recognized by herbalists for its astringent and binding properties which made it good for coughs, chest complaints, mouth and throat ulcers, headaches, eyeaches and eye inflammations.

The use of roses in cooking and cosmetics has never lost its popularity and Mességué is full of praise for its tonic properties. He recommends an infusion of rose petals for sore throats and runny noses as well as diarrhoea, claiming that it is excellent for replacing the intestinal flora killed by courses of antibiotics. He also claims to have cured arthritis, rheumatism and liver complaints using rose preparations.

To make a concentrated decoction for use as a general tonic for convalescents, old people and children put a handful of dried rose petals into 1 1/2 pt of boiling water and infuse for ten minutes. Drink two cupfuls a day. A weaker

Rosa 'Complicata' in the walled herb garden at Hollington's nursery

infusion can be used as a lotion or as a compress for conjunctivitis.

To make rose honey to ease sore throats or use as a gargle or enema put 20 g/²⁄₃ oz of petals from buds into 100 g/4 oz of honey, boil for ten minutes then strain through muslin.

To make rose vinegar, highly acclaimed on the Continent for headaches caused by the sun, fill a jar with rose petals collected in the morning. Cover with best distilled vinegar. Leave to stand in the sun for three weeks then strain. Soak a cloth in the liquid and apply to the forehead. This can also be used as a skin lotion, gargle or eyebath.

The Apothecary's Rose can easily be grown in the garden. It likes deep rich soil and a sunny position.

Pick the petals on a dry day while the flowers are still not fully open, remove the stamens and dry quickly to retain the colour and smell. Store in a dry tin or tinted glass jar and use within four months or else their medicinal properties will be lost.

Rosa gallica 'Versicolor' is a variegated form of the Apothecary's Rose which has been known since the sixteenth century and often reverts to its non-variegated parent.

Rosa 'Complicata' is a Gallica or Gallica hybrid that forms a large shrub with single flowers that can be up to 13 cm (5 in) across.

Dog Rose, Wild Briar or **Wild Rose** *Rosa canina* is a deciduous shrub, native to Europe, North Africa and south-west Asia and also

naturalized in North America. It is commonly found growing wild in hedgerows, woods and scrubland. Dog rose has a long, fibrous root and arching stems which grow up to a height of 3 m (10 ft). The stems have curved or hooked thorns and numerous branchlets with oval or elliptical pointed leaves that are usually smooth on both sides. The pink or white five-petalled flowers grow singly or in small clusters of three or four flowers and they bloom from June to July. They are followed by the round, smooth, red hips which contain the seeds in hairy achenes.

The common name of the plant, dog rose, is either derived from the ancient belief that the root would cure the bite of a mad dog or, more probably, is a corruption of the Old French *dague*, 'dagger' (alluding to its prickly thorns). In the language of flowers, dog rose symbolizes pleasure mixed with pain.

Dog rose hips have been eaten for thousands of years. Their seeds have been found in the 2000-year-old skeleton of a neolithic woman unearthed in Britain. The ancients learned how to cultivate roses but wild species have still been used over the centuries – the petals to scent water, pot pourris and food; the hips either eaten in times of fruit scarcity or used to make wines, syrups, jams and preserves. Petals and hips were also used medicinally. Rosehips are an important source of vitamin C with an even higher vitamin C content than citrus fruit. The hips of the dog rose contain the highest amounts of vitamin C of all the varieties and the further north the plant is found the higher the vitamin C content.

This, along with their high level of calcium,

phosphorus and iron, means rosehips are astringent and tonic and so increase the body's resistance to infectious diseases such as colds, flu and dysentery. They are very useful for beating coughs, sore throats and bronchial problems as well as for bleeding gums and diarrhoea.

Rosehips can either be eaten raw (six to eight per day) or made into a tea. Put 30 g/1 oz of rosehip rind into ½ l/1 pt of water, bring to the boil, simmer for five minutes, leave to stand for five more minutes, strain, sweeten as necessary and take two cupfuls a day, after meals. A stronger decoction (double quantity of hips to water) has a mildly diuretic effect and is recommended for kidney complaints. A tiny pinch of the down found on the hips and coated with honey is said to be an excellent way of curing intestinal worms, particularly in children. In North America, the Mescalero Apaches drank tea made from wild dog rosebuds to beat gonorrhoea. Syrup, purée, jam and wine can all be made from rosehips and all have a marvellously tonic effect.

Dog rose is easy to grow in the garden and it soon makes a decorative hedge. Make sure to space it out well.

Gather the hips after the first frost when they are bright red and slightly soft to the touch. Handle them gently to prevent loss of vitamin C. Cut lengthwise and dry rapidly in a well-ventilated place. Shake well in a wire sieve to remove hairs, then store in a cool place. Do not keep for more than a year as they lose their vitamin C. Use only stainless steel, wood or plastic in preparation and cooking, as other metals break down the vitamin C.

Calamint or **Mountain Balm** *Calamintha grandiflora*

Wood Calamint *Calamintha sylvatica*

Calamint or **Mountain Balm** *Calamintha grandiflora* is a hardy, aromatic perennial native to southern Europe and North Africa. It grows wild along hedgerows, roadsides, dry banks, in woods and waste places, and is also cultivated. Calamint is an erect, bushy plant with a creeping rootstock and square, downy stems that grow to a height of 20–60 cm (1–2 ft). The broadly ovate, stalked, downy leaves are toothed and the somewhat drooping, pale purplish flowers bloom in July and August.

Closely related to the thymes and ground ivy, calamint has been valued medicinally as a diaphoretic, an expectorant and an aromatic. Gerard said it helped cure 'melanchole and sorrowfulness' and Culpeper recommended it for jaundice, nerves, convulsions, cramps and 'all afflictions of the brain'.

With its pleasant aromatic taste it makes a delightful infusion. Steep the whole plant in boiling water for twenty minutes. Strain, sweeten if necessary, and drink as a tonic. A poultice made with a wad of leaves, gently heated with an iron, may help soothe bruises and relieve rheumatic pains.

The plant can be propagated by seeds sown outdoors in dry soil in April or by putting cuttings in cold frames in the spring or by root division in either spring or autumn. Collect the leaves in July, then dry and store in an airtight jar to use for making tea.

Common Calamint *Calamintha ascendens* synonym *Calamintha officinalis* has a short creeping rhizome, an erect stem and few branches. The flowers are lilac or pale reddish-purple with darker spots.

The generic name is derived from the Greek *kale*, 'good' and *minthe*, 'mint' and the former specific name refers to its official recognition as a medicinal herb in the Middle Ages.

Lesser Calamint *Calamintha nepeta* has a long, creeping rhizome and an erect stem, bearing lilac flowers, smaller than calamint's. The numerous branches are grey with long, soft, spreading hairs.

Wood Calamint *Calamintha sylvatica* has an erect stem with few branches, and the purple-pink flowers are large with a deep purple blotch on the lower lip.

Nepeta camphorata is a perennial plant, native to Greece, which has white flowers with purple spots.

Wild Catmint or **Catnip** *Nepeta cataria* is a strongly scented perennial herb, native to Europe but also naturalized in North America and South Africa, which is found growing in hedgebanks, roadsides, near streams and in mountainous areas. Wild catmint has erect, branched woolly stems that reach a height of 40–100 cm (16–40 in). The heart-shaped leaves are coarsely toothed at the edge and very downy, almost white on the underside. The small whitish or pinkish flowers have red spots and grow in dense whorls in the leaf axils. They bloom from July to September.

The common names for this plant arise from the fact that it seems to have an overwhelming attraction for cats on which it appears to act as an aphrodisiac – the smell of it being similar to the pheromones of cats of the opposite sex. The

Garden Catmint *Nepeta × faassenii*

smell of it is also slightly reminiscent of mint
which might account for the name catmint.

In France, wild catmint is used in salads as a
seasoning and, before the advent of China tea, it
was commonly drunk as a beverage.

Medicinally, wild catmint has been used for
centuries. It is useful for fevers, colds and
nervousness and induces sleep. Its mildly
sedative properties have made it particularly
useful for children's ailments and it is used to
ease colic, restlessness, pain and flatulence. It is
also reputed to be good for nervous headaches
and as an aid to restoring regular menstruation.
Smoking the leaves is said to stop hiccups and
chewing them to relieve heachaches.

To make an infusion, steep 30 g/1 oz dried
leaves or flowering tops in ½ l/1 pt of boiling
water for five to ten minutes. Give children 2–3
tsps several times a day; adults may take
stronger doses to ease pain and flatulence.

Attractive to bees as well as cats, wild catmint
can either be found in the wild or grown in a
herb garden from seed. It makes a very pretty
border plant and will grow in almost any kind of
soil, requiring less moisture than other, true
mints. Sow seeds in spring or divide existing
plants. Protect your plants until well
established, otherwise cats will destroy them.
Gather the leaves and flowering tops when in
full bloom and dry for winter use.

Garden Catmint *Nepeta × faassenii* is a
perennial herb with blue flowers and aromatic
grey leaves. It grows easily from seed in
ordinary soil, favouring a sunny position, and is
frequently cultivated in a herb garden as a
pretty edging plant.

Lesser Calamint *Calamintha nepeta*

Wild Catmint or **Catnip** *Nepeta cataria*

Common Calamint *Calamintha ascendens*

Nepeta camphorata

English Lavender *Lavandula angustifolia*

Lavundula 'Loddon Pink'

Lavender or **English Lavender** *Lavandula angustifolia* synonyms *Lavandula officinalis* and *Lavendula spica* is a hardy, aromatic shrub native to the mountainous regions of the western Mediterranean but now found all over the world. It sometimes grows wild in hilly regions but is also extensively cultivated for perfume and grown in gardens for ornament. Lavender has a short, much branched stem with numerous straight, woody, quadrangular, downy, grey branches that reach a height of 100 cm (40 in). The opposite, stalkless, long, narrow leaves are pale greyish-green. The lovely bluish-violet flowers, which grow in dense whorls, forming a terminal spike, bloom from June to August.

The generic and common names are thought to derive from the Latin *lavare*, 'to wash', because the Romans and Carthaginians put lavender in their bath water both for its fragrance and its therapeutic properties. The antiseptic and disinfectant qualities of lavender were recognized from early times and the plant used as a strewing herb, placed among clothes and linen to deter moths and hung in rooms to keep them free of flies and mosquitoes. It was also used to treat some snake bites. A small amount of chopped leaves will give an aromatic tang to salads and honey from bees that have visited lavender is much sought after.

Modern research has shown that the medicinal properties ascribed to lavender are well-founded scientifically. The essential oil extracted from the plant is a powerful antiseptic which will kill many of the common bacteria – typhoid, diphtheria, streptococcus, pneumococcus – as well as being a powerful antidote to some snake venom.

Lavender has a sedative, antispasmodic, tranquillizing effect when taken as a mild infusion so it is prescribed for headaches, insomnia, nervous digestion, fainting, convulsions, nausea, flatulence and colic. As a stronger infusion it is also a tonic and stimulant given for respiratory complaints, tonsillitis, chills, influenza and fever. Externally, a lotion or compress is good for burns, infected wounds, eczema and acne. A tincture strengthens hair and prevents hair loss and also relieves rheumatism and painful joints. In veterinary practice lavender is commonly used as a germicide and vermifuge and in France it is increasingly used to embalm corpses. The dried flowers are frequently made into lavender bags and added to pot pourris and oil of lavender is used extensively in the making of soaps, powders and perfumes.

To make a mild infusion, put 5–10 g/⅙–⅓ oz of dried sprigs into 1 1/2 pt of boiling water, leave to infuse for five minutes, then strain and drink two to three cupfuls a day. To make a stronger infusion, use 30 g/10 oz of sprigs to the same amount of water. To make lavender oil, put 30 g/1 oz of fresh flowers in 1 1/2 pt of olive oil, leave to macerate for three days in the sun, strain through muslin, then repeat several times until the oil is highly perfumed. Use internally for migraines and nervous indigestion and externally as a lotion or on compresses for

Lavandula stoechas subsp. *pedunculata*

French Lavender *Lavandula stoechas*

Lavandula 'Hidcote'

burns, eczema and bronchitis. (These recipes come from *Grandmother's Secrets* by Jean Palaiseul.) Lavender vinegar can be made in a similar way by steeping freshly gathered flowers in white vinegar for a week, shaking the stoppered bottle daily, then straining the resulting liquid through blotting paper.

Lavender is very easy to grow in the garden. It can either be grown from seed or propagated from autumn cuttings, kept in compost under cover during the winter and planted out the following spring in an open, sunny position. Prune the bush after flowering to encourage denser growth.

Collect the flowers just as they are coming into bloom and tie up in small bundles to dry.

Lavandula 'Hidcote' is a small-growing form with lovely deep purplish flowers.

Lavandula 'Loddon Pink' is a tall-growing pink-flowered form.

French Lavender or **Gentle Lavender**
Lavandula stoechas is found in dry, sandy areas, often along the coast, of Mediterranean Europe. It is a small shrub with velvety, whitish leaves and very pretty, dark purple flowers. It was probably this variety that was used by the Romans in their baths. Its smell is more like rosemary than other lavenders and it is not generally used for distillation. It is more frost-sensitive than English lavender.

Lavandula stoechas subsp. *pedunculata* is a very pretty garden variety.

Curry Plant *Helichrysum angustifolium* synonym *Helichrysum italicum* is a grey-leaved shrubby perennial plant that reaches a height of 60 cm (24 in). It has yellow flowers that bloom from July to September; the silvery, curry-smelling leaves can be used to flavour salads and meat dishes.

It is commonly grown as a decorative garden plant because of its pretty scented foliage. It looks particularly good in a tub, best positioned near a path so that, as you walk past, you can rub against it to release the odour.

Curry Plant *Helichrysum angustifolium*

Cotton Lavender *Santolina chamaecyparissus*

Cotton Lavender *Santolina chamaecyparissus*

Cotton Lavender *Santolina chamaecyparissus* is a hardy, aromatic dwarf shrub native to the western and central Mediterranean area, but also widely cultivated worldwide. It grows wild in neglected fields and waste ground, particularly on calcareous soil. Cotton lavender has a woody root and an erect, ascending, numerously branched stem that reaches a height of 10–50 cm (4–20 in). The linear, pinnately lobed leaves are greyish-white with dense woolly hair and the little cream to yellow flowers bloom in July and August.

Although no longer used much, cotton lavender was once esteemed for its stimulant and antiseptic properties. It was used to expel intestinal worms and dried twigs were put among linen to keep away moths. Dried flowers and leaves can be powdered and applied to insect bites to allay pain and if added to herb sachets they will help repel insects. The Arabs are said to have made a lotion from the plant to soothe sore eyes and one modern herbal says a compress applied to a surface wound will help healing and promote scar formation.

It is a pretty plant to grow in a herb garden because of its silver-grey leaves. It likes ordinary, sandy soil and sun.

Santolina chamaecyparissus nana

Santolina neapolitana 'Edward Bowles'

Santolina serratifolia

Santolina chamaecyparissus nana is a dwarf form which grows into a small, compact shrub. It has coarse, grey leaves and yellow flowers.

Santolina neapolitana 'Edward Bowles' has fine grey leaves and cream-coloured flowers.

Santolina serratifolia has fine, grey leaves and lemon yellow, button flowers.

Camphor Plant *Balsamita major* var. *tomentoşum* has white, daisy-like flowers, silver-grey leaves and a camphor scent. The dried leaves can be tied in bunches or put in little bags to keep moths away.

Camphor Plant *Balsamita major* var. *tomentosum*

75

Cheddar Pink *Dianthus gratianopolitanus*

Clove Pink or **Carnation** *Dianthus caryophyllus*

Maiden Pink *Dianthus deltoides* a dark variety

Maiden Pink *Dianthus deltoides* 'Wisley variety'

Jerusalem Sage *Phlomis fruticosa*

Clove Pink or **Carnation** *Dianthus caryophyllus* is a perennial herb, native to southern Europe and North Africa, commonly cultivated in gardens but sometimes found in old walls as an escape. Clove pink is a tufted herb with a woody stock and shoots that reach a height of 20–50 cm (8–20 in). The narrow, bluish-green leaves are smooth-edged and the beautifully fragrant, deep-pink single or double flowers bloom from July to August.

Clove pink, the old-fashioned carnation, was one of the earliest flowers to be cultivated in Britain. It was grown for its decorative, culinary and medicinal properties. It was used for its spicy, clove-like fragrance in vinegars, ales, wines, sauces and salads. The petals were candied to decorate cakes and dried as an important ingredient in pot pourris.

Although no longer much used medicinally, they traditionally had a reputation for being good for fevers because they were said to promote perspiration and quench thirst. According to Jean Palaiseul in *Grandmother's Secrets ratafia* taken one liqueur-glassful a day is an excellent remedy for indigestion, distension and flatulence. To make the *ratafia* macerate 300 g/10–12 oz of fresh petals in 1 1/2 pt of spirits of alcohol for eight to ten days then strain through a cloth and sweeten to taste.

Cheddar Pink *Dianthus gratianopolitanus* synonym *Dianthus caesius* is a densely tufted plant with long, creeping, non-flowering shoots.

Maiden Pink *Dianthus deltoides* is a perennial herb, native to Europe and temperate Asia and introduced into North America. Maiden Pink has narrow green leaves and single pink flowers that bloom all summer.

Phlomis russeliana

Jerusalem Sage *Phlomis fruticosa* is a shrub, native to the Mediterranean but naturalized elsewhere in Europe, which is found growing in rocky and bushy places and often cultivated in gardens. Jerusalem sage is a handsome shrub, with white felty branches, that reaches a height of 1.5 m (5 ft). The aromatic, elliptical to ovate leaves are silver-leathery above and densely covered in white felt below. The compact whorls of bright orange-yellow flowers bloom from June to August.

This attractive plant is frequently grown for ornament because of its pretty silver leaves that give off an aromatic odour.

Phlomis russeliana synonym *Phlomis samia* is a good evergreen plant with large rough leaves that make an excellent ground cover.

Korean Mint *Agastache rugosa*

Anise Hyssop *Agastache anethiodora*

Mexican Orange *Choisya ternata*

Hedge Hyssop *Gratiola officinalis*

Anise Hyssop *Agastache anethiodora* is a perennial plant, native to central North America, which is found growing on prairies and plains. Anise hyssop has a slender, leafy, generally branched stem that reaches a height of 60–120 cm (24–48 in). The anise-scented leaves are short-stalked, ovate to triangular with a pointed tip and a sharply toothed margin. The longish spikes of lovely mauve-purple flowers bloom from July to September.

Anise hyssop is an important bee plant, and its aniseed-flavoured leaves make a good herbal tea and can be used as an interesting seasoning in salads.

Korean Mint *Agastache rugosa* is a perennial plant native to the East and similar to anise hyssop except that its smell and taste is more minty. It is also a good bee plant and used for making a refreshing tea and flavouring mint dishes.

Hedge Hyssop *Gratiola officinalis* is a perennial herb, native to central and southern Europe, which is found wild in wet meadows, moist ground, river banks and ditches. Hedge hyssop has a creeping rhizome and an erect, hollow, quadrangular stem that grows to heights of 20–50 cm (8–20 in). The narrow, lance-shaped, finely-toothed leaves are smooth, pale-green and in opposite pairs. The creamy or yellowish flowers with reddish stripes grow singly in the axils of the upper leaves and bloom from June to August.

Known in earlier times as *Gratia Dei*, 'grace of the Lord', because of its active medicinal properties, hedge hyssop is a powerful cathartic and emetic with diuretic properties. It used to be recommended for dropsy, scrofula, liver infections and jaundice and was also believed useful in expelling worms. It is recognized in modern phytotherapy as an emmenagogue so it should not be taken by pregnant women as it could cause abortion. Because of its powerful action, hedge hyssop should only be taken in doses prescribed by a qualified practitioner.

Mexican Marigold *Tagetes minuta* is an aromatic annual, native to South America and locally naturalized in Europe, where it is found growing in waste places and cultivated ground. Mexican marigold has erect, smooth stems with short branches that reach a height of 100–180 cm (40–72 in). The pinnate leaves have three to seven narrow segments and small, yellow, daisy-like flowers that bloom from August to October.

This plant is cultivated in parks and gardens for the weed-suppressing chemicals supposedly secreted by its strong roots. It is used to protect potatoes from eelworm and it may also kill bindweed, ground elder and, to some extent, couchgrass. It needs a long growing season so raise the seeds in early spring and plant out in April.

French Marigold *Tagets patula* is a half-hardy, strong-smelling annual that reaches a height of 23 cm (9 in) and has lovely flowers that are either yellow or red or a combination of both.

Long used by organic gardeners for its insecticidal properties, it can be grown amongst tomatoes and other crops to repel whitefly and soil nematodes.

Mexican Orange *Choisya ternata* is an evergreen shrub, native to south-western North America, which is found growing on chalky soil or near the sea. Mexican orange grows to a height of 3 m (10 ft) and has widely spreading branches with shiny leaves. The clusters of pretty white flowers bloom at any time of year but mainly from March to May.

It is generally cultivated in gardens for ornament and because of the attractive, sweet, vanilla-like scent of its flowers. The leaves also have a strong, pleasant aromatic smell especially when crushed.

French Marigold *Tagetes patula*

Mexican Marigold *Tagetes minuta*

Wormwood *Artemisia absinthium* is a bitter, aromatic, perennial plant, native to Britain and Europe and widely distributed in Siberia, Eurasia, North and South America and New Zealand. It is found along roadsides, in waste places, on rocky hillsides and in pastures. Wormwood has a firm, woody, silky-haired, grooved stem that reaches a height of 1 m (40 in). The basal leaves are lobed with a long leaf-stalk and stem leaves are bipinnate: both are whitish with silky hairs. The small, tubular, yellow flowers grow in round, terminal clusters and bloom from July to October.

The generic name derives from Artemis, (Diana), the Greek goddess who was said to have given this group of plants to Chiron the centaur. The specific name is derived from the Latin *absinthium*, 'without sweetness', referring to the very bitter taste of the plant. The common name wormwood refers to its frequent use as a vermifuge, as a strewing herb and as a moth and insect repellent amongst clothes. Ever since Egyptian times, wormwood has been valued for its powerful medicinal properties. Galen recommended it as a tonic; the Salerno school advocated it as an aid against seasickness. Overall it was renowned for having a stimulating effect on the whole body.

However, despite its beneficial medicinal properties, wormwood, if used excessively, can become a harmful and addictive poison. Absinthe, the bitter principle extracted from the root, was the basis of the French liqueur absinthe which was so addictive and deadly that is killed, amongst others, Verlaine and Toulouse Lautrec; it was made illegal in 1915. Also used at one time instead of hops for brewing, absinthe is still used to flavour liqueurs, vermouth, wines, tonic waters and aperitifs and if taken in large doses over a period of time can cause chronic poisoning, epeleptiform convulsions and degeneration of the central nervous system.

Mességué says that he has found it to be an excellent tonic and appetite stimulant. He gave it to a young girl suffering from anorexia nervosa and found it restored her taste for life. He also recommends it for liver malfunction, jaundice, viral hepatitis and for late or irregular menstruation. However, it is important with such a powerful drug not to exceed the recommended dose and it should never be taken by pregnant or breast-feeding women or people with severe stomach or bowel problems.

To make an infusion put 7 g/¼ oz of dried leaves into ¼ l/½ pt of boiling water. Infuse for four minutes, strain, sweeten and drink one or two cups a day for indigestion, heartburn, regularizing periods, relieving fevers, rheumatism and as a tonic for the liver and gallbladder. Infused in brandy it is a remedy for gout.

Wormwood is easy to grow. Propagate by root division or cuttings in spring, in heavy clay soil, or by sowing the seeds in a shady position in the autumn, after they are ripe, and keep free from weeds. Gather the flowers and leaves on a dry sunny day during the flowering season from July to September then dry and store in airtight boxes.

Mugwort or **St John's Plant** *Artemisia vulgaris* is an aromatic, perennial plant, native to Europe and most of the temperate regions of the northern hemisphere, which is commonly found in waste places, along hedgerows and roadsides. Mugwort is a vigorous spreading plant with a woody rhizome and erect, angular, sometimes

Roman Camomile or **Lawn Camomile** *Chamaemelum nobile* synonym *Anthemis nobilis*

purplish stems, branching at the top, that reach a height of 60–120 cm (24–48 in). The pinnately lobed leaves with pointed, lance-shaped segments are dark green and smooth above, whitish and downy below. The small yellow or reddish-pink flowers grow in flat oval groups, forming a long spike at the end of the stem, and bloom from July to September.

The generic name comes from the Greek goddess Artemis who, like the Roman goddess Diana, was the patron not only of the hunt but also of women. Her role was to help women in all their illnesses, particularly those relating to menstruation, conception, childbirth and menopause. Its common name, mugwort, probably alludes to its use as a flavouring for beer before the common use of hops. Alternatively it might have derived from Old English *mucgwyrt*, from 'midge' and 'wort', and allude to the plants' use as a repellent to insects.

Mugwort has a history of use going back to ancient times. Believed to have magical powers, it was worn as a talisman against tiredness, diseases and evil spirits. St John the Baptist is said to have worn a girdle of mugwort when he went into the wilderness. Although no longer used to flavour beer, mugwort has been used in the liqueur industry for flavouring absinthe and vermouth because of its somewhat bitter but aromatic taste and smell. It is a good antidote to overindulgence in rich food and aids the digestion of fatty meat and oily fish. On the Continent it is often used to season such things as goose, duck and eel. A sparing amount can also be added to salads.

Its main medicinal use has been for difficult

or irregular menstruation and as an aid for women during the menopause. However, pregnant women should not take mugwort because it has a strong decongestant effect on the uterus. Culpeper says: 'It is boiled among other herbs for drawing down the courses, by sitting over it, and for hastening the delivery, and helps to expel the afterbirth.' He also says that the fresh herb or juice from it is a good remedy for those suffering from 'over-much taking of opium'. A mild tea of mugwort was prescribed for poor digestion and stomach upsets and also for soothing hysteria, nerves, fevers and rheumatism.

To make a mild infusion, put 10 g/⅓ oz of dried mugwort herb into 1 l/2 pt of boiling water and leave for five minutes. Strain and drink two cupfuls a day.

Mugwort can easily be picked from the wild or grown in the garden in any kind of soil. Propagation by cuttings or root division, in spring, is best. Harvest the flower heads when they are fully developed but not open, and dry them whole. Pick and dry leaves for winter use.

Southernwood *Artemisia abrotanum* is a strongly aromatic shrub, probably native to southern Spain but naturalized in many parts of southern, eastern and central Europe and North America. It is rarely found in the wild but widely cultivated in gardens for ornament. Southernwood has a creeping, woody rhizome and erect, downy, irregularly branched stems which reach a height of 100 cm (40 in). The finely cut grey-green leaves are smooth above, downy below and the small yellow flowers, in

Wormwood *Artemisia absinthium* 'Lambrook Silver'

Mugwort or St John's Plant *Artemisia vulgaris*

Wormwood *Artemisia absinthium*

Southernwood *Artemisia abrotanum*

Old Warrior *Artemisia pontica*

heads, bloom in August.

The generic name (see Mugwort) comes from the goddess Artemis, while the common name is from the Old English for 'southern wood', referring to its southern European origin, and to its use as a vermifuge. The leaves of southernwood have a bitter lemony taste and are used to flavour cakes in France and Italy. It is also added to salads and to aromatic vinegars, and the essence is added to perfumes to give subtle tones. Like mugwort, it was thought that the plant warded off tiredness and infection and it was given to children to expel worms. It is also a moth and insect repellent.

However, its principal uses medicinally were as an abortifacient, emmenagogue, stimulant, tonic, and astringent. Because of its ability to restore the menstrual flow, it should under no circumstances be taken by pregnant women.

Easy to grow in any soil.

Roman Wormwood or **Old Warrior** *Artemisia pontica* most delicate of the aromatic wormwoods, is native to central and eastern Europe. It is used to flavour vermouth and is recommended for strengthening the stomach and aiding digestion. According to the eighteenth-century apothecary Dr John Hill, the reason why Germans traditionally could eat so much without sickness or indigestion was because they alternated every mouthful of food with a mouthful of wormwood wine!

Old Lady *Artemisia campestris* subsp. *borealis* is aromatic, with finely cut grey foliage, and is native to the Alps and Arctic Russia.

Roman Camomile or **Lawn Camomile**
Chamaemelum nobile synonym *Anthemis nobilis* is a pleasantly scented, perennial herb, native to Europe, North Africa and the temperate regions of Asia, which is found either growing wild as an escape on roadsides or wasteland or cultivated in gardens, commons or pastures. Roman camomile is a low-growing, creeping plant with a fibrous root and erect, branched hairy stems that grow to a height of 10–40 cm (4–16 in). The leaves, 1.5–5 cm (½–2 in), are divided into fine thread-like segments, creating a feathery appearance. The flowers have white ray-florets and yellow centres and are borne singly on long stalks. They bloom from May to September.

Roman camomile has long been a favourite garden herb not only for its medicinal properties but also for its agreeable smell, reminiscent of apples. This gave rise to its generic name. Camomile is derived from the Greek *kamai*, 'on the ground', and *melon*, 'apple'. Similarly the Spanish common name Manzanilla means little apple and a light sherry has also been called Manzanilla as it is flavoured with camomile. It has probably been cultivated in Britain since pre-Roman times and it never seems to have lost its popularity. During the Middle Ages it was frequently used as a strewing herb because of the lovely aromatic smell it emits when trodden on. Camomile was also known as the 'Plant's Physician' because, if it was planted near an ailing plant, the sickly one was supposed nearly always to recover!

Roman camomile has a rather bitter taste so it is not generally used for making tea.

There has been considerable controversy as to whether Roman camomile or German camomile (see page 67) is the most efficacious medicinally but Weiss suggests that as they both have the same constituents they can be combined to achieve a good effect. Medical opinion of Roman camomile has changed considerably in the last half century. Previously it was known to be a popular herbal remedy but thought not to be very effective. Now, however, it is scientifically acknowledged as having at least some of the curative powers that a long history of empirical use had claimed for it. The most active principle in camomile oil is azulene and this, combined with a whole complex of other active substances, has three medicinal actions: it reduces inflammation and fever, relieves spasm, and counteracts flatulence and stomach cramps. Camomile has been shown scientifically to be very beneficial for treating ulcers and also to have anti-toxic and antibiotic properties. If given with lactose or lactic acid, it will restore balance to the intestinal flora. However, for all treatments – acute gastritis, ulcers, diseases of the upper respiratory tract, blocked sinuses – the condition will only improve if camomile tea is drunk several times a day over an extended period, possibly up to three months.

Roman camomile should be sown in the spring in a sheltered, weed-free seed bed of rich, loamy soil, and kept moist and protected from birds. Alternatively the seeds can be germinated in a seed tray, transferred to small pots and the young plants planted out in time. For German camomile see pages 66–7.

Meadowsweet *Filipendula ulmaria*

Variegated Meadowsweet

Meadowsweet *Filipendula ulmaria* synonym
Spiraea ulmaria is a perennial, aromatic herb,
native to Europe and temperate Asia as far east
as China and also found in eastern North
America. It grows wild in fens, marshes,
swamps and by rivers, wet woods and meadows.
Meadowsweet has erect, furrowed, angular,
red-tipped stems which grow to a height of 60–
120 cm (24–48 in). The leaves have finely
serrated edges and are dark green above and
white and downy below. The highly scented
clusters of tiny, creamy white flowers bloom
from June to August.

Also known as Queen of the Meadow,
meadowsweet was one of the most popular
strewing herbs in olden times because its
delightful perfume would completely fill the
room. It was said to be one of the herbs held
sacred by the Druids. The addition of the flowers
to beer or wine was supposed to make a heady
drink; Gerard claimed that the flowers boiled in
wine were good for ague and made 'the heart
merrier', while distilled water from the flowers
was supposedly good for itching and inflamed
eyes.

Its main medicinal use has been as a diuretic
but Jean Palaiseul in *Grandmother's Secrets* claims
it is effective in numerous other ways because it
contains methyl salicylate and salicylic aldehyde
– both of which have been used chemically to
produce acetylsalicylic acid, most commonly
known as aspirin. He says 'when it
(meadowsweet) is dried, the methyl salicylate
changes into salicylic acid and salicylates of
sodium, potassium, magnesium etc. These salts
are the principal antidotes for, firstly, uric acid
which, by depositing its crystals in the joints, is
responsible for gout, and secondly, oxalic acid
which, together with uric acid, is one of the
causes of renal and urinary calculi'. Therefore,
he suggests using meadowsweet for many of the
illnesses for which one would prescribe aspirin:
colds, influenza, articular rheumatism, gout, as
well as for kidney and bladder complaints,
cellulitis, arteriosclerosis and insomnia.

Make an infusion from flowers picked when
fully open, dried in the shade and separated from
the stem. Put 30–60 g/1 ½–2 oz of flowers in
1 1/2 pt of *almost* boiling water (do not use boiling
water as the steam will carry away the salicylic
acid). Cover, infuse for ten minutes, strain and
drink three to four cups a day between meals.
This infusion is also excellent for treating
diarrhoea. A strong decoction of the boiled root
is said to be good, used externally, for bathing
sores and ulcers.

Can be grown from seed and planted out in
damp areas.

Variegated Meadowsweet *Filipendula ulmaria*
'Variegata' has yellow-variegated foliage and is
an attractive garden plant.

Sweet Woodruff *Galium odoratum* synonym
Asperula odorata is a perennial herb, native to
northern and central Europe as far east as the
Balkans, North Africa and Siberia. It is found
growing wild in shady, woody places with
dappled light. Sweet woodruff has slender,
creeping rhizomes and erect, quadrangular
stems that reach a height of 15–45 cm (6–18 in).
The narrow, green leaves grow in star-like
whorls and the small white flowers grouped in
terminal clusters above them bloom from May
to June.

Also known as *Waldemeister*, Master of the
Wood, in Germany, sweet woodruff is still
steeped in Rhine wine to make a delightful
drink known as the *Maibowle* which is drunk on
the first of May.

The dried plant gives off a delightful smell
which has been described as a mixture of hay,
honey and vanilla. In the Middle Ages sweet
woodruff was used for strewing or hanging in
churches; it was put amongst linen to give a
lovely smell and to ward off moths and insects.
High in fragrant coumarin, it was used in pot
pourris, added to fancy snuffs and used in
perfumery, not only because of its own
fragrance but also because of its ability to fix or
disguise other odours.

It was also considered to have numerous
medicinal properties. It was formerly
recommended for menstrual pains, menopause,
uterine cramps and gynaecological complaints.
It was also advocated for liver and kidney
disorders, dropsy, poor digestion and varicose
veins. But, most importantly, according to Jean
Palaiseul, it remains an excellent tranquillizer

Sweet Woodruff *Galium odoratum*

for the nerves. Sweet woodruff tea soothes, calms and relaxes – some would say more effectively than modern tranquillizers but with none of the worrying side effects.

Put 30 g/1 oz dried leaves into ½ l/1 pt boiling water and infuse for five minutes. Strain and drink one or two cups a day and particularly one at night to induce sleep and relieve tension.

Clare Loewenfeld and Philippa Back in *The Complete Book of Herbs and Spices* give the following suggestion for *Maibowle*: 'Take a small handful of fresh woodruff and leave it to dry out in a heated airing cupboard for three hours. Cut off stems and put leaves in a large bowl. Pour over juice of a lemon and ½ bottle of light, white wine so leaves are covered, and leave in a warm place for three to four hours. Add 4–6 tbsps of sugar according to taste, and 1½ bottles of white wine. Chill in refrigerator. Just before serving add one bottle of sparkling white wine or champagne. For a stronger drink add a measure of brandy when adding the sparkling wine. A lovely addition to the cup is strawberries, cut up and sprinkled with lemon juice and sugar, and floated on top.'

Weiss reports that coumarin has recently been said to cause liver damage and cancer in animals, in high doses, but, he adds, many medicinal plants' isolated principles taken in very large doses can have toxic effects but these findings should not be applied to small therapeutic doses of the whole complex of active principles contained in the plant.

Sweet woodruff can be collected from the wild or from seed in a herb garden to make an attractive ground-cover. The seeds take a long time to germinate so it is best to plant in August in a shady spot with plenty of space between them. Alternatively propagation can be done by root division of older plants. Once established sweet woodruff will self-seed.

Lady's Bedstraw *Galium verum*

Lady's Bedstraw *Galium verum* is a perennial herb, native to Europe and western Asia which is also found all over North America, and grows abundantly by the roadside in waste land, dunes and hedgebanks. Lady's bedstraw has a cylindrical, creeping, woody rhizome and erect, quadrangular, branching stems that reach a height of 25–100 cm (10–40 in), and blacken when dried. The very narrow leaves with prominent veins on the underside grow in whorls of six to eight. The small bright yellow flowers, closely clustered in pinnacles at the end of the stalks, bloom in July and August.

The generic name comes from the Greek *gala*, 'milk', and probably refers to the plant's unusual ability to curdle milk. Also known in the sixteenth century as cheese renning or cheese rennet, Lady's bedstraw was used in Tuscany to give a sweeter taste to goat's cheese, and in Britain it was used in the making of cheeses to give them a richer colour and flavour. The English common name comes from its use

as a stuffing for mattresses and may have originated in the Christian legend that it was one of the cradle herbs used in the manger at Bethlehem.

Lady's bedstraw is one of a group of plants that yield natural dyes: red from the roots and yellow from the flowering tops. The flower tops distilled in water also make a refreshing drink.

Medicinally, the plant was thought to be effective for epilepsy and hysteria and was a popular remedy for gall stones and urinary diseases. Culpeper recommended it to stop nose bleeds and internal bleeding and an infusion made from the leaves is said to be laxative; an ointment is 'soothing for the weary traveller' according to Gerard.

To make an infusion put a handful of leaves in ½ l/1 pt of boiling water and leave to stand for ten minutes. Strain and drink as required.

Easily gathered from the wild. Gather the flowering tops in summer and dry in the sun.

Woad *Isatis tinctoria* (the flowers in the centre)

Woad *Isatis tinctoria* is a biennial or short-lived perennial herb native to central and southern Europe and Asia which has been widely introduced elsewhere as a result of its cultivation since ancient times. It is found growing naturalized on cliffs or in cornfields or cultivated for its dye. Woad has a stout tap-root and branched stock bearing several rosettes and leafy flowering shoots that are branched above and reach a height of 50–120 cm (20–48 in). The heads of small, fluffy, yellow flowers bloom from April to July, succeeded by large, black, tongue-shaped seed heads.

Woad, or wad as it was called in Anglo-Saxon times, has been extensively cultivated since Roman times principally as a dye for cloth which is made from the fermented leaves. Caesar found the natives stained with it when he visited Britain but later it had to be imported by the Saxons to dye their homespun cloth probably because its great popularity during Roman times had made it less common. Although it is still extensively grown on parts of the Continent, it is used less for the dye itself than for its ability to improve the colour and quality of indigo. It is also used to form a base for black dye.

Medicinally the herb is so astringent it is only used externally, as a plaster for the spleen, or as an ointment for ulcers and inflammation and to staunch bleeding. Culpeper says: 'A plaister made thereof, and applied to the region of the spleen which lies on the left side, takes away the hardness and pains thereof. The ointment is excellently good for such ulcers as abound with moisture and takes away the corroding and fretting humours'.

Woad can easily be raised from seed. It likes good, well-drained soil and a sunny aspect. The first crop can be gathered as soon as the leaves are fully grown and probably two or three more gatherings can be made after a few weeks.

Weld, Dyer's Rocket or **Yellow Weed** *Reseda luteola* is a biennial herb, native to central and southern Europe, western Asia and North Africa and also introduced into North America. It is commonly found growing wild on arable land, walls and in waste places, favouring chalky soils. Weld has a deep tap-root which produces a rosette of leaves in its first season and a flowering stem in the second season. The stem is erect, ribbed and hollow, sometimes with a few erect branches and it reaches a height of 50–150 cm (20–60 in). The basal leaves are spear-shaped and stalkless, the stem leaves narrowly oblong with a stalk-like base or no stalks: both have smooth or slightly wavy margins. The yellowish-green flowers grow in long, slender, spike-like clusters at the end of the flowering stem and bloom from June to September.

Weld has been principally cultivated for its yellow dye which has been used in textile-making and painting.

Cleavers or **Goosegrass** *Galium aparine* is an annual herb, native to Europe and north and western Asia but also widely introduced into other parts of the world, which commonly grows wild in hedgerows, fields and waste places. Cleavers has a creeping rhizome and scrambling, diffusely branched, angular, hooked stems that reach a height of 15–120 cm (6–48 in). The narrow, spear-shaped leaves are spiny and grow in whorls. The greenish-white, star-like flowers grow on stalks arising from the leaf axils and bloom from May to September, followed by paired fruits covered in hooked bristles.

The generic name comes from the Greek *gala*, 'milk', and alludes to the fact that many species in this group have the ability to curdle milk. The specific name is derived from the Greek *aparo*, 'to seize', an allusion to the plant's habit of clinging with its stem or, more especially, fruit. The common name cleavers also refers to this and the other popular name, goosegrass, refers to the fondness which geese have for the plant as food.

Cleavers has a long history of use among country folk and herbalists. The roots yield a red dye and the seeds make a very palatable substitute for coffee. The young leaves have been extolled as a vegetable but some find them bitter and unpalatable. However they make a useful addition to vegetable soup and Culpeper says: 'It is familiarly taken in broth, to keep them lean and lank that are apt to grow fat.' The juice of the fresh herb was reputed to stop bleeding and be good for wounds and ulcers. An infusion of the dried herb was thought to be good for inducing calm sleep as well as being used as a skin lotion to reduce freckles and sunburn. A good general tonic and ingredient in many old-fashioned country spring tonics, cleavers is also said to be good for scurvy and skin diseases as well as urinary infections and stones in the bladder. As an ointment it is used for scalds and burns and as a poultice for sores and blisters. It has been reputed to be effective in the treatment of cancer but these claims have been neither disproved nor confirmed by modern research.

Woad *Isatis tinctoria* (in seed)

Weld or **Dyer's Rocket** *Reseda luteola*

Cleavers or **Goosegrass** *Galium aparine*

Hedge Bedstraw or **White Bedstraw** *Galium mollugo*

To make an infusion, put 30 g/1 oz of the dried herb in ½ l/1 pt of boiling water, infuse for five minutes, strain and drink several wineglassfuls a day.

Cleavers can easily be found in the wild and the leaves should be picked and used before the hard, round seeds appear.

Hedge Bedstraw or **White Bedstraw** *Galium mollugo* is a perennial herb native to Europe and northern Asia, which commonly grows wild in hedge banks, open woods, scrub and grassland.

Similar to Lady's bedstraw *Galium verum*, (see page 83) except that it grows more vigorously and its flowers are white instead of yellow, it also has very similar properties and has been used in the same way.

Dyer's Woodruff *Asperula tinctoria* is a perennial herb, native to northern and central Europe, which grows in meadows and rocky places.

Dyer's Woodruff has pretty pinky-white flowers and the roots yield a red dye.

Dyer's Woodruff *Asperula tinctoria*

85

Indigo *Indigofera tinctoria*

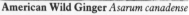

American Wild Ginger *Asarum canadense*

Wild Indigo *Baptisia tinctoria*

Dyer's Broom or Dyer's Greenweed *Genista tinctoria*

Indigo *Indigofera tinctoria* is a sub-shrubby plant native to India and cultivated in sub-tropical countries.

Indigo is a very ancient dye plant that has been used for centuries to produce a clear, fast, blue dye which is exported from India in great quantities. In fact the dye does not come ready-formed in the plant but is produced from a constituent in the plant called indican, after a period of fermentation. At one time it was used medicinally but no longer, as it is said to cause vomiting.

It can be grown from seed in the garden but it has a long germination period and needs to be sown in early spring, preferably under cover.

Wild Indigo *Baptisia tinctoria* is a bushy perennial, native to south-eastern North America, which is found growing on dry, burnt land. Wild indigo has a black, woody root with numerous rootlets and a smooth, round, branched stem that grows to a height of 90 cm (36 in). The small, alternate leaves are palmate with three wedge-shaped leaflets and the numerous, bright-yellow flowers which grow in long terminal clusters bloom from August to September.

The generic name is derived from the Greek, *bapto*, 'to dye', because the black root yields an inferior dye, sometimes used as a substitute for true indigo. The American Indians used a decoction of the root steeped in water externally as an antiseptic wash and American colonists, recognizing its astringent and antiseptic properties, applied it to sores, ulcers and eczema. It also has purgative properties

and was taken internally for scarlatina and typhus.

Asarabacca, Hazelwort or **European Wild Ginger**, *Asarum europaeum* is a perennial, evergreen herb, probably native to Britain and parts of Europe, but only rarely found in the wild, in moist woods, particularly beech woods. Asarabacca has a thick, creeping rhizome and short, fleshy downy stems that reach a height of 5 cm (2 in) and bear two large, dark-green, kidney-shaped leaves and a single drooping, purplish-green flower which blooms in May.

Asarabacca, with its strong, peppery taste and smell, was used in the past as a purgative and emetic and in head-colds for promoting sneezing. There have been doubts about its toxicity if taken in anything but tiny amounts so

Broom or **Scotch Broom** *Cytisus scoparius*

it is no longer used much in medicine. A bright apple-green dye extracted from the plant was formerly used for dyeing wool.

American Wild Ginger *Asarum canadense*, found in North America, is very similar to its European counterpart. It was used for chest complaints, dropsy and spasms in the bowels and stomach. One Indian tribe boiled the root slowly in a little water for a long period and drank the resulting decoction, believing it to have contraceptive properties.

Dyer's Broom or **Dyer's Greenweed** *Genista tinctoria* is a small shrub, native to Europe and Asia Minor and also established in eastern North America. It is found growing wild in meadows, pastures and heaths. Dyer's broom is an ascending plant with slender, branched stems that reach a height of 30–75 cm (12–30 in). The branches are erect and stiff and the spear-shaped leaves, placed alternately on the stem, are smooth with hair-fringed margins. The spikes of bright yellow, pea-like flowers open in July, followed by the compressed pods containing five to ten seeds.

Dyer's broom has been collected and used since Roman times for the marvellous yellow dye that can be extracted from the whole plant and particularly the flowering tops. Mixed with woad, the dye becomes an excellent green and is particularly good for dyeing wool.

Although it has never been an official drug, a decoction of the plant has been used as a treatment for gout, dropsy and rheumatism. The powdered seeds are said to be a mild purgative and were, at one time, used in a plaster for broken limbs.

The plant can either be collected from the wild or grown from seed. It likes lime-free soil and a sunny position.

Broom or **Scotch Broom** *Cytisus scoparius* synonym *Sarothamnus scoparius* is an erect shrub, native to temperate Europe and northern Asia and also naturalized in parts of North America. It is found growing wild in sandy soils on heaths, waste ground, in woods, pastures and on sea cliffs. Broom grows to a height of 60–200 cm (24–80 in) and has numerous, long, straight, slender, bright green branches which are tough, smooth and prominently angled. The alternate, lower leaves are stalked with three oblong leaflets; the upper leaves are stalkless, smaller, and often reduced to one leaflet. The bright yellow, fragrant flowers are borne in axillary stalks and bloom from April to July, followed by the flattened pods which burst with a distinctive pop when the seeds are ripe.

The generic name of the synonym is derived from the Greek words meaning 'to sweep' and 'a shrub', and the specific name is derived from the Latin *scopa*, 'a besom'.

Known in olden times as *Genista scoparius*, Broom has a history in both medicine and heraldry going back at least to medieval times. Geoffrey of Anjou thrust a sprig of broom into his helmet as he rode into battle and, from then onwards, it was adopted as the badge of Brittany. Henry II, claimant of the province, also adopted it, its medieval name *Planta genista*, giving the name of Plantagenet to his family line. An even older tradition about broom relates that, when Mary and Joseph were fleeing from Herod with the infant Jesus, all the plants spread their branches wide to make a path, except broom which remained stiff and unbending. Because of this, legend has it, it was condemned to remain stiff and dry to the end of its days. This legendary curse gave broom a bad reputation and it was associated with witches' broomsticks and also with magic philtres to keep witches at bay.

Over the centuries broom has been put to many uses. It binds earth together making it a useful shelter for game and other more delicate shrubs. The twigs and branches are used for making brooms and baskets, for building huts, thatching cottages and heating bakers' ovens. The bark yields an excellent fibre which has been employed in making rope and yarn and the fibrous shoots have been used in the manufacture of paper and cloth. The bark also contains a great deal of tannin, formerly used for dyeing.

Before hops were introduced, the tender green tops added a bitter taste and increased potency to beer and pickled broom buds were a great delicacy in Elizabethan times.

Medicinally broom has been used down the centuries to cure numerous ills and it has, undoubtedly, considerable therapeutic properties. It is a powerful diuretic and may be beneficial for bladder, liver and kidney infections. Weiss reports that broom has always been known to have cardiac properties but research has established that it contains an alkaloid, sparteine, which has a similar action to quinine and is very useful for treating cardiac arrhythmias. It also stimulates uterine contractions and is used in obstetrics. The great advantage of the plant is that it is non-toxic and can be given over an extended period and, in fact, seems more effective over the long term.

Broom can easily be grown from seed in rough, sandy soil. Transplant the seedlings in spring or autumn and prune immediately after flowering if the shoots have not been gathered.

Safflower *Carthamus tinctorius* Photographed August 16

Safflower *Carthamus tinctorius* is an annual or biennial herb probably native to Africa and grown in southern Europe, India, China, North Africa and most hot, dry areas of the world. It is extensively cultivated or grown in gardens for ornament. Safflower has numerous roots and an erect, ridged stem that branches near the top and reaches a height of 60–100 cm (24–40 in). The leaves are oval to lance-shaped, spiny, distinctly veined and generally stalkless. The yellow or orange flowerheads bloom from August to October, and the shiny, white fruits look like little shells.

It is also known as false saffron because it is frequently used as a food colouring, in place of the much more expensive saffron, and sometimes called parrot plant because its seeds are so beloved by these colourful birds.

Safflower is in great demand because the flowers contain two colouring matters – yellow and red. The yellow, as has been said, is used as a saffron substitute or yellow food colouring. The Hopi Indians used it to dye their wafer bread yellow. The red is used for dyeing silk various shades of rose and scarlet, or, mixed with fine talcum powder, to make 'rouge' – a cosmetic for colouring the cheeks. Safflower is also in great demand as a basic ingredient of certain margarines and cooking oils. The seeds yield a purified, low-cholesterol oil which is useful in the diets of the obese or those with heart problems.

An infusion made from the flowers 15 g/½ oz steeped in ½ l/1 pt boiling water, strained and sweetened, acts as a mild purgative and promotes perspiration. In the past this was given to children suffering from measles and fevers.

Yellow Camomile, Golden Marguerite or **Dyer's Camomile** *Anthemis tinctoria* is a biennial or perennial herb native to southern and central Europe, north to Scandinavia and western Asia and also in Britain and North America, which is found as an escape in waste places. Yellow camomile has erect, woolly, branched stems and grows to a height of 20–60 cm (8–24 in). The long leaves, 4–8 cm (1½–3 in) are more or less smooth above and woolly below. The disk florets and the ray florets are yellow and are visited by a great variety of insects. They bloom from July to October.

The flowers yield a distinctive yellow dye, hence its common name.

Coreopsis or **Calliopsis** *Coreopsis tinctoria* is an annual herb, native to North America, which is found growing wild in waste places and along roadsides and cultivated for its pretty flowers. Coreopsis has numerous, smooth, slightly angled branches and grows to a height of 60–120 cm (24–48 in). The long, opposite leaves are dissected with numerous linear segments and the showy, yellow, daisy-like flowers are blotched reddish-brown at the base and have reddish-brown discs. They bloom from June to September.

The flowers yield a bright yellow-orange colour which is used to dye cloth.

Saw Wort *Serratula tinctoria* is a perennial herb, native to Europe and North Africa, which grows on the edges of woods, in clearings, damp meadows and on open grassland. Saw wort has a short, stout root and a slender, erect, wiry, grooved stem that reaches a height of 30–90 cm (12–36 in). The large, deeply cut leaves are deep green with fine bristle-tipped teeth on the margins. The bright purple, cornflower-like flowers bloom from July to October.

Yields a yellow dye.

Yellow Camomile, Golden Marguerite or **Dyer's Camomile** *Anthemis tinctoria*

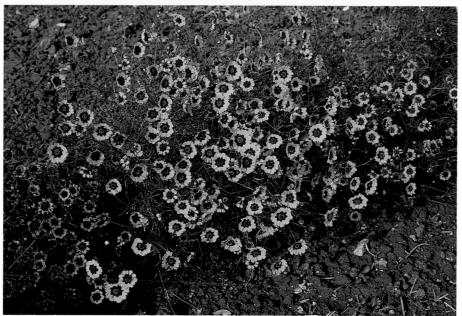

Coreopsis or **Calliopsis** *Coreopsis tinctoria*

Saw Wort *Serratula tinctoria*

89

Christmas Rose or **Black Hellebore** *Helleborus niger*

Christmas Rose or **Black Hellebore** *Helleborus niger* is a perennial plant, native to central and southern Europe and also naturalized in some other areas. It is found growing wild in woods and thickets in mountainous areas, favouring limy soil, and it is also widely cultivated. Christmas rose has a short underground root and flowering stems that rise directly from the root and reach a height of 30 cm (12 in). The long-stemmed basal leaves are dark green and glossy, divided into leaflets with toothed margins. The pure white or pink-tinged flowers bloom in December or January.

The specific name *niger*, means 'black', and alludes to the dark rootstock, while the common name refers to its winter-time flowering.

According to Pliny, the black hellebore was used hundreds of years before the birth of Christ as a purgative in the treatment of mania. More recently, the dried and powered root has been prescribed for hysteria and nervous conditions but undoubtedly the plant is a violent purgative and highly poisonous and although used for centuries as a medicinal plant it should only be taken on a physician's

prescription. The fresh root can be a violent irritant to sensitive skin. Probably because of its strong narcotic properties, Christmas rose seems to be associated with witchcraft and magic. One source claims that the roots were dug up accompanied by mystic incantations and then waved over cattle to protect them from evil. Another story claims that sorcerers used hellebore to make themselves invisible.

Christmas rose is frequently cultivated for ornament and will readily grow from seed or by root propagation to form a good flowering plant within two or three years. However it dislikes being transplanted, and ideally should be left for six or seven years before division. Although it will grow in any soil, it prefers a good combination of peat and manure. It will flower best in a moist, sheltered position.

Daisy, Bruisewort or **Bairnwort** *Bellis perennis* is a perennial herb, native to Europe and western Asia, and naturalized as a lawn weed over most of the world. It grows wild, in great abundance, wherever there is grass, from the coast to mountainous areas. Daisy has a small, stout tap-root and many rootlets. It has a simple, downy

stem and grows no higher than 10 cm (4 in). The egg-shaped, slightly toothed, basal leaves form a ground-hugging rosette and the stem bears one flower with a bright yellow disk and numerous white or pale pink petals which blooms from April to July.

The generic name is either derived form the Latin *bellus*, 'pretty' or 'charming', or from a dryad named Belidis, while the common name is a corruption of the Old English name day's eye. The common name bruisewort testifies to its vulnerary use and the Scottish common name Bairnwort presumably refers either to its medicinal use for children's complaints or the fun children have in making daisy chains from it. A charming old proverb associated with daisies goes, 'When you can put your foot on seven daisies summer is come'.

In times past daisy was considered to have numerous medicinal properties though nowadays it is rarely used except in homoeopathy. Its chief reputation was as a wound herb and it was prescribed for stiff neck, lumbago, painful aches and bruises as well as a cure for fresh wounds. Taken internally it was thought to ease inflammatory disorders of the liver. A strong decoction of the roots has been recommended for scrobutic complaints and eczema although it needs to be taken for some time before its effects are obvious. A mild decoction may also ease complaints of the respiratory tract, rheumatic pains and painful or heavy menstruation. Finally, chewing fresh leaves will help cure mouth ulcers. Many people are reverting to the long practised habit of adding the young leaves to spring salads to 'clean the blood' at the end of winter.

Collect from the wild in a non-polluted area.

Purple Trillium or **Beth Root** *Trillium erectum* is an unpleasant-smelling perennial, native to eastern North America, which is found growing wild in rich soil in damp, shady woods, and is cultivated for ornament in gardens. Purple trillium has a compact, knotty rhizome from which arises a slim, erect stem that reaches a height of 20–40 cm (8–16 in). The dark-green, pointed, oval leaves are wavy and distinctly veined and grow in groups of three. The maroon to reddish-brown or occasionally white flowers grow singly on stalks that arise from the leaf axils and bloom from April to June, succeeded by the oval, dark red berries.

The generic name derives from the Latin for 'three' and alludes to the fact that the leaves and flowers are arranged in groups of three. The specific name refers to the upright nature of the stem. The common name beth root is a corruption of birth root so-called when early American settlers adopted the native Americans' habit of using the plant in childbirth, mainly to stop bleeding after parturition. Early American colonists and, later, the Shaker community, used purple trillium to assist in uterine problems, to stop haemorrhaging and excessive menstruation. The root has astringent, antiseptic properties which gave rise to its external use for treating sores, ulcers and gangrene and, made into a lotion, as a wash for sore nipples. The roots boiled in milk were considered helpful for diarrhoea and it was thought that smelling the fresh roots would stop a nose bleed.

Although purple trillium was listed in the National Formulary between the wars, many of the uses claimed for it are not accepted today.

Pasque Flower *Pulsatilla vulgaris* synonym *Anemone pulsatilla* is a perennial herb, native to northern and central Europe and western Asia, which is found growing wild on dry, grassy, chalky slopes. Pasque flower has a thick, rather

Daisy or **English Daisy** *Bellis perennis* cultivated (above), wild (below)

Purple Trillium or **Beth Root** *Trillium erectum*

woody, root-stock and a flowering stem that reaches a height of 10–30 cm (4–12 in) elongating in fruit. The leaves form a basal rosette of finely divided leaves covered with silky hairs, and they do not usually appear until after the flowers. The violet-purple, bell-shaped flowers are borne singly on downy stems and bloom from April to June.

The specific name is derived from *pulsa*, 'beat', alluding to the way the downy seeds are beaten about by the wind, and the common name is either a reference to the fact that the plant was used to colour Paschal eggs in some countries or, according to Gerard, because he himself named it pasque flower or Easter flower because of its appearance at that time of year.

The fresh leaves and flowers of pasque flower are poisonous and can cause marked skin irritation in some people but, when used with care or in homoeopathic doses, it is considered a very useful medicinal plant. It is used for respiratory and digestive problems, to beat the spasmodic cough of asthma, whooping cough and bronchitis. Weiss says it has been regarded as beneficial for spasms in the genital region and it is said to restore the menstrual flow, relieve headache and neuralgia and remedy nervous exhaustion in women. In homoeopathy, it is a specific for measles, prescribed for nettle rash, toothache and earache and bilious indigestion. In modern herbalism, it is used externally to treat eye conditions such as diseases of the retina, senile cataract and glaucoma.

Pasque flower can be grown in average garden soil in a sunny or partially sunny position.

Gather the whole herb soon after it flowers, dry and preserve carefully in airtight jars. Do not keep for longer than a year as it loses its active medicinal properties.

Purple Trillium or **Beth Root** *Trillium erectum*

Pasque Flower *Pulsatilla vulgaris*

Stinging Nettle *Urtica dioica* Photographed March 20

Stinging Nettle *Urtica dioica* is a perennial plant, found throughout the temperate regions of the world, which commonly grows wild in hedgerows, rubbish tips, waste places, field edges, grassy places and wherever there is litter or rubble, favouring nitrogen-rich soil. Stinging nettle has tough, yellow creeping roots and hairy stems that reach a height of 30–150 cm (12–60 in). The ovate leaves with toothed margins are light green and covered like the stems in stinging hairs. The tiny greenish flowers grow in small hanging clusters, male and female on separate plants, and bloom from June to September.

The common name is thought by some people to be derived from the Anglo Saxon *noedl*, a needle, alluding either to its sharp sting or to the fact that it provided thread for sewing in olden times before the introduction of flax. Nettle fibre is very similar to hemp or flax and was used for fine textiles as well as for sail cloth and rope. However as flax was cheaper to produce the use of nettle fibre died out until shortages of flax and hemp in Germany in the First World War resulted in its use for many articles of army clothing. Some manufacturers believe that nettle fibre is superior to cotton for making velvet and plush. Nettle fibres have also been used in paper manufacture.

Nutritionally nettle is high in vitamins and minerals and is a valuable addition to the diet not only of humans but of animals too. Cattle and poultry fed on fodder containing nettle give more milk and eggs than those whose diets have not been enriched. Nettle juice is good for curdling milk, making a good rennet substitute for vegetarians. The roots yield a yellow dye

formerly used by Russian peasants and the leaves yield a permanent green colour used to dye woollens in Russia.

Nettles have a long history as a culinary plant. They are used in salads and soups and as a spinach-like vegetable. Nettle beer was a favourite country drink. They are easy to digest and are an excellent tonic and purifier of the system at the start of spring.

Stinging nettle has several medicinal properties: it is astringent, tonic, anti-asthmatic and diuretic. It promotes urinary secretion so is prescribed for dropsy, diabetes and excessive weight, rheumatism and gout. An infusion is said to improve liver, gall bladder and intestinal functions and to stop diarrhoea. It halts nosebleeds and makes an excellent gargle for sore throats and mouth ulcers. It is reputed to regulate women's menstruation and increase the milk flow of breastfeeding mothers. In some parts of the world, beating the body with a bunch of nettles is believed to cure rheumatism, and Mességué claims an old Frenchman said the same treatment improves virility! Nettle compresses or lotions are good for cleaning the skin, reducing acne and eczema and helping the hair to grow.

To make an infusion for use as a general restorative tonic, put 45 g/1½ oz of fresh leaves into 1 1/2 pt of boiling water, infuse for ten minutes, then strain. Drink three cupfuls a day. Alternatively put 30–45 g/1–1½ oz of dried root in 1 l/2 pt of water, bring to the boil, simmer for two minutes, then infuse for ten minutes. Strain. A decoction using 100 g/4 oz of root can be made and used externally as a hair tonic. To stop nosebleeds, soak a small piece of cotton

wool in nettle juice and insert into the bleeding nostril for rapid relief.

Collect from the wild or cultivate a patch around the compost heap in your garden or near the vegetable patch: some claim they make other plants more resistant to disease.

Gather the leaves in spring and use fresh, or dry for future use. Harvest the roots in autumn. Wear gloves while collecting, but drying or cooking nettles will eliminate the sting.

Small Nettle *Urtica urens* is an annual herb, native to north temperate regions, which grows wild in cultivated ground and waste places. Smaller than the stinging nettle, it generally has both male and female flowers on the same panicle. It can be used in the same way as stinging nettle.

Roman Nettle *Urtica pilulifera* is native to southern Europe but often found naturalized or as a casual in other parts.

Coltsfoot *Tussilago farfara* is a perennial herb, native to Europe, northern and western Asia and North Africa, which has also been introduced into North America. It is commonly found growing wild in hedgerows and arable fields and on roadsides, banks, waste places and shingly screes or dunes. Coltsfoot has a creeping rhizome with stout, white stolons and flowering stems covered in pinkish, woolly scales that reach a height of 15–20 cm (6–8 in). The leaves, which appear after the flowers have faded, form a rosette and are heart-shaped with toothed, lobed margins. The yellow flowers, similar to those of dandelion, are borne singly at the top of

Small Nettle *Urtica urens*

Roman Nettle *Urtica pilulifera*

White Deadnettle *Lamium album*

Coltsfoot *Tussilago farfara*

the flowering stem and bloom from March to May.

The generic name derives from the Latin *tussis agere*, 'to take away cough', and it has been used since ancient times for treating all kinds of bronchial problems. In the Middle Ages it was also known as *Filius ante patrem*, 'the son before the father', alluding to the advent of the flowers before the leaves.

Although not much used as a culinary plant, a few coltsfoot leaves can be added to salads to enrich the vitamin C content or be made into a tisane.

The roots, leaves and flowers are all used medicinally and are high in mucilage, making it a soothing expectorant and anti-inflammatory when served in the form of a tea, decoction or syrup. Pliny recommended smoking the leaves to ease a cough and other herbalists combined coltsfoot with betony, eyebright, rosemary, thyme, lavender and camomile to make a herbal tobacco that was recommended for asthma, catarrh and other lung troubles. Because of its soothing effect on the mucous membranes, it can also be helpful for gastritis. Weiss reports that coltsfoot is still a very popular plant for treating coughs and because it contains both mucilage and tannin it is also a good tonic. It is particularly recommended for chronic emphysema and silicosis because it helps to relieve the persistent cough associated with these conditions. Recent reports have claimed that coltsfoot contains carcinogenic compounds, but the doses given to animals in the experiments on which these claims are based are very high and administered over an extended period. Weiss says this has no bearing on the tiny therapeutic doses prescribed to humans for short periods and says that he and other herbalists feel that the 'cancer scares' can be disregarded. Fresh crushed leaves mixed with honey are also recommended for external use on varicose veins, ulcers, wounds and sores.

To make an infusion that can either be drunk or applied to varicose veins, put 30 g/1 oz of dried leaves or flowers into ½ l/1 pt of boiling water and steep for ten minutes. Strain, sweeten with honey and drink several cups a day.

Coltsfoot is generally gathered from the wild but it will grow in a garden in any soil. Harvest the flowers in March or April and the leaves

from May to July. Remove any damaged ones and dry in the sun or in a warm, well-ventilated room and store for winter use in an airtight container.

White Deadnettle *Lamium album* is a hairy, perennial plant, native to most of Europe, the Himalayas and Japan and naturalized in North America. It is commonly found growing wild along roadsides, in fields, hedgerows and on waste ground. White deadnettle has a creeping rhizome from which spring several erect, angular, hollow stems, that grow to a height of 20–60cm (8–24in). The bright green, oval- to heart-shaped leaves are rough, pointed, distinctly veined with a toothed margin, and grow in opposite pairs at right angles to each other. The white flowers grow in dense whorls in the axils of the upper leaves and bloom from May to November.

White deadnettle has leaves similar in appearance to the stinging nettle and they like the same kind of habitat so often grow side by

side. However, they are no relation botanically: the two main differences are that the white deadnettle doesn't sting and it has completely different flowers.

The young leaves and plant tips are boiled like spinach and either eaten hot as a vegetable or added to salads. Medicinally, the flowers and flowering tips are made into an infusion or a decoction that is prescribed for respiratory or urinary catarrh, diarrhoea, liver malfunctions and menstrual problems, particularly leucorrhoea. It may also be used as a compress and applied externally to piles and the distilled water is claimed to be an effective eye-lotion.

Gather from the wild in an unpolluted spot.

Symphytum ibiricum × uplandicum 'Hidcote Blue'

White Comfrey *Symphytum orientale*

Comfrey *Symphytum officinale* Photographed April 15

Caucasian Comfrey *Symphytum caucasicum*

Bulbous Comfrey *Symphytum bulbosum*

Lungwort or **Soldiers and Sailors** *Pulmonaria officinalis*

Pulmonaria saccharata

Lungwort or **Soldiers and Sailors** *Pulmonaria officinalis* is a perennial herb, native to central Europe and naturalized in other areas too, which is found growing in moist grasslands, damp woods and hedgerows. This and other lungworts have been planted all over the world as garden plants. Lungwort has a fleshy, cylindrical rhizome, and an erect, slender, hairy stem that reaches a height of 10–30 cm (4–12 in). The basal leaves are oval and hairy with pale green blotches. They form a rosette at the base and are arranged alternately on the flowering stems. The clusters of pink flowers which turn lilac-blue at the end of the stems are bell-shaped and bloom from March to May.

The generic name is derived form the Latin *pulmones*, 'lungs', from the supposed resemblance of the blotchy leaves to lungs. Both this and the common name allude to the fanciful Doctrine of Signatures which held that the plant resembled what it should treat. Hence lungwort has long been prescribed for all manner of lung complaints.

It is doubtful whether it ever cured consumption as some have claimed but it is probably beneficial in soothing coughs, sore throats, bronchitis and similar complaints. The distilled water from lungwort has been considered an effective eyewash for tired eyes.

To make an infusion put a generous 30–40 g/ 1 oz of dried plant into 1 1/2 pt of cold water, bring to the boil, boil for two minutes, then infuse for ten more. Strain and sweeten with honey. Drink three to four cupfuls per day to soothe coughs and chest complaints.

Lungwort is also used in liquor-distilling – it is an ingredient of vermouth – and the tender young leaves made a palatable cooked vegetable.

The plant can either be collected in the wild or grown from seed in the garden in a damp, shady spot. Gather the whole plant in May or June and dry in the shade.

Pulmonaria longifolia is a similar species, native

to Europe, which is easily distinguished by its much longer and narrower leaves with white spots; the flowers are a vivid blue.

Pulmonaria angustifolia from central Europe has plain dark green leaves. The flowers are pink in bud and when open a rich blue.

Pulmonaria saccharata From central Europe, has large, white-spotted leaves and red-violet or dark violet flowers.

Comfrey *Symphytum officinale* is an erect, hairy perennial, native to Europe and temperate Asia and naturalized in North America and many other countries. It grows wild in damp, shady places, particularly near rivers and streams. Comfrey has a thick, fleshy, branched root up to a foot long, black on the outside, white inside, and a hairy branched stem that reaches a height of 30–120 cm (12–48 in). The long, pointed, lance-shaped leaves are dark green, downy and distinctly veined. The bell-shaped flowers grow in drooping clusters and can be blue, purple, pink, cream or white and they bloom from May to October.

The generic name is derived from the Greek *symphyo*, 'to unite', alluding to the plant's renown for healing broken bones. The specific name tells us that it was on the official list of medicinal plants. Some of its other common names – Knitbone, Boneset, Bruisewort – testify to its reputation as a vulnerary.

For centuries comfrey has been valued for its medicinal properties, particularly its ability to help broken bones set, to heal wounds, cuts, swellings, ulcers, sprains and bruises. Modern research has shown that it contains two substances, allantoin and choline, which promote healthy growth of red blood corpuscles – vital after excessive loss of blood from wounds or injuries.

Comfrey used to be taken internally for medicinal purposes and was also considered a good culinary plant. However, Weiss reports

that recent research has suggested that comfrey may have carcinogenic properties – it contains Pyrrozolidine alkaloids which are known carcinogens. However, this only applies to the internal use of the root and herb, not the external use. There is no evidence to suggest that the external use of the root in compresses to treat ulcers and wounds has any harmful effect.

For external use, make a compress from either fresh, grated root or dried powdered root mixed with water, and apply to the afflicted area to soothe inflamed joints, sprains, twists, bruises, burns, scalds or falls.

Comfrey can be easily grown in the garden from seed or by root division. It likes any kind of damp soil and a shady position. The leaves should be harvested in June or July and dried and stored for winter use. The roots should be dug up from October to March.

It makes an excellent compost and added to other plant material will help that to decompose quickly. Some gardeners use it fresh in the bottom of a trench when planting, knowing that in a matter of days it will have composted down.

White Comfrey *Symphytum orientale* is native to south-west Asia and grows in Europe in hedgebanks and as a garden escape. It is smaller and paler green in colour than comfrey and its white flowers bloom earlier, from April to May.

Bulbous Comfrey *Symphytum bulbosum* is native to southern Europe, and grows in woods and shrubby places. It has a slender, creeping rhizome which produces roundish tubers and the stems and leaves are densely covered in very small, hooked hairs. The flowers are pale yellow.

Caucasian Comfrey *Symphytum caucasicum* has bright blue flowers. Beware! It is a rapid spreader.

Tuberous Comfrey *Symphytum tuberosum* has a creeping rhizome, with alternate thick tuberous and thin sections and yellowish white flowers.

Cowslip *Primula veris* (above left), **Oxlip** *Primula elatior* (above right), **Primrose** *Primula vulgaris* (bottom)

A field of **Cowslips** *Primula veris* in the Chiltern Hills

Primrose *Primula vulgaris* is a perennial plant, native to western Europe, Asia Minor and North America, which commonly grows wild in woods, hedgerows, pastures and on railway embankments. Primrose has a knotty rhizome with cylindrical branched rootlets on all sides. The egg-shaped to oblong leaves are hairy, prominently veined and irregularly toothed at the margin. The yellow flowers are on separate stalks and flower from April to May, sometimes earlier in sheltered spots during mild winters.

Primrose has similar medicinal properties to cowslip – it is astringent, antispasmodic and emetic. In early times, Pliny says, it was commonly prescribed for muscular rheumatism, paralysis and gout. Nowadays, an infusion on the root is sometimes prescribed for nervous headaches, and a teaspoon of dried powdered root given as an emetic. The plant has sedative and expectorant properties. In America, a tincture is given for restlessness and insomnia and, formerly, an ointment was made for skin wounds.

Primrose can be collected from the wild or grown in the garden. It likes ordinary soil and at least some shade.

Oxlip *Primula elatior* is a perennial plant native to central and western Europe, and very local in Britain, which is found growing in damp meadows and woodlands on chalky boulder clay. Oxlip has a short rhizome and slender flowering stems that reach a height of 20 cm (8 in). The leaves form a basal rosette and are usually egg-shaped, narrowing into a winged stem; they are wrinkled, veined and downy on the under surface. The sulphur-yellow flowers hang in one-sided clusters and bloom from April to May.

Oxlip is similar to cowslip and primrose in its medicinal properties and can be used in the same way.

Cowslip *Primula veris* is a downy perennial plant, native to Europe and temperate Asia but

nevertheless rare in the Mediterranean region. It is found growing wild in meadows, pastures, fields and woods, favouring calcareous soil, and also cultivated in many varieties in gardens. Cowslip has a short, stout, ascending rhizome with numerous rootlets and downy flower stems that reach a height of 10–30 cm (4–12 in). The rough-textured leaves are arranged in a basal rosette, ovate-oblong in shape with a slightly indented margin and a downy under-surface. The deep yellow flowers have orange spots at their base and are grouped in a nodding cluster at the end of the flower stem. They bloom from April to May.

According to Geoffrey Grigson the origin of the word cowslip comes from the Old English *cuslyppe* referring to a cowpat. The common name *paigle* is of Anglo-Saxon origin and means St Peter, alluding to the resemblance of the hanging flower heads to the bunch of keys held by St Peter at heaven's gate. Its other common names, herb Peter, key flower, key of heaven, also draw their origin from this source.

Cowslip has many culinary and medicinal uses and, although no longer considered the kind of general panacea it was in former times, it undoubtedly has many uses. Cowslip leaves can be eaten fresh or cooked as a vegetable. The flowers can also be used to decorate salads, eaten fresh with cream, candied with sugar to decorate cakes, infused into a refreshing tea or fermented into cowslip wine. The eating or drinking of all or any of these will enable one to benefit from the antispasmodic and sedative properties of this plant. Cowslip wine was recommended as an excellent sedative by country herbalists and the flowers were thought to strengthen the nerves and brain, relieve restlessness and insomnia and paralytic ailments. Cowslip tea is recommended for headaches, vertigo, nervous stomach spasms, insomnia and constipation. Compresses applied to the head may ease migraine, and cowslip lotion or ointment helps to remove spots, blotches, wrinkles and other skin blemishes.

Primrose *Primula vulgaris*

Cowslip oil can be used, like arnica, to reduce pains, swellings or bruises. Modern herbalists use it to treat chronic bronchitis and persistent coughs because it is a good expectorant. Some people may have a slight allergic reaction to cowslip: it can create a burning, itching sensation known as *primula dermatitis*.

To make cowslip tea infuse 30 g/1 oz fresh or dried flowers in 1 l/2 pt boiling water for fifteen minutes. Strain and drink three cupfuls a day after meals.

To make cowslip oil, macerate a handful of fresh flowers and a handful of fresh chopped root and put in a tightly stoppered jar. Leave in the sun or a warm place for six weeks. Strain through a muslin and store in corked jars. (From *Grandmother's Secrets* by Jean Palaiseul.)

It can be collected in the wild but over-picking has contributed to the great reduction of this plant in many areas, although loss of habitat is a more significant factor. It makes much more sense to grow it from seed in a herb garden, for use in wines or medicines or just as a pretty border plant. Seeds should be sown in spring in open sandy soil mixed with peat or leaf-mould in a shady, damp position.

Bogbean *Menyanthes trifoliata* (leaves)

Bogbean or **Buckbean** *Menyanthes trifoliata*

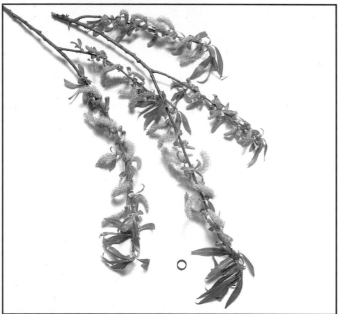

White Willow *Salix alba*

Greater Celandine *Chelidonium majus*

Bogbean or **Buckbean** *Menyanthes trifoliata* is a perennial aquatic or bog plant, native to Europe, northern and central Asia and North America, which is found quite commonly in bogs, fens, marshes, river and pond edges, and shallow water from lowland to mountain elevation. Bogbean has a creeping rhizome and many rootlets and a fleshy, procumbent stem covered by leaf sheaths. The trifoliate, egg-shaped to elliptical leaves are borne on long stalks and they are thick and glossy. The bell-shaped flowers are white inside and rose-coloured outside, and they grow in a spike on stalks that can reach a height of 45 cm (18 in). They bloom from May to July.

The generic name is derived from the Greek *men*, ' month', and *anthos*, 'flower', and it is thought to allude to its flowering period, but in fact it often flowers for much longer than a month! The specific name is a reference to the form and number of its leaves. The German common name *Scharbock* is a corruption of the Latin *Scorbutus*, the old medical name for scurvy for which the plant was thought to be a useful remedy.

Both in Europe and America, bogbean has long been valued for its tonic, cathartic and fever-reducing properties. Made into an infusion or used as a powder, it has been taken for liver and gall-bladder complaints, rheumatism, scurvy and ague. Taken in large doses it may have an emetic effect, so caution should be used when self-prescribing. Bogbean has been incorporated into herbal teas and tobaccos and is widely used in making bitter-based alcoholic drinks.

Bogbean is primarily collected from the wild but may be grown in a garden if there is a sufficiently wet spot or if planted in peat with the roots permanently in water. For use fresh or to dry, collect the leaves and flowering stems between May and June.

White Willow *Salix alba* is a tree, native to Europe, North Africa and western Asia, which has been introduced into North America and is commonly found growing wild or planted along river banks, streams, ditches, in fens and wet woods. White willow has a strong trunk with deeply fissured, ash-grey bark and ascending branches, and it reaches a height of about 10–25 m (33–83 ft). The twigs are somewhat silky-haired and the alternate leaves are long, oval and pointed – smooth above and downy below – with a toothed margin. The flowers are grouped into male and female catkins and appear at about the same time as the leaves from March to June.

The generic name for this tree derives from the Celtic *sal lis*, 'near water', and alludes, of course, to its preferred habitat. The specific name from the Latin *alba*, 'white', refers to the pale hairs on both sides of the young leaves which give a silver-white appearance to the whole tree.

White willow has been used medicinally for centuries for its pain-killing and fever-reducing properties. It was also prescribed for rheumatism and dyspepsia.

Research during this century has shown that fresh willow bark contains salicin which probably decomposes into salicylic acid in the human system. Aspirin is the synthetic equivalent of this and as that is generally used for headaches, migraine, colds, flu and

Butterbur *Petasites hybridus*

rheumatism it is perhaps not surprising that white willows has been prescribed for treating similar illnesses for hundreds of years.

Greater Celandine *Chelidonium majus* is a perennial herb, native to Europe, western Asia and North Africa, and naturalized in North America. It is found growing wild in banks, hedgerows, old walls and waste ground near habitations. Greater celandine has a thick, fleshy tap-root that branches out in all directions and erect, branched, leafy stems which are brittle and grow to a height of 30–90 cm (12–36 in). The yellowish-green, downy leaves are deeply pinnate and form pairs of leaflets with a large terminal leaflet. The golden-yellow, four-petalled flowers are grouped at the end of the stems in loose clusters and bloom from May to August. The plant emits a bright orange milk where its stems or leaves are broken.

The generic name derives from the Greek *khelidon*, 'a swallow', alluding to the fact that the plant flowers about the time swallows return from their migration and fades about the time they depart again. The common name celandine is a corruption of this.

Greater celandine has a history of medicinal use dating back to Roman times. It was a popular drug plant of the Middle Ages prescribed for plague, jaundice, blood disorders and blindness. However, greater celandine is poisonous and great care must be taken as large doses can be extremely dangerous. It should only be used externally or in homoeopathic (i.e. minute) doses, and not taken internally unless prescribed by a doctor.

Used externally, the plant is very useful. The orange juice obtained from the leaves and stems has long been used to cure warts, ringworm and corns and, mixed with milk or water, it is said to be an effective eye-lotion. (Make sure to protect the area surrounding the eyes.)

Culpeper says: 'This is a herb of the sun and under the celestial Lion, and is one of the best cures for the eyes, for all that know anything in astrology know that the eyes are subject to the luminaries.'

Mességué recommends 2 tbsps of fresh juice, mixed with a glassful of water or rose water, for use as an eyebath. He also suggests making a concoction from the roots (macerate thirteen dried roots in 1 l/2 pt of sweet white wine for twelve hours) and using this externally as a massage for insomnia, anxiety, asthma and nerves. Mességué also says the same concoction can be used as a vaginal douche to regularize periods, ease frigidity, sterility and inflammation of the uterus.

Weiss reports that modern opinion is rather mixed about the efficacy of this plant for gall-bladder conditions. Studies have shown that the effective alkaloid, chelidonine, which the plant contains, is similar to papaverine and has an anti-spasmodic and sedative action on the bile ducts and bronchi. However, results have been inconsistent, particularly if the preparations used were not fresh. When fresh juice was used it seemed to give marked relief for up to six months but stopped working after that. Preparations from old plants seemed to have no effect. Weiss concludes that it is an interesting plant but difficult to judge its beneficent properties while there are no methods of standardizing it. The plant can be gathered from the wild between May and July, or grown in a herb garden. Gather the whole plant from the garden as all parts are active and dry it carefully in the shade. Of the fresh plant, use only the juice and remember, never exceed the stated dose.

Butterbur *Petasites hybridus* is a perennial herb, native to Europe and north and western Asia, which has also been introduced into North

America. It is found growing wild in wet meadows and copses and by marshy riverbanks. Butterbur has a stout, fleshy, creeping rhizome and branches that reach a height of 150 cm (60 in). The leaves appear in April, after the flowers, and are very large, sometimes up to 90 cm (36 in). They are roundish with a heart-shaped base, downy but green above and greyish beneath, and toothed. The flowers appear before the leaves in March and form in crowned clusters on a dense spike: some spikes have male flowers, some female flowers. The petals are flesh-coloured or pale reddish purple, bell-shaped in the male flowers and full of nectar, thread-like in the female flowers with no nectar, and they are followed by the white feathery pappus which crowns the seeds.

The generic name is derived from the Greek *petatos*, 'a shepherd's felt hat', and alludes to the leaves which are so large they can be used as a headcovering. The common name comes from the use of the large leaves to wrap up butter in warm weather in early times.

In the Middle Ages it was considered 'a soveraigne medicine against the plague' and Gerard wrote: 'The powder of the roots cureth all naughty filthy ulcers, if it be strewed therein.' Butterbur root has been employed as a heart stimulant and a diuretic and it and coltsfoot are specific homoeopathic remedies for neuralgia in the back and loins. Widely considered an effective cough remedy, recent experiments have shown butterbur to have remarkable anti-spasmodic and pain-relieving properties. It is now also used to treat gastrointestinal complaints and biliary diskynesia.

Butterbur can be collected from the wild or grown in a garden but, once it takes hold, it can take over: no other vegetation can live where it grows because the large leaves exclude light and air from all beneath it.

Virginian Skullcap or **Mad-dog Skullcap** *Scutellaria lateriflora*

Cape Aloe *Aloe ferox*

Milk Thistle *Silybum marianum* (flower)

Milk Thistle *Silybum marianum*

Coolwort or **Foamflower** *Tiarella cordifolia*

Cape Aloe *Aloe ferox* is a succulent shrub, native to South Africa and naturalized in North and South America. It is also cultivated for ornament in Mediterranean gardens. Cape Aloe is a large, fleshy succulent with an erect simple stem that reaches a total height of 2–4 m (6–12 ft). The dull green leaves, about 50 cm (20 in) long, are convex-triangular shaped with spiny margins and are arranged in a huge rosette at the top of the stem. The flowering stem, up to 1 m (40 in), grows out of this rosette and is covered with cylindrical clusters of red or orange flowers that bloom from April to August.

Cape Aloe contains aloin, principally used as a purgative, particularly for sedentary or phlegmatic types. Aloe tincture or extract is very gentle and slow-acting although too frequent use is said to induce piles. Taken in large doses, it can have a drastic effect, even causing abortion, so it should never be taken by pregnant women. It is also made into an ointment for mild skin rashes and a decoction of its juice acts as a mosquito repellent. Cape aloe is sometimes blended with other bitter ingredients to flavour alcoholic drinks.

The resinous milky juice can be collected throughout the year by draining it from the cut-off leaves and drying in the sun. Although Aloes may be grown outdoors in sheltered positions, they are best grown in a greenhouse or conservatory.

Milk Thistle *Silybum marianum* is a biennial, native to south-western Europe and now naturalized throughout most of Europe and North America. It is found wild along roadsides

Pale-flowered Fritillary *Fritillaria pallidiflora* (in China growing for medicinal use)

and in waste places and on cultivated land, as well as being grown in gardens for ornament. Milk thistle grows to a height of 1.5 m (5 ft) and has large crinkly leaves with white veins and sharp yellowish prickles. The purple flowerheads with pink or white flowers bloom from June to August.

Historically, milk thistle has been used both in cooking and medicine. The stalks can be boiled for a vegetable, the leaves used in salads and the roots eaten like salsify. According to the seventeenth-century diarist, John Evelyn, 'Disarmed of its prickles and boiled, it is worthy of esteem and thought to be a great breeder of milk and proper diet for women who are nurses.'

Weiss reports that although traditionally used as a medicinal plant, milk thistle had fallen into disuse until research in this century showed the plant in a completely different light. Numerous studies into the toxicology of the plant have shown it to be very useful in treating liver complaints: chronic hepatitis, fatty liver and even cirrhosis of the liver. Very recent research explains the action of silymarin – the active principle contained in milk thistle – which acts on the membranes of the liver cells, preventing the entry of virus toxins and other toxic compounds and thus preventing damage to the cells or arresting further damage. In the same way it has also proved useful in treating those suffering from poisoning from the Death Cap mushroom, *Amanita phalloides*. As soon as the stomach has been pumped of all poison, silibinin (the principal component of silymarin) should be given intravenously to prevent further damage to the liver and kidneys.

Young plants can easily be grown and its variegated leaves will form an attractive area in the herb garden.

Pale-flowered Fritillary *Fritillaria pallidiflora* is a bulbous perennial, native to north-western China and neighbouring USSR in the Boro Horo Shan mountains, which is found growing in alpine meadows, woods and scrub. These fritillaries have small white bulbs, and solitary leafy stems which reach a height of 30 cm (12 in). The large, nodding, bell-shaped, greenish flowers have reddish square spots and speckles inside and are produced in April and May. The seed pods are upright, with broad wings.

Species of fritillary called Bei Mu are a popular traditional medicine in China and Japan, used to cure chronic coughs, wheezing and bronchitis. The active ingredient, imperialin, an alkaloid, has been found to prevent spasm in the throat and chest muscles. Large quantities are collected in the wild, and several species are cultivated. The bulbs are dried, powdered and an infusion is drunk or made into tablets.

The bulbs of fritillary can be bought and grown but they are rather expensive so buy the powder or tablets for consumption and leave the ones you do buy to beautify the garden.

Virginian Skullcap or **Mad-dog Skullcap** *Scutellaria lateriflora* is a perennial plant, native to eastern North America and as far west as New Mexico, which is found growing wild in wet places. Virginian skullcap has slender stolons and thin, leafy stems, branched above, that reach a height of 10–75 cm (4–30 in). The ovate to linear, pointed leaves are coarsely toothed, getting smaller towards the top of the stem. The small, blue flowers grow in one-sided racemes and bloom from June to September.

Virginian skullcap was used, in an infusion, by the Cherokee Indians for bringing on retarded menstruation and later became popular as a treatment for rabies – hence its common name. Since the middle of the nineteenth century it has been considered a marvellous nervine because of its sedative and antispasmodic properties. Small doses are recommended for all kinds of hysterical and nervous complaints: convulsions, St Vitus's Dance, neuralgia, nervous headaches and epilepsy. However, in larger doses it can cause giddiness, stupor, twitchings, etc., so care must be taken in prescribing this plant.

Virginian skullcap can be easily cultivated to good effect in European gardens. It likes ordinary soil and an open, sunny border and can be propagated either by seeds or root division in April.

Coolwort or **Foamflower** *Tiarella cordifolia* is a pretty, perennial plant, native to north-eastern North America, which is found growing wild in rich woods. Coolwort grows to a height of 15–30 cm (6–12 in) and has lobed leaves that are sharply toothed, sometimes hairy, with deep red veins. The basal leaves turn a deep orange-red. The tiny, white flowers bloom from April to June.

The generic name derives form the Greek *tiara*, a turban worn by the Persians, and alludes to the shape of the pistils. The common name foamflower arose from the tiny flowers and fine-textured stamens which resemble foam.

Coolwort has tonic and diuretic properties and infusions or decoctions have been prescribed for bladder and liver problems. It may help to correct acidity and relieve indigestion.

Marsh Marigold, Kingcup or **May Blobs** *Caltha palustris*

Ribwort or **English Plantain** *Plantago lanceolata*

Hoary Plaintain *Plantago media*

Lesser Celandine or **Pilewort** *Ranunculus ficaria*

Marsh Marigold, Kingcup or **May Blobs**
Caltha palustris is a smooth, perennial herb,
native to central and northern Europe,
including Iceland and arctic Russia, and also
temperate and arctic Asia and North America.
It is found growing, sometimes abundantly, in
marshes, streams, wet meadows, ditches and
by mountain brooks and streams. Marsh
marigold has a short, fleshy rhizome and
numerous tufts of thin rootlets. The erect,
somewhat spongy stem reaches a height of
about 30 cm (12 in). The basal leaves are large,
glossy, toothed and kidney-shaped with long
stalks, while the stem leaves are stalkless but
also toothed. The single, widely spaced, bright
yellow flowers are composed of five petaloid
sepals and bloom from mid-March to mid-
June.

The generic name derives from the Greek
world *calathos*, 'a cup' or 'goblet', while the
specific name comes from the Latin *palus*, 'a

marsh', alluding to its habitat. The common
English name marigold is a reference to the fact
that in the Middle Ages it was one of the flowers
devoted to the Virgin Mary in religious
ceremonies. Marigolds were also made into
garlands for May Day festivals. Three other
synonyms are *Verrucaria* because it is supposed
to cure warts, and *Solsequia* and *Sponsa solis*
because the flower opens at dawn and closes at
dusk.

Medically, the plant should be used with
caution because it has highly irritant properties.
In the past a tincture made from the whole
flowering plant was used to cure anaemia and an
infusion from the flowers was considered
efficacious for fits. However, it is now
considered inadvisable to use the plant
internally to avoid any risk of poisoning.

To propagate marsh marigolds, part the roots
in autumn and plant in moist soil or at the edge
of a pond.

Ribwort or **English Plantain** *Plantago lanceolata*
is a perennial herb, native to Europe and
northern and central Asia, which has been
introduced into North America and many other
temperate regions of the world. It is found
growing wild on ordinary or neutral soils in
grassy places. Ribwort is a dark green, slender
plant with silky-haired flowering stems that
reach a height of 50–75 cm (20–30 in). The long,
lance-shaped leaves narrow towards the stalk
and have three to five prominent ribs. The
flowerheads vary greatly in size but generally
form a blunt, dense spike. The brownish sepals
give it a rusty appearance but the white stamens
are its most attractive feature. They bloom from
May to September.

The leaves of ribwort, which contain active
principles, including tannins, mucilage and silic
acid, are rather bitter but they are regarded as
beneficial for diseases of the upper respiratory
tract. Taken internally as an infusion or mixed

Bugle *Ajuga reptans*

with other herbal teas, it is said to be good for chest colds caused by chilling. The fresh juice, extracted from the whole plant and boiled with honey, then stored in the fridge, is considered a very good cough remedy. Externally, the fresh leaves made into a poultice and applied to wounds will soothe and speed up the healing process.

Ribwort is not generally grown in the garden as it is so easy to find in the wild. All species and plantain can become obnoxious weeds if not kept under control.

Hoary Plantain *Plantago media* is a downy perennial plant, native to most of Europe and temperate Asia, which is found in grassy places.

Like all the plantains, it was valued in the Middle Ages as a medicinal plant and used as an astringent, a vulnerary and as an eye-wash for conjunctivitis.

It is a pretty species for growing in a herb garden.

Lesser Celandine or **Pilewort** *Ranunculus ficaria* is a perennial herb, native to Europe and western Asia, which has also been introduced into North America. It is commonly found growing in damp woods, meadows, grassy banks and stream edges. Lesser celandine has fibrous roots with many fig-shaped root tubers and ascending, branched stems that reach a height of 5–25 cm (2–10 in). The stalked leaves are smooth, fleshy, dark green and heart-shaped: the basil ones sheathing the stem and forming a rosette; the stem ones similar but smaller. The bright golden-yellow flowers grow individually at the end of the stem and bloom from February to May.

The generic name is derived from the Latin *rana*, 'a frog', alluding to the preference this genus of plants has for the same kind of habitat a frog favours – moist and marshy. The specific name is derived from the Latin *ficus*, a fig, and alludes to the fig-like shape of the plants' tubers. The common name pilewort alludes to its supposed efficacy in curing haemorrhoids. Gerard grew this plant in his garden and called it Lesser Celandine, probably because it bloomed at about the same time as *Chelidonium majus*, which he called Greater Celandine, but they are not in any way related botanically. Poetically, this inconspicuous little flower has achieved fame because it was a great favourite of Wordsworth's and it has been immortalized in his verses and on his tombstone.

Lesser celandine was well-known to medieval herbalists, who valued it for its astringency and mainly used it for curing piles – indeed it is still widely recommended for this purpose. An infusion can be drunk daily and ointment or poultices or a lotion can be applied externally – all of which are said to bring relief and eventually cure the condition, although Weiss says his experiments with it, both internally and externally, have failed completely. It was also used to treat varicose veins, and other hard 'wens and tumours'. People with sensitive skin should use this plant with caution as it can cause irritation and sores. In fact, it was said that beggars used to rub the plant on their skin to induce repulsive sores and ulcers which aroused sympathy and encouraged the rich to give alms.

Rainbow Bugle *Ajuga reptans* 'Multicolor'

Bronze Bugle *Ajuga reptans* 'Atropurpurea'

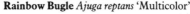

Afterwards the beggars cured themselves by applying fresh mullein leaves to their sores.

To make an infusion to be taken internally, put either 15 g/½ oz of dried root or herb in ½ l/1 pt of boiling water, leave for five minutes, then strain. Take three wineglassfuls daily.

Loewenfeld and Back in *The Complete Book of Herbs and Spices* suggest the following ointment to be used externally for relieving piles: melt 120 g/4 oz Vaseline, add 30 g/1 oz dried herb and stir well. Cover and simmer gently for forty-five to sixty minutes. Strain, then cool before using.

Lesser celandine can be gathered from the wild or grown in a moist, shady spot in the garden, providing good spring ground cover but tending to became invasive and hard to eradicate subsequently. The whole plant is best collected in March, dried thoroughly and stored in an airtight jar. The roots can be dug up towards the end of summer.

Bugle *Ajuga reptans* is a perennial plant, native to Europe, Asia, north Africa, and naturalized in North America, which is found in damp woods, grassy fields and mountain pastures. Bugle has a short rhizome and long, leafy, rooting stolons. The erect, four-sided stems reach a height of 10–30 cm (4–12 in) and are downy on two sides. The oval-shaped basal

leaves are slightly toothed and have stalks, the upper leaves in opposite pairs are stalkless. The purplish-blue flowers are in whorls on a spike and bloom from May to July. The fruit consists of small blackish seeds but they do not often mature and propagation is mainly from the rooting runners.

For many centuries bugle has been valued as a vulnerary (a plant useful for healing wounds). It has astringent properties and was formerly used for stopping haemorrhages. In homoeopathy, it is added to preparations for throat irritation and mouth ulcers. Its effect is rather similar to that of digitalis: it slows the pulse. Some have claimed it useful for bad hangovers!

To make a decoction that is soothing for an irritant cough, infuse 30 g/1 oz of dried herb in ½ l/1 pt of boiling water for ten minutes. Drink three to four wineglassfuls daily.

Bugle can either be picked in the wild or propagated in a herb garden. Put in ordinary damp soil in a semi-shady spot and gather in May or early June.

Bronze Bugle *Ajuga reptans* 'Atropurpurea' is a garden form that has deep purple-bronze leaves.

Rainbow Bugle *Ajuga reptans* 'Multicolor' is a most attractive garden form.

Solomon's Seal *Polygonatum multiflorum* Photographed at Bateman's, Rudyard Kipling's Garden

Solomon's Seal *Polygonatum multiflorum* is a perennial plant, native to Europe, which is found growing in woods and scrubland. Solomon's seal has a stout, white, creeping rhizome, twisted and knotted with circular scars, and erect, round, pale green stems that reach a height of 30–80 cm (12–32 in). The large, oval leaves grow alternately on the stems, with clasping bases, and have distinctive ribs on the surface. The small, drooping clusters of cream-coloured flowers hang from the leaf axils, in the opposite direction to the foliage and bloom from May to June, succeeded by small, blue-black berries in the autumn.

Several explanations are given for the origin of the common name. Some believe that it arises from the resemblance of the flat, round scars on the rootstocks to the impressions of a seal. Others suggest that as, when the root is cut transversely, it somewhat resembles Hebrew characters, Solomon, who knew the virtues of roots, set his seal upon them to show men its value as a medicinal root. Gerard believed that its name arose because of its efficacy in sealing up wounds. Whatever explanation is correct, the fact that there are so many indicates that the plant has had a long history of use – both culinary and medicinal.

The young shoots, boiled and eaten like asparagus, are a favourite vegetable in Turkey, and the macerated roots, which contain a large quantity of starch, were commonly made into bread by native Americans and also used in time of famine in Europe. The flowers and roots were powdered and taken as snuff to induce sneezing, and it was also fashionable at one time as an aphrodisiac. Distilled water made from the whole plant was reputed to be excellent as a skin tonic and was a commonly used ingredient of expensive cosmetics; Italian women were said to be particularly fond of it for their complexion.

Medicinally, Solomon's seal has astringent, demulcent and tonic properties. Because it is mucilaginous it has a very soothing effect and has been given for pulmonary complaints, inflammation of the stomach and bowels, piles, dysentery and menstrual cramps. The

powdered roots make excellent poultices for bruises, wounds and piles, as do the bruised leaves, mixed with lard to make an ointment. A decoction of the root, steeped in wine and drunk, was said by Gerard to knit bones wonderfully, not only of humans, but cattle too.

Solomon's seal can easily be grown in a herb garden. It likes light soil and a shady spot. It can be either grown from seed or the roots may be divided and transplanted at any time but not more often than every three or four years.

Lily of the Valley *Convallaria majalis* is a perennial, native to Europe and north-east Asia, which is also found in eastern North America. It sometimes grows abundantly in thin, dry shady woodland, clearings and meadows and it is also widely cultivated. Lily of the valley has a deep rhizome from which the leaves and the stalks on which the flowers grow arise. The plant grows to a height of 30 cm (12 in) and the broad, pointed oval leaves, 8–20 cm (3–8 in) long, are deeply ribbed and backward-slanting. The flower stalk bears little, fragrant, white, nodding bell-shaped flowers with scalloped edges which bloom in April and May, and by August or September they have developed into poisonous red berries.

The generic name is derived from the Latin *convallium*, 'of the valleys', and the specific name *majalis* refers to the month of May when it commonly flowers. One legend claims that the fragrance from lily of the valley encouraged the nightingale to forsake the hedgerow to find his mate in the shady woods. Apuleius in his fourth century Herbal claims that lily of the valley was found by Apollo and given to the leech Aesculapius.

It is now known that among other compounds lily of the valley contains two glycosides called convallarin and convallamarin which are a powerful cardiac tonic and diuretic. Yet our forefathers knew centuries ago that the plant was beneficial for weak hearts. Matthiolus, in the sixteenth century, wrote that lily of the valley will 'strengthen the heart and combat

spasms and palpitations'. The action of the drug closely resembles that of foxglove, *Digitalis purpurea*, slowing down the disturbed action of a weak and irritable heart while at the same time strengthening its power. Grieve claims that it is a perfectly safe remedy even if taken in full and frequent doses but modern writers say that the inconsistency of the drug could be dangerous and therefore it should only be used when prescribed by a physician. Weiss reports that a new lily of the valley preparation called Convacard has been developed by a method which largely preserves the complex active principles contained in the plant. The pills are film-coated so that, taken internally, absorption is rapid with no irritant effect on the gastric mucosa and elimination is fast too, making it a valuable alternative for those suffering from bradycardiac forms of heart failure which are particularly sensitive to digitalis.

Lily of the Valley can either be found in the wild or cultivated in the garden by root division. Plant at the end of September in well-drained, sandy loam with some leaf mould if possible. Collect the flowers in May before they have faded; then cut and dry the whole stalk for future use. You will notice that their sweet fragrance will be replaced by a rather narcotic smell. The root can also be collected in autumn and dried for further use.

Mayapple or **American Mandrake** *Podophyllum peltatum* is a poisonous, perennial herb, native to central and eastern North America, which is found growing wild in moist woods and clearings and wet meadows. Mayapple has a long, creeping rhizome composed of numerous long-jointed, brown runners. The single, generally unbranched stems reach a height of 30–45 cm (12–18 in). The large, smooth, stalked leaves grow in pairs and are composed of five to seven wedge-shaped divisions, lobed at the top. The solitary, drooping, unpleasant-smelling white flowers grow between the leaf stalks and bloom from April to June succeeded by the large, fleshy, lemon-like berries.

The generic name is derived from the Latin

Lily of the Valley *Convallaria majalis*

Green False Hellebore *Veratrum viride*

Mayapple *Podophyllum peltatum*

Indian Podophyllum *Podophyllum emodi*

Green False Hellebore *Veratrum viride* (leaves)

podos, 'a foot', and *phyllon*, 'a leaf', alluding to some supposed resemblance of the leaf to the foot of an aquatic fowl. One of its common names, duck's foot, also alludes to this, while the term wild lemon refers to the similarities of the berries to tiny lemons.

Mayapple is a highly toxic plant long recognized by the native Americans for both its poisonous and healing qualities. Taken in large doses, the leaves, roots and seeds are extremely dangerous and can even cause death – some Indian tribes used it to commit suicide – but taken in very small doses mayapple is a useful purgative and vermifuge; its resin is now considered good for curing venereal warts and it is generally a good stimulant for the bowels and liver. It should only be taken under medical supervision. The berries are slightly acidic but sweet and edible and can be used to make jellies.

Mayapple can be grown from seed or by root division in loamy soil and it likes a warm sheltered spot such as a shady border free from

weeds. Once established, it is a hardy plant and won't be injured by frost.

Indian Podophyllum *Podophyllum hexandrum* synonym *Podophyllum emodi* is a native of India with stouter, knottier roots. Although it is used medicinally in India, it should not be substituted for mayapple roots as it is much stronger than the American species and contains far higher quantities of podophyllotoxin, with drastic laxative effects.

Both plants have been used to treat cancer – particularly ovarian cancer – but alopecia is said to be a common side effect.

Green False Hellebore or **Indian Poke**
Veratrum viride is a poisonous perennial plant, native to eastern North America, which is found growing wild in swamps and damp meadows. Green false hellebore has a thick, cylindrical rhizome with numerous roots and a tubular flowering stem that reaches a height of 1.5 m (5 ft). The large, elliptical leaves sheathe the

stem at the base and are longitudinally veined and pleated. The small, green, star-shaped flowers bloom from May to July but do not usually appear every year.

White False Hellebore *Veratrum album* is a poisonous perennial plant, native to Europe, which is found in damp woods and meadows. It is very similar both in appearance and in active principles to green false hellebore except that it has yellowish white flowers.

Both plants are highly poisonous and should never be taken internally unless prescribed by a medical practitioner. White false hellebore was formerly used on daggers and arrows as a poison and it was prescribed for mania and epilepsy. Nowadays it is mainly used in veterinary medicine. A large dose will cause severe vomiting, diarrhoea, stupor and convulsions.

Green false hellebore lowers the pulse and slows respiration and it has been used in acute cases of pneumonia, peritonitis and threatened apoplexy.

Geranium macrorrhizum 'Album'

Herb Robert *Geranium robertianum*

Herb Robert *Geranium robertianum* is an annual or biennial plant, native to Europe, southern temperate Asia and North Africa and naturalized in North and South America. It is found growing wild in shady, moist hedgerows, undergrowth, woods, among rocks and on shingle. Herb Robert is an unpleasant-smelling, leafy, hairy plant with a small tap-root and an erect, red stem reaching a height of about 30 cm (12 in). The palmate, deeply cut, slightly hairy leaves are tinged with red. The five-petalled flowers which grow in groups of 2 or 4 in the leaf axils at the top of the stem are pinkish-red and bloom from May to June.

The generic name is derived from the Greek *gheranos*, 'a crane', because of the resemblance of the fruit to the beak of this bird. The specific name is a corruption of *ruberta* from *ruber* meaning 'red', alluding to the reddish fruit of the plant and its flowers. According to the seventeenth-century Doctrine of Signatures, its red colour denoted its therapeutic qualities: it was considered good for regenerating the blood and was prescribed for internal haemorrhages and diabetes (modern tests have shown it does indeed lower the blood sugar level).

Herb Robert was often used as a lotion or compress for eye inflammation and as a mouthwash for sore throats and mouth sores. It was also thought to be a wound herb capable of mending fractures and a remedy for milk retention in the breasts. The freshly crushed leaves are said to ward off mosquitoes. To make a decoction for external use as a gargle or lotion put 100 g/4 oz dried plant in 1 1/2 pt water, soak for a few minutes then gently bring to the boil and leave to infuse for fifteen minutes. Strain before use. Gather the plant from the wild when in flower and dry in the shade.

Geranium macrorrhizum is a perennial, native to southern Europe. It has magenta to pink flowers that bloom from May onwards. It makes an excellent ground cover in either sun or light shade. The leaves are strongly scented; they contain geranium oil, which is used in perfumery and for scenting pot-pourri.

Scurvy Grass or **Spoonwort** *Cochlearia officinalis* is a small, biennial or perennial plant, widely distributed in western, central and southern Europe, Asia and North America. It is found, sometimes abundantly, on cliffs and banks near the sea, in salty soil and brackish marshes. Low-growing with a long tap-root, scurvy grass has one or several smooth shoots, reaching a height of 5–50 cm (2–20 in). The basal leaves form a loose rosette and are broad, fleshy, long-stemmed and spoon-shaped (hence spoonwort); the upper leaves are stalkless, pale green, ovate-pointed with bluntly toothed margins, and they clasp the stem. The small, white, four-petalled, fragrant flowers form clusters at the end of the stem and bloom from April to August.

High in vitamin C, this plant derives its common name from the fact that the leaves were eaten by sailors during long sea voyages to prevent them from developing scurvy, a disease caused by ascorbic acid (vitamin C) deficiency. The plant was also valued as an aperient, diuretic and a stimulant and the oil extracted from the leaves was reputed to be beneficial for rheumatism. Scurvy grass ale was a popular tonic in times past. Nowadays an infusion made from 60 g/2 oz leaves in 1 1/2 pt of boiling water, steeped for five minutes, strained and sweetened and drunk in small wineglassfuls several times a day, can be beneficial for those deficient in vitamin C.

According to Barbara Griggs in *Green*

Scurvy Grass or **Spoonwort** *Cochlearia officinalis*

Ground Elder or **Goutweed** *Aegopodium podagraria*

Variegated Ground Elder or **Goutweed** *Aegopodium podagraria* 'Variegata'

Pharmacy, during the seventeenth century scurvy was considered a 'New Disease' because as journeys become longer, sailors were vulnerable to it once fresh fruit and vegetables ran out – as were people crowding into the slums around the big cities, who often had a poor diet. Although no one seemed to know the cause of scurvy, a herbal remedy had been used for centuries; scurvy grass was, as Gerard pointed out, 'a singular medicine against the corrupt and rotten ulcer, the stench of the mouth; it perfectly cureth the disease called the scurvie'. The learned medical profession would not accept the simplicity of this. Instead all kinds of violent treatments and ineffectual medicines were recommended: repeated bleedings and coolings, purges and mercurial medicines. In 1720 during the winter siege of Belgrade thousands of the Imperial troops in Hungary went down with scurvy. Mercury was administered and 'they all died in a salivation'. Later, naval surgeon, James Lind (1716–1794) undertook an empirical study involving twelve sailors suffering from scurvy. He treated two with cider, two with garlic and gum myrhh, two with elixir of vitriol, two with vinegar, two with sea water, and two with oranges and lemons. At the end of a fortnight, those treated with oranges and lemons were back at their duties, the rest showed little or no improvement. It took another fifty years before the Admiralty bowed to irrefutable evidence and ordered every sailor in the British Navy to have an ounce of lemon juice issued after the sixth week at sea. By 1879, scurvy in the British Navy was a thing of the past.

Collect from the wild in an unpolluted spot.

Ground Elder or **Goutweed** *Aegopodium podagraria* is a stout, erect perennial found in most parts of Europe, Asia Minor, the Caucasus and Siberia. Probably introduced into Britain in the Middle Ages it is now well naturalized; it is also found naturalized in North America. It can

be a persistent weed in gardens and is commonly found around roadsides and in waste places. Ground elder has a creeping root system that spreads rapidly, smothering other plants. Its round, hollow, grooved stem reaches a height between 40–100 cm (16–40 in) and the large, alternate leaves 10–20 cm (4–8 in) have ovate, sharply toothed lobes. The flat, umbrella-like flower clusters are quite large with numerous small white flowers that bloom from June to August. These are followed by flattened seed vessels which open when ripe so that the seeds can be scattered by the wind.

The generic name is a corruption of the Greek word *aigos*, 'a goat', and *podos*, 'a foot', because someone imagined a resemblance between the leaves and a goat's foot! The specific name is derived from the Latin word *podagra* 'gout', and refers to its medicinal use in treating this complaint; hence also the common name, goutweed. It is also known as Herb Gerard because it was dedicated to St Gerard, the patron saint of gout sufferers. Its other common

names, bishopsweed and bishopswort, arose because it was formerly cultivated in monastery gardens as a medicinal and pot herb and is frequently found near ecclesiastical ruins.

In Sweden and Switzerland the young leaves are picked in spring, cooked like spinach and tossed in butter and make a delicious vegetable; or they can be eaten raw in a salad. Medicinally the plant has been used internally or externally to help relieve aching joints, gout pains and sciatica.

To make an infusion add 15 g/½ oz of dried leaves to ½ l/1 pt of boiling water. Drink small glassfuls several times a day, simultaneously applying a hot poultice to the affected area. In modern herbal practice it is now generally considered obsolete. As this herb is such a rampant weed, it is probably advisable not to introduce it into your garden but make a note of a good wild source where you can pick it freely in spring to eat as a vegetable and then take some home to dry and store for medicinal use.

Iris pallida

Orris *Iris germanica* var. *florentina*

Orris *Iris germanica* var. *florentina* has big, whitish flowers and is also cultivated for ornament and for its root. Probably a native of the eastern Mediterranean, it is now naturalized in most parts of Europe except the north.

Iris pallida is a perennial plant with sweet-smelling blue to lilac flowers, that is native to the eastern Mediterranean and naturalized elsewhere in southern Europe. It is found growing wild and cultivated extensively for ornament and for its root.

These two beautiful plants are cultivated in gardens all over the world, but in Italy, they are grown on mountain slopes for their roots, which yield the highly prized Orris Root, used since ancient times for making perfumes and unguents and medicinally as a purge and for certain chest complaints. The juice is used cosmetically for bleaching freckles. The powdered root was used in medieval times to scour linen, and in Russia was added to a honey and ginger beverage to flavour it. When fresh the root is very bitter but this bitterness disappears as it dries and gradually after two or three years it acquires its lovely, characteristic violet odour. Oil of Orris, extracted from the root, is used extensively to perfume scents, soaps, powders, toothpastes and sweets. Large roots are sometimes turned into ornamental forms or made into infants' teething shapes.

Both species will grow happily in the garden in ordinary soil and can be increased by dividing the root-stock in April and replanting in rich soil. It takes at least three years for the root to reach maturity. It then takes a further two years' drying before it can be ground into Orris powder.

Sweet Flag *Acorus calamus* is a stout, aromatic, aquatic perennial, native to southern Asia and central and western North America, which was introduced into Europe by the botanist Clusius

who grew it at the Vienna Botanical garden and then distributed it to other botanists in Belgium, Germany and France. It was introduced into Britain at the end of the sixteenth century and it can now be found in most parts of Britain, especially in the Fen districts although it is scarce in Scotland. It grows in shallow water, by pond edges, ditches, marshes, rivers and canals. Sweet flag has a large, branched, creeping, cylindrical rhizome which can become immersed in the mud and has numerous roots. Sheathed and pinkish at the base, the erect yellowish-green leaves are 50–100 cm (20–40 in) high and about 2.5 cm (1 in) wide. Similar to iris, they have a central rib on both sides, are narrow, spear-shaped and pointed with wavy or crimped edges. The leaves' pale yellow-green colour and the smell of tangerines they emit when bruised, distinguish sweet flag from irises and other similar plants. The triangular stem has a solid, cylindrical spadix, 5–10 cm (2–4 in) long, set at an angle from the stem and covered with tiny, yellowish-green, sweet-scented flowers which bloom in June and July.

Also known as sweet sedge, calamus and myrtle grass, the generic name is said to be derived from the Greek *Coreon*, meaning 'pupil' (of the eye), as the plant was used by the ancients to cure eye complaints. The specific name is derived from the Greek *calamos* meaning 'reed' or 'cane'. Because of its pleasant smell, sweet flag was traditionally strewn on the floors of churches and private houses, a tradition kept up at Norfolk Cathedral for important festivals until quite recent times.

Recently there has been a cancer scare associated with sweet flag because certain polyploid forms of the plant have been found to contain asarone, a carcinogenic substance that is not apparently present in the diploid form. Furthermore, Weiss points out, this plant has a

very long history of medicinal use and there are no reports of cancer developing from it. While it would probably be unwise to use sweet flag for an extended period, used medicinally for a limited time it can undoubtedly be beneficial.

It is the root of sweet flag that contains its medicinal property. It possesses to 1 to 4 per cent of an aromatic volatile oil, as well as acorin, and tannin, choline and an essence containing azarone, eugenol and pinene. Taken internally the drug stimulates the digestion, is mildly diuretic and relieves flatulence. Weiss says it has wonderfully tonic powers of stimulating the appetite because it activates stomach secretions and is, therefore, recommended for anorexia nervosa. Children or adults with appetite disorders often respond very well if regularly given a few drops of sweet flag tonic before meals. Weiss claims he has also seen it used successfully to give symptomatic relief to patients suffering from stomach cancer.

Sweet flag root is also used by people who are trying to give up smoking. Chewing the rhizome stimulates salivation and has a tonic effect on the mouth and throat. In the same way, a few bits of chopped rhizome tied up in a piece of muslin can be beneficial for babies with teething problems. The candied root has been used for coughs or infused to make a gargle for sore throats. Because of its stimulating tonic properties, morning baths of sweet flag are recommended for convalescents or those suffering from anaemia or diabetes. It is also used to add a bitter tang to beer and an aromatic odour to toothpaste and perfume. Powdered, the root can be used as a substitute for cinnamon, nutmeg or ginger.

The leaves can be used to flavour creams and custards in the manner of a vanilla pod. Normally in tropical countries up to 12 per cent of rice is lost through insect pests but Indian scientists recently discovered that adding chopped sweet flag rhizome to the rice before storage reduced loss because its oil sterilized the male rice weevils.

To make a tonic, infuse 30 g/1 oz of root in ½ l/1 pt of boiling water for five minutes and drink freely in small cupfuls. Alternatively, boil the root in several changes of water, then boil it in a sugar syrup to make a candy that can be chewed to ease coughs, sore throats or dyspepsia.

Sweet flag can be found in the wild or grown in rich, moist or frequently watered soil in the garden, and it can easily be propagated by root division in the early spring or early autumn. The roots should be gathered in autumn when sufficiently large and firm, generally after two or three years, before they become hollow. When dry the root loses 70 per cent of its weight but improves in smell and taste. However, it does deteriorate when stored for too long.

Yellow Flag *Iris pseudacorus* is an erect perennial, native to Europe, west Asia and North Africa, which is found growing wild in marshes, swampy woods, shallow water at river edges and in ditches. Yellow flag has a thick, horizontal rhizome from which smooth, erect stems grow to a height of 30–100 cm (12–40 in). The smooth, sword-shaped leaves with parallel veins also arise from the root. The beautiful yellow flowers with purple veins at the base bloom from May to July.

The genus is named after the rainbow goddess Iris because of the variety of colours it displays. The specific name comes from the Greek *pseudo*, 'false', and *acorus*, the generic name for sweet sedge which this iris resembles: when not in flower the plants resemble one another and favour a similar habitat. Also known as the *Fleur de Lys*, it is the heraldic emblem of the kings of France. One theory says the name is a corruption of Fleur de Louis, after Louis VII who adopted it as his heraldic symbol in his crusade against the Saracens. Another theory says that it was named after the Lys River near Flanders because it grew there in such profusion.

Yellow flag has been used since ancient times as a medicinal plant. It has a very powerful purging effect and was used to cure 'evil spleens', coughs and convulsions. The powdered root was used as a snuff and the juice inhaled up the nostrils provokes violent sneezing so was recommended for persistent head colds. A slice of root held against an aching tooth was said to cure the pain immediately. Because of its extremely acid taste yellow flag is rarely used nowadays and it should only be taken under prescription as it can cause violent vomiting and diarrhoea.

The flowers yield a beautiful yellow dye and the root, with sulphate of iron, a good black dye. The seeds, well-roasted, are reputed to be an excellent coffee substitute.

Yellow flag can be grown in a moist, shady place in the garden. Propagate by dividing roots in spring or autumn.

Stinking Iris or **Gladwin** *Iris foetidissima* is an unpleasant-smelling, smooth perennial, native to western Europe and North Africa, which is found growing wild in hedge-banks, open woods and on sea cliffs, favouring calcarous soil. Similar to yellow flag but with shorter, narrower, darker leaves and dull purple or yellow flowers that bloom sparingly from June to August.

Stinking iris, as its name implies, has a strong, unpleasant odour when crushed. Like yellow flag, it has been used medicinally since ancient times as a purge and also an emmenagogue and taken in infusion for nervous and hysterical complaints. Nowadays it is not generally used.

Easily grown in the garden, the seed pods burst open in autumn to show the attractive red seeds.

Yellow Flag *Iris pseudacorus*

Sweet Flag *Acorus calamus*

Stinking Iris *Iris foetidissima* var. *citrina*

Lady's Mantle *Alchemilla mollis*

Lady's Mantle *Alchemilla mollis*

Lady's Mantle *Alchemilla vulgaris* is a perennial herb, native to Europe, north and west Asia, Greenland and north-eastern North America, but also found in high mountain ranges, such as the Himalayas, in southern latitudes. It is found growing in damp grassland, open woods and rock-ledges in mountainous areas. Lady's mantle is a low to medium-sized downy plant that reaches a height of 5–45 cm (2–18 in). It has a stout, black rootstock and large, kidney-shaped, toothed leaves with delicate little pleats that are arranged in rosettes. The basal leaves have long stalks and the stem leaves are stalkless. The tiny, greenish-yellow flowers have no petals and bloom from June to August.

The generic name is derived from the Arabic *alchimia*, 'alchemy', and originated from alchemists' belief that it has numerous wonder-working properties. The common name is thought to have arisen from the fact that the lobed leaves are considered to resemble the scalloped edge of a mantle. Two other common names, lion's foot and bear's foot, arise from the supposed resemblance of the spreading basal leaves to these.

Used since ancient times as a vulnerary to stop bleeding wounds and promote healing, lady's mantle is considered to be particularly helpful for menstrual problems. It helps stop vaginal discharge and reduces excessive bleeding and it heals lesions after pregnancy. No wonder it is sometimes called Woman's Best Friend. It has also been used as a heart tonic, diuretic and a mild sedative. The freshly pressed juice will help to heal skin troubles such as acne and a weak decoction can be used for conjunctivitis. Weiss says that little is known scientifically about lady's mantle but it probably contains tannins which would account for its long history of use in female disorders.

To make a tea put 45 g/1½ oz of dried lady's mantle into ½ l/1 pt of boiling water. Infuse for ten minutes, strain, sweeten and drink one or two cups a day.

To make a poultice for healing wounds, take a pad of fresh leaves, heat for two minutes with a warm iron and apply to the affected area. Change the poultice after ten minutes.

Apart from its medicinal uses, lady's mantle leaves are sometimes blended into tea in Switzerland and in mountain areas the fresh young leaves are added to salads. If foraged by cows, they yield more milk and the cheese made from this milk has a very distinctive flavour.

Lady's mantle can be gathered wild or easily grown from seed. Sow the seed in spring – it will spread rapidly – and gather the leaves in mid-summer while the flowers are still in bloom. Dry thoroughly and store in an airtight container.

Alchemilla mollis is a robust, perennial herb, introduced into Britain from Asia Minor, commonly found in gardens and occasionally as an escape. Generally much more hairy than *Alchemilla vulgaris* and more frequently grown in gardens.

Wallflower *Cheiranthus cheiri* is a short-lived perennial herb, probably native to the eastern Mediterranean region but widely naturalized throughout Europe as a result of cultivation. It is found growing wild or as a garden escape on old walls, quarries and sea cliffs. Wallflower has a slender, woody tap-root and an erect, branching, leafy stem that reaches a height of 20–60 cm (8–24 in). The basal leaves form a rosette while the stem leaves are alternate and crowded; both are oblong to lance-shaped. The fragrant, yellowish-orange flowers are grouped in clusters at the top of the stem and bloom from April to August.

Wallflower was, in the past, used as a diuretic but it has recently been discovered that the chemical compound, cheiranthin, that the plant contains has cardiotonic properties which are more active than digitalis. Therefore if taken in large doses it can be poisonous and should not be used unless advised by a physician. The oil has a pleasing perfume if diluted.

Aconite or **Monkshood** *Aconitum napellus* is a very poisonous, hardy, perennial herb introduced into Britain before the tenth century and also found wild or cultivated throughout the northern temperate zone to the Himalayas. It is found growing in clumps on shady stream banks, ditches, pastures and alder groves or in high mountain meadows. Aconite has a fleshy, spindle-shaped tap-root which puts out 'daughter' roots each year. The erect, green stem is minutely downy and grows to a height of 50–100 cm (20–40 in). The glossy, dark green leaves are pale green or whitish underneath and deeply divided in palmate fashion. The erect clusters of irregularly formed dark blue or purple flowers are thought to resemble the shape of a monk's hood and are very attractive and accessible to bees. They bloom in June.

Some claim the generic name for aconite is derived from the Greek *akontion*, 'a dart', because barbarian races used it to poison their arrows; others that it derives from *akone*, 'cliffy' or 'rocky', referring to one of the plant's habitats. Pliny thought the name derived from Aconae, its supposed place of origin. The specific name *napellus* means 'a little turnip' and refers to the shape of the plant's roots. Well-known to the ancients for its poisonous properties, aconite was said to be one of the constituents of the potion given to the old and infirm on the island of Ceos to facilitate their departure from the world when they were no longer useful and it is also said to have been the poison that Medea put in the cup she prepared for Theseus.

Aconite, mentioned in herbals and lists of plants since the tenth century, has long been recognized as highly dangerous. Its primary use was thought to be as an antidote against other poisons, particularly those from snake bites. Aconite contains amongst others, aconitine, mesaconitine, aconitic acid, malic acid and acetic acid. Extracts can be highly poisonous in large concentrations, first stimulating and then paralysing the central and peripheral nervous system. Symptoms of aconite poisoning are a burning sensation on the tongue, vomiting, stomach pain and diarrhoea leading to paralysis and death. The poisons are principally contained in the root but are found throughout the plant. All medicines obtained from aconite come under Table 1 of the Poison Schedule, and medicinal doses must only be taken on a doctor's prescription. Its main uses in modern times are as an ointment for the treatment of terminal neuralgia and rheumatic pains and as a tincture for coughs and laryngitis.

Aconite is probably best grown apart from the culinary herbs in a herb garden and children should be warned against its dangers.

Aconite likes moist, loamy, shady soil. It can either be grown from seed which will then take two to three years to flower or it can be propagated by root division in the autumn. Small 'daughter' roots should be selected and replanted about 30 cm (12 in) apart, in December or January. Harvest roots for storing in the autumn. Wash, trim, dry and store in airtight containers in the dark. Leaves and flowers can be cut just before the flowers bloom. Always wash your hands thoroughly after handling this plant.

Wallflower *Cheiranthus cheiri*

Aconite or **Monkshood** *Aconitum napellus*

Viper's Bugloss *Echium vulgare*

Viper's Bugloss *Echium vulgare* is a bristly biennial, native to Europe from central Scandinavia to central Spain and eastwards to Asia Minor, and naturalized in North America. It is found growing wild in uncultivated fields and by the roadside, also in grassy places in dry soil by sea-cliffs and dunes, particularly in chalky areas. Viper's bugloss has a spindle-shaped root and erect stems that are very bristly, spotted red and reach a height of 100 cm (40 in). The leaves are oblong to lance-shaped and hairy with a prominent midrib – the lower ones are stalked, the upper ones are not. The funnel-shaped flowers grow numerously, in curved spikes, and turn from rose-coloured to bright blue or occasionally white. They bloom in June or July.

The generic name derives from the Greek *ekios*, 'a viper', referring to the supposed resemblance of the seeds to a snake's head or alluding to the red-spotting on the stem. The common name is partly a translation of this, while 'bugloss' has its origin in a Greek word meaning ox's tongue and alluding to the roughness and shape of the leaves.

Traditionally viper's bugloss was considered an effective cure for venom and snake bites. Culpeper writes: 'It is an herb of the sun. It is an especial remedy against both poisonous bites, and poisonous herbs. The seed drunk in wine produces abundance of milk in nurses' breasts.' It was thought also to be comforting to those who were full of 'swoonings, sadness and melancholy'. Nowadays, the juice is used as a soothing emollient for sensitive skin and in a poultice for treating boils. The infusion can be drunk as a diuretic and to alleviate fevers and headaches. The young leaves are similar to those of borage and can be added to salads.

Collect from the wild or grow from seed by planting in ordinary, well-drained soil in a sunny position. Gather the flowering tops in July and the young leaves earlier, before they become hairy, to add to salads.

Hound's Tongue *Cynoglossum officinale* is an erect biennial, native to Europe and Asia and introduced in North America. It grows wild in dry, grassy areas and wood edges, often in sandy or chalky soil or near the sea. Hound's tongue has a black, spindle-shaped root and an erect, branched, downy stem that reaches heights of 40–100 cm (16–40 in). The long, oblong to lance-shaped, downy basal leaves form a rosette and the upper leaves are also downy but stalkless, with the base clasping the stem. The funnel-shaped flowers are red or dull purplish red and bloom from May to August.

The generic name is derived from the Greek *cynoglossum*, 'dog's tongue', alluding to the shape and texture of the leaves. The specific name indicates that it was included on official lists of medicinal plants in former times.

Long recognized for its effectiveness in relieving piles, hound's tongue was also reputed to have a soothing effect on the digestive system. In Culpeper's day, the root was used to make a decoction for coughs and colds; the leaves were boiled in wine to alleviate dysentery, and the bruised leaves or juice, made into an ointment, were thought to prevent balding and used to treat head wounds, scalds and burns. Modern phytotherapy uses hound's tongue in compresses, ointments and pastes to treat leg ulcers, bruises and thrombophlebitis. Nowadays, homoeopathic preparations made from hound's tongue are claimed effective for treating insomnia, but large doses of the plant should not be taken as it is known to have narcotic effects.

Sweet Violet *Viola odorata* is a sweet-smelling perennial herb, native to Europe and north Africa, which has also been introduced into eastern Asia and North America. It is found growing wild in fields, hedgebanks and scrub and also cultivated in gardens and meadows, favouring calcareous soil. Sweet violet has a short, thick rhizome with long, creeping, rooting stolons and reaches a height of 15 cm (6 in). The stalked, basal leaves are roughly heart-shaped, bright, dark green with distinctive veining. The pretty, scented, deep violet or white flowers are borne on long stalks and bloom from March to May.

The origin of the generic name is a little uncertain but one suggestion has been that *viola* is the Latin form of the Greek *Ione*. Io, beloved of Jupiter, was turned by him into a heifer to protect her from Juno's jealousy and at the same time violets sprang up around Io to provide her with food.

The specific name, of course, refers to the strong scent of the flowers which has been used since ancient times to perfume confectionery, wine, cosmetics and medicines. To the Greeks, violets were a symbol of fertility and a frequent component in love potions. Both the Greeks and the Romans drank violet wine and Hippocrates and Pliny declared it good for hangovers, Pliny recommending a garland of violets be worn to dispel headaches and dizziness, particularly those caused by over-indulgence. A tenth-century herbal tells us that the ancient Britons mixed violets with goat's milk to make a skin lotion. Essence of violets is much used in the perfume and cosmetic industries although nowadays this essence is increasingly synthesized chemically as it needs over 100 kg (220 lbs) of flowers to extract 60 g/2 oz of essence.

From the earliest times herbalists have recognized the medicinal properties of sweet violet and recent research has given a scientific explanation for some of the claims made for the plant. For instance, sweet violet has traditionally been recommended for headaches, migraine and insomnia, and it is now known to contain the glycoside of salicylic acid which, derived from White Willow, *Salix alba*, has been used in the synthesis of aspirin. The roots contain an alkaloid, violine, which is very similar to emetin from Ipecacuanha. A decoction made from the roots is often prescribed as a laxative; the flowers are also mildly laxative and, in the form of a tea or syrup, often recommended for constipation in children, particularly if combined with almond

Viper's Bugloss *Echium vulgare*

Hound's Tongue *Cynoglossum officinale*

Sweet Violet *Viola odorata*

Burnet Saxifrage *Pimpinella saxifraga*

oil. Tea or syrup made from the leaves is also recommended for whooping cough, sore throats, tuberculosis, bronchitis and similar complaints. Claims have been made for its use in curing cancer but these have not been clinically substantiated. Used externally, violet infusion can relieve inflammation of the eyes, throat and mouth and compresses made from the crushed leaves were traditionally used for reducing swellings. Culpeper says: 'The flowers of the white violet ripen and dissolve swellings. The herb or flowers, while they are fresh, or the flowers that are dry, are effectual in the pleurisy, and all diseases of the lungs . . . and hoarseness of the throat, heat and sharpness of urine, and all pains of the back, or veins, or bladder'.

To make an infusion, put 15 g/½ oz of flowers into 1 1/2 pt of cold water, soak for three minutes, then bring to the boil and leave to infuse for ten minutes. Drink two to four cups a day for coughs, colds, respiratory or digestive problems.

To make a syrup, put 125–150 g/5–6 oz fresh flowers into 1 1/2 pt of boiling water, cover and leave to macerate for twelve hours. Strain the liquid through a cloth and add it and 1 kg/2 lb of sugar to a saucepan; boil for an hour or until

it acquires a syrupy consistency. Store in a stoppered glass jar and take three or four teaspoons a day as an expectorant, sedative or laxative.

Sweet violet can easily be grown in the garden from cuttings taken from the last season's runners. Plant in moist, peaty soil in a shady spot and make sure they have plenty of moisture until firmly rooted. Gather the leaves and flowers in spring. Dry them carefully in the shade so that they retain their colour and scent but make sure that they don't get damp. When dry, store them in stoppered glass jars, well away from the light.

Burnet Saxifrage *Pimpinella saxifraga* is a perennial herb, native to Europe, (except the most southerly parts), the Middle East and western Siberia, which has also become established in North America. It is found in dry grassy meadows and pastures, on railway embankments and in waste places. Burnet saxifrage has a slender rootstock and a slender round, lined stem that reaches heights of 30–100 cm (12–40 in). The numerous root-leaves grow in five to ten pairs of oval, pinnate leaflets; the lower stem-leaves are sparse and the leaflets narrower, while the uppermost leaves are small,

sheath-like and purplish. The small white flowers grow in flat-topped clusters, and bloom from June to October.

Cultivated in parts of Europe since the sixteenth century and introduced into North America by the settlers, burnet saxifrage was held in high esteem by the old herbalists, who recommended it as a wound herb and claimed it was efficacious for gout, rheumatism and against the plague. Nowadays, it is generally used internally to ease digestion, soothe respiratory problems and treat kidney and urinary diseases. Externally it is used for hoarseness and throat infections.

Commonly grown in the herb gardens of the past for its fragrance, its young leaves were added to salads, stews and sauces. It was also added to beer tankards and cups to impart a cool, aromatic flavour.

Burnet saxifrage can be picked in the wild or grown from seed in a herb garden. Scatter seeds in the autumn and plants will come up plentifully. If kept well-weeded, they last for several years if the soil is sufficiently dry. Gather the leaves while young and tender for use in salads but harvest the roots in autumn. Clean and dry in natural heat then store in airtight containers for future use.

Wintergreen or **Creeping Wintergreen** *Gaultheria procumbens*

Salal, Shallon or **Western Wintergreen** *Gaultheria shallon*

Wintergreen or **Creeping Wintergreen**
Gaultheria procumbens is a perennial shrub
native to eastern and northern North America
and Canada, which is found growing wild on
sandy or barren plains, cool damp woods, and
mountainous forests. Wintergreen is a creeping
evergreen that grows to a height of 15 cm (6 in).
The shiny alternate leaves are dark green, paler
underneath, and rather thick and leathery to
touch. The drooping white waxy flowers are
produced singly from the base of the leaves and
bloom from about June to September, followed
by bright red berries that ripen in the autumn
but remain on the plant all winter.

Best known for the oil of wintergreen which
can be distilled from its leaves, it was very
popular in American domestic medicine in the
nineteenth and early twentieth centuries as well
as being commonly used by American Indians
prior to that time.

Oil of wintergreen contains methyl salicylate,
closely related to acetylsalicylic acid or aspirin,
and is widely regarded as an effective remedy
for acute rheumatic pains. It is also considered a
good diuretic and is said to encourage milk flow
in nursing mothers.

The leaves can be used to make a tea and the
berries are edible, favoured by partridges,
grouse and deer. The oil is used to flavour
toothpastes, often mixed with menthol and
eucalyptus oil.

Salal, Shallon or **Western Wintergreen**
Gaultheria shallon is a native to western North
America, and is found growing there in woods
and clearings. It is also grown in gardens all over
the world as an undershrub. It is an upright
shrub with numerous spreading branches. The
plant is used in a similar way to wintergreen.
The purple fruits are edible and rather delicious
when fully ripe.

Hawthorn or **May** *Crataegus monogyna* is a
deciduous shrub or small tree, native to Europe,
western Asia and North Africa, which has been
introduced into North America. It grows wild in
hedges and thickets and is often cultivated as a
hedge. Hawthorn is very branched and spiny
and can reach a height of 10 m (33 ft). The white
flowers bloom in masses, in May, and have a
strong smell. The red 'haws' or berries ripen in
September.

The generic name is derived from the Greek
kratos, 'hard', referring to the hardness of the
wood, and the specific name derives from *mono*,
'one', and *gyna*, 'female', alluding to its single
carpel. Hawthorn has a long history of legend
attached to it, the most famous being that it was
reputedly used for Christ's crown of thorns. In
Normandy, they still believe that lightning will
not strike a house protected by hawthorn as
lightning is the devil's work and cannot strike
the plant that touched Christ's brow.

In ancient times hawthorn was used for gout,
fever, pleurisy and insomnia. Nowadays science
has confirmed that it has antispasmodic and
sedative chemical components, which are
considered useful for various heart conditions
such as valvular inefficiency, although the
treatment needs to be taken over a long period
to have its full effect. In recent years hawthorn
has become a widely used herbal remedy for
certain heart conditions, although its precise
action is not fully understood. However, it does

Hawthorn or **May** *Crataegus monogyna* Photographed near Wensley, Derbyshire

not contain digitalis-like substances and it is a well-tolerated drug with no risk of habituation. Weiss says 'Crataegus is particularly useful for long-term prophylactic use, in middle-aged patients showing the first signs of coronary involvement and also in older patients where the rather vague term 'senile heart' has come to be widely used.'

A medicinal tea made from dried berries, 30 g/1 oz in 1 1/2 pt of boiling water, may be used to treat diarrhoea or, made double strength, as an excellent gargle for sore throats.

The green leaf buds make a crunchy addition to spring salads and the ripe haws make a delicious jelly or jam.

Sanicle *Sanicula europaea* is a perennial herb, native to Europe, Africa and southern, central and eastern Asia, which is found growing wild in woods, hedges, shady damp areas and some mountainous regions and is especially prolific in alkaline areas. Sanicle has a creeping, fibrous rhizome and an erect stem that reaches heights of 30–40 cm (12–16 in). The three to five lobed leaves have toothed margins, are glossy green and are on long stalks. The small pink or white flowers are arranged in clusters at the top of slender stalks and bloom from May to July.

The generic name comes from the Latin *sano*, 'I heal or cure', and indicates in what high esteem sanicle used to be regarded. Unfortunately, inflated claims were made for its powers and when they proved unfounded the plant was discredited and it is not commonly used today.

Sanicle *Sanicula europaea*

Lemon Verbena or **Lemon Vervain** *Lippia triphylla* synonym *Lippia citriodora*

Vervain *Verbena officinalis*

Vervain *Verbena officinalis* is a hardy perennial herb, native to Britain and Europe, North Africa and West Asia, which is widely distributed around the world including China, Japan and North America. It commonly grows wild in waste places, along roadsides and pastures and among ruined buildings. Vervain has a spindle-shaped root and several tough, erect stems that grow to a height of 60 cm (24 in). The branched stem is squarish and the opposite leaves, 2.5–8 cm (1–3 in), are arranged in pairs and deeply divided in unequal lobes with the upper leaves being less divided or almost entire. The small, mauve, five-lobed flowers are arranged in long slender spikes at the top of the stalks and bloom from July to September.

Not to be confused with Lemon Verbena, *Lippia triphylla*, which was only introduced into Europe at the end of the eighteenth century, vervain has been known and used in Europe for many centuries. The name vervain is derived from the Celtic *ferfaen*, 'to drive away a stone', and refers to its use in bladder infections, especially calculus. It is also known as *Herba veneris* because of its supposed aphrodisiac qualities and *Herba sacra* because it was used by the ancients for sacrifices. The Druids regarded it almost as highly as mistletoe and in the Middle Ages magicians used it for casting spells or adding to potions, particularly love potions. It was used to foretell the future and protect houses against wicked spirits, and worn around the neck as a general good-luck charm.

Medicinally it was thought to cure every ill: it healed war wounds and conferred immortality; it was a protection against plague; it cured poisonous snake bites, jaundice, toothache, headache, ulcers and heart disease. Culpeper says: 'This is a herb of Venus, and excellent for the womb to strengthen and remedy all the cold distempers of it . . . it helps the yellow jaundice, the dropsy and the gout . . . corrects the diseases of the stomach, liver and spleen; helps the cough, wheezings, shortness of breath' etc. etc.! Possibly its numerous reputed powers stem from the legend that it was found on Mount Calvary and used to staunch the wounds of the crucified Christ.

It has been rather neglected in recent times

except by homoeopaths but recent research has shown interesting and promising results in the treatment of certain tumours. Vervain tea made with 15–30 g/½–1 oz of dried leaves infused in a pint of boiling water taken three or four times a day is used to bring relief from indigestion and jaundice; also for painful and irregular menstruation, nervousness, coughs and insomnia. A stronger decoction is used externally to treat wounds, cuts and burns, soothe sprains and neuralgia or as a gargle for tonsillitis and sore throats. An even more concentrated decoction, 250 g/8 oz infused in 1 l/2 pt of boiling water, added to the bath is very refreshing.

Vervain can easily be gathered in the wild or grown in a herb garden. It adapts well to most kinds of soil although it will probably thrive best in well-drained, rich soil. Sow seeds in early spring or take cuttings or propagate by root division. Gather the leaves before the flowers fully ripen, dry and store for future use.

Verbena × *hybrida* 'Silver Anne' is a tender perennial that should be kept in a greenhouse until ready for transplanting to a sunny, well-drained spot. It is a lovely garden variety used only for decoration.

Verbena 'Sissinghurst' also tender, is another superb garden plant, grown only for ornament in a herb garden.

Lemon Verbena or **Lemon Vervain** *Lippia triphylla* synonyms *Lippia citriodora, Aloysia citriodora, Verbena triphylla* is a highly aromatic, deciduous shrub, native to Chile and Peru, introduced into the Old World in 1784 and now commonly cultivated particularly in warm Mediterranean gardens for ornament. Lemon verbena, which can grow to 175 cm (6 ft), has lance-shaped, yellow-green leaves that are shiny above and dull below and grow in groups of three, each 8–10 cm (3–4 in) long. When crushed they give off a strong lemony scent. The small, pale lavender flowers grow in slim panicles and bloom in July or August.

Often confused with its wild cousin Vervain, *Verbena officinalis*, which has been known in Europe since ancient times, lemon verbena is

Larkspur *Consolida orientalis*

in fact quite a different plant and used in different ways.

The essence contained in its leaves is most commonly used in the making of liqueurs and perfume. A refreshing tea, very popular in Spain and France, is made by infusing 30 g/1 oz of dried leaves or flowering tops in a ½ l/1 pt of boiling water. This can be drunk three or four times a day to relieve acidity, indigestion and flatulence or as a stimulant for lethargy or depression. Mességué says it is also useful for stomach cramps, palpitations, asthma, neuralgia, migraine and vertigo.

Lemon verbena can be grown in rich or poor soil and it favours a warm, damp climate although it will grow in milder climates if it is put in a sheltered position. In winter the roots should be covered with wood ash or leaf-mould for protection. Pick leaves and flowers just before they flower and dry in a warm, shady place. The dried plant will keep its scent for years.

Larkspur *Colsolida ambigua* is an annual herb, native to Mediterranean Europe and naturalized in many other areas, which grows wild in corn fields and is also cultivated for ornament. Larkspur has a simple or branched stem that reaches a height of 100 cm (40 in). The basal leaves have oblong segments, the stem leaves linear ones. The deep blue flowers grow in a racemose spike and bloom from May to September, followed by the flattened, black seeds which are poisonous.

The generic name of the plant refers to its ability to consolidate and heal wounds. The juice from the leaves is considered a remedy for piles and an infusion of flowers and leaves was formerly prescribed for colicky children.

The seeds are poisonous and emetic if taken internally and children should be warned against picking this plant in the garden but, applied externally, the tincture made from the seeds is used as an insecticide and said to be effective against hair nits.

Consolida orientalis is a common garden annual, native to Mediterranean Europe, which often becomes temporarily naturalized in corn fields and waste places. Its flowers are usually purplish-blue or they may be pink or white.

Verbena × hybrida 'Silver Anne' (top), *Verbena* 'Sissinghurst' (centre)

Verbena 'Sissinghurst'

Perennial Flax *Linum perenne*

Purging Flax *Linum catharticum*

Blue Pimpernel *Anagallis monellii*

Common Flax *Linum usitatissimum* is an annual herb found in almost all tropical and temperate regions, cultivated for its fibre and oil, and sometimes occurring as a casual. Common flax has a tap-root from which usually a single stem grows to a height of 60 cm (24 in). The sparse, alternate leaves are narrow, pointed and heavily veined on the lower surface. The beautiful blue flowers grow in a sparse, flat-topped cluster and bloom from May to August followed by round fruits that contain about ten small, glossy, pip-like seeds.

The history of flax goes back so many centuries that its origins are unknown. Flax seeds and linen woven from flax were found in Egyptian tombs and it is mentioned several times in the Bible. Numerous traditions are associated with flax. In German mythology the goddess Hulda was believed to have shown mortals the art of spinning and weaving flax and the Bohemians believed that if seven-year-old children danced among the flax fields they would be favoured with the gift of beauty. In the Middle Ages it was believed that flax flowers were a protection against witchcraft. The fibre from flax has been used to make linen for clothing, fish nets, thread, ropes and string. The oil expressed from the seeds is used in furniture polish and is an ingredient in printers' ink.

Medicinally, the oil extracted from the seeds is used in numerous ways. Linseed oil, as it is known, has soothing and lubricating properties, and is used in medicines to relieve tonsillitis, sore throats, coughs, colds, constipation, gravel and stone. Linseed oil mixed with an equal quantity of lime water is recommended for burns and scalds, and the crushed seeds can be used as a poultice for ulcers, wounds and inflamed swellings.

To make linseed tea, put 30 g/1 oz crushed seeds in ½ l/1 pt of boiling water and infuse for fifteen minutes. Strain and sweeten with a little honey and drink several glassfuls a day to soothe coughs, colds, bronchial catarrh and urinary infections.

Common flax can be cultivated in a garden but it requires a very rich, deep, loamy soil. The seeds should be planted in March and harvested in August. When the seeds ripen they can be threshed, dried and stored for winter use.

Perennial Flax *Linum perenne* is a perennial herb, native to central and eastern Europe, including Britain, where it is very local. It is found growing wild on calcareous grassland. Perennial flax has many decumbent or ascending stems that grow to a height of 30–60 cm (12–24 in). The numerous, alternate leaves are narrow and pointed. The sky-blue flowers grow in a loose cluster and bloom from June to July, succeeded by the seeds.

Like common flax, perennial flax can be used for making fibre (although it is coarser) and for extracting the medicinal linseed oil.

Purging Flax *Linum catharticum* is a slender smooth annual, native to Europe and western Asia, which grows on heaths, moors, hilly pastures and dunes, favouring calcareous soil.

Praised by Gerard for its purgative properties (hence its name) and used in the past by herbalists for its gently laxative action as well as for muscular rheumatism and catarrhal problems, it is little used by modern herbalists and is dismissed as obsolete by Weiss.

Blue Pimpernel *Anagallis monellii* is a perennial herb, native to south-western Europe, where it grows in dry, open places, along field edges or on waste ground. Blue pimpernel is a form with intensely deep-blue flowers. Traditionally, pimpernels were used extensively in medicine and thought to cure a wide range of complaints, particularly in diseases of the brain, but modern research warns against its use unless prescribed by a medical practitioner: large doses can cause excessive urination.

Red Poppy or **Field Poppy** *Papaver rhoeas* is an annual or occasionally biennial herb, native to

Opium Poppy *Papaver somniferum* in Eccleston Square

Red Poppy or **Field Poppy** *Papaver rhoeas*

Europe, North Africa and temperate Asia, which has also been introduced into North America, Australia and New Zealand. It is found wild in corn fields and waste places. Red poppy has a slender tap-root and erect or ascending stems which are finely hairy and channelled and reach heights of 40–75 cm (16–30 in). The basal leaves are lance-shaped, form a rosette and are pinnately divided; the upper leaves are three-lobed and pinnately cut – all the leaves are green and hairy. The flowers, which are borne on long, hairy stalks that arise from the leaf axils, are bright red shading to black at the base of the broad petals and bloom from June to October.

Use of red poppy – a relative of opium poppy, *Papaver somniferum*, but not addictive – dates back to ancient times. Remains of poppy garlands were found in Egyptian tombs and the Greeks and Romans used the seeds as a condiment and ate the young leaves in salads.

Nowadays the flower petals and light seeds are recognized as being mildly narcotic, soothing and sedative. Taken as an infusion, red poppy leaves are recommended for chest complaints, asthma, pleurisy and pneumonia, and Mességué claims they are good for treating insomnia, nerves, anxiety and stomach spasms, although most writers suggest red poppy should only be taken under medical supervision as its alkaloid content is still under investigation. Red poppies can be gathered in the wild. The leaves should be picked very carefully before they fade and quickly dried in the air. They should then be stored in hermetically sealed jars for future use.

Opium Poppy *Papaver somniferum* is an annual herb, native to the eastern Mediterranean, Asia Minor and central Asia, which is also extensively cultivated in Europe, India, China and North America and occasionally found as an escape. Opium poppy has a spindle-shaped tap root and an erect, hollow stem with a few branches that reach heights of 50–150 cm (20–60 in). The big, alternate, ovate leaves are toothed and wavy-edged. The large, solitary flowers range from white to lilac to pinkish-purple, sometimes with a darker blotch at the base, and they bloom from July to August, succeeded by egg-shaped capsules containing numerous tiny white or black seeds.

The specific name is derived from the Greek meaning 'sleep-bearing', and the narcotic properties of the opium poppy have been known and used for centuries by different civilizations. The ancient Egyptians used the sedative properties of opium poppy, and Cretan women worshipped a Poppy Goddess in 1400BC. Mohammed's missionaries were largely responsible for spreading its cultivation to Europe, where it was widely used for treating cholera and dysentery and, during the Middle Ages, highly regarded as a spice. It was not until the seventeenth century that the opium-smoking habit swept through China and it became an abused drug.

The opium drug is obtained by slitting the wall of the ripening capsule which exudes a white milky juice that is collected when it has hardened (overnight). The crude opium thus obtained contains a large number of important alkaloids which are used in a great many pharmaceutical preparations: morphine, narcotaline, papavarine, codeine, thebaine and noscapine.

Opium poppy is a very poisonous plant and the drug extracted from it highly addictive and dangerous. It should never be taken except under strict medical supervision and, in most countries, opium poppy can only be cultivated by authorised growers.

Poppy seeds, however, contain no drug and because of their pleasant, nut-like flavour, they are frequently added to breads and pastries. Crushed seeds are added to curries for flavouring and thickening, and an edible oil, obtainable from the crushed seeds, can be used as a substitute for olive oil.

Rhubarb *Rheum rhaponticum*

Turkey Rhubarb *Rheum palmatum*

Rhubarb *Rheum rhaponticum*

Turkey Rhubarb *Rheum palmatum* is a herbaceous perennial plant, native to north-western China but now cultivated extensively in the USSR and Germany and also grown for ornament throughout Europe. Turkey rhubarb has a large rhizome with many fibrous roots and an erect, hollow, branching stem that reaches a height of 2 m (6½ ft). The leaves grow from the base on a strong stalk that encircles the stem. The large leaf-blades have five lobes and are broadly toothed at the margin; they are also

distinctly veined. The loose clusters of greenish-white flowers bloom in June and July.

The generic name is thought to derive from the Greek *rheo*, 'to flow', alluding to the purgative properties of the plant, while the specific name is a reference to the shape of the leaves. The common name arose because it was through Asiatic Turkey that this species of rhubarb reached Europe.

For centuries the rhizome of the Turkey rhubarb was highly regarded by the Chinese for its medicinal properties. Modern research has justified its reputation. It contains anthraquinones, which have a purgative effect, and tannins and bitters which have the opposite effect. If taken in small quantities the tonic, aperient effect predominates and it is therefore useful in cases of appetite loss and acute diarrhoea; if it is taken in larger quantities, it will have the laxative effect for which it is generally well-known.

Only the rhizome is used medicinally as the leaves are toxic. The root is scraped clean and dried, then either powdered or made into a syrup or tincture. The variety most used for medicine is *Rheum palmatum* var. *tanguticum*. Medicinal Rhubarb, *Rheum officinale*, is also used as a laxative.

The species most commonly grown in gardens, cultivated for use in the distilling industry or to make jellies and jams, are *Rheum rhaponticum* and *Rheum rhabarbarum*. These contain only small amounts of the principles found in the medicinal species and so are mildly laxative.

Alder Buckthorn *Rhamnus frangula* synonym *Frangula alnus* is a deciduous shrub or small

tree, native to Europe (though rare in the Mediterranean region), central and Northern Asia and North America. It is found growing in scrub, around raised bogs, damp heath and woodland, in thickets and fens, particularly on peaty soil. Alder buckthorn reaches heights of 4–5 m (13½–16½ ft). The long, slender branches have smooth, dark-brown or greyish-brown bark which is yellow inside. The shiny green, oval, veined leaves turn yellow or red in the autumn and the greenish-white flowers appear on short stems from the leaves' axils. They bloom from April to June succeeded by round, green berries which turn red, then glossy black by the autumn.

Since the Middle Ages it has been recognized for its gentle laxative properties. It so effectively but gently eases constipation it can even be prescribed for children, pregnant women, and those recovering from an abdominal operation. Externally a decoction can also be used as a lotion or compress for minor skin irritations. To make a mild laxative put 10 g/⅓ oz dried bark into 1 1/2 pt of water, boil for ten minutes, leave to macerate for six hours, strain, flavour with mint or orange zest if desired and drink a cupful at night on retiring or a cupful before meals three times a day.

Note: The fresh bark must never be used as it can be a toxic irritant – use only dried bark that is one or two years old. Collect the bark either from three-to four-year-old shrubs found in the wild or cultivate from seeds sown as soon as they are ripe. Keep the seedlings free from weeds and plant in the nursery in the autumn, when the bark should be cut off in strips and thoroughly dried in a well-drained, shady place and then kept for a year before use.

Buckthorn *Rhamnus catharticus*

Cascara Sagrada *Rhamnus purshiana*

Fumitory *Fumaria officinalis*

Alder buckthorn also provides several important commodities: its straight stems are used to make wickerwork furniture; the juice from the berries makes a particular green pigment to dye textiles and water colours and the wood stripped of its bark makes a very fine, light, inflammable kind of charcoal, much sought after by gunpowder makers.

Cascara Sagrada *Rhamnus purshiana* is a shrub or small tree, native to western North America, which is found growing at the base or sides of canyons forming the undergrowth of great forests. Cascara sagrada grows to heights of 4.5–6 m (15–20 ft). The bark is grey with white markings and its dark green, elliptical leaves have prominent veins and toothed margins. The small greenish-white flowers grow in short-stemmed clusters from the leaves' axils and bloom from May to July succeeded by green berries which are glossy black when ripe, and poisonous.

The common name is Spanish for 'Sacred Bark' which was what the early Spanish priests named this plant, probably when they learnt about it from the Indians of Mendocino, California. Many Indian tribes in western North America knew and used the plant for its gentle laxative effect. By the end of the nineteenth century it entered the United States Pharmacopoeia and it is still an official medicine as well as a very popular one for treating the bowel because it not only relieves the problem but appears to restore tone to the relaxed bowel thus making repeated use of the drug unnecessary.

Cascara sagrada is exported from America to Europe where it is now more popularly used

than Alder Buckthorn *Frangula alnus*. Because of its mildness it is considered useful for frail and elderly people. It is also very commonly used in veterinary medicine as a mild purgative for dogs.

Buckthorn *Rhamnus catharticus* is a rather thorny, deciduous bush native to Europe, North Africa and western Asia, which grows wild in hedges, scrub and in ash or oak woods, favouring calcareous soil.

The bark and berries of buckthorn are highly purgative as the specific name suggests and it has been used for centuries as a laxative. The berries, collected when ripe, contain an acid, bitter juice that, mixed with sugar and aromatic herbs, make a syrup that was highly valued by herbalists and country people. However, its action on the bowels is so violent that it is no longer listed in the British Pharmacopoeia, nor used in human medicine, though it is still extensively used in veterinary practice, particularly for dogs.

Fumitory *Fumaria officinalis* is a sub-erect or climbing annual plant, native to Europe, south to the Canary Islands and east to Iran, which is also found in North America, Australia and South Africa. It grows in fields, wasteland and on old walls. Fumitory has robust, slender, climbing, regular stems which grow to heights of 25–30 cm (10–12 in). The silvery grey leaves are divided into many segments with flat, lance-shaped lobes. The small, pinkish-white flowers with purple tips form loose clusters at the end of the stems and bloom from April to October.

There has been much discussion over the years as to how fumitory acquired its strange

name. Some claim that the ancients called it Earth Smoke because it was born of the 'vapours of the earth', others that its appearance from a distance is reminiscent of a field on fire, and others that it was because the juice would clear the eyesight by bringing tears to the eyes like smoke does.

Since Roman times, physicians have valued fumitory for its purifying properties and it has been used as a general tonic and as a treatment for liver complaints, especially jaundice, arteriosclerosis, arthritis and urine retention. Weiss reports that recent studies have shown that fumitory has a remarkable regulatory effect on the biliary system and is particularly beneficial for relieving biliary colic, biliary migraine and chronic dyskinesia.

Externally it has been used as a skin lotion for fading freckles, treating eczema and scabbing and for cradle-cap in babies. However, although fumitory is known as an effective tonic, if taken for more than eight days it has hypnotic and sedative qualities so dosages should be adjusted according to the desired effect.

To make a skin lotion, put 60 g/2 oz dried plant into ½ l/1 pt milk, boil for five minutes, remove from heat, then strain and apply cold to the affected area.

Collect fumitory from the wild from late spring to autumn. Pick stems that are very leafy and full of flowers. Dry in small bunches hung from the ceiling, then store in a dry, dark place for winter use.

Motherwort *Leonurus cardiaca*

Motherwort *Leonurus cardiaca*

Couch Grass *Elymus repens* synonym *Agropyron repens*

Great Burdock *Arctium lappa*

Motherwort *Leonurus cardiaca* is a hairy perennial, native to many parts of Europe and introduced elsewhere, which is found on banks under hedges and on waste ground, favouring gravelly or calcareous soil, sometimes as a garden escape. Motherwort has a stout rhizome and square, stout, erect branched stems that grow to heights of 90–120 cm (3–4 ft). The lower leaves are roundish and palmately five-lobed; the upper leaves are trifid and spear-shaped: both are stalked and somewhat hairy. The pinkish-white flowers grow in numerous, many-flowered whorls and bloom in August.

The generic name is derived from the Greek *Leonurus*, 'a lion's tail', an allusion to some imagined resemblance. The common name comes from the plant's long-standing reputation for being invaluable in female disorders. It was also said to calm nervous irritability and hysterical complaints and strengthen and gladden the heart. As a tonic, it is used for delirious fevers and some heart diseases. Weiss reports that his own investigations have convinced him of the plant's medicinal action for functional heart complaints due to autonomic imbalance; it is also used in antithyroid treatment. In both instances, the effects are only felt if the plant is taken for a period of several months. It has a pungent odour and bitter taste so, although it can be made into an infusion, it is more palatable made into a conserve or syrup.

Motherwort is very hardy and will readily grow in a herb garden in ordinary soil. It will quickly increase if its seeds are scattered.

Couch Grass *Elymus repens* synonym *Agropyron repens* is an erect perennial plant, native to Europe, North Africa, Siberia, North Asia and North America, which is found growing wild in fields and waste places, favouring clay soils. Couch grass is a weedy plant with numerous far-creeping rhizomes and stems that reach heights of 25–100 cm (10–40 in). The flat, rough leaves have a long, cleft sheath and the round, hollow flower stems, with flowers in terminal spikes, resemble rye or beardless wheat and bloom from June to August.

The generic name is derived from the Greek *agros*, 'field', and *puros*, 'wheat'. Its common name is thought to be a corruption of the Anglo-Saxon *cwice*, 'vivacious', referring to its tenacious hold on life. It is disliked by farmers and gardeners because it is a persistent weed that spreads quickly and is very difficult to eradicate once it has taken hold. Another of its common names, Dog Grass, is a reference to its avowed ability to heal sick dogs: they, and cats, will chew it to reduce vomiting when ill.

Although often regarded as a troublesome weed, couch grass is used for cattle fodder in Europe and in times past the dried roots were ground into meal and added to bread dough. For centuries the plant has been valued for its medicinal properties. Dioscorides claimed it was a useful remedy for those having difficulty passing urine or suffering from bladder-stones. Pliny prescribed it for urinary calculus and ulcers of the bladder and Culpeper praised it for treating diseases of the kidney. Among other things couch grass contains vitamins A and B, potassium salts, organic acids and starch so it has long been used as a tonic in deficiency diseases; also as a diuretic, for cystitis and diseases of the bladder, for gout and rheumatism. The fresh young leaf shoots can be eaten raw in salads or the juice can be drunk in spring to cleanse the body after the winter months. The French commonly drink a tisane made from couch grass roots. To make an infusion put about 30 g/1 oz of dried, chopped

Common Agrimony *Agrimonia eupatoria*

root in ½ l/1 pt of boiling water and infuse for ten minutes. Drink up to two cups a day.

Collect the roots in spring. Remove all traces of leaves and rootlets, cut into short lengths and dry thoroughly before storing in an airtight container.

Great Burdock *Arctium lappa* is a tall, biennial herb, native to Europe and Asia, which is also widely distributed in North America. It is found growing wild in waste places and roadsides, particularly in calcareous soil. Great burdock has stout, furrowed, somewhat woolly, branched stems that reach heights of 90–200 cm (36–80 in). The large, rough, basal leaves are ovate to heart-shaped and bigger than the stem leaves. The flower heads are round and the purple flowers, which bloom from July to September, are encased in an involucre of long stiff scales with hooked tips: these stick to whatever they come into contact with and especially if to the coats of animals, are thus disseminated far and wide.

The generic name comes from the Greek *arktos*, 'a bear', alluding to the rough burrs, and the specific name from *lappa*, 'to seize', referring to their ability to cling. Children have always liked playing with the burrs which are known as Beggar's Buttons.

Medicinally burdock has been used for centuries. Henry III is reputed to have been cured of syphilis thanks to burdock and, it is, without doubt, a very effective remedy for many skin conditions because of its mucilaginous soothing properties. It has been used to treat eczema, acne, impetigo, herpes, ringworm and cutaneous conditions; also for measles, boils, bites, bruises and inflamed skin. Other uses include relief of rheumatism, indigestion, kidney trouble and dropsy, treatment of premature balding and to stimulate hair growth after alopecia.

For poor skin conditions make a decoction with 30–60 g (1–2 oz) of fresh root infused in 1 l/2 pt of boiling water. Strain, sweeten and drink four or five times a day. Also apply this decoction externally to the affected areas or make a similar decoction from the leaves or a poultice from the fresh, crushed root. The same decoction is said to facilitate the eruption of measles and help recovery. To treat hair loss make a lotion by macerating 100 g/4 oz of fresh burdock root with 50 g/1½–2 oz of fresh nettle root in ½ l/1 pt of rum for eight days then strain. Massage daily into the scalp.

Fresh young stalks boiled lightly until tender and served hot with melted butter make a tasty vegetable or they can be eaten raw in a salad. In times past the stalks were sometimes candied like angelica and had a mildly laxative effect.

Collect plants from the wild. Use the leaves fresh as they are bitter when dried and collect the roots in the autumn for slow drying then store in an airtight jar for future use.

Common Agrimony *Agrimonia eupatoria* is an erect, perennial herb, native to Britain but also distributed throughout northern, central and eastern Europe to Iran and North Africa; it can be found as an introduction in North America. It is commonly found growing wild along roadsides, hedgerows, paths, wood edges, meadows and waste ground up to 480 m (1600 ft). This faintly aromatic and very downy plant has a small, twisted rhizome with numerous rootlets and an erect, furrowed stem that grows from 30–60 cm (12–24 in). The numerous, downy, serrated leaves which can be up to 20 cm (8 in) long near the ground are green above and whitish below, while the upper leaves are much smaller and simpler in outline and interspersed with tiny leaflets on the stem. The small, five-petalled yellow flowers grow in a long upright spike at the end of the stem, flowering from the bottom upwards. They bloom from June to August. The seeds are contained in urn-shaped fruits in the form of burrs that may stick to clothes or animals' fur, so giving rise to its other common names cockle burr and sticklewort.

The generic name for agrimony probably comes from the Greek *agremone* meaning 'a plant that can heal diseases of the eye'; although others claim that it is from the Latin *agrimonia* meaning 'defender of the field', referring to the fact that it grows around field edges. The specific name was given in honour of Mithridates IV Eupator, King of Pontus, who was fond of dabbling in herbal medicine.

Long valued for its medicinal properties, the virtues of agrimony have been extolled by most of the major herbalists over the centuries. Dioscorides valued it as a general purgative; Galen recommended it for jaundice, complaints of the liver and the bowels; Culpeper praised it for numerous things including curing sores, wounds and bruises, colic, ague and coughs. Although it was at one time included in the London *Materia Medica* as a vulnerary herb, its virtues are no longer recognized by modern official medicine, although still appreciated by herbal practitioners.

Its main uses are as an astringent, a tonic, a diuretic and a mild anti-diarrhoetic. It contains 5 per cent tannin which may explain its long use as a healer of wounds and as an excellent gargle. Mességué claims he has found agrimony very effective in the treatment of sore throats, tonsillitis and mouth ulcers, as well as being useful for treating kidney troubles.

An infusion of leaves and flowers (15 g/½ oz of dried leaves and ¼ l/½ pt of water) can be taken internally as a tonic or diuretic, or used externally to dress wounds or bathe problematic skin. To make a gargle put 100 g/3–4 oz of dried leaves into 1 l/2 pt of water and boil until reduced to ⅔ l/¾ pt, sweeten with honey and use two to three times a day.

Agrimony is hard to cultivate because of the poor germination of the seed so it is best to collect it from the wild. The flowering tops should be gathered before the seeds have dried in the usual way. Sadly the faint, aromatic smell is lost in the drying process but not its medicinal properties.

Male Fern *Dryopteris filix-mas*

Polypody *Polypodium vulgare*

Common Horsetail *Equisetum arvense*

Giant Horsetail *Equisetum telmateia*

Male Fern *Dryopteris filix-mas* is a fern, native to Europe and temperate Asia, and also found in parts of North and South America, Africa and India. It commonly grows in damp woods and hedge banks in hilly and mountainous areas. The male fern has a big, scaly rhizome, reddish outside and greeny-white inside. The large, compound fronds usually grow to 60–120 cm (24–48 in) and are wide, spreading and broadly lance-shaped. They are bipinnate and stalked, with opposing leaflets that are blunt and scallop-edged. The veins on the underside of the fronds are covered with sori, rich in sporangia.

Commonly used since ancient times and mentioned by the great medical writers – Dioscorides, Galen and Avicenna – the root of the male fern is well known as a powerful and effective vermifuge.

Gerard wrote: 'The roots of the Male Fern, being taken in the weight of half an ounce, driveth forth long, flat worms as Dioscorides writeth, being drunk in mede or honied water'.

Male fern is still considered an effective remedy against tapeworm infestations and is also frequently used by veterinary practitioners. Care must be taken with the dosage: too small a dose will not expel the worms, too large a dose will be an irritant poison causing, eventually, coma and lesions of the optic nerve that may result in blindness.

No preparation containing male fern should ever be taken by pregnant women or those with heart trouble.

The old herbalists thought that an ointment made from the bruised, boiled root mixed with lard was soothing for wounds, and the powdered root cured children of rickets. The dried fronds stuffed into cushions and mattresses were believed to ease rheumatism.

Many species of fern have been used as food by various nations but modern research has suggested there is a strong possibility that some species are carcinogenic. This research dealt in particular with Bracken *Pteridium aquilinum* but it is probably best to avoid all species until the situation has been clarified.

Polypody *Polypodium vulgare* is a fern, native to Europe, Tibet, China, Japan, South Africa and eastern North America, which is found growing wild in damp woods, shady hedgebanks, tree stumps, moist rocks and old walls. Polypody has a stout, creeping rhizome densely covered when young with reddish-brown scales. Its flesh is pale yellow with a distinct, liquorice-like taste. The leathery fronds are stalked, lanceolate and pinnatifid. The long, narrow, smooth leaflets are arranged alternately on the stalk and joined together at the base. They have a central vein and bear round, rust-coloured sori below. The fronds come out in May but in sheltered places remain almost evergreen.

The generic name is derived from the Greek *poly*, 'many', and *podos*, 'a foot', from the many foot-like divisions of the caudex. This fern was used by the ancients as a purgative. It frequently grew on the roots of oaks and was thus attributed magical powers. In North America the western species of this fern, the California polypody, *Polypodium californicum*, was used by native American tribes both as a source of food (in times of scarcity they ate the root) and as a medicine; they rubbed the juice on to areas of rheumatic pain.

Principally the plant has been prescribed as a mild laxative, particularly for children, if mixed with convolvulus powder and honey. It is also said to encourage expectoration and sooth dry coughs and was prescribed for consumptive cases. The root used to be used as an adulterant for liquorice and is still used as a sweetener.

Common Horsetail *Equisetum arvense* is a perennial plant, native to Europe but also found in central China and North America. It is found growing wild in moist loamy or sandy soil and usually near water in fields, hedgebanks, waste-places and dunes. The common horsetail is a cryptogam, that is, a plant without flowers or seeds. It has a branched rhizome which sends up brownish-yellow, fertile, hollow, jointed stems that reach heights of 20–50 cm (8–20 in). These stems terminate in cone-like catkins

containing the spores from which young horsetails grow.

The generic and common names for this extraordinary and large genus, of which the common horsetail is one of the most well-known species, allude to the shape of the plant; the Latin derives from *equus*, 'a horse', and *setrum*, 'a tail'.

These plants are very interesting because fossil remains indicate that our modern dwarf varieties originated from giant varieties of horsetail which existed in the Carboniferous period. Also, they are exceptional because of the high quality of silica, acids, minerals, vitamins and salts that they contain. Because of the granular texture of the silica, one species of horsetail was used by country people to scour pots and pans and to polish wood used in marquetry and cabinetmaking and one species is still used in China today for polishing wood. It is an effective organic fungicide for black spot and mildew on garden plants and young horsetail shoots can be cooked and eaten with butter.

Medicinal virtues have been claimed for horsetail since Roman times: as a general tonic, an astringent and useful for staunching the flow of blood in wounds and nosebleeds. Horsetail tea has been recommended for chest complaints and tuberculosis, for anaemia, loss of blood, kidney and urinary diseases; the high silicic acid content for enriching the blood, encouraging the formation of white blood corpuscles and strengthening the connective tissue. The fresh juice may alleviate mouth ulcers, glandular swelling and inflamed tonsils.

To make an infusion soak 30 g/1 oz of horsetail in ½ l/1 pt of cold water for one to two hours. Simmer gently for ten minutes, leave to stand for a further ten minutes then strain and drink lukewarm, one or two cupfuls a day.

Collect from the wild and harvest in June and July. Pick stems carefully and dry. Store in airtight containers and keep in a dark cupboard.

Giant Horestail *Equisetum telmateia* is found growing on shady banks in heavy or marshy soil and reaches heights of 20–40 cm (8–10 in).

Hemlock *Conium maculatum*

Hemlock *Conium maculatum*

Hemlock *Conium maculatum* is an erect, foetid, biennial plant native to Europe, Asia and North Africa, which has been introduced into North and South America and New Zealand. It is commonly found growing wild along roadsides, on waste ground, damp places, near water and in open woods from coastal to mountainous areas. Hemlock has a long tapering root and smooth, hollow stems, with purple blotches, that reach heights of 1–2 m (40–80 in). The large, feathery, toothed leaves are long-stalked and tripinnate lower down but smaller and pinnate, with tiny stalks, higher up the stem. The small, white flowers grow in large clusters and bloom from June to August. The egg-shaped fruits have wavy ridges.

The generic name is derived from the Greek *konas*, 'to whirl about', alluding to the fact that when eaten the plant causes vertigo and death. The common name is thought by some historians to be derived from the Anglo-Saxon words *hem*, 'border or shore', and *leac*, 'plant or leek' referring to the plant's partiality to damp and watery habitats.

Hemlock is poisonous and has been recognized as such since ancient times. The juice of hemlock was administered to criminals, and Socrates chose to drink this fatal poison rather than renounce his philosophical teachings. Plato's account of his death is considered to be a superb description of the plant's effect on the body. Hemlock contains a volatile, oily, alkali called coniine which has a bitter taste and a disagreeable, mouse-like smell. It is highly narcotic and has a paralysing effect on the motor functions although the mind remains completely clear. If an overdose is taken, complete paralysis occurs and the respiratory function is quickly depressed, then ceases altogether, so that death follows through asphyxia.

In medieval times hemlock was used with a mixture of herbs to create an anaesthetic preparation and later it was used as an antidote to strychnine poisoning. Because of its sedative properties hemlock was used in the past for nervous spasms, cramp, teething in children (!),

epilepsy, whooping cough, spasms of the larynx and gullet and acute mania. It was also used by Greek and Arabian physicians to cure tumours, swellings and pains in the joints. Baron Storch recommended it as a poultice for cancerous ulcers and open sores. A homoeopathic tincture is used to treat arteriosclerosis and prostate complaints but otherwise hemlock is little used in medicine these days.

Hemlock belongs to the Umbellifer family – the same group that contains parsley, fennel, parsnip and carrot. Great care must be taken when collecting these edible umbellifers, because mistaking them for this plant could have fatal consequences.

Wood Avens or **Herb Bennet** *Geum urbanum* is a perennial herb, native to Europe, Asia and North Africa, which is also found in North America and Australia. It grows in woods, hedgerows, shady places and scrub. Wood avens has a short, thick rhizome which smells of cloves and thin, erect, slightly branching stems that are reddish and hairy and reach heights of 20–60 cm (8–24 in). The large, stalked, basal leaves are pinnate with toothed margins, the stem leaves are smaller and divided into three. The bright-yellow flowers have five petals and bloom from June to October or sometimes even as late as December and they are succeeded by a brown ball of seeds covered with hairs or bristles.

The generic name is derived from the Greek *geno* meaning 'to yield up an agreeable fragrance', in reference to the pleasant clove-like smell which the freshly dug root emits. The common name herb bennet is a corruption of *Herba benedicta*, the blessed herb, because in times past the plant was worn as an amulet and believed to have the power to ward off evil spirits and venomous beasts. In medieval times the graceful, trefoiled leaf and the five-petalled flower were used in architectural decoration to symbolize the Holy Trinity and the five wounds of Christ.

Paracelsus recommended wood avens root for catarrh of the stomach and intestine and Gerard

also said that a decoction was beneficial 'against stomach ills and bites of venomous beasts'. It was made into a cordial for use against the plague and chewing the root sweetened foul breath. As well as its medicinal uses, wood avens was also used to flavour ale and Angsberry Ale is said to owe its special flavour to the addition of a small bag of wood avens in each cask. Wood avens roots were put in linen as a protection against moths and to impart a pleasant smell.

In modern herbal medicine an infusion of wood avens is taken for chills, catarrh and diarrhoea and, used externally as a lotion, it will remove spots and freckles. Taken as a tincture, it is considered an excellent spring tonic or purifier, particularly for the liver, and it is known to have mildly sedative properties.

Collect from the wild or grow in the herb garden in ordinary soil, in a shady spot. The roots should be dug up in spring (the old herbalists specified 25 March as the best day) as they are then thought to be at their most fragrant. It must be dried carefully and slowly as it easily loses its fragrance and then sliced and powdered for storage as it retains its odour better this way.

Bistort *Polygonum bistorta* is a herbaceous perennial, native to northern and central Europe, the mountains of southern Europe, Asia Minor and central Asia, which is also naturalized in North America. It is found wild in moist meadows, by waterways and along grassy roadsides. Bistort has a stout, horizontal, twisted, red-brown rhizome and an erect, knotted stem that grows to heights of 25–50 cm (10–20 in). The basal leaves are long and spear-shaped, narrowing into a long stalk; the top leaves are also narrow and spear-shaped but they are wavy and clasp the stem at their base. The dense, spiked flower stalk bears small pink flowers which bloom from May to June and September to October.

The common name is derived from the Latin *bis*, 'twice', *torta*, 'twisted', in reference to its contorted, serpentine shape, as are its other

Wood Avens or **Herb Bennet** *Geum urbanum*

Bistort *Polygonum bistorta*

Water Pepper or **Smartweed** *Polygonum hydropiper*

common names: snakeroot, adderwort and snakeweed. In the Middle Ages bistort was popularly cultivated in herb gardens for both culinary and medicinal purposes. The leaves and young shoots were eaten in spring as a vegetable and were an essential ingredient in Herb Pudding – a favourite country recipe still eaten in Westmorland and Cumberland before the war. The roots too are sometimes eaten in times of scarcity in Russia and Siberia because they contain a great deal of starch and are very nutritious when soaked in water and roasted or made into bread.

Medicinally, bistort is one of the strongest vegetable astringents known, being very rich in tannin. In the sixteenth and seventeenth centuries it was used for smallpox, fevers and plague but nowadays the root is used more to stem external and internal bleeding or discharge. It may be effective in treating cases of diarrhoea, dysentery, cholera, haemorrhages from the lungs and stomach and piles. It is also useful as a gargle for mouth ulcers or spongy gums and sore throats. It may help stem profuse menstruation and ease uterine difficulties. As a compress, the roots or crushed leaves help to heal wounds and soothe bruises or snake bites.

Bistort can be particularly attractive in a moist garden rockery. Propagate by root division in spring or early autumn. It likes ordinary soil and is happy in sun or shade.

Water Pepper or **Smartweed** *Polygonum hydropiper* is an annual herb, native to Europe, North Africa, temperate Asia and North America, which is found in shallow water in ponds and streams and in damp places. Water pepper has a branched stem that reaches heights of 25–75 cm (10–30 in). The lance-shaped leaves are short-stalked and wavy, glandular below and sometimes fringed with hairs. The greenish-pink flowers grow in long, loose, somewhat drooping clusters and bloom from June to October.

Water pepper has no smell but a peppery taste. Indeed, in ancient times the ripe seeds were used as a pepper substitute. One old tradition has it that if you place this plant underneath your horse's saddle it will go long distances without feeling hungry or thirsty. Apparently the Scythians used it for this reason.

For medicinal purposes, the flowering heads and leaves are mostly used but occasionally the fresh roots too. Principally it is used as an infusion to stem bleeding and relieve menstrual pain. A cold water infusion used to be prescribed for gravel, dysentery, coughs, sore throats, colds, and gout. A fomentation is good for chronic ulcers and bleeding tumours. Some herbalists of old thought it effective in nervous diseases – vertigo, lethargy, apoplexy and palsy.

Great Mullein or **Aaron's Rod** *Verbascum thapsus*

Great Mullein or **Aaron's Rod** *Verbascum thapsus*

Jacob's Ladder *Polemonium caeruleum*

Columbine *Aquilegia vulgaris*

Great Mullein or **Aaron's Rod** *Verbascum thapsus* is an erect, biennial (rarely annual) herb, native to Europe and Asia east to western China and naturalized and common in North America. It is commonly found growing wild on sunny banks, waste places, field and road edges, particularly on dry soil. Great mullein, which is densely clothed with soft, whitish, woolly hairs, has a white tap-root and a simple stem than can reach a height of 2 m (6½ ft). The alternate, oval to lanceolate leaves are woolly with a small stalk, forming a rosette at the base, while the stem leaves are smaller and with a less decurrent stalk. The yellow flowers grow in a dense, spike-like cluster climbing up the top of the stem and bloom from June to September.

The generic name is thought to be a corruption of *barbascum* from the Latin *barba*, 'a beard', alluding to its shaggy, woolly appearance. The plant has numerous common names: Aaron's rod probably arose from its stiff, upright appearance, and candlewick plant, hag's taper and torches are three common names that allude to its use as a wick before the introduction of cotton. The stalks of the plant were dipped in suet or pitch and used as candles.

Historically, the use of mullein goes back many centuries. It was attributed with the power of driving away evil spirits and according to Homer, was the plant that Ulysses took with him to protect himself from the charms of Circe.

Medicinally, mullein has been used in many countries; it is recommended for all kinds of chest complaints, sore throat, tonsillitis, asthma, children's dry coughs and hoarseness. The plant is very mucilaginous with soothing, softening and antiseptic properties. Externally an ointment or compress of mullein may be effective against piles, burns, wounds, ulcers, chilblains, skin infections, neuralgia and painful rheumatic joints. It is also mildly sedative. Dried leaves are often put in herbal cigarettes smoked to relieve asthma. Several old writers also claim that a decoction from the flowers was used as a dye to lighten the hair.

Remember, however, that before you drink or use any preparation made from mullein it is essential to strain it through a fine muslin to eliminate the tiny hairs which can cause considerable irritation inside the mouth and on the skin.

To make a decoction that is excellent for sore throats or persistent coughing put 30 g/1 oz of leaves and flowers in 1 1/2 pt of boiling water and infuse for ten minutes. Strain and use as a gargle and drink.

To make a lotion for piles, wounds etc. put 30 g/1 oz of fresh flowers plus 60 ml/2 fl oz of olive oil in a pan; macerate over a low heat, then cook until no moisture remains. Press the mixture through a muslin and store in an airtight jar.

Mullein can easily be collected from the wild (find an unpolluted spot) or grown in the garden from seed in well-drained, chalky soil in a sunny windless position. The seeds should be planted in a frame in spring and moved outside in the summer. The following year they should produce flowers and from then on they should flourish without much attention.

Collect the flowers in summer and either use fresh or dry very carefully, in a dark place at a low temperature so that they retain their colour and, therefore, their medicinal properties.

Verbascum phlomoides looks very similar but differs from great mullein in having non-decurrent leaves. However, the seeds contain traces of a poisonous saponin and, with their slightly narcotic properties, have been used by poacher anglers to intoxicate fish.

Jacob's Ladder *Polemonium caeruleum*

Arnica *Arnica montana*

Columbine *Aquilegia vulgaris* is an erect perennial, native to south and central Europe, North Africa, temperate Asia to China and also naturalized in North America. It is found growing wild in woods, damp and shady sites and hilly areas, preferring calcareous soil, and cultivated in gardens. Columbine has a blackish, often branched stock and smooth or downy, leafy, branched, flowering stems that grow to heights of 40–100 cm (16–40 in). The biternate basal leaves are long-stalked with crenate lobes; the stem leaves are short-stalked and smaller. The purplish-blue flowers have five sepals, five petals and a hooked spur. They bloom from May to July.

The generic name of the plant is probably derived from the Latin *aquila*, 'an eagle', because the spurs of the flowers were thought to resemble an eagle's talons. The common name comes from the Latin *columba*, 'a dove' or 'pigeon', because the flowers were held to resemble a flight of those birds. A favourite, old-fashioned garden, window or pot flower since the Middle Ages, columbine is mentioned in Shakespeare's *Hamlet*.

Originally used in lotions for sore mouths and throats because of its astringent properties and also, according to Culpeper, for obstructions of the liver and yellow jaundice, it is no longer used in medicine and should not be used in home-made remedies as it contains hyrocymic acid which is both poisonous and dangerous.

Jacob's Ladder *Polemonium caeruleum* is a perennial herb, native to northern and central Europe, the Caucasus, Siberia and North Africa, which has also been introduced into North America. It is found on grassy slopes and screes or in bushy places and alongside streams, also as an escape from gardens. Jacob's ladder has a short, creeping rhizome and an erect, hollow, angled, leafy stem which has glandular

hairs on the upper section and reaches heights of 30–90 cm (12–36 in). The leaves comprise numerous pairs of entire leaflets and the many blue flowers grow in tall spikes, blooming from June to August.

The generic name is derived from the Greek *polemus*, 'war', but why is unknown. The common name is a reference to the arrangement of the leaves (Genesis). Culpeper says it is under the sign of Mercury and helpful in malignant fevers and nervous complaints and it was even reputed to cure epilepsy in some cases. In north-west North America, the Thompson Indian tribe boiled the entire plant and used the resulting decoction as a hair rinse. Although it is commonly grown in gardens for its attractive flowers, Jacob's ladder is no longer used medicinally.

Jacob's ladder likes good rich soil and a sunny position in the garden.

Arnica *Arnica montana* is a perennial herb, native to central Europe, which is found in mountain pastures and woods. Arnica has a dark brown, cylindrical rhizome from which rises a flower stalk that can grow to a height of 30–60 cm (1–2 ft). The leaves form a flat rosette at the base and are arranged in opposite pairs up the hairy stem. The orange-yellow flowers are rather like daisies and they bloom from June to August.

Also known as sneezewort because the freshly crushed flowers cause sneezing, and mountain tobacco because it is used as a tobacco substitutes by mountain dwellers in central Europe, arnica has been known and used for centuries as a medicinal plant. Another one of its common names, tumblers' cure all, comes from its well-known external use as a soothing remedy for bruises, sprains and wounds. In North America the Cataulsa Indians drank the tea made from the roots of one species of arnica

to cure back pains. It is still a favourite homoeopathic treatment for sprains as well as for trauma, muscular fatigue, vertigo, seasickness and hoarseness.

It has also been used internally as a stimulant and a diuretic. It is said to activate the nervous, digestive and circulatory systems, reduce fever, clear phlegm and be useful in the treatment of gout, lumbago and sciatica. Arnica is also given to treat acute weakness of the heart because it is said to improve the supply of blood through the coronary vessels. However, it should only be taken under medical supervision as arnica can cause severe skin inflammation and if taken internally can cause dizziness, trembling or fatal poisoning. In fact the 1968 Medicines Act said that licensed herbal practitioners could only prescribe arnica for external use. As it contains such a strong and active drug, the amateur herbalist is strongly advised not to use it internally. However, externally, it is beneficial for all kinds of rheumatic and arthritic conditions and acute inflammations of the joints.

To make a tincture for external use, macerate 100 g/3–4 oz of dried flowers or roots or leaves in ½ l/1 pt of alcohol (60%) for ten days in a closed container and shake periodically. Strain through a fine muslin and store in a tinted glass bottle with a tight stopper. Dilute 1 tbsp of the tincture in ¼ l/½ pt of water and apply to bruises. Rubbed on to the scalp it is reputed to induce hair growth; added to a foot-bath, it soothes aching feet.

Arnica likes soil that is a mixture of peat, loam and sand and it can be propagated either by sowing seeds in March under a glass frame and then planting out in May or by root division in spring. The entire flowers should be gathered when in bloom during the summer and the roots should be collected in the autumn after the leaves have died down.

Golden Hop *Humulus lupulus* var. *aurea* in Mrs Verey's vegetable garden in Gloucestershire

Hop *Humulus lupulus* is a climbing herbaceous perennial, native to Europe, Asia and North America, and widely cultivated in the temperate regions of the Northern Hemisphere as well as in South America and Australia. It is found growing wild in hedgerows and thickets. Hops have a thick, fleshy root from which arise long, climbing stems that twist in a clock-wise direction to heights of 3–6 m (10–20 ft). The large, heart-shaped, deeply lobed leaves are dark green, toothed and veined. The small, yellowish-green male flowers are in loose bunches while the female flowers are contained in small, cone-like catkins which bloom from June to September. After flowering, the catkins become enlarged to form fruits – the hops used by brewers. These have resinous glands from which the bitter substance lupulin is extracted.

The generic name is possibly derived from *humus*, 'earth', alluding to the rich ground in which the plant flourishes, while the specific name *lupulus*, 'a wolf', is said to refer to the way the plant strangles as it climbs as a wolf strangles its prey. The common English name is derived from the Anglo-Saxon word *hoppan*, 'to climb'.

Hops were first mentioned by Pliny, who wrote that they were cultivated in Roman gardens as a vegetable. The young shoots were eaten in spring, like asparagus. Hops have been used in Britain since the sixteenth century for brewing beer though they were apparently used two centuries earlier in the Netherlands for the same purpose. Initially many Britons resisted the adulteration of their ale with hops and Henry VIII forbade their use but during the seventeenth century the aromatic bitter flavour which they imparted to beer and their preservative qualities were recognized. Hop growing in Britain became centred around Kent which remains a major hop-cultivating area.

Medicinally, hops have long been recognized for their sedative, calming properties. They are a good general pick-me-up tonic and help to balance the digestion. In some countries a pillow filled with hops is considered beneficial for insomnia and nervous irritation as well as toothache and earache. An infusion made from 30–60 g/1–2 oz of crumpled hop cones in ½ l/1 pt of boiling water is considered an aid to sleeplessness and useful for indigestion, jaundice, stomach and liver disorders and menstrual cramps. Applied externally, the infusion relieves neuralgic inflammation and rheumatic pains. The drug lupulin is considered mildly sedative, inducing sleep without headache and in tablet form is sometimes given to nursing mothers to promote the flow of milk.

Hops are easy to grow in gardens, even in towns and cities, and will quickly cover fences and walls. Propagation is by cuttings or suckers taken from healthy old roots and planted out in the autumn. Hops like deep, rich soil and prefer a sunny position, although they can tolerate some shade. They need to be well watered and mulched in dry weather and are not generally full bearing until the third year.

Golden Hop *Humulus lupulus* var. *aurea* is a golden-leaved variety that is especially pretty in a herb garden, though the leaves may become scorched in full sun.

Rue or **Herb of Grace** *Ruta graveolens* is an evergreen, perennial aromatic plant, native to southern Europe but found cultivated in many different countries all over the world. It is found on dry rocky slopes and limestone screes, and frequently cultivated or naturalized as a garden escape. Rue has a woody root and an erect, branched stem that reaches heights of 15–45 cm (6–18 in). The alternate, stalked leaves have three lobes, and are fleshy, blue-green, with small oil glands. The small, greenish-yellow flowers grow in clusters and bloom from July to August.

The generic name is from the Greek *reuo*, 'to set free', and thought to allude to the plant's efficacy in freeing the body from numerous diseases. The common name, herb of grace, is thought to have arisen because holy water used to be sprinkled from brushes made of rue. The use of rue goes back many centuries. The Greeks considered it useful against the witchcraft of strangers and in the Middle Ages it was used in incantations against witches. It was one of the ingredients of the famous Four Thieves' Vinegar, drunk by robbers who plundered the bodies of plague victims, yet never themselves fell prone to the infection. Rue is mentioned in Milton and Shakespeare and it was undoubtedly one of the most popular herbs in English gardens from the time the Romans introduced it into Britain.

Country people treated sick cattle with rue and it was used to ward off infection, diseases, fleas and insects.

Rue has a strong, aromatic smell and bitter taste and is used as an ingredient in grappa and

Rue or **Herb of Grace** *Ruta graveolens*

Variegated Rue *Ruta graveolens* 'Variegata'

Phytolacca clavigera

other alcoholic drinks.

Medicinally, it should only be taken under medical supervision because it has toxic properties if taken in large doses. It should also be handled with great care as it can cause dermatitis to those with sensitive skin and serious burning if the sap comes into contact with the skin in warm weather. In small doses it can be a tonic and a stimulant which aids digestion. It is said to help with menstrual difficulties but it should not be taken by pregnant women as it has abortive properties. Fresh leaves applied to the head are said to cure headaches and chewing a leaf to refresh the mouth may help to relieve tension headaches or giddiness.

To make an infusion, put 15 g/¼ oz of chopped leaves in ½ l/1 pt of boiling water. Infuse until the water is cold and strain. Drink one cupful a day – no more.

Rue can easily be grown from seeds or cuttings or root division in the garden, in the poorest of soil, but it does like sun. Space plants well to allow for bushy growth and prune in spring to prevent straggling and encourage new growth.

Variegated Rue *Ruta graveolens* 'Variegata' has very pretty cream-variegated leaves.

Pokeweed *Phytolacca americana* is a poisonous perennial plant, native to North America, found naturalized in Mediterranean countries but now cultivated in other parts of Europe. It is found among ruined buildings and on waste land. Pokeweed has a thick, tap-rooted rhizome and a smooth, hollow stem, which divides into two above the base, and grows to a height of 3 m (10 ft). The alternate leaves are ovate-lanceolate and the flowers, which have a white calyx but no petals, bloom from May to July, succeeded by distinctive long clusters of deep purple berries.

The native American tribes had long used pokeweed as an emetic and as a cure for rheumatism before it was adopted by the settlers and made official in the United States Pharmacopoeia from 1820 to 1916. Dried pokeweed root was used to relieve pain and allay inflammation, ease chronic rheumatism and treat skin parasites.

In Europe it was recognized for its slow emetic, purgative, and narcotic properties, and used for chronic rheumatism and granular conjunctivitis. Some authorities have also claimed its usefulness in treating cases of breast cancer.

The beautiful purple dye which can be extracted from the roots is sometimes used to colour wines and liqueurs and the young, pale shoots are delicious eaten as an asparagus-type vegetable. However, never eat the mature stems, berries or leaves as they contain phytolaccin, a slow-working but powerful emetic.

Pokeweed should only be taken internally under proper medical supervision.

Phytolacca clavigera has large green leaves and spikes of pale pink flowers which bloom in July and August, succeeded by maroon berries. The root is purgative and sometimes used to treat throat infections but it should only be taken if prescribed by a medical practitioner.

Pokeweed *Phytolacca americana*

Caper Spurge *Euphorbia lathyrus*

Golden Creeping Jenny *Lysimachia nummularia* 'Aurea'

Caper Spurge *Euphorbia lathyrus* is a biennial herbaceous plant, native to southern Europe as far east as Greece and as far north as France and Britain, but doubtfully native to central Europe. It is commonly found growing as an escape anywhere from coastal areas to lower mountain slopes. Caper spurge has a tap-root and an erect, hollow stem, branched at the top, which reaches a height of 1 m (40 in). The lance-shaped leaves are pointed with a smooth edge. The flowering head consists of a cluster of two to six rayed flowers, with lance-shaped bracts, which bloom from June to August.

The milky juice collected from cuts made in the fleshy branches is very bitter. Although it has been used as a depilatory, it has a revulsive effect. The leaves cause blistering and were used by beggars to induce ulcers and thus incite pity. The seeds of caper spurge yield a fine clear oil called Oil of Euphorbia which is a violent purgative and can cause severe poisoning; it is no longer used. The root of the plant is an emetic and a purgative, as are the seeds, which country people in France take in small quantities as a purgative. Do not use this plant unless prescribed by a qualified doctor.

Creeping Jenny or **Moneywort** *Lysimachia nummularia* is a creeping perennial, native to Europe from central Sweden and the Caucasus, which has naturalized in North America. It is found growing in moist hedgerows, damp meadows and along stream edges. Creeping Jenny has smooth, quadrangular stems that reach a length of 60 cm (24 in). The leaves are also smooth and rounded, dotted with glands and the golden cup-like flowers grow singly in the leaf axils and bloom from June to July.

The specific name comes from the Latin *nummulus*, 'money', because of the circular coin-like shape of its leaves, which also gives rise to its common name moneywort. However it is more commonly known by other names such as creeping Jenny, wandering Jenny, running Jenny and creeping Joan – all of which allude to the way it rapidly trails across the ground. Another of its names, strings of sovereigns, is probably in reference to its large, golden flowers.

Creeping Jenny was traditionally reputed to have many virtues. Old herbalists thought it one of the best wound herbs. An ointment or compress made from the fresh leaves was applied externally to wounds or sores, and a decoction of fresh leaves was thought to alleviate internal bleeding. Boiled with wine or honey, it was considered a good specific for whooping cough. Boerhaave, the Dutch physician, recognizing the anti-scorbutic properties in its leaves, recommended them, dried and powdered, to ward off scurvy.

Creeping Jenny very rarely produces fruit, but propagates by its creeping stolons that trail over-ground. It thrives very well in a herb garden if planted in a damp place and the whole herb should be collected in June, either for immediate use or to dry and store for use in the winter.

Golden Creeping Jenny *Lysimachia nummularia* 'Aurea' is a lovely golden leaved variety.

Kidney-vetch or **Ladies' Fingers** *Anthyllis vulneraria* is an erect or low-lying perennial, native to Europe and North Africa, and naturalized in North America. It is found in dry or calcareous soil in hilly areas and on sea cliffs. Kidney-vetch has a spindle-shaped root stock and a downy stem that grows to 1 m (40 in) long. The lower leaves are simple; the upper ones, arranged in pairs of leaflets, are narrow

Kidney-vetch or Ladies' Fingers *Anthyllis vulneraria*

Variegated Lemon Balm *Melissa officinalis* 'Variegata'

Golden Lemon Balm *Melissa officinalis* 'Aurea'

and spear-shaped – the terminal ones being broader and larger than the rest. The red or yellow flowers are clustered into heads and bloom from April to September.

Containing saponin, tannin and mucilage, kidney-vetch has soothing and astringent properties which are used in medicine for healing wounds, relieving coughs and as a laxative. Because the plant dries so well, it is also frequently used in dried flower arrangements.

Not generally grown in herb gardens.

Lemon Balm *Melissa officinalis* is a sweet-scented perennial herb, native to southern Europe but introduced and naturalized elsewhere many centuries ago, which is found in moist, waste places from coastal plains to mountainous areas. Lemon balm has a short rhizome and erect, branched, downy stems that reach heights of 30–60 cm (12–24 in). The light-green, ovate to heart-shaped leaves are deeply veined and downy with toothed margins and they give off a strong lemony odour when bruised. The white, yellowish or pinkish flowers grow in small, loose bunches in the leaf axils and bloom from June to October.

The generic name is derived from the Greek *melissa*, 'a honeybee' because the flowers are very attractive to bees, which produce extremely good honey from them.

Lemon balm has been used for centuries for medicinal and culinary purposes. The Romans introduced it to Britain and it became an important plant in the monastic apothecary garden. Avicenna and Paracelsus both recommended it for its ability to 'make the heart merry' and revive the spirits. Lemon balm has anti-spasmodic, soothing and sedative properties and it is often an ingredient in herbal teas for promoting relaxation and sleep. It is also recommended for colic, vomiting, poor digestion, palpitations, menstrual cramps, vertigo and feverish complaints. Weiss reports that experiments with spirits of melissa showed that it acts on the limbic system in the brain which is the part that governs the autonomic functions and protects the cerebrum from excessive external stimuli; thus supporting the long-held belief in the efficacy of lemon balm for the treatment of autonomic nervous disorders such as loss of bladder control arising from diseases like multiple sclerosis or motor-neurone disease.

Lemon balm is also used in making perfumes, toilet waters and liqueurs. In cooking it is added to fish and poultry dishes, herb sauces and marinades. It can also be used to flavour jams, jellies, custards and fruit salads and the fresh leaves can be added to any salad or vegetable dish for a refreshing and invigorating lemony flavour.

Lemon balm is particularly good combined with peppermint; 1 teaspoon of each in a cup of hot (not boiling) water will ease a nervous stomach and induce sleep.

Lemon Balm Tisane. Add 30 g/1 oz of leaves or flowering tips to ½ l/1 pt of boiling water. Infuse for five minutes and drink sweetened with honey. It is said to promote longevity.

Lemon Balm Cordial for indigestion. Take 15 g/½ oz each of the following herbs: Lemon balm, basil, hyssop, mint, sage, wormwood and angelica root and macerate for fifteen days in 1½ l/3 pt of spirit or alcohol (45°). Strain and store in tightly stoppered bottles. (From *Grandmother's Secrets* by Jean Palaiseul)

Lemon balm can easily be grown from seeds, divisions or cuttings. Plant in any soil in early spring, allowing room for the lower leaves to develop fully. Keep well-weeded. Harvest the leaves two or three times in the summer but use the first cutting for drying and storage as on subsequent cuttings the leaves will be smaller.

Variegated Lemon Balm *Melissa officinalis* 'Variegata' has pretty golden-variegated leaves that can be used in the same way as lemon balm.

Golden Lemon Balm *Melissa officinalis* 'Aurea' is a lovely golden-leaved variety that makes a good border plant.

Pellitory-of-the-Wall *Parietaria diffusa*

Goat's Rue or **French Lilac** *Galega officinalis*

Pellitory-of-the-Wall *Parietaria diffusa* is a herbaceous perennial, native to southern and western Europe as far north as southern Britain, which grows wild on rocks and old walls, in hedgebanks and stony waste land. Pellitory-of-the-wall has an elongated rhizome from which arise several reddish, brittle stems that grow to heights of 30–60 cm (12–24 in). The ovate to lanceolate leaves are smooth and veined above, downy below, and the tiny green, stalkless flowers grow in compact whorls in the leaf axils and bloom from June to October.

The generic name is derived from the Latin *paries*, 'a wall', alluding to the fact that walls are one of its favourite habitats; the common English name as well as deriving ultimately from *paries*, also refers to this.

In the Middle Ages pellitory-of-the-wall was widely used to treat a number of ills but in this century only a few herbalists and country folk who have learnt of its medicinal tradition still continue to use it. Related to and almost as common as the nettle (though without the sting), it may prove efficacious in treating problems of the urinary tract: urinary calculus, stone in the bladder or kidney, dropsy, cystitis, nephritis and oedema. Externally poultices or compresses of the fresh leaves have a soothing effect on scalds and burns.

The young plant can be used as a salad ingredient but hayfever sufferers should note that pellitory pollen is one of the earliest and most active of the hayfever pollens: get someone else to do the collecting!

To make an infusion for treating urinary problems, add 30 g/1 oz to ½ l/1 pt of boiling water, leave for five to ten minutes then strain and drink a wineglassful between meals.

Gather from the wild and use fresh if possible, as it loses most of its efficacy unless dried very quickly.

Goat's Rue or **French Lilac** *Galega officinalis* is an erect perennial, native to Europe from Italy eastwards and introduced to many other areas. It is often found growing wild on roadsides, in moist waste places and by ponds and streams and also widely cultivated in gardens. Goat's rue is a stout plant with erect, striate stems that grow to heights of 60–150 cm (24–60 in). The pinnate leaves have six to eight pairs of bright green lance-shaped leaflets with an odd terminal leaflet on short stalks. The white, lilac or pinkish-purple flowers in axillary racemes bloom from June to August.

Recommended by old herbalists for fever and the plague because of its ability to promote sweating, it was also considered a good remedy for worms and serpents' bites. In the early nineteenth century attention was drawn to the fact that the flow of cow's milk increased by up to 50 per cent when the cattle had goat's rue as fodder. Weiss recommends it as a lactagogue, claiming that it not only increases the amount of milk produced but also the proportion of milk solids so that the quality as well as the volume remains high. The plant also has a high level of nitrogen which makes it a valuable plant food when ploughed back into the soil. The juice extracted from goat's rue contains a chemical compound known as galegin which reduces the level of sugar in the blood. Used fresh, it will clot milk so it is sometimes used in cheese-making.

Goat's rue can easily be grown from seed. It is happy in ordinary soil on open borders with plenty of moisture. Gather the whole plant in late summer and dry for winter use. To increase the sturdy growth of the plant, cut back in October.

Valerian or **All Heal** *Valeriana officinalis* is an erect, perennial plant, native to Europe and northern Asia, which has become naturalized in North Americá and is cultivated for medicinal use in central and eastern Europe. It grows wild in rough, bushy places by streams, ditches and marshy thickets and sometimes in drier soils. Valerian has a short rhizome, many bundles of hollow rootlets and a grooved, hollow stem that grows to heights of 50–150 cm (20–60 in). The bright green, opposite, pinnate leaves are lance-shaped with either a smooth or toothed margin; the lower ones on long stalks. The numerous clusters of pale pink flowers bloom from June to August.

The generic name derives either from Valerius who was thought to be the first person to have used the plant medicinally, or from the Latin *valere*, 'to be in health', alluding to its medicinal properties.

Valerian has been used medicinally for centuries. Hippocrates recommended it in the fourth century BC and it was a constituent of the recipes for leeching used by Anglo-Saxon herbalists. Its traditional common name All Heal is indicative of the high esteem in which it was held during the Middle Ages, when it was widely grown in monastery gardens and used as a spice and as a perfume. Roots were laid among clothes to scent them. Although the scent no longer appeals generally today, in parts of Asia, other species of valerian are still used in the manufacture of scents and ointments.

Valerian is a very powerful medicinal drug. Although the exact mechanism of its action is not fully understood, it has long been recognized as having powerful sedative, anti-depressant and anti-spasmodic properties. Its usefulness in cases of epilepsy was first recognized in the sixteenth century by Fabius Calumna, who cured himself with it, and it has been prescribed ever since for all kinds of nervous disorders – hysteria, St Vitus's dance, vertigo, migraine, palpitations, insomnia, stomach cramps, etc. It reduces pain, induces sleep and minimizes feelings of stress and strain. However, large doses should not be repeated too often as it can cause headaches and stupor. Valerian also has an extraordinary effect on the nervous system of some animals, particularly cats and rats. It has been suggested that possibly the Pied Piper of Hamelin had valerian roots in his pockets which made the rats follow him irresistibly, plunging to their deaths in the River Weser!

In medieval times it was recommended for several other complaints. Culpeper writes: 'The decoction of this herb takes away pains on the sides, provokes women's courses, and is used in antidotes; the root boiled with licorice, raisins and aniseed, is good for difficulty of breathing, coughs and to expectorate phlegm, and clear the passages. If boiled in wine and drunk, it is good for venomous bites and stings; it helps to drive wind from the belly and is of excellent property to heal inward sores or wounds and for outward cuts or wounds, and driving away splinters or thorns from the flesh.' Long before Europeans colonized North America, certain Indian tribes used a native species of valerian to heal cuts and wounds. A cold valerian tea will calm nerves, ease tension and headaches and soothe digestive upsets caused by emotional stress; it can also be used as a lotion to soothe skin rashes and swollen joints or veins.

Soak 10 g/⅓ oz of root in 100 ml/4 fl oz of cold water for at least twelve hours. Strain and drink two or three cups a day for general nervous disorders or take one cup an hour before bedtime to promote sleep.

Several other decorative valerians are grown in gardens but only *Valeriana officinalis* has the full medicinal properties. It will grow in any soil but if grown from seed there is only a 50 per cent success rate so it is better to propagate it by root division. The young plants probably won't flower the first year and the roots shouldn't be harvested until their second autumn. Cut the flowering tops in spring and summer to encourage rhizome growth. As the roots dry, the characteristically bitter, rather disagreeable odour will increase and this, together with the whitish or yellowish internal colour of the roots differentiates it from other, similar drugs.

Scopolia *Scopolia carniolica* is a poisonous perennial herb, native to central and south-eastern Europe, which has been introduced into North America and is found on damp, stony hillsides. Scopolia has a fleshy, curved horizontal rhizome and smooth simple or branched stems which reach a height of 30 cm (12 in). The lower leaves are thin, oblong, and scale-like, the upper ones elliptical to egg-shaped. The flowers are dark, brownish-violet outside, yellowish to brownish-green inside, and they bloom from April to May.

Similar in its constituents to belladonna, scopolia contains hyoscine and is used extensively in the United States for making belladonna plasters. Its medicinal properties are narcotic and very similar to belladonna and it has been used in the treatment of mania, hysteria and drug addiction. At the beginning of the twentieth century, it was used as a form of anaesthetic, in combination with morphine, and known as Twilight Sleep. It causes loss of memory and pain, but fell into disuse as the effects were unpredictable and often fatal.

This plant should never be taken unless prescribed by a medical practitioner, as it can produce alarming toxic symptoms.

Valerian or **All Heal** *Valeriana officinalis*

Scopolia *Scopolia carniolica*

Selfheal *Prunella vulgaris*

Cut-leaved Selfheal *Prunella lacinata*

Large Selfheal *Prunella grandiflora*

Selfheal *Prunella vulgaris* is a small, herbaceous perennial native to southern Europe, temperate Asia, North Africa, North America and Australia, and commonly found growing wild in grassland, woodland clearings and waste places. Selfheal has a short, twisted root and numerous rootlets. The slender, downy, erect stems reach heights of 10–30 cm (4–12 in). The oval or diamond-shaped opposite leaves have smooth or slightly indented margins; the lower ones stalked, the upper ones not. The purple or violet flowers are like lips and arranged in a short compact flower spike. They bloom from June to November.

The generic name is supposedly derived from the German *die Breaüne* which then became *brunellan* and then *Prunella* referring to quinsy or inflammation of the throat which the plant is reputed to be so good at healing. Brunella was the medieval Latin name for tonsillitis. The common name denotes that he who is ill may cure himself by using this plant.

According to Cole, a seventeenth century writer who favoured the Doctrine of Signatures, the throat-shaped flowers of selfheal indicated that it was especially good for throat problems.

Recommended by Gerard and Culpeper as a wound herb, selfheal does have astringent properties and is still much used in modern medicine for sore throats, mouth ulcers, piles and internal bleeding. An infusion is also considered a good general tonic.

Large Selfheal *Prunella grandiflora* has larger flowers and is often grown as a garden plant.

Cut-leaved Selfheal *Prunella lacinata* has creamy white flowers, occasionally tinged violet, and cut leaves.

Rock-rose *Helianthemum nummularium* synonym *Helianthemum chamaecistus* is an undershrub, native to Europe and western Asia, which is found growing on grassland and scrub. Rock-rose has a woody stock and a vertical tap-root with procumbent or ascending branches that reach heights of 5–30 cm (2–12 in). The oblong leaves are green above and white-hairy below, and the bright yellow flowers, which grow in a loose cluster, bloom from May to September.

Rock-rose *Helianthemum nummularium*

The generic name comes from the Greek words *helios*, 'sun' and *anthos*, 'flower', alluding to the fact that the flowers only open in the sunshine. The Rock-rose was one of Dr Bach's Twelve Healers – plants that he believed would help to cure physical diseases brought on by a person's psychological condition. He recommended rock-rose for the following: 'Emergencies, sudden illness or accident, for very great fear, terror, panic, hysteria, when life is despaired of, for the horror and dread of nightmares, when there has been a close encounter with evil. Symptoms may include paralysis, unconsciousness, sudden deafness, dumbness, icy coldness, trembling, loss of control.'

Love-in-a-Mist *Nigella damascena* is an annual herb, native to southern Europe, and sometimes naturalized, which is cultivated in gardens for ornament and for its aromatic seeds. Love-in-a-mist reaches a height of 45 cm (18 in) and has spirally arranged, bipinnate leaves and lovely blue flowers that bloom from June to July, succeeded by seeds in a globular capsule.

The seeds of this plant and a similar species *Nigella sativa*, found more commonly in Asia, have a strong, aromatic odour and a spicy taste and are used as a condiment or spice to flavour cakes, breads and curries. In India, they also put them among clothes and bed-linen to repel moths and Indian doctors consider the seeds to be a stimulant, an aid to menstruation and milk-flow in nursing mothers. They are also used medicinally to relieve digestive upsets and bowel complaints.

Easily grown from seed, it makes a very attractive garden plant.

Love-in-a-Mist *Nigella damascena*

Digitalis ferruginea at Kew Gardens

White Foxglove *Digitalis purpurea* 'Alba'

'fox's glove' but another interpretation is that it is a corruption of 'folksglove', meaning the glove of the good folks or fairies who, like the flowers, lived in woody dells. Other common names are Fairy's Glove, Fairy's Cap, Fairy Thimbles, Witches Gloves, Bloody Fingers and Dead Men's Bells; the last three no doubt alluding to the plant's highly poisonous properties.

Purple foxglove does not seem to be among the herbs used by the ancients but from the sixteenth century it was recommended by Gerard, Parkinson, Dodoens and Culpeper for a variety of ailments such as sores, ulcers and fresh wounds. It was not until 1785, when Dr Withering published *An Account of the Foxglove*, that its use as a treatment for heart problems was recognized. Apparently Withering had been asked his opinion about a recipe for dropsy kept secret by an old Shropshire woman who seemed to have effected some dramatic cures with it. Withering wrote: 'This medicine was composed of twenty or more different herbs; but it was not very difficult for one conversant in these subjects to perceive that the active herb could be none other than foxglove.' After a detailed study of numerous cases Withering was convinced of the efficacy of foxglove in the treatment of dropsy, particularly when associated with heart disease, but he also cautioned against large doses or prolonged use – a caution that was not always heeded and doubtless quite a number of patients died from injudicious use of the plant.

Modern research has confirmed Withering's claims and a clearer understanding of the chemical construction of the plant has enabled scientists to understand the way the plant works. Its cardiotonic activity is due to various glycosides it contains which increase the tone of the cardiac muscle, causing the heart to be more effectively emptied and slowing and strengthening the heartbeat. However it is also recognized as a highly toxic drug and sustained use causes severe digestive upsets and dangerously lowers the blood pressure. It should never be taken unless prescribed by a physician. Purple foxglove has also been effectively used in cases of pneumonia and dropsy.

Purple foxglove is easily found in the wild and it is also grown in gardens for ornament, although children should be cautioned about its dangers. Fortunately, the unpleasant smell and taste of the leaves acts as a natural deterrent to its consumption. It can be grown from seed and likes light, well-drained soil and some shade. The seeds should be sown in April and it will produce leaves the first year but not flowers until the second year. It is a great favourite with bees and small insects.

Woolly or Austrian Foxglove *Digitalis lanata* is found in south-eastern Europe and cultivated extensively for the pharmaceutical industry. It has largely replaced the use of *Digitalis purpurea* in the commercial market because of its greater potency.

Yellow Foxglove *Digitalis lutea* is a smooth or slightly hairy perennial found in western and central Europe. Its flowers are whitish or pale yellow. It has similar medicinal properties to *Digitalis purpurea*.

Digitalis ferruginea is a perennial or biennial plant found in southern Europe, in woods and scrubland. The flowers are reddish or yellowish-brown, veined.

Common or Purple Foxglove *Digitalis purpurea* is an erect, biennial or occasionally perennial plant, native to western and central Europe, as far south as Sardinia but not in Italy or Switzerland and also naturalized in North America and many other countries. It commonly grows wild in light dry soil in woods, clearings, heaths, mountain slopes and is also cultivated for ornament and for medicinal purposes. Purple foxglove has a simple, greyish, often finely-hairy stem that reaches heights of 50–150 cm (20–60 in). The large, ovate to lance-shaped leaves are long-stemmed, green and somewhat hairy above, grey and downy below. The tall stem bears many purple, pale pink or white bell-shaped flowers, with spots inside, that bloom from June to July.

The generic name comes from the Latin *digitabulum*, 'a thimble', in reference to the shape of its flowers, while the specific name alludes to their purple colour. The generally held belief is that the common name is from

Common or **Purple Foxglove** *Digitalis purpurea* in a disused coalpit in Wales

Woolly or **Austrian Foxglove** *Digitalis lanata*

Yellow Foxglove *Digitalis lutea*

Prickly Restharrow *Ononis spinosa*

Toadflax, Eggs and Butter or **Eggs and Bacon** *Linaria vulgaris*

Eyebright *Euphrasia rostkoviana* synonym *Euphrasia officinalis*

Prickly Restharrow *Ononis spinosa* is an erect or ascending perennial, native to Europe, Asia and North Africa, which is found in rough, grassy places or dry, stony ground, especially in chalky areas. Prickly restharrow is woody at the base but very branched and spiny on the stems, which grow to heights of 30–60 cm (12–24 in). The leaves consist of three small leaflets with short stalks and the pretty pink flowers bloom from June to September.

The generic name comes from the Greek *onos*, 'an ass', alluding to the fact that it is one of the favourite foods of that animal. Its specific name refers to the prickly spines that grow up its stems and the common name, restharrow, arose from the fact that it is so tough it arrests the progress of the plough. One tradition has it that this was the plant out of which Christ's crown of thorns was plaited.

Medicinally, it has a long history of use as a diuretic and has been recommended for the treatment of cystitis, engorgement of the prostate and bladder stone. Weiss reports that opinion has differed as to the effectiveness of prickly restharrow as a diuretic. Experiments show that the plant's efficacy depends on the root's saponin content, which is in turn dependent on the type of soil in which the plant grows. Also the root contains a volatile element which has diuretic properties that are lost when a decoction of the plant is made. Only an infusion will have an effective diuretic result.

Prickly restharrow is sometimes grown in cottage gardens as a decorative border plant and the flowers make a pretty addition to salads; it is also grown as a major field crop in the USSR.

Not generally grown in herb gardens.

Toadflax, Eggs and Butter, Eggs and Bacon *Linaria vulgaris* is a perennial plant, native to Europe and western Asia but also naturalized in North America. It grows wild in hedgerows, waste ground, grassy meadows and fields, favouring shady or gravelly soil. Toadflax has a small creeping rhizome with several rootlets and slender, erect stems that reach heights of 30–75 cm (12–30 in). The stalkless leaves are long, narrow and bluish-green in colour, with an irregularly toothed margin, and the dense spikes of pretty yellow and orangey flowers are similar to the snapdragon and flower from July to October.

The generic name is derived form the Latin *linum*, 'flax', because the leaves resemble those of flax. Part of its common name also alludes to this. The reference to toads derives either from the supposed resemblance of the flowers to little toads or from the fact that toads were thought to shelter under the branches of the plant. The common names eggs and butter or eggs and bacon refer to the two-tone colour of the flowers.

In times past a golden yellow dye was extracted from the plant for dyeing clothes and in Sweden the plant used to be boiled in milk and left to stand where flies were troublesome, country folk believing it to be an effective fly poison.

Medicinally, it has astringent, purgative and diuretic properties. Old herbalists believed it to be excellent for dropsy and also recommended it for jaundice, liver complaints, skin diseases and scrofula. The fresh plant was used either as a compress for healing piles or made into an ointment for sores, ulcers and wounds and the distilled water was considered a good remedy for eye irritation.

Toadflax can be gathered wild or easily cultivated in a herb garden, preferably in dry soil. Seeds can be sown in spring or the plant propagated by root division in the autumn. The

Centaury *Centaurium erythraea*

Rupturewort *Herniaria glabra*

plant should be gathered just when it is coming into flower and either used fresh or dried for winter use.

Eyebright *Euphrasia rostkoviana* synonym *Euphrasia officinalis* is an annual plant, native to Europe and north and west Asia, which is found on heaths, pastures and chalky hills. Eyebright is a small plant with a creeping woody root and wiry, slender, branched, erect stems that grow to heights of 10–40 cm (4–16 in). The deeply cut, jagged leaves are dark green and generally lance-shaped. The white or lilac flowers are purple-veined with yellow centres and bloom from June to September.

The generic name is derived from the Greek *Euphrosyne*, 'gladness', the name of one of the three Graces and presumably a reference to the gladness this plant brings when it relieves those suffering from poor eyesight. The same word is also given to the linnet, which, according to Greek fables, used eyebright to clear the sight of its young and passed on this knowledge to mankind. Despite its Greek name there does not appear to be any reference to this plant in ancient writings but from the Middle Ages it was frequently recommended as an effective remedy for eye disorders. Its French and German common names, *casse-lunette* and *angentrost* confirm that in these countries it was used for the same purpose. As well as being widely used for eye ailments, eyebright was also said to strengthen the head, eyes and memory and be an effective remedy against head colds and hayfever as well as being a digestive tonic.

To make an infusion that can be either drunk or used as an eyebath, steep 30 g/1 oz of the dried herb in ½ l/1 pt of boiling water for several minutes. Strain and drink it or bathe the eyes with it three to four times a day.

As eyebright is a semi-parasitic plant, relying on the roots of other plants for part of its nourishment, it can be difficult to cultivate

unless it is surrounded by grass and other plants off which it can feed. Eyebright is best collected in July and August when it is in full flower. Either use fresh or dry and store in a dark place for future use.

Centaury *Centaurium erythraea* synonym *Erythraea centaurium* is a smooth annual, native to Europe, North Africa and south-western Asia, which is naturalized in North America. It is commonly found growing in dry grassland, on dunes, cliff edges, along wood margins and on mountain slopes, favouring chalk or limestone. Centaury has a fibrous, woody root and one or several stiff, erect stems that branch at the top and reach heights of 5–50 cm (2–20 in). The basal leaves are wedge-shaped, smooth, shiny and prominently veined; the stalkless stem leaves are narrower, more lance-shaped and grow in opposing pairs at distant intervals on the stalk. The clusters of pretty, star-like flowers are rose-coloured and bloom from July to September.

The generic name is derived from the Greek centaur, Chiron, who was reputed to have used this plant to cure himself of an arrow wound Hercules accidentally inflicted on him. The specific name is derived from the Greek *erythros*, 'red', alluding to the colour of the flowers.

Centaury flowers are very sensitive to light, opening only in fine weather, and not until midday, and closing up as evening falls. The ancients believed the plant had magical powers and it was hailed, exaggeratedly, as a universal purifier. However, it is still recognized as a tonic, an aid to digestion, beneficial for liver and kidney disorders, and a treatment for intermittent fever (hence its Saxon name, feverwort).

Weiss feels that centaury has an important role to play where there is a general weakness and lack of tone in the digestive system and also for loss of appetite. The bitter principle

contained in the plant positively stimulates the gastric juices and has a general tonic and stimulant effect on the whole body. To be effective, treatment should be continued for some time, but an infusion drunk before meals will, over a period of several days, help to improve the appetite. He recommends it for cases of anorexia (along with psychotherapy in extreme cases). Make an infusion 30 g/1 oz of flowering tips in 1 l/2 pt of boiling water, leave for ten minutes, then strain and sweeten (as it is rather bitter) and drink three cupfuls a day before meals. For external use on varicose veins, wounds, and to prevent hairloss, make a decoction 60 g/2 oz flowering tops boiled for a few minutes in 1 l/2 pt of water and apply as a lotion or on a compress.

Rupturewort *Herniaria glabra* is an annual to short-lived perennial herb, native to western, central and southern Europe, North Africa and Asia and introduced into North America. It grows in sandy fields and pastures or on dry paths, byways and between paving. Rupturewort has a tap-root and numerous low-lying stems that reach a length of 30 cm (12 in). The stems are smooth or slightly hairy and green with short alternate branchlets. The ovate to lance-shaped leaves are tiny and the minute, green flowers which grow in axillary clusters and crowd along the stems intermixed with the leaves, bloom from May to October.

It is known medicinally for its antispasmodic effect on the urinary tract. The leaves and flowering stems are made into an infusion (which must not be boiled) to treat inflammation of the bladder, kidney stones and prostate gland. However, Weiss points out, the plant must be used fresh or it loses its effectiveness.

Grown in a herb garden, in ordinary soil, in sun or shade, rupturewort provides a useful evergreen ground cover.

Feverfew *Tanacetum parthenium* synonym *Chrysanthemum parthenium*

Feverfew *Tanacetum parthenium* grown for medicinal research at Chelsea Physic Garden

Feverfew *Tanacetum parthenium* synonym *Chrysanthemum parthenium* is a strongly aromatic annual to perennial herb, probably native to south-eastern Europe but now found throughout Europe and North and South America. It is found in hedgerows, walls, waste ground and rocky places, usually as an escape from gardens. Feverfew has an erect, furrowed, downy stem that reaches a height of 25–60 cm (10–24 in). The yellowish-green leaves are divided into ovate, pinnate leaflets with toothed margins. The flowerheads are small, numerous and daisy-like, with yellow centres and white rays, and they bloom from May to November.

The common name of this plant is an allusion to its fever-reducing properties and it has been used medicinally for centuries as a general tonic for nervous and hysterical complaints and a treatment for arthritis. The aromatic leaves are sometimes used in cooking to impart a distinctly bitter flavour. An infusion made from adding 30 g/1 oz of leaves to ½ l/1 pt of boiling water, straining and cooling was recommended for pain relief to those suffering from facial aches, earache and rheumatism. As a poultice, it was used to reduce bruising and applied to insect bites, stings and swellings for instant relief. Some people believe that sponging exposed areas of skin with a strong infusion of feverfew repels insects. As early as 1772 the herbalist J. Hill was writing of feverfew: 'in the worst headache there is no more efficacious remedy'.

In recent years feverfew has been exciting much interest in medical circles as research has gradually established that it can bring relief to some migraine sufferers. Two doctors in Britain, P. J. Hylands and E. P. Thomas, and others in America have conducted small clinical trials which have shown that feverfew has a potent physiological effect – perhaps acting on substances such as histamine, bradykinin, prostaglandins and others which are believed to be the cause of migraine attacks. More controlled clinical studies are needed to understand how it works and why feverfew is so useful but many sufferers are finding it a life-saver. Regular migraine sufferers have found that taking feverfew daily decreases the number and severity of their attacks over several months. The traditional method of taking the herb is to eat about one to four fresh leaves daily. However, the bitter taste makes it very unpalatable to some and occasionally it may cause a slight allergic reaction to sensitive skin, resulting in mouth ulcers. For this reason, the leaves are usually eaten sandwiched between bread, or taken in readily available capsule form.

In order to keep a good supply of leaves during the winter months, a syrup can be made. Boil sugar and water to make a syrup, then cool and add fresh leaves. Alternatively chop fresh leaves and root into honey – it acts as both a preservative and a palliative. Fresh leaves can also be frozen in ice for later use.

Feverfew can be either collected from the wild or easily grown from seed. Sow the seeds under glass in March, then plant out in early June in well-drained soil, preferably in a sunny position, although it thrives well almost anywhere and will self-seed very freely.

Note: feverfew was traditionally considered useful for regularizing menstruation so it is probably best avoided by pregnant women.

Double Feverfew *Tanacetum parthenium* 'Flore Pleno'

Golden Feverfew *Tanacetum parthenium* 'Aurea'

Purple Loosestrife *Lythrum salicaria*

Purple Loosestrife *Lythrum salicaria* is a perennial herb, native to European and also found in central Asia, Australia, North Africa and very commonly in North America. It is frequently grows wild in wet or marshy places, often forming large stands. Purple loosestrife has a creeping rhizome and several erect, angled, reddish-brown stems that reach heights of 60–120 cm (24–48 in). The long, lance-shaped leaves are in opposite pairs or whorls of three and the reddish-purple flowers grow in dense whorls forming a long terminal spike and bloom from June to August. Three slightly different flower forms are found, depending on the area.

The generic name is derived from the Greek *Inthron*, 'gore', alluding to the blood-like colour of the flowers, and the specific name derives either from *salix*, 'willow' (referring to their preference for growing under willows along stream or river banks) or from *Salicaria*, 'willow-like', referring to the shape of the leaves, which resemble the grey sallow.

Although not greatly used nowadays, purple loosestrife was valued by the old herbalists for relieving dysentery, diarrhoea, internal haemorrhage, excessive menstrual flow, nosebleeds and stomach pains. A more concentrated decoction was also used as a compress to relieve skin complaints such as eczema and an ointment was said to ease sores and ulcers. In fact, modern tests have proved that it does have an antibiotic effect on the typhus bacillus and dysentery amoeba.

To make a decoction for relieving diarrhoea put 30–45 g/1–1½ oz dried plant (treble the quantity of fresh plant) in 1 1/2 pt of water. Boil for five minutes, infuse for ten minutes then strain and sweeten if necessary. Take three to five small cupfuls a day between meals.

A striking addition to the garden, it is best grown in damp areas.

Figwort *Scrophularia nodosa* is a perennial herb, native to Europe and temperate Asia, and naturalized in North America. It is commonly found growing wild in damp woods, wasteland and hedgebanks. Figwort has a short, swollen, knotted rhizome and square stems that reach heights of 40–80 cm (16–32 in). The big, ovate, pointed leaves have double-toothed margins. The dingy pink flowers form a long terminal spike and bloom from June to August.

Figwort was also known as scrofula plant because, according to the 'Doctrine of Signatures' the knots or protuberances on the root looked like the enlarged lymphatic glands caused by scrofula and so it was used to treat all kinds of abscesses, wounds, gangrene and skin diseases. It is diuretic and slightly purgative; a decoction made from the whole plant is used for sprains, swellings and inflammations. In some country areas the bruised leaves are applied directly to burns and swellings.

Collect from the wild or grow it in a dampish place, and pick the flowering stalks in June or July. Dry and store in an airtight jar for winter use.

Water Figwort *Scrophularia auriculata* native to Europe is found on pond and stream edges and wet meadows and woods.

Variegated Figwort *Scrophularia nodosa* 'Variegata', is similar in every way but has the added advantage of being a very striking garden plant, with its variegated foliage.

Soapwort or **Bouncing Bet** *Saponaria officinalis* is a perennial herb, native to Europe and western Asia, which has been introduced into central and eastern Asia and North America. It is found growing by streams, roadsides and in waste places, often as a garden escape. Soapwort has a stout, branched, creeping rhizome and erect, reddish-green stems that reach heights of 30–90 cm (12–36 in). The opposite, broadly ovate leaves are pale green with veins along the length of the leaf blade. The large, pink, white or flesh-coloured flowers are grouped in small, terminal clusters and bloom from July to September.

As its common name indicates, this is a plant that has traditionally been used for cleaning.

Because of its high saponin content and its gentle lathering properties it has been used for centuries in place of soap – for washing clothes, particularly delicate fabrics, and for washing the body. It is also a very effective cleaning agent for pictures and furniture and it is used in shampoos and skin lotions.

In the past a decoction of the root was taken as an expectorant for respiratory conditions, for gout, rheumatism and jaundice. However, taken internally in large doses, soapwort may cause muscular paralysis and should only be taken under the guidance of a medical practitioner. Externally, it has been used in compresses to soothe skin complaints. Formerly, it was considered a good cure for venereal disease when mercury had failed.

To make a decoction to use either as a shampoo or skin lotion or to clean delicate fabrics, boil pieces of root in water for four to five minutes. Cool and strain.

Soapwort can be grown easily in the garden either from seed or propagated from cuttings or by root division; indeed, it can become invasive. It likes a good loamy soil and a sunny position. Dig the roots up in autumn and use fresh or dry and store.

Goat's Beard or **Jack-go-to-bed-at-noon** *Tragopogon pratensis* is an annual to perennial herb, native to Europe and the Near East and naturalized in North America. It is quite commonly found in meadows, pastures, dunes, roadsides and waste places. Goat's beard has a long, brownish, cylindrical tap-root and an erect, hollow stem that reaches heights of 30–70 cm (12–28 in). The long, narrow, grass-like leaves have distinctive white veins and the basal ones sheathe the stem. The large, yellow flowerheads, with numerous rays, grow at the end of the main flowering stems and bloom from June to July, followed by seeds in a large, feathery clock, similar to that of a dandelion.

The generic name is derived from two Greek words synonymous with Goat's beard. The other common name alludes to the plant's habit of opening its blossoms at dawn and closing

Figwort *Scrophularia nodosa* (flowers)

Water Figwort *Scrophularia auriculata*

Variegated Figwort *Scrophularia nodosa*
'Variegata'

Goat's Beard or **Jack-go-to-bed-at-noon**
Tragopogon pratensis

Soapwort or **Bouncing Bet** *Saponaria officinalis*

them again at midday.

In medieval times the roots were eaten, boiled and buttered, like parsnips, and the young stalks were eaten like asparagus. Modern research has shown that the roots of the plant are high in inulin, which gives them a delicious sweet flavour. An infusion of goat's beard petals is said to lighten freckles and the distilled water makes a good lotion for dry skin. Culpeper recommended the boiled roots for lean and consumptive types and also said that a decoction of the roots was good for heartburn and loss of appetite, while a modern herbal recommends making a syrup from the root to ease coughs and bronchitis.

It can either be collected from an unpolluted spot in the wild or easily grown in a kitchen garden.

Tree Lupin *Lupinus arboreus*

Tree Lupin *Lupinus arboreus* is an upright shrub, native to western North America and also grown in Europe for ornament and naturalized in many areas, which grows in waste places. Tree lupin can be trained to produce a branching stem that grows to a height of 3 m (10 ft). The leaves are broadly lance-shaped, smooth above and downy below, and the scented yellow or whitish flowers bloom from May to August.

The bruised seeds, soaked in water, are said to be diuretic and an emmenagogue if taken internally. Externally they are sometimes used on ulcers and sores.

Indian Physic or **American Ipecac** *Gillenia trifoliata* is a perennial herb, native to eastern North America and also cultivated in gardens in Europe and other parts of the world, which grows wild in woodlands. Indian physic has an irregular-shaped, brownish root with several erect stems that reach a height of 90 cm (36 in). The leaves are variously shaped and the white flowers with red tinges which grow in loose clusters at the end of the stems bloom from May to July.

Well-known to the American Indians as a mild but efficient emetic, Indian physic root was quickly adopted by the colonists not only for its ability to induce vomiting but also for its toxic, cathartic and expectorant qualities, and it was recommended for dyspepsia, dropsy and rheumatism.

The roots were collected in September when they were said to be at their most potent. They are not much used in modern herbalism.

Purple Coneflower *Echinacea purpurea* is a perennial herb, native to central North America, which grows in rich soil in open woods and on prairies. Purple coneflower has a stout, generally smooth stem that reaches heights of 60–150 cm (2–5 ft). The lower leaves are ovate and sometimes toothed, the upper leaves are more spear shaped and smooth edged. The

numerously rayed purple, crimson or, rarely, pale flowers bloom from July to October.

Purple coneflower has a long history of use among the American Indians. The tribes of the western plains used it to soothe all kinds of insect bites and stings and also to treat snakebite. A piece of the fresh root was chewed to alleviate toothache and one tribe used to wash their hands in a decoction of the plant to enable them to withstand heat. It is a component in many modern ointments for healing wounds.

The plant also has a reputation for increasing the body's resistance to infection and for being a good blood purifier. Advances in immunology have shown that a whole range of plants, with *Echinacea purpurea* and *Echinacea augustifolia* in the forefront, have a marked effect on the body's resistance to infectious diseases of all kinds, particularly the influenza and herpes viruses. Their action is almost equivalent to the body's own interferon, a protein produced in the body to overcome infections. The latest research has established that *Echinacea* increases interferon production in the body, thus enhancing the defence system. The hope that it might prove useful in the treatment of cancer has not yet been substantiated, however it may help to activate a certain improvement in well-being for a limited period and bring symptomatic relief.

Purple coneflower can be grown in the garden, where it favours deep, light, loamy soil and a sunny position.

Alecost or **Costmary** *Balsamita major* synonym *Chrysanthemum balsamita* is an aromatic perennial herb, native to the Orient but grown all over Europe for centuries. It grows wild along roadsides, river banks and in waste places and is extensively cultivated for ornament. Alecost has a creeping rootstock and branched, leafy stems that reach heights of 30–150 cm (12–60 in). The long slender leaves have finely toothed margins and the yellow button flowers which grow in loose clusters bloom from August to October.

The common name alecost arose from the use

of the plant as a spicy flavouring for beer or ale, and its North American name, bibleleaf, arose from the early colonists' custom of using the long, slender leaves as bookmarks in their bibles. Costmary is derived from the Latin *costus*, 'an oriental plant', and Mary alludes to the Virgin Mary with whom the plant was widely associated during the Middle Ages, (hence its French name Herbe Sainte-Marie).

Commonly found in kitchen gardens in the Middle Ages, it has largely gone out of fashion in this century. The plant has a minty smell which becomes rather lemony when cooked. The fresh leaves were added to salads and soups and used to flavour roast meat as well as home-brewed beer. The leaves, added to pot pourri, intensify the scent of other plants.

Medicinally, alecost has astringent and antiseptic properties: an infusion was drunk to relieve upset stomachs, dysentery and ague. It was said to expel worms from children and be an excellent tonic for those suffering weight loss as well as being recommended for liver and gall-bladder complaints.

To make an infusion put 15–20 g/½–1 oz of dried herb in 1 1/2 pt of boiling water. Infuse for five to ten minutes. Strain and drink two cupfuls a day.

Alecost can easily be grown in a herb garden. Propagate by root division in spring or autumn and plant in a dry, sunny position. It will thrive in any kind of soil. The creeping roots spread quickly but should be thinned every year.

Catsfoot *Antennaria dioica* is a small, stoloniferous perennial, native to Europe, Asia and North America up to the Arctic. It grows on heaths, pastures and dry mountain slopes, often over limestone or leached soil, up to 3,000 m (10,000 ft). Catsfoot has erect stems which can grow to a height of 20 cm (8 in). The basal leaves are spoon-shaped and form a rosette; while the stem leaves are alternate and lance-shaped: both have a white to grey woolly appearance. The short-stalked, white, pink or

Indian Physic or **American Ipecac**
Gillenia trifoliata

Alecost or **Costmary** *Balsamita major*

Purple Coneflower *Echinacea purpurea*

Catsfoot *Antennaria dioica*

yellow flowers form a close terminal cluster of between two and eight heads and bloom in June. The fruits are single-seeded achenes with a bristly, protruding pappus.

Also known as life everlasting or mountain everlasting, catsfoot derives its generic name from the Greek word *antenna* as the pappus hairs of the florets resemble a butterfly's antennae. Gerard refers to it as 'Live for Ever' because it can be kept fresh in the medicine chest or elsewhere for a whole year. It is used as an everlasting cut flower because it dries well and keeps its colour.

It contains tannins, essential oils, phytosterol and mucilage and it is used medicinally for its astringent properties. It is said to be efficacious for treating mumps, some poisonous reptile bites and loose bowels. It is included in many chest remedies because of its mucilage content. An infusion of 30 g/1 oz of catsfoot in ½ l/1 pt of boiling water can be used as a mouthwash or throat gargle, taken in a wine glass during the day.

Catsfoot can be found in the wild or bought at a nursery and propagated in ordinary soil, in a sunny spot, by root division. The plant is generally gathered in May before it flowers.

147

Ribbed Melilot, Yellow Melilot or **Common Melilot** *Melilotus officinalis*

Sneezewort *Achillea ptarmica*

having properties that are effective for certain specific ailments. In homoeopathic medicine ribbed melilot is prescribed for headaches arising from hypertension and menopause and herbalists recommend an infusion to relieve catarrh and ease flatulence and digestive problems. It is used by herbalists in the treatment of varicose veins and thrombophlebitis but experiments have also indicated it might be useful in the treatment of lymphoedema. The active substance coumarin which the plant contains makes it useful for culinary purposes. Dried it can be used for flavouring stews and in stuffings, particularly for rabbit. In Switzerland it is an essential ingredient in the green cheese called 'Schabzieger'. It can also be used in marinades and to flavour snuff and pipe tobacco as well as added to herbal tea mixtures and pot pourris.

Yellow melilot can be grown in a herb garden in any kind of soil but it is usually gathered from the wild.

Sneezewort *Achillea ptarmica* is a perennial herb, native to Europe, except the southern Mediterranean, Asia, Caucasus and Siberia and also found in North America. It grows in damp meadows, marshes and near streams. Sneezewort has a long, thin, fleshy root and erect, angular stems that reach heights of 20–60 cm (8–24 in) and are hairy above but smooth lower down. The long, lance-shaped leaves have sharply toothed margins and no stalks. The white flowers grow in loose clusters and bloom from June to August.

Sneezewort earned its common name from the fact that the powdered herb, taken as a snuff, induces sneezing 'and cleanses the head of tough slimy humours', according to Culpeper. The leaves were also added to salads; the root was reputed to cure toothache and infusions made from the leaves were used in a similar way to Yarrow *Achillea millefolium*.

To cultivate in a herb garden, plant in any kind of soil, in sun or shade.

Common Fleabane *Pulicaria dysenterica* is a perennial herb, native to Europe, Asia Minor and North Africa and naturalized in North America, which is commonly found growing wild in marshes, wet meadows, ditches and rivers. Common fleabane has a creeping rootstock and erect, woody stems that are branched and leafy above and reach heights of 20–60 cm (8–24 in). The oblong, woody leaves are heart-shaped at the base, clasping the stem and irregularly wavy. The bright yellow flowers bloom from July to September.

The generic name is derived from the Latin *pulex*, 'flea', because the smoke of the plant drives away fleas; the specific name refers to the plant's use in treating dysentery. The Arabians called the plant *Parajeub*, 'Job's Tears', because it was believed that Job used a decoction of common fleabane to cure his ulcers.

This plant has a rather soap-like smell and bitter, astringent medicinal properties which some herbalists rank highly. It used to be recommended, in infusion, for dysentery, skin disorders and ulcers.

Birthwort *Aristolochia clematitis* is a smooth, perennial herb, native to central and southern Europe, west to northern Asia and introduced and occasionally found in the wild in Britain and North America. It has long been cultivated as a medicinal plant and is found growing naturalized in fields, meadows, along roadsides and near old ruins. Birthwort is a foetid plant, with a long, creeping rhizome and numerous straight stems that reach a height of 25–75 cm (8–30 in).

Ribbed Melilot, Yellow Melilot or **Common Melilot** *Melilotus officinalis* is an annual, or sometimes biennial, scented plant, native throughout most of Europe and eastwards to China; naturalized in North America and elsewhere. It grows wild or naturalized by the roadside, in fields and in waste places. Ribbed melilot has a partially woody tap-root and erect, simple or sometimes branched stems that reach a height of 150 cm (60 in). The leaves are on long stalks and each consists of three narrow, pale green leaflets with finely toothed margins. The small, yellow flowers grow in slender, one-sided clusters from the leaf axils and bloom from June to September.

The generic and common names are derived from the Greek *meli*, 'honey', and *lotos*, 'lotus', alluding to the sweet-scented flowers which are so attractive to bees.

Ribbed melilot was extensively grown for cattle fodder in the eighteenth century and has been used for culinary and medicinal purposes since Egyptian times. The Egyptians used it for earache and worms and over the centuries it was credited with curing numerous ills. However, in more recent times it has been recognized as

Common Fleabane *Pulicaria dysenterica*

The large ovate-cordate leaves, 5–15 cm (2–6 in), are finely toothed and the dull yellow flowers have a roundish base and a curved tube with a long, oblong limb at the end. They bloom from May to August.

The generic name is derived from the Greek *lochos*, 'parturition' which, like its common name, refers to its long use as an aid in childbirth. It was also traditionally an emmanagogue, helping to restore menstrual flow. However, if taken in large doses the results can be dangerous, causing abortion, enteritis and vomiting and finally respiratory paralysis. Externally, a decoction has been used to treat ulcers or other skin complaints. All over the world species of *Aristolochia* have been used medicinally for centuries for bites, as tonics or stimulants, as diuretics and purgatives, as emmenagogues and for fevers, gout and neuralgia. The most famous is probably Snakeroot or Virginia Snakeroot *Aristolochia serpentaria* which North American explorers quickly learnt about from the Indian natives because, as its common name implies, it was considered particularly efficacious as an antidote to snake bites. It fame travelled so rapidly that it had entered the London Pharmacopoeia by 1650.

According to Weiss, scientific research has confirmed the plant's efficacy in strengthening the body's defence mechanism. However, experiments on animals have shown that one of its components, aristolochic acid, has carcinogenic properties, and in Germany, products containing aristolochic acid have been banned. So far, there has been no evidence of it causing cancer in humans.

Birthwort *Aristolochia clematitis*

149

Dropwort *Filipendula vulgaris*

Tansy *Tanacetum vulgare*

Dropwort *Filipendula vulgaris* synonym *Spiraea filipendula* is a perennial herb, native to Europe, Asia Minor and North Africa, where it is found on chalky soil in dry pastures or grassland. Dropwort has a short rhizome and roots bearing ovoid tubers. The stem grows to heights of 15–75 cm (6–30 in) and the feathery leaves are composed of leaflets cut into narrow serrated segments. The creamy white flowers which grow in erect, crowded, compound clusters are scentless and bloom from June to August.

According to Culpeper, dropwort roots, powdered or made into a decoction with white wine and honey, were good for kidney infections, lung diseases, wheezing and shortness of breath and were an aid to expectorating phlegm. The flowers can be used to flavour herbal beers and wines.

An excellent perennial to grow in ordinary soil in a sunny position.

Tansy *Tanacetum vulgare* synonym *Chrysanthemum vulgare* is a strong-smelling perennial, native to Europe, which has also become naturalized in North America. It is found growing wild on waste ground, by hedgerows and roadsides, and is extensively cultivated for ornament. Tansy has a creeping rootstock with many rootlets and erect, tough stems that reach heights of 30–100 cm (12–40 in). The alternate, feathery leaves are broad, finely divided and toothed and the flat clusters of yellow flowers bloom from July to September.

The common name tansy is thought to be derived from the Greek *athanatoia*, 'immortality', shortened to *thansa*, either because the flowers last so long, or because it was reputed to have been given to Ganymede to make him immortal, or because the plant was used to preserve the dead from putrefaction.

Tansy has a long history of use since ancient times when it was used at burials. In the Middle Ages it was one of the 'strewing herbs' and was especially favoured because of its reputation as an insecticide. For centuries tansy has been used medicinally to expel worms, especially in children, to keep away fleas and bed-bugs and rid dogs of fleas.

Tansy was also reputed to be an excellent tonic and stimulant to be taken in spring after the Lenten fast. It was thought to be good for failing appetite, nausea, ague, hysterical and nervous disorders, jaundice, high blood pressure and menstrual problems. However, tansy is now considered dangerous taken in large amounts as toxicosis with epileptic convulsions can occur and it can be a violent irritant to the stomach. As it is a plant used to restore the menstrual flow it should not, under any circumstances, be taken by pregnant women.

Tansy has also had a long history of culinary use. The fresh young leaves were eaten in spring, in cakes, puddings and pancakes. The hot peppery flavour of tansy which many dislike was valued in medieval times as a substitute for the expensive spices nutmeg and cinnamon. It was used to flavour custards, puddings, cakes, omelettes, fish and Irish sausages.

Tansy tea can be taken as a lotion for toothache or ear and eye swellings. Infuse 30 g/1 oz of finely chopped leaves in ½ l/1 pt of boiling water for five minutes. Strain and sweeten.

Tansy can either be picked from the wild (find an unpolluted source) or grown in a herb garden, in any kind of soil. Propagate by root division in the spring or autumn.

Tansy *Tanacetum vulgare* on the Cornish coast

Tansy *Tanacetum vulgare* var. *crispum*

Dalmatian Pyrethrum *Tanacetum cinerariifolium*

Cornflower *Centaurea cyanus*

Curled Tansy *Tanacetum vulgare* var. *crispum* is a variety with curled, bright green, fern-like leaves. It can be used in the same way as tansy.

Dalmatian Pyrethrum or **Dalmatian Pellitory** *Tanacetum cinerariifolium* synonym *Chrysanthemum cinerariifolium* is a perennial plant, native to western Yugoslavia and Albania and now grown in many parts of the world, where it may occasionally be found naturalized on rocky ground. Dalmatian pyrethrum has stems up to heights of 15–45 cm (5–18 in) and dark green, lance-shaped pinnatifid leaves. The small, white flowers bloom from May to September.

Dalmatian pyrethrum has superseded Persian pyrethrum because it was discovered to yield a more effective insecticide.

Dalmatian pyrethrum is deadly to flies but harmless to humans so it can be used as a powder or lotion to dab on the skin as a protection against insect bites. The smoke from the burnt flowers is also a useful fumigator. The flowers contain the active ingredient and they will retain their insecticidal properties indefinitely if kept carefully. The unopened but fully-developed flower buds are the most active part of the plant and fetch the highest prices. The more pollen the insect powder contains, the better the quality, and this can be tested by capturing some houseflies and putting them and some powder under a tumbler – they should be stupefied within a minute.

Easily grown from seed.

Cornflower *Centaurea cyanus* is an annual plant sometimes overwintering, which is native to Europe and western Asia. It is found wild in cornfields, by roadsides, in waste places, and as an escape, and is often cultivated in gardens for ornament.

Cornflowers have beautiful, brilliant blue flowers that are used to make an ink that is used in water-colour drawing. The dried petals are often put into pot-pourris to add colour and incorporated into dried flower arrangements. Medicinally, they have been chiefly renowned for yielding an eyewash used to treat conjunctivitis and sore eyelids.

Easily grown from seed planted in the spring.

Asian Mallow *Malva verticillata* var. *crispa*

Musk Mallow *Malva moschata*

Common Mallow or **Wild Mallow** *Malva sylvestris* is a perennial herb, native throughout Europe and introduced into North America, which is found growing wild along roadsides and in waste places. Common mallow has quite a fleshy tap-root and an erect or decumbent, sparsely haired stem that reaches heights of 40–100 cm (15–40 in). The dark green leaves are five-lobed with toothed margins and the pinkish rose-purple to bluish-mauve flowers which form small clusters in the leaf axils bloom from May to October.

The genetic name of the plant is derived from the Greek *malake*, 'soft', alluding to the softening, healing properties of this and other mallows. Common mallow has long been a favourite remedy with country people who used it when they were unable to get marsh mallow. The leaves and flowers were applied as poultices to wounds and an infusion was drunk to soothe coughs. Common mallow was also cooked and eaten as a vegetable.

Common mallow can either be picked from the wild or grown from seed in a herb garden. It likes quite damp, nitrate-rich soil and plenty of sun. If you want to harvest twice, cut it right back in late June, water well and you should get a second crop in September.

Collect the leaves and plants in June before they have come into full flower and dry quickly but thoroughly in the shade so the flowers turn a pretty blue colour. Make sure they are really dry before storing in an airtight jar, otherwise they will rot.

Musk Mallow *Malva moschata* has large rose-pink flowers clustered towards the top of the stem and a faint musky smell is given off from the leaves, particularly in warm weather, if they are run through the hand.

The white root and light green leaves have the same properties as the common mallow and are used in a similar way.

Asian Mallow *Malva verticillata* var. *crispa* is a biennial herb with curly edged leaves and whitish flowers. Native to eastern Asia, it has been introduced into Europe and is now becoming widely naturalized due to its cultivation as a salad plant.

Marsh Mallow *Althaea officinalis* is a perennial herb, native to Britain, central and southern Europe, North Africa and central Asia, which has also been introduced into North America. It is found growing wild in ditches, near the sea and on the edges of salt marshes, damp meadows and on the banks of tidal rivers, and cultivated in gardens. Marsh mallow is a pretty, decorative plant with a long, tough, fleshy, whitish, tapering root and a simple or slightly branched, velvet-haired stem which grows to heights of 60–120 cm (2–4 ft). The round, three to five lobed, irregularly toothed leaves are soft, thick and velvety with dense whitish hairs. The large, pale pink flowers grow in small clusters at the axils of the leaves and bloom during August and September, followed by the round flat fruits, commonly called 'cheeses', which contain the smooth dark seeds.

The generic name *Althaea* is derived from the Greek word *altho*, 'to cure', while the specific name *officinalis* refers to its long history of use as a medicinal plant.

According to Barbara Griggs in *Green Pharmacy*, a species of *Althaea* was among the flower pollens found scattered around the grave of a Neanderthal man who had been buried in a cave in Iraq some 60,000 years ago and she speculates that as it and six of the other pollens discovered around the grave were plants which

Marsh Mallow *Althaea officinalis*

Hollyhock *Althea rosea*

are still used for medicine by the local people today it is highly likely that they were scattered there to strengthen the dead man on his journey to the next world.

Horace and Cicero mention the laxative properties of the plant. Pliny said 'Whosoever shall take a spoonful of the Mallows shall that day be free from all diseases that may come to him'. Barbara Griggs also tells us how Henry VIII, who took a keen amateur interest in medicine, used marsh mallow as an ingredient in his 'King's Grace's oyntement', invented 'to coole and dry and comfort the member'. Most of the mallows have also been used as food and are often mentioned in the context by classical writers. Marsh mallow in particular was considered a delicacy by the Romans. Syrians, Greeks and Armenians often subsisted for weeks on the abundantly available marsh mallow when cultivated crops failed. In France the young tops and tender leaves are eaten raw in spring salads to stimulate the kidneys.

Marsh mallow is valued particularly for its high mucilage content, present throughout the plant but particularly in the root; it has special softening and healing properties for which it has been used down the ages. It is used internally to soothe irritation and inflammation caused by coughs, colds, bronchitis, sore throats, stomach ulcers, constipation or cystitis.

Externally it is used as a gargle for sore throats, tonsillitis, dental abscesses, gingivitis and sinusitis. An old-fashioned remedy for teething babies and toddlers is to give them a stick of marsh mallow to suck.

To make a tea take 30 g/1 oz of finely chopped root, leaves or seeds and steep in *cold* water for eight hours, strain and heat to lukewarm. Drink three or four times a day.

Common Mallow or **Wild Mallow** *Malva sylvestris*

If you can find marsh mallow in the wild, take stem cuttings from old plants and put into a good rich layer of soil. They should grow well. Alternatively you can grow them from seed in March or April, July or August.

Leaves and flowers should be cut in the summer just before they bloom. Pick on a fine day after the dew has dried; if cut when damp they blacken and spoil. The roots should be harvested in autumn and cleaned by brushing or scraping (not washing) and then dried.

Hollyhock *Althea rosea* is a biennial to perennial herb thought to be a native of China which was introduced into Europe in the sixteenth century and is now widely naturalized. It is cultivated in gardens or found growing as a garden escape. Hollyhock has a stout, erect, hairy stem that

grows up to 3 m (10 ft). The long-stalked, roundish to heart-shaped leaves, 30 cm (12 in) across, are lobed, crenate and hairy. The clusters of flowers, which vary from white to yellow, red or dark purple, form a long irregular spike and bloom from June to August.

As well as being grown for its ornamental value, hollyhock can be used medicinally as a substitute for marsh mallow. It has similar soothing and diuretic properties which make it particularly useful for coughs and some chest complaints. It is also used as a mouthwash for ulcers and a lotion to remove redness or blotching on the face. The purple flowers yield a dye which was formerly used for colouring wine but new chemical substitutes have now, sadly, taken their place.

Easily grown from seed, in any soil.

Evening Primrose *Oenothera erythrosepala*

Evening Primrose *Oenothera erythrosepala* is a perennial herb probably introduced into Europe, and a member of the rather confused evening primrose genus which is native to North America. It grows wild by roadsides, in waste places, fields, dunes and railway banks and is often cultivated in gardens. Evening primrose has a large, fleshy rootstock and erect, leafy, hairy stems with red bulbous bases that reach heights of 50–100 cm (20–40 in). The stalked, basal leaves are ovate-lanceolate, crinkled and distantly toothed, the stem leaves hardly stalked with a white, sometimes reddish, midrib. The large, fragrant, yellow flowers grow singly in the leaf axils to form a terminal spike and bloom from June to September.

The common name arose from the plant's unusual habit of opening its flowers between six and seven o'clock in the evening. Native American Indians ate young stems and leaves of several different varieties of evening primrose and this custom soon spread to Europe when the plant was introduced there in the seventeenth century. Although tougher, the young roots can also be eaten if boiled or pickled.

Medicinally, the plant has astringent and sedative properties and a syrup made from the flowers is prescribed for whooping cough and asthma. It has also been used for gastro-intestinal problems and dyspepsia. The finely ground flowering tops are used in face-masks to give the skin a pretty pallor. Recent research has shown the plant to be rich in an oil containing gammalinolenic acid – an essential fatty acid that is used by the body to produce hormone-like substances called prostaglandins which assist the body in maintaining healthy body tissue and limit inflammatory reactions. Evening primrose oil can be bought in capsule or liquid form and is recommended for eczema, brittle nails, coughing, cramp and arthritis. It is also believed to contain an anti-clotting factor that is said to aid prevention of heart attacks.

Evening primrose can be grown from seed, either in cold frames in the autumn or in a sheltered spot outdoors in late spring ready for transplanting to a sunny spot a few weeks later. Keep well weeded and transplant again the following spring, being careful not to break the roots.

Gayfeather or **Dense Blazing Star** *Liatris spicata* is a perennial plant native to parts of central and eastern North America, which grows wild in moist ground and is cultivated in gardens. Gayfeather has a tuberous root and an erect, leafy stem that reaches heights of 30–180 cm (12–72 in). The numerous, linear leaves are crowded on the stem and decrease in size as they ascend. The rose-purple flowers form a beautiful long, dense spike and bloom from July to September.

The plant is bitter in taste but very pleasant-smelling owing to the coumarin in its leaves and roots so, when dried, they are sometimes added to pot-pourris.

Medicinally, gayfeather is said to be a very effective diuretic and has apparently been used to treat kidney complaints, sore throats and gonorrhoea.

As long as it is kept well watered in dry weather, gayfeather can easily be grown in the garden from seed. It likes light, rich or ordinary soil and sunny, open borders.

Golden-rod *Solidago virgaurea* is a perennial herb, native to Europe, Asia and North America, which grows wild in dry woods, rocks, cliffs, dunes and uncultivated fields. Golden-rod has a stout, tap-rooted rhizome from which arise branched, leafy stems that reach heights of 10–75 cm (4–30 in). The stalked, basal leaves are oval to elliptical, pointed and toothed; the stem leaves are narrower, stalkless and generally smooth-edged. The flowers grow in spikes composed of small, golden-yellow flowerlets which bloom from late July to October.

The generic name comes from the Latin *solidare*, 'to make whole', and alludes to its ancient reputation as a vulnerary or wound herb, which is echoed by another of its common names – woundwort.

Extensively prescribed in homoeopathic medicine for its ability to cleanse the body by stimulating the liver and kidneys to eliminate waste matter, it has long been and is still considered an excellent diuretic. It is also considered very efficient for eliminating stones in the bladder. One American Indian tribe chewed the blossoms to extract their juice which they believed cured sore throats.

Golden-rod tea has a very pleasant taste and can be taken either internally to act as a mild diuretic or used as a lotion to staunch bleeding.

Put 60 g/2 oz of dried leaves and flowers in 1 1/2 pt of water, boil for a minute, then steep for ten minutes. Strain and drink three to four cups a day.

Golden-rod is easily propagated by root division in the autumn. It likes ordinary, damp soil in sun or shade.

Gather the whole plant (except the root) during the flowering period and dry carefully at a low temperature so that the flowers and leaves retain their colour. Crush coarsely and store in an airtight jar.

Golden-rod *Solidago canadensis* a perennial herb, native to North America, is frequently cultivated in gardens and often found as an escape. Golden-rod is a tall, hairy plant with a rhizome and stems that reach heights of 30–250 cm (12–100 in). The lance-shaped, veined leaves are roughly hairy and toothed. The golden yellow flowers form in dense one-sided clusters and bloom from July to September.

Golden-rod *Solidago canadensis*

Gayfeather or **Dense Blazing Star** *Liatris spicata*

Golden-rod *Solidago virgaurea*

155

Black Horehound *Ballota nigra* (left), **White Horehound** *Marrubium vulgare* (right)

White Horehound *Marrubium vulgare*

White Horehound *Marrubium vulgare* is a hairy perennial, native to Mediterranean Europe and central Asia, and also established in central and northern Europe and North and South America. It grows wild in waste places, pastures and along roadsides from coastal to mountainous regions. White horehound has a short, stout, woody root and angular branched, hairy stems that reach heights of 40–80 cm (16–32 in). The egg-shaped, wrinkled, roughly toothed, dull-green pairs of leaves are felty and deeply veined and get smaller towards the top of the stem. The small, cream-white flowers are grouped in clusters in the leaves' axils and bloom from June to September.

The generic name is possibly derived from the Hebrew *marros*, 'bitter juice', as it is thought to be one of the five bitter herbs that the Jews ate at Passover to commemorate the exodus from Egypt. White horehound has been used medicinally since Egyptian times to treat numerous ailments. It contains a bitter principle, marrubin, as well as tannins, essential oil and mucilage. Because of its softening action, it has long been taken for respiratory problems, bronchial catarrh, asthma, coughs, digestive problems and as an appetite stimulant. It has also been used to correct irregular and rapid heart action. Candied white horehound makes a soothing sweet for coughs and sore throats. In syrup form, it is very useful, not only for children's coughs and croup but also for minor stomach upsets and as a digestive tonic. It has been used as a vermifuge and a salve to treat dog bites. White horehound makes an appetizing and healthful drink which was popular in Norfolk and other country districts before the war, according to Grieve. It also has a specific use in herbal medicine as a substitute for quinine when the latter is proving ineffective.

To make an infusion for use in treating catarrh, asthma or coughs, put 30 g/1 oz fresh or dried leaves in ½ l/1 pt of boiling water. Infuse for ten to fifteen minutes, strain, sweeten and drink lukewarm, three to four glassfuls a day.

Best grown in a herb garden. It flourishes well in poor soil and can either be grown from cuttings or root division or seeds. Plant in spring and weed well. It will not blossom for two years.

Black Horehound *Ballota nigra* is a hairy, unpleasant-smelling perennial, native to Europe, Morocco and East Iran, which commonly grows wild along roadsides and in hedgerows and waste places. Black horehound has a short, stout, woody root and branched stems that reach heights of 40–100 cm (16–40 in). The stalked, roughly toothed, dull-green, egg-shaped leaves are arranged in pairs on the stem and covered in soft grey hairs and conspicuously veined. The dull purple flowers are arranged in dense whorls in the leaves' axils and bloom from June to October.

The generic name is derived from the Greek *ballo*, 'to reject', and the specific name from the Latin *nigra*, 'black'. It is sometimes called black stinking horehound because of its very unpleasant smell; even cattle tend to avoid it.

It has long been reputed an antidote for the bites of mad dogs, as well as a vermifuge, stimulant and antispasmodic.

Easy to grow in the garden but take care, it spreads like wildfire.

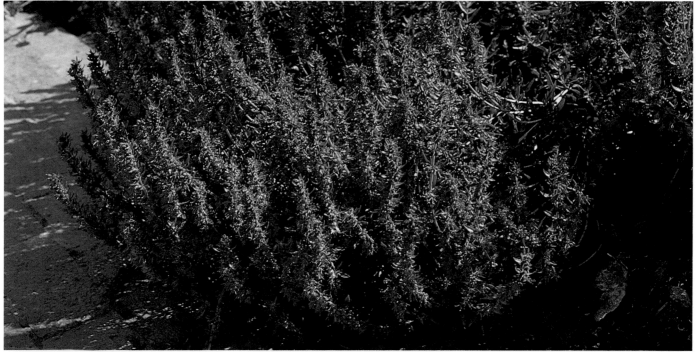

Hyssop *Hyssopus officinalis*

White Hyssop *Hyssopus officinalis* 'Alba'

Rock Hyssop *Hyssopus officinalis aristatus*

Dragonhead *Dracocephalum ruyschianum*

Hyssop *Hyssopus officinalis* is an aromatic perennial, native to southern Europe and eastern Asia and naturalized as far north as southern England, which has been introduced into North America. It is sometimes found wild on dry rocky slopes or walls and often cultivated for ornament. Hyssop is a partially evergreen plant with a short, fibrous rhizome and a stalk that divides into numerous, woody, square stems which are herbaceous around the top and reach a height of 60 cm (24 in). The lance-shaped leaves are arranged in whorls, and the long dense spikes of tubular-shaped light-blue, purplish-white, pink or white flowers bloom from June to August.

The generic name is derived from the Greek *azob*, 'a holy herb', and refers to its use in cleaning holy places. Hyssop is mentioned in the bible as a cleansing plant 'Purge me with Hyssop and I shall be clean' (Psalms LI, 7) although botanical experts disagree as to whether it was *Hyssopus officinalis* that was meant. But there is no doubt that hyssop has been used in the Mediterranean countries since pre-Christian times for medicinal and culinary purposes.

The strong aromatic odour of the flowers, leaves and young shoots make a delicious addition to salads, game soups and fruit pies, but it does need to be used sparingly. It aids the digestion of fat and is recommended as an accompaniment to greasy meat or fish. The fine oil extracted from the plant is used in the manufacture of liqueurs, particularly Chartreuse, and also in perfumery. Honey from bees that have fed on hyssop flowers is delicious.

Medicinally, hyssop oil has stimulative, carminative and sudorific properties and it was formerly used to relieve flatulence and calm hysterical conditions. Nowadays it is mainly used in an infusion to aid digestion, ease coughs, sore throats, hoarseness and bronchial catarrh. Hyssop tea and hyssop baths are old country remedies for rheumatism and, as a lotion, it may be used to treat ear, eye and throat infections and to relieve bites and stings.

To make hyssop tea infuse 30 g/1 oz hyssop flowers in 1 1/2 pt of boiling water for ten minutes. Strain, sweeten if necessary, and drink small glassfuls three times a day. However, it should never be taken by pregnant women as it is an emmenagogue.

Hyssop is a fairly hardy plant and can be easily grown in a herb garden to make a pretty edging plant. Propagation is by root division, cuttings or seeds. Cuttings should be taken in spring or autumn and seeds sown in April. When large enough, they should be planted out a foot apart in light dry soil in a warm spot and kept well watered until established.

The flowers and green tops should be collected just as flowering begins, then dried and stored in an airtight container.

Rock Hyssop *Hyssopus officinalis* subsp. *aristatus* is similar to hyssop but is a smaller, more compact plant with blue flowers that bloom in August.

Dragonhead *Dracocephalum ruyschianum* is a perennial plant, native to Russia and central Europe as far west as the Pyrenees. It is found growing wild in dry, open habitats and often cultivated in gardens for ornament. Dragonhead has erect stems that reach a height of 60 cm (24 in). The leaves are smooth and linear to lance-shaped; the lower leaves with short stalks, the upper leaves with none. The blue to violet leaves grow in whorls on a dense, terminal spike and bloom from June to July.

This is a good bee plant and easily grown from seed.

St John's Wort *Hypericum perforatum*

St John's Wort *Hypericum perforatum*

Henbane or **Hogbean** *Hyoscyamus niger*

Mandrake *Mandragora officinarum*

White Henbane *Hyoscyamus albus*

American Ginseng *Panax quinquefolius*

Henbane or **Hogbean** *Hyoscyamus niger* is a poisonous annual or more commonly biennial herb, native to Europe, western Asia and North Africa and also introduced into eastern Asia, Australia and North America. It is found growing wild on waste ground, roadsides and sandy places near the sea. Henbane is a hairy, unpleasant-smelling plant with a spindle-shaped tap-root and a stout, simple or branched, erect stem that can reach a height of 80 cm (32 in). The ovate, hairy leaves are alternate and slightly lobed. The bell-shaped flowers on terminal spikes are yellow with purple veins and bloom in May or June (possibly later on annuals). The fruit contains many small, kidney-shaped seeds.

The generic name is derived from the Greek *hyos* and *cyomos*, 'the bean of the hog' because that animal was thought to relish it and from this arises one of its common names. The other is thought to allude to the fact that the seeds are poisonous to poultry.

Henbane has a long history of medicinal use dating back to ancient times. The plant was recommended by Dioscorides for inducing sleep and allaying pain but it fell into disrepute because of its deadly poisonous properties. In medieval times it was associated with black magic; witches were purported to use it to throw their victims into convulsions. It contains the powerful alkaloids hyoscyamine and scopolamine which have antispasmodic, hypnotic and narcotic properties. In small doses it has been used for its tranquillizing effect on people suffering from nervous irritability and sleeplessness. Its antispasmodic effect on brain and spine has made it a popular medicine in mental asylums for treating acute mania and delirium tremens. It is also used externally to relieve rheumatism and arthritis, earache, toothache and asthmatic conditions. However, it is a very poisonous plant which can cause acute symptoms and in large doses even death. It should never be gathered or taken except under prescription from a qualified practitioner.

White Henbane *Hyoscyamus albus* is very similar to henbane with white to pale-yellow flowers and is considered to have very similar medicinal properties and uses.

St John's Wort *Hypericum perforatum* is a poisonous perennial plant, native to Europe, western Asia and North Africa, which has also become naturalized in eastern Asia, Australia, New Zealand and North and South America. It commonly grows in open woods, grasslands, waste places and clearings. St John's Wort has a short rhizome and erect, angular stems, woody at the base and branched at the top, which grow to a height of 1 m (40 in). The ovate, veined leaves are arranged in opposite pairs and covered with translucent dots that contain an essential oil which is also found in the flowers. These are small, golden yellow, generally in clusters of three, with five petals each and numerous stamens, and they bloom from May to September.

The generic name is derived from the Greek *hypericum*, 'over an apparition', a reference to the fact that the herb was so unpleasant to evil spirits that one whiff of it would cause them to disappear. The specific name, the Latin *perforatum*, alludes to the tiny, transparent, oil-bearing dots on the leaves which give them a perforated appearance if held up to the light. Its English name is derived from its traditional association with St John the Baptist.

Medicinally, the plant is highly regarded for the soothing and healing properties of the red oil which can be made from the flowers and leaves. In the Middle Ages it was used by the Crusaders to heal their wounds. Internally, the oil has also been taken for colic, worms and abdominal pains and an infusion was recommended for bronchial catarrh, asthma, irregular menstruation, ovarian inflammation, depression, insomnia, fainting fits and toothache! Modern phytotherapy recognizes St John's Wort as yielding a useful psychotropic drug which induces euphoria in those suffering from depression.

To make the oil, place flowers and leaves in a large glass container, cover with any kind of cooling oil (sunflower is good), place a muslin on top to prevent flies and insects getting in, then stand the jar in the sun for about three to four weeks until the oil becomes a good red colour. Strain through the muslin into clean bottles and stopper firmly. Rub on painful joints, for rheumatism, arthritis, strained muscles, bruises or tumours. As a compress, it relieves deep bruises or sprains and it can be used to treat wounds, inflammation and skin rashes. It will keep the skin soft and in good condition. Note that the plant contains a red pigment which is photosensitive. Some people can develop a skin irritation if exposed to the sun for a long time after taking internally.

To make a tea, put 30–60 g/1–2 oz of dried flowering tips or flowers in 1 1/2 pt of water, bring gently to the boil, leave to infuse for ten minutes then strain. Drink three cupfuls a day.

St John's Wort can easily be found in the wild or cultivated in a herb garden. It likes any kind of soil and some sun and some shade.

Yellow Gentian *Gentiana lutea* is a perennial plant, native to central and southern Europe and introduced into North America. It is found wild in mountainous pastures and on slopes. Yellow gentian is a herbaceous plant with a very long, thick tap-root and an erect, stout, smooth stem that reaches heights of 50–125 cm (20–50 in). The pointed, oval leaves have five to seven prominent veins and grow in opposite pairs. The yellow flowers are arranged in whorls in the axils of the upper leaves and bloom from June to August.

The generic name is derived from Gentius, King of Illyria in 180BC, because it was he who was said to have discovered the medicinal value of the plant.

From the Middle Ages yellow gentian was thought to be a panacea for all ills and seemed to be an ingredient of almost every 'miracle' medicine. Although some of the claims made for it were undoubtedly preposterous, it is nevertheless a marvellous tonic and the bitter principle contained in the root is beneficial for many digestive ailments, loss of appetite, sickness, fainting and general debility from chronic illness. Yellow gentian improves the blood by stimulating increased production of blood corpuscles, so it is very useful for anaemia and weakness of the heart or nerves, but it must not be taken by those with hyperacidity or high blood pressure, or by pregnant women. In Germany and Switzerland the fresh root is used for various bitter liqueurs and aperitifs. A simple bitter, yellow gentian is more palatable mixed with orange peel and cardamom.

To make a tincture, put 60 g/2 oz dried yellow gentian root, 30 g/1 oz dried orange peel and 15 g/½ oz crushed cardamom seeds in 1 1/2 pt brandy. Take ½ to 1 tsp of this liquid in a small glass of water, three times a day.

Yellow gentian can be cultivated easily in a garden. It can either be grown from seed or propagated by root division. If grown from seed, plant them in a nursery bed and then transplant the seedlings into deep, rich, loamy soil, allowing plenty of room for the long roots

to grow. Yellow gentian takes about three years to grow to flowering size. Make sure the plant is well-sheltered from cold winds but exposed to sunshine; keep the soil moist.

Yellow gentian root can be dug in the autumn and carefully cleaned (but not washed) before being dried either slowly, whole, or cut in slices lengthwise and dried quickly.

Note: Do not confuse yellow gentian with the poisonous False Hellebore *Veratrum album* (page 105) whose leaves are similar but alternate and whose flowers grow in spikes.

American Ginseng *Panax quinquefolius* is a perennial herb, native to central and south-eastern North America, which is now only rarely found wild in cool, moist woods but extensively cultivated for export to China. American ginseng has a large, fleshy, many-headed tap-root and a smooth, round stem that reaches a height of 40–60 cm (16–24 in). Two or three stalked, dark-green leaves at the end of the stem are divided into five leaflets and the greenish-white flowers growing in a single cluster at the top of the stem bloom from May to August.

The generic name comes from the Greek *panakos*, 'a panacea', alluding to the numerous powers attributed to it, and the common name is a corruption of the Chinese *Jin chen* meaning 'like a man', alluding to the humanoid shape of the roots. The Latin specific name means 'five leaved', in reference to the five leaflets of which each leaf is comprised.

For centuries the Chinese have valued the root of ginseng for its medicinal properties. They consider it an aphrodisiac (as did several American Indian tribes), a tonic for mental and physical fatigue, a heart stimulant and a general aid to prolonging life and vitality. A great deal of research has been done into the constituents of ginseng and it has been found that there is no one principle that has a specific action on the heart or circulation but the combined action of all the principles does seem to have a general tonic effect on the whole body, which possibly accounts for the wide variety of therapeutic claims made for it.

Mandrake *Mandragora officinarum* is a perennial herb, native to south-eastern Europe and cultivated in gardens in other parts of Europe. Mandrake has a large, brown, parsnip-like root which is sometimes divided and runs deep into the ground. From it arises the big, dark-green, ovate, pointed leaves which grow erect, up to 30 cm (12 in) high and 13 cm (5 in) wide until full-grown, when they flatten out on to the ground. The greenish-white, bell-shaped flowers grow on short stalks at the base of the leaves and bloom in March or early April, succeeded by smooth, round fruits, like green tomatoes, which turn deep yellow when ripe, with a pineapple-like odour.

The generic name is derived from the Greek word *mandra*, meaning 'a stall or herd of cattle', and probably alludes to the fact that it is harmful to them. The specific name alludes to its inclusion in the ancient lists of officially recognized medicinal herbs. One of its English names, Satan's Apple, alludes to its apple-like fruits and to its strange powers: it was considered by Anglo-Saxon herbalists to free a person who was possessed by demons.

Mandrake roots, because of their habit of dividing in two, were often thought to resemble human forms and frequently made into amulets, which gave rise to the many superstitions surrounding the plant. Mandrake amulets in the house were supposed to bring good fortune and it was believed that mandrake could cure sterility. Others claimed mandrake grew under murderers' gallows and death pursued those who dug it up.

Yellow Gentian *Gentiana lutea*

Yellow Gentian *Gentiana lutea* (young leaves)

Mandrake, like other members of the potato family, contains highly poisonous alkaloids that, suitably modified, have a sedative effect. In ancient times mandrake root was used to allay pain and induce sleep; in Pliny's day, the root was chewed by a patient about to undergo surgery because of its anaesthetic properties and it is thought that the crucifixion sponge given to Christ was probably dipped in a solution containing mandrake. So realistic was the death-like stupefaction that could ensue, that the Romans took to mutilating the bodies of crucifixion victims by sticking spears in them, to ensure that the apparently 'dead' bodies did not come to life again when the effects of the sedation wore off. The juice expressed from the the finely grated root was also given to relieve rheumatic pains, ulcers and scrophulous tumours, as well as being administered to those suffering melancholy, convulsions or mania. However, large doses were said to excite delirium and madness. Mandrake is still used in modern medicine because the root contains the alkaloid, hyoscine, which is the standard pre-operative medication given to soothe patients and reduce bronchial secretions. It is also used to treat motion sickness.

The plants are very difficult to get hold of for growing in one's garden.

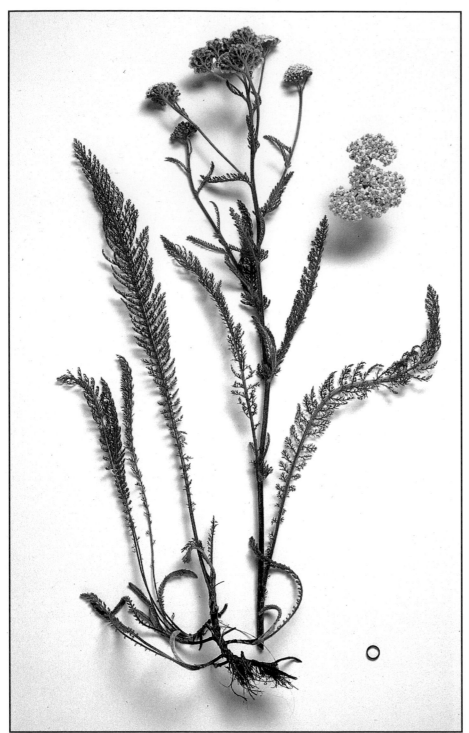

Yarrow *Achillea millefolium*

Woodsage or **Sage-leaved Germander** *Teucrium scorodonia*

Yarrow *Achillea millefolium* is a hairy, strongly scented, perennial herb, native to the British Isles but also found in the temperate areas of southern Europe and western Asia and introduced into North America, Australia and New Zealand. It commonly grows in meadows, pastures, hedgerows and roadsides, and as a garden weed. The yarrow has erect, furrowed stems which usually reach heights of about 45–60 cm (18–24 in). Its bottle-green, two- or three-pinnate leaves are lance-shaped with a feathery appearance. The numerous small, white, pink or lilac flowers form a dense, flat-topped cluster and bloom from June to November.

Its generic name is said to be derived from Achilles who was reputed to have used it to staunch the bleeding wounds of his soldiers. Its specific name means 'a thousand leaves' and refers to the numerous segments of its foliage, and gives rise to other common names such as milfoil and thousand weed. The common name yarrow may be a corruption of the Greek *hiera*, 'holy herb', for it was thought to possess numerous medicinal properties, or it may be a corruption of *gearwe*, the Anglo-Saxon name, or *gerwe*, the Dutch name. Herbe Militaris, staunchweed, bloodwort and carpenter's weed are other synonyms which testify to its use for treating wounds, cuts and nosebleeds. Yarrow has up to 0.5 per cent of an essential oil containing chamuzulene, therapeutically the most effective constituent, and also achillein, choline, valeric acid, formic acid, methyl alcohol, flavones and tannins.

Yarrow is primarily anti-spasmodic, anti-inflammatory, carminative and tonic. It is good for the digestive system and Mességué particularly recommends an infusion to aid stomach cramps, stimulate the digestion and help expel acid from the intestine. It may also have a beneficial effect on blood circulation and be used internally to treat lung and kidney haemorrhage and menstrual problems. Weiss says that yarrow, used regularly over a long period, has a generally beneficial effect on women suffering from gynaecological problems such as spastic parametropathy (vegetative dystonia of the small pelvis) and leukorrhoea. Note that it should not be taken by pregnant women. Yarrow promotes perspiration so it is useful at the onset of colds or fevers. It has also been recommended as a cure for piles, sores, ulcers, bruises, acne and toothache.

Yarrow tea can be made by infusing 30 g/1 oz of the dried herb 60 g/2 oz of fresh leaves and flowers in ½ l/1 pt of boiling water for ten minutes and drinking warm two or three times a day or using in the bath.

Very easy to grow in any kind of soil.

Wall Germander *Teucrium chamaedrys* is a perennial plant, native to central and southern Europe and sometimes naturalized in more northern parts. It is found wild in dry, sunny waste ground or rocky walls, and cultivated in gardens as an escape. Wall germander has a slender rhizome with many rootlets and ascending, hairy stems, which are woody at the base, and can reach a height of about 100 cm (40 in). The lower leaves are opposite, short-stalked, oval and shiny with a crenate margin, while the upper leaves are stalkless and almost entire. The rosy pink flowers grow in small whorls on leafy terminal spikes and flower from June to July.

Commonly used in the past for various medicinal purposes, wall germander has a reputation for being good for gout and is said to have been used to cure Charles V, the Holy Roman Emperor, of this. It was an important ingredient in the popular Portland Powder.

Culpeper recommended a decoction of the leaves taken with honey for a wide range of ills ranging from serpent bites to fevers, headaches and epilepsy. It was also considered helpful for removing uterine obstructions and soothing asthmatic coughs. Nowadays, it is sometimes used externally to treat gum diseases but because of its stimulant and tonic properties it is most extensively used in making alcoholic drinks.

Wall germander will grow in almost any soil and can be propagated either by seeds, cuttings or root division. Gather the herb in summer and dry quickly to store for winter use.

Woodsage or Sage-leaved Germander

Teucrium scorodonia is a perennial plant native to south and western Europe, from Norway to Spain and across to northern Italy, which commonly grows in woods, heaths, grasslands and dunes. Woodsage is a downy plant with a creeping rhizome and erect, branched, square stems that reach heights of 15–45 cm (5–18 in). The ovate, heart-shaped leaves are coarsely toothed, wrinkled and greyish-green. The small, yellowish-green flowers grow in spike-like clusters and bloom from July to September.

The generic name is thought to be a reference either to the legendary archer at Troy, Teucer or to a medical botanist called Dr Teucer. The common names allude to its similarity to sage. In taste and smell, the species resembles Hop and in some areas it has been used as a substitute for it in beer-making.

Commonly used since medieval times, it has a reputation as a diuretic, tonic, and emmenagogue. It restores the menstrual flow and dispels clotted blood beneath bruises and falls. It is valuable as a tonic and promotes the appetite, particularly after an attack of gout or rheumatism.

To make an infusion, put 30 g/1 oz of the dried herb in boiling water and infuse for five minutes. Strain and drink three to four wineglassfuls a day.

Woodsage can either be collected in the wild or easily grown from seed or by cuttings or root division in ordinary soil in a herb garden. Collect the whole herb, for drying, in July.

Cat Thyme

Teucrium marum is a small shrub, native to the islands of the western Mediterranean but also naturalized in Spain and southern Europe, which is found growing on dry soil.

Cat thyme has aromatic leaves and branches which cause sneezing and so have been used for head disorders. The powdered leaves macerated in wine have been prescribed for nervous disorders and the bark, which is very astringent, used for stopping haemorrhages.

Not commonly grown in herb gardens.

Elecampane

Inula helenium is a large, perennial herb probably native to central Asia, which has been introduced and become naturalized into many parts of Europe, Asia, North America and Japan. It is occasionally found growing wild in fields, waysides, copses and waste ground but more commonly found cultivated for ornament. Elecampane is a sturdy, attractive plant with a thick, fleshy rhizomatous root and stout, erect, furrowed hairy stems that reach heights of 60–150 cm (24–60 in). The large, stalked, slightly toothed basal leaves form a rosette while the smaller, stalkless, stem leaves are more heart-shaped and very thick and rough although soft and downy on the underside. The large, bright-yellow flower heads are reminiscent of sunflowers and bloom from June to August.

The generic name is thought to be a

Wall Germander *Teucrium chamaedrys*

Cat Thyme *Teucrium marum*

Elecampane *Inula helenium*

corruption of the specific name from the Greek *helenion*, 'Helen', probably alluding to Helen of Troy. One explanation is that Helen was holding a bunch of elecampane when snatched away by Paris; another is that the plant grew from the tears that she shed. The common name is derived from the combination of Latin *inula* and *campane*, 'of the fields'.

Elecampane root (now known to contain inulin) was used for centuries for its medicinal properties although it is now no longer used much in European countries. Hippocrates noted the beneficial effect it had on the uterus, urinary passages and respiratory areas and herbalists have long used the roots in infusion or decoction to soothe coughs, sore throats, whooping cough and bronchitis. It was also thought to have a beneficial effect on the digestive organs and to be an excellent general tonic, according to Mességué, with antiseptic and cleansing properties. It may help soothe itchy skin, herpes and acne, minor wounds and cuts.

The root used to be candied and eaten as a sweetmeat or made into lozenges for sore throats and whooping cough. In Europe, it is used in

distilling liqueurs, particularly in the making of absinthe.

To make an aromatic infusion soak 45–60 g/ 1½–2 oz of root in cold water for an hour, then boil for one minute in 1 1/2 pt of water and leave to infuse for ten minutes. Strain and sweeten if desired and take three glassfuls a day before meals to promote expectoration and soothe coughs, sore throats and bronchial problems.

A strong decoction, 45 g/1½ oz to ½ l/1 pt boiling water, can be used externally as a lotion for scabby skin disorders and minor cuts and wounds.

Elecampane is a lovely flower to grow at the back of a herbaceous border. It can be cultivated from seed in the spring or propagated by off-cuts from the old root, in autumn, with a bud or eye on each. Plant in ordinary, rich soil in a moist, sunny bed which is well weeded. The root will be ready for use after two years. Harvest the root in August, carefully brush clean, cut into rounds and leave to dry. After a while it will emit a delightful smell of violets. Store in an airtight container for future use.

Betony or **Bishopswort** *Stachys officinalis*

Betony or **Bishopswort** *Stachys officinalis*

Great Lobelia *Lobelia siphilitica*

Betony or **Bishopswort** *Stachys officinalis* synonym *Betonica officinalis* is a hairy perennial, native to Britain, Europe and Algeria, which is found quite commonly and widely distributed throughout its range in moist fields, open woods, hedgerows and heaths, up to 450 m (1500 ft). Betony has a small, woody rhizome from which arise erect stems to a height of 15–60 cm (6–24 in). The aromatic, coarsely toothed, opposed pairs of leaves are oblong to ovate and those near the base are hairy and have long stalks while those near the apex are stalkless. The small purplish or crimson flowers are arranged in an interrupted terminal spike – in dense rings or whorls in short spikes in the axils of the upper leaves. The flowers bloom in July and August.

The generic name is derived from the Greek word *stachys*, 'an ear of corn', alluding to the way in which it flowers. The former generic name is thought to be derived from the Celtic words, *bew*, 'head', and *ton*, 'good', alluding to its frequent use in head complaints. *Officinalis* refers to its official status in lists of medicinally valuable plants. Since ancient times betony has been considered a panacea for all ills. Antonius Musa, physician to the emperor Augustus, wrote a treatise claiming it was a specific cure for forty-seven diseases. It was grown in physic gardens, monastery gardens and around churches and graveyards as it was also thought to give protection from the evils of witchcraft.

During the eighteenth century it was rejected by doctors but country people still used it. Betony has always been considered to be very good in cases of head colds. A pinch of dried leaves causes violent sneezing, thus clearing the head, and a decoction may help cure a severe headache. It is also used for sore throats, asthma, catarrh, clogging of the respiratory tract, gout, rheumatism and nervous conditions. Externally, a poultice of fresh leaves, steeped for several minutes in boiling red wine and applied to an open wound, will quickly cleanse this and facilitate scar-formation. To make a decoction, put 25 g/¾ oz of dried or chopped plant in ½ l/1 pt of boiling water and steep for five minutes, strain and take a wineglassful three times a day.

Collect from the wild, in an unpolluted spot, on a fine, dry day in July and hang it up in loose bunches to dry as quickly as possible, then store in airtight tins for future use.

Cardinal Flower *Lobelia cardinalis* is a beautiful annual native to eastern North America, where it is found growing wild in damp sites along streams and cultivated in gardens for ornament. Cardinal flower has an erect stalk that reaches a height of 60–120 cm (24–48 in). The alternate leaves are lance-shaped with a toothed edge and the brilliant red tubular flowers form an elongated cluster and bloom from July to September.

The specific and common names allude to the similarity of the flower colour to the bright red robes worn by Roman Catholic cardinals.

One Indian tribe powdered the roots of either the cardinal flower or the blue lobelia and used them as an aphrodisiac, putting them into the food of an arguing couple. They believed it made the couple love each other again. This plant may contain poisonous alkaloids and should therefore only be taken if prescribed by a qualified medical practitioner.

Great Lobelia or **Blue Lobelia** *Lobelia siphilitica* is very similar to the cardinal flower except that it has bright blue flowers. The Iroquois Indians used to make a strong tea from the roots, believing this an effective remedy

Cardinal Flower *Lobelia cardinalis*

Gipsywort *Lycopus europaeus*

against venereal disease (hence its specific name) and also effective in the treatment of asthma. This plant may also contain poisonous alkaloids and should only be taken if prescribed by a medical practitioner.

Indian Tobacco *Lobelia inflata* is a poisonous annual, native to central and eastern North America, which is found wild in fields, open woods and dry waste places and grown in gardens. Indian tobacco is an erect herb with simple or branched hairy stems that grow to heights of 30–60 cm (12–24 in). The ovate leaves with a wavy-toothed margin are thin, alternate and light green. The tiny lavender flowers grow in elongated clusters at the end of the stem and bloom from June to October.

The generic name commemorates the botanist Mathias de l'Obel who died in 1616, while the specific name is a reference to the inflated, balloon-shaped seeds. The common name, Indian tobacco, arose because American Indians chewed and smoked the leaves. Nowadays, certain anti-smoking preparations use Indian tobacco in them but controversy exists about how poisonous the plant is.

In the past Indian tobacco was used to treat a variety of disorders – epilepsy, convulsions, diphtheria and asthma. Externally, it was used as a poultice for sprains and bruises but, taken internally, in large doses Indian tobacco proved a violent emetic, causing depression, nausea, cold sweats and even death in some instances. Indian tobacco should never be taken unless prescribed by a medical practitioner.

Gipsywort *Lycopus europaeus* is a perennial herb, native to Europe and western and central Asia, which is also naturalized in North America. It grows by river banks, streams, ditches and in marshes and fens. Gipsywort has erect, somewhat hairy stems with ascending branches, and it reaches heights of 30–100 cm

(12–40 in). The large, deeply cut, pointed leaves are roundish, spear-shaped and the small white or pale flesh-coloured flowers which grow in whorls in the axils of the upper leaves bloom from July to September.

Gipsywort is grown for its astringent and sedative properties and used to ease palpitations in thyroid patients. Gipsywort, as its name implies, was most commonly used by gipsies, apparently to stain their skin darker. The plant yields an excellent black dye which gives a permanent colour to wool and silk.

Easily grown from seed but beware; it self-seeds and will rapidly spread all over the garden!

Bugleweed *Lycopus virginicus* is a perennial plant native to North America, which commonly grows in damp, shady ground. Bugleweed has a creeping rhizome and smooth, quadrangular stems that reach heights of 15–60 cm (6–24 in). The leaves grow in opposite pairs, the upper ones lance-shaped with a toothed margin, the lower ones wedge-shaped with smooth margins. The purplish flowers grow in clusters in the leaf axils and bloom from July to September.

Like gipsywort, bugleweed has astringent and sedative properties and has also been used as an anti-thyroid remedy. Modern research has suggested that both bugleweed and gipsywort may have hormonal properties that could give a contraceptive effect if taken over a long period.

Put 30 g/1 oz dried herb in ½ l/1 pt of boiling water. Infuse for five minutes, then strain and drink frequently in small glassfuls to ease coughs.

Easily grown from seed.

Field Scabious or **Blue Buttons** *Knautia arvensis* is a perennial herb, native to Europe, which has escaped and naturalized in North America. It is found growing wild in dry, grassy fields, pastures and banks. Field scabious has a

Field Scabious *Knautia arvensis*

dark, somewhat woody tap-root and erect, simple or branched stems that are bristly below and reach heights of 25–100 cm (10–40 in). The leaves are variable but generally they grow in pairs on the stem and are hairy: the stalked, basal leaves are ovate, lance-shaped cut into large teeth on the margin; the stalkless stem leaves are deeply cut into lobes. The clusters of purple flowers grow on the end of the stems and bloom from June to October.

The generic name is derived from the name of the seventeenth-century Saxon botanist, Dr Knaut, and the common name is believed to be a corruption of the Latin *scabies*, a form of leprosy, for which this species was reputedly used as a remedy.

In medieval times it was taken as a precaution against infection and for coughs, shortness of breath and lung diseases. This old medicinal herb is probably best known for helping to remove freckles, pimples, dandruff and scurf.

It can be cultivated in a herb garden in chalky soil with a sunny aspect.

Tormentil *Potentilla erecta*

Silverweed *Potentilla anserina*

Sundew *Drosera rotundifolia* is a perennial plant native to northern and central Europe, North Asia and North America, which grows wild in damp, peaty ponds, bogs, marshes, heaths and moors, often among *Sphagnum*. Sundew is an insectivorous plant with a short, fibrous root and spoon-shaped leaves that grow from it on long stalks in rosette form. The upper surface of the leaves is covered with red, glandular hairs that secrete a sweetish fluid which is attractive to, and traps, insects. Once caught, they are dissolved by a digestive fluid. The tiny white flowers are only grouped on one side of the flowering stem and bloom from July to September.

The enzymes emitted from this plant to digest insects are very similar to those in the human stomach and milk will curdle if heated with sundew. However, its principal use has been in a tincture, infusion or herbal tea for treating whooping cough, asthma, bronchitis and respiratory congestion. It is also considered effective for treating old-age diseases: arteriosclerosis and hypertension.

Silverweed *Potentilla anserina* is a perennial plant, native to Europe and found all over the temperate world, which commonly grows in waste places, ditches, dunes, roadsides and moist pastures, favouring calcareous soils. Silverweed has a slender, dark brown rhizome and long, creeping, rooting and flowering stems that reach a length of 80 cm (32 in). The silky, downy leaves are composed of numerous pairs of oval, toothed leaflets and the yellow, buttercup-like flowers are borne on the end of a long stalk, arising from the leaf axil, and flower from June to September.

The generic name is derived from the Latin *potens*, 'powerful', alluding to the strong medicinal properties of some of the species. The specific name is derived from the Latin *anser*, 'a goose', and alludes to the fact that this plant is a great favourite with geese.

Although not as strong as its 'sister', Tormentil, *Potentilla erecta* (see below) silverweed has similar astringent, anti-inflammatory and sedative properties. All parts of the plant contain tannin: the flowering parts are more commonly used in herbal medicine but the astringent roots are also used sometimes. An infusion taken internally has been prescribed for colic and diarrhoea, and a stronger decoction applied externally to treat piles, but Weiss is rather scathing about the effectiveness of this plant, claiming that personal experiment has led him to believe that the anti-spasmodic and astringent actions are very minor. Distilled water of silverweed is used in cosmetic preparations for soothing reddened skin, spots and pimples. Curiously, when the plant is fresh it is said to be slightly radioactive and so is said to have an analgesic effect when placed on a painful area.

To make an infusion put 30 g/1 oz of fresh or dried herb with ½ l/1 pt of boiling water. Leave for ten to fifteen minutes, then strain, sweeten and drink three cupfuls a day after meals.

Gather from the wild in June or July on a dry day, dry rapidly and thoroughly then pack into airtight containers for winter use.

Tormentil *Potentilla erecta* is a perennial herb, native to Europe, western Asia and North Africa, which grows in grassland, heaths, mountain bogs and meadows and sometimes open woods, favouring light acid soil. Tormentil has a thick, woody, cylindrical, reddish-fleshed root with many branched, slender stems growing from it to reach heights of 10–40 cm (4–16 in). The stalked basal stems are three to five-lobed, the stalkless stem leaves are three-lobed and toothed. The four-petalled yellow flowers are borne on long, slender stems and bloom from June to October.

The specific name *erecta*, 'upright', is rather misleading as it implies that tormentil is an upstanding plant, whereas in fact it varies from trailing to ascending and creeping rather than upright. The common name is derived from the Latin *tormentum*, 'gripes', which this herb is effective at relieving.

Tormentil has a faint, aromatic odour and a strong astringent taste. It contains 18 to 30 per cent tannin and 18 per cent of a red colouring principle; the root has been used both in the

Orkney Isles and Lapland to tan leather and to stain it red. Tormentil is considered one of the safest and most effective natural astringents and is used extensively in herbal medicine to arrest diarrhoea, at the same time giving nourishment and support to the bowels. A strong decoction is used to soothe piles, chapped anuses and cracked nipples. It is also recommended as a wash for inflamed eyes and a gargle for sore throats, mouth ulcers and pyorrhoea. A compress of fresh leaves will tone up flabby skin and fresh juice made into a cream will soothe sores and wounds. Lint soaked in the fresh juice or a strong decoction and applied regularly to warts will make them disappear.

Tormentil can easily be found in the wild. Collect the roots in spring or autumn, clean thoroughly, cut into thin layers and dry carefully before storing.

Heather or **Ling** *Calluna vulgaris* is an evergreen shrub, native to Europe and north-west North Africa and also found in eastern North America. It commonly grows wild on heaths, moors, bogs, wood edges and roadsides. Heather has numerous twisting stems and small branches and it reaches a height of 60 cm (24 in). The tiny, overlapping leaves are triangular and stalkless. The small pink flowers grow in leafy spikes and bloom from July to September.

The generic name derives from the Greek, *kallynein*, 'to clean', presumably alluding to its diuretic and purifying properties. Medicinally, it has been used to clear infections of the urinary tract and the kidneys. Added to the bath or made into an ointment, it is considered excellent for relieving rheumatic and arthritic pain. Bees are very fond of heather and produce delicious honey from it. The roots are sometimes made into briar pipes and the branches were used in broom making.

To relieve rheumatism, try adding a small armful of heather to the bath. Take two baths a day! For urinary infections, drink 3 cupfuls of heather tea. Put 30–46 g/1–1½ oz of flowers in 1 l/2 pt of cold water. Bring to the boil and simmer for five minutes. Strain.

Collect heather from the wild, cutting the flower spikes while they are still in bud and hanging little bunches in an attic or dry shed for winter use. Alternatively, sow from seed in the spring, in a mixture of peat and sand.

Canadian Fleabane *Conyza canadensis* is an annual, herbaceous plant, native to North America, which was introduced into Europe in the seventeenth century and has become widely naturalized. It is found growing on waste land, in fields and along roadsides. Canadian fleabane has a branched root and numerously branched, stiff, hairy, erect stems that reach heights of 20–100 cm (8–40 in). The basal leaves are lance-shaped and stalked and quickly dying; the stem leaves narrow, linear and hairy. The scaly flower heads bear numerous, small, white or pink flowers which bloom from June to September.

Its common name is derived from its use for destroying fleas and gnats, according to an early American herbalist, Samuel Stearns. The plant contains an oil that is thought to have similar properties to oil of turpentine. Apparently, it was used by American Indians not only to cure diarrhoea but also to regulate menstruation and to treat haemorrhage; externally it was also used for gonorrhoea. It is now claimed to be effective against mouth ulcers, inflamed tonsils and bleeding piles.

Collect from the wild in early autumn when the flowers are in bloom. Gather the whole plant and dry in bunches. It is also a very common garden weed.

Canadian Fleabane *Conyza canadensis*

Heather or **Ling** *Calluna vulgaris*

Sundew *Drosera rotundifolia*

Black Cohosh *Cimicifuga racemosa*

Liquorice *Glycyrrhiza glabra*

Stinking Cohosh *Cimicifuga foetida*

Liquorice *Glycyrrhiza glabra*

Black Cohosh *Cimicifuga racemosa* is an unpleasant-smelling perennial plant, native to North America, which grows in rich woods. Black cohosh has a stout, knotty, blackish underground rhizome and delicate stems that reach a height of 1.5 m (5 ft). The biternate leaves are sharply toothed and the small, white flowers grow in several long, narrow clusters on a leafy stalk. They bloom from June to October.

The generic name is derived from the Latin *cimicus*, 'insect', and alludes to the supposed ability of the plant to drive away insects, as do two of its other common names, bugbane and bugwort. The specific name is an allusion to the way the flowers grow, in racemes.

The root of black cohosh has a long history of use among American Indians. It was primarily used to treat irregular menstruation and relieve the pains of childbirth; hence another common name – squawroot. Modern research has confirmed the traditional uses of this plant. The root contains oestrogenic, hormone-like substances which are now used specifically in modern phytotherapy for conditions involving oestrogen deficiency. Regular courses of treatment over an extended period have proved effective in spastic parametropathy and climacteric depression.

However, the plant can be poisonous in large doses, causing nausea and vomiting, so this plant should only be taken under the guidance of a medical practitioner.

Stinking Cohosh *Cimicifuga foetida*, native to eastern Europe, is also unpleasant-smelling and has drooping clusters of greenish flowers.

Liquorice *Glycyrrhiza glabra* is a perennial herbaceous plant native to south and eastern Europe as far as Persia, which is occasionally found growing wild in dry, open habitats but more often found extensively cultivated. Liquorice has a thick, dark reddish-brown root, which is yellowish inside, from which spring horizontal stolons and very long rootlets. It grows to a height of 150 cm (60 in) and has leaves divided into several pairs of almost opposite leaflets with a central, apical leaflet, and they contain numerous oil glands which make them sticky. The bluish-purple flower spikes spring from the leaf axils and bloom from

Teasel *Dipsacus fullonum*

Fullers' Teasel *Dipsacus sativus*

July to September, succeeded by small, smooth pods containing dark, oval seeds.

The generic name and common names are derived from the Greek *glycyrriza*, 'sweet root', and the specific name *glabra*, 'smooth', is a reference to the smooth seed pods. Liquorice has been used medicinally for many centuries: the ancient Egyptians, Greeks and Romans, all recognized how beneficial it was for coughs, colds and chills. Liquorice was often called scythic by the ancients because the Scythians, redoubtable warriors, were reputed to be able to go for ten days without other food or water by eating liquorice.

Since Hippocrates' day liquorice has been prescribed for dropsy because it does, indeed, prevent thirst – probably the only sweet thing that does. The chief medicinal action of liquorice is as a demulcent and emollient. Its soothing properties make it excellent in throat and chest complaints and it is a very common ingredient in throat pastilles and cough mixtures. It is also widely used in other medicines to counteract bitter tastes and make them more palatable.

Liquorice is also a popular confection which can be safely eaten by diabetics; Pontefract or Pomfrey cakes are made from liquorice grown around the town of the same name in Yorkshire. Liquorice is used by brewers to give body and colour to porter and stout as well as being employed in the manufacture of tobacco. Recent research has shown that it has a pain-killing effect on stomach ulcers and prolonged use raises the blood pressure.

To make a decoction that can be taken for coughs, colds, sore throats and stomach ulcers, put 45–60 g/1½–2 oz liquorice root into 1 1/2 pt of water, boil for ten to fifteen minutes, strain and drink as required.

Liquorice can be propagated by root division. It favours well-manured, stone-free soil. Take side roots or runners with eyes or buds from well-established roots and cut them into sections. Plant them in groups of three at intervals of 30 cm (12 in), covered with 8 cm (3 in) of soil. Growth will be slow for two years but once established liquorice grows luxuriantly. Harvest roots in the third or fourth autumn, wash, trim and dry for future use.

Teasel *Dipsacus fullonum* is a biennial plant, native to Europe, North Africa and the Canary Isles and sometimes found in North America. It grows wild on waste land, hedgerows and by streams and is also cultivated. Teasel has a thick, contorted, yellowish tap-root and smooth, erect, angled stems that reach heights of about 50–200 cm (20–80 in). The basal leaves are long, lance-shaped with spines and they form a rosette; the stem leaves are narrower, prickly on the mid-rib, and fuse to form a water-collecting cup at the base. The lilac flowers are arranged in ovoid heads at the top of each stem – each flower equipped with spiny bracts – and they bloom from July to August.

The generic name is derived from the Greek *dipsao*, 'to be thirsty', alluding to the cup-formation of the leaves which hold water. The common name comes from the Anglo-Saxon *taesan*, 'to tease', referring to the use of the flower heads by cloth workers to 'fleece' woollen cloth.

Culpeper and other herbalists have advocated using the water collected in the leaves as a cosmetic and an eyewash and the roots are also considered to have cleansing properties. The root is recommended for strengthening the stomach and for jaundice and a tincture made from the flowering plant to treat skin disease. Florists use the dried flowers in their flower arrangements because they retain their pretty colour well but most teasel is cultivated for use by clothmakers. Indeed the arms of the Clothmakers' Company are composed of three teasel heads.

A tall, decorative garden plant that can easily be grown from seed.

Fullers' Teasel *Dipsacus sativus* has spines which are strongly developed into a hooked form. This variety is specifically cultivated for raising the nap on woollen cloth, particularly the green baize used on billiard tables.

167

Colchicum speciosum

Colchicum speciosum above Trabzon in north-east Turkey

Tobacco *Nicotiana tabacum*

Meadow Saffron *Colchicum autumnale* is a perennial herb native to central and south-eastern Europe, which grows in damp meadows, marshes, roadsides, railway banks and woods. Meadow saffron is a pretty, colonizing plant growing from a deeply rooted, oval corm with brown outer scales. It reaches heights of 25–40 cm (10–16 in). The two or three glossy, green, parallel-veined, lance-shaped leaves arise from the corm in spring and the leafless, white flowering stem 10–20 cm (4–8 in) high, bears pale mauve, six-pointed flowers which bloom from September to October.

Although this plant has a long history of medical use, all parts of it are poisonous and it should only be used under the direction of a physician.

Its reputation is largely based on its efficacy in treating gout and it is still considered the most effective remedy for an acute attack. The active principle which the plant contains, colchicine, interferes with cell division, causing doubling of chromosomes: experiments which have made use of this ability have been carried out for cancer research. It has also been used in the past as an emetic but overdoses can cause violent purging and undue depression.

Easily grown from bulbs which will multiply to form attractive clumps.

Colchicum speciosum (illustrated here) is very similar to meadow saffron and is grown extensively in Turkey for commercial use.

Tobacco *Nicotiana tabacum* is a viscid annual or short-lived perennial herb, native to tropical America, which is now extensively cultivated and often found naturalized in other parts of the world, growing along roadsides and field edges. Tobacco has a long, fibrous root and an erect cylindrical stem, which is hairy and sticky, and reaches heights of 100–300 cm (40–120 in). The numerous, alternate, pale-green leaves are very large, ovate to lance-shaped, slightly sticky and hairy, with a sickly bitter taste and narcotic smell. The funnel-shaped flowers are pale green to mauve and bloom from August to October.

The generic name is derived from Jean Nicot, a Portuguese who introduced the plant into France. Walter Raleigh brought it to England in 1586 and at first it was violently disapproved of; however, by the mid-nineteenth century it was

Knapweed *Centaurea nigra*

official in the British Pharmacopoeia. In this century smoking is a social habit practised by millions of people world-wide, despite its known addictive properties and its well-established health risks – an estimated 2½ million people world-wide die of tobacco-related diseases each year.

In North America several Indian tribes used tobacco for medicinal purposes. Blowing tobacco smoke into the ear was recognized as a cure for earache and applying the wet leaves to bee stings was reputed to cure them. Many early explorers also chewed the leaves to extract the juice which they then rubbed on their bodies as an insect repellent.

The most important constituent of tobacco is the alkaloid nicotine, which is highly poisonous. Taken internally it has a disturbing effect on the digestion and circulation as well as being sedative, diuretic and emetic. Taken in large doses it causes vomiting, nausea and sleepiness. The smoke injected into the anus – or a rolled tobacco leaf suppository – will evacuate the bowels and help in cases of strangulated hernia. A wet tobacco leaf applied to haemorrhoids will help cure them and a cigarette or pipe smoked after breakfast usually results in a speedy evacuation of the bowels.

Nicotine is still an important insecticide in the horticultural industry.

Knapweed, Lesser Knapweed or **Black Knapweed** *Centaurea nigra* is a perennial herb, native to Europe, eastwards to Sweden and southwards to central Italy and naturalized in North America. It is found growing on grassland, along waysides and on cliffs. Knapweed has a stout, branching stock and tough, rigid, grooved stems that are branched in the upper part and reach heights of 60–90 cm (24–36 in). The leaves are variable with the basal ones generally somewhat lobed or toothed, with stalks; the upper ones narrower and stalkless. The whole plant is dull green and rather hairy. The flowerheads are composed of tubular, dark purple florets with black fringed bracts and they bloom in July and August.

Knapweed was once highly regarded as a

White or **Red Bryony** *Bryonia cretica* subsp. *dioica*

wound herb and included in a fourteenth-century ointment for pestilent wounds. It is also said to be a useful tonic and diuretic and, according to Culpeper: 'of special use for soreness of throat . . . and very good to stay bleeding at the nose and mouth'.

White or **Red Bryony** *Bryonia cretica* subsp. *dioica* is a perennial plant, native to Britain, which is also widely distributed in central and southern Europe, west Asia and north Africa. It commonly grows in scrub, copses and hedgerows. White bryony has a thick, tuberous, branched rootstock and very long, brittle, rough-haired stems that branch from the base and climb over hedges and bushes for several yards, assisted by their long tendrils. The deeply lobed leaves are covered in rough hairs and have a curved stalk. The small, greenish flowers grow in clumps of three and four in the leaf axils and bloom in May. The berries which follow on female plants are red or orange.

The generic and common names are derived from the Greek *bryo*, 'to thrust or sprout',

alluding to the speed at which the plant grows. The subspecific name *dioica* tells us that white bryony is dioiecious, i.e. has separate male and female plants. The French call the root *navet de diable*, devil's turnip, because of its violent and dangerous action. All parts of the plant are poisonous and should only be taken under the guidance of a physician.

The medicinal properties of the plant have been recognized since Hippocrates' time. The root exudes a milky juice which is very bitter and nauseous to the taste. It is violently purgative or cathartic and was used by the Romans and Greeks for this reason but it is no longer used as a purgative or an emetic because of its highly irritant nature. It was also used in the past for dropsy, rheumatism and sciatica and it is still used in homoeopathic medicine for the treatment of whooping cough, pleurisy and bronchitis as well as for chilblains.

Joe Pye Weed, Gravelroot or **Purple Boneset** *Eupatorium purpureum* Photographed August 28

Hemp Agrimony *Eupatorium cannabinum*

Squirting Cucumber *Ecballium elaterium*

Hemp Agrimony *Eupatorium cannabinum* is a perennial herb, native to Europe, western and central Asia and North Africa, which is commonly found growing wild in damp woods, ditches, river banks, fens and marshes. Hemp agrimony has a woody rootstock and erect, downy, reddish stems that are pleasantly aromatic when cut and grow to heights of 30–125 cm (12–50 in). The basal leaves are long-stalked, the stem leaves have very short stalks – all leaves being arranged in opposite pairs, bearing short hairs and tiny resinous dots. The crowded clusters of dull lilac, pinky-red or purplish flowers are arranged at the top of the stem or branches and bloom from August to September.

Used since ancient times as a gentle laxative and to treat eye-rheum, it was also considered to have diuretic and anti-scorbutic properties. The leaves are used to make an infusion that will relieve catarrh, influenza, coughs, colds, arthritis and rheumatism. It was widely used as a wound herb in the Middle Ages and is said to be good for problem skin and for scurvy. Modern research has suggested that the plant may have immune-boosting properties which would account for its use in treating colds and fevers and it is possible that it may prove useful in the treatment of Aids. Note that large doses are purgative.

Gather from the wild in the summer. Dry and store in a dark place for use during the winter months.

Joe Pye Weed, Gravelroot or **Purple Boneset** *Eupatorium purpureum* is a perennial herb, native to North America, which is found growing in moist soil and rich, swampy, low ground. Joe Pye weed has a stout, erect, unbranched stem that grows to heights of 90–300 cm (36–120 in). It is purple above the point of leaf attachment and the coarsely serrated, oblong-pointed leaves are generally arranged in whorls of three to six.

The numerous, elongated flowers are white, pinkish or purple and bloom from July to October. The whole plant emits a vanilla-like odour when crushed.

The plant was given the common name Joe Pye weed in memory of an American Indian doctor from New England who became famous curing typhus with this plant. Its other common names allude to its supposed efficacy in curing gravel and healing the pain that arises from a species of influenza common in the United States, known as break-bone fever.

Joe Pye weed is especially valuable as a diuretic, tonic and stimulant and useful for gout, rheumatism, dropsy and renal problems. The Meskwaki Indians also considered it 'a love medicine to be nibbled when speaking to women when they are in the wooing mood'!

This tall perennial is easily grown from seed.

Squirting Cucumber *Ecballium elaterium* is a perennial, herbaceous plant, native to Mediterranean Europe and naturalized in southern Britain, which is found growing quite abundantly near the shore. Squirting cucumber has a long, white, fleshy root and several round, thick, trailing stems from 20–60 cm (8–24 in) long. The rough, heart-shaped leaves are toothed or crinkled at the edge and the yellowish male flowers are bell-shaped and grouped in clusters; the female flowers are solitary and bloom in July. The green fruits are large, hairy and fleshy and when ripe they burst, ejecting the seeds quite a distance.

Squirting cucumber can be very dangerous and must never be taken except on prescription. In large doses it can cause nausea, vomiting, abortion in pregnant women and even death. In correct doses and combined with other substances it has been used to treat constipation and obesity.

This plant is an interesting novelty to grow from seed.

Bear's Breech or Acanthus *Acanthus spinosus*

indoors in a large pot. It likes well-drained loamy soil and full sun or partial shade. Propagation is by root division during the autumn and if the weather is very cold it is advisable to mulch the plants or cover them with litter for protection.

Acanthus spinosus is very similar but with much more divided leaves and is more commonly found in gardens.

Sea Holly or **Eryngo** *Erynium maritimum* is a smooth perennial, native to Europe from the North Sea to the Mediterranean and eastwards to the Black Sea, which is found growing wild on sandy or shingly soil by the sea. Sea holly is an intensely bluish plant with large, brown, fleshy, brittle roots reaching a long way into the soil. The solid, slightly ribbed stems grow to a height of 30 cm (12 in). The irregularly lobed leaves terminate in sharp prickles and the clusters of stalkless, blue flowers grow in the whorls of the uppermost leaves. They bloom in July and August.

The generic name is derived from the Greek *eruggarein*, 'to eructate', and refers to the plant's supposed efficacy in flatulent disorders. The specific name refers to its preference for a seaside habitat as does its common name, which also alludes to its spiny leaves, like those of holly.

Known since ancient times as an excellent flavouring, vegetable and medicine, sea holly roots were thought to contain aphrodisiac qualities. The roots have a sweetish taste and are very mucilaginous; boiled or roasted they resemble chestnuts in taste and are very nutritious – alternatively they can be candied and eaten as a sweet or used to flavour jams, jellies and toffees. The young flowering shoots and leaves are tasty boiled and served with butter.

Medicinally, sea holly is a diuretic and said to be useful for those with bladder complaints and painful urination. It also promotes perspiration and is an expectorant so it is helpful for long-standing coughs or consumption. It has been prescribed for those with nervous diseases. Made into an ointment, it may help heal the skin after splinters, bites and stings have been removed.

Clare Loewenfeld and Philippa Back in *The Complete Book of Herbs and Spices* recommend the following cough syrup:

'Cover 250 g/9 oz sea holly root with 1 l/ 40 fl oz cold water. Bring slowly to the boil and simmer gently until tender. Strain through a jelly cloth. To each ½ l/20 fl oz extract, add juice of one lemon, grated rind of half a lemon and 450 g/1 lb sugar. Boil hard for ten minutes and test for jelling. Pot and cover. Use a teaspoonful at a time in a little hot water.'

Sea holly can be found in the wild or easily cultivated. If you live near the sea and have sandy soil, cultivation of large fleshy roots should be easy but it will also grow in the garden if planted in a warm spot in well-drained, preferably gravelly soil although the roots will not be so large or fleshy. Sun is essential wherever it is grown. Either transplant young roots in the autumn and keep well-weeded or propagate by seeds. As the germination period is long, it is best to show the seeds in autumn in the place where you want them to grow as they do not transplant well.

Blessed Thistle or **Holy Thistle** *Cnicus benedictus* synonym *Carduus benedictus* is an annual herb, native to southern Europe, locally naturalized in central and south-eastern Europe, and also found in parts of the USSR, South

Bear's Breech or **Acanthus** *Acanthus mollis* is a hardy perennial, native to the west Mediterranean and introduced into Britain in the Middle Ages, becoming naturalized in western Cornwall and the Scilly Isles but now rarely found growing wild. It is commonly grown in gardens throughout Europe. Bear's breech has several sturdy simple stems that can grow to a height of 100 cm (40 in) and beautiful broad, glossy, dark-green leaves 63–150 cm (25–60 in) which are deeply pinnate. The white, purple or pale blue flowers are tube-shaped with a three-lobed lip and grow in a dense cluster at the top of the flower spikes. The leaves can be gathered from spring to summer and the flowers appear from August to September.

The generic name comes from the Greek

akanthos, 'spine'. Dioscorides, the classical physician, wrote a description of bear's breech in his *De Materia Medica*. It is said that the beautiful symmetry of the leaves and plant inspired the Greek architect Callimachus in his design for the columns at the temple of Corinth.

Bear's breech contains mucilage, tannins, glucose and pectin-like substances. It was formerly used as a healing herb and was regarded as soothing: the crushed leaves were used in cases of gout and to soothe burns and scalds. It is not reputed to have any culinary uses.

John Evelyn, the herbalist, grew this stately ornamental plant in his physic garden and it well deserves a place in a herbaceous border or herb garden; alternatively it can be grown

Sea Holly or **Eryngo** *Eryngium maritimum*

Blessed Thistle or **Holy Thistle** *Cnicus benedictus*

Africa and South America. It grows wild in stony, waste ground and cultivated fields. Blessed thistle has a cylindrical, white tap-root and a slender reddish, downy, branched stem that reaches a height of 60 cm (24 in). The long, dark green leaves are deeply lobed and prickly with prominent, pale veins. The pale yellow flowers are grouped in single, prickly heads and bloom from June to August.

Blessed thistle was so called because in the Middle Ages it was considered a cure-all for many diseases, and it is praised by most of the great herbalists for numerous curative properties. In *Much Ado About Nothing* Shakespeare wrote: 'Get you some of this distilled Carduus Benedictus and lay it to your heart; it is the only thing for a qualm.'

It was a common ingredient in medicines used for curing the plague and it was also used as a tonic and stimulant for encouraging appetite and preventing sickness. One modern study has shown that the essential oil contained in the plant has antibiotic properties against *Staphylococcus aureus* and *Staphylococcus faecalis* which may explain its empirical use against infections and sickness. In large doses, blessed thistle is a strong emetic and thus useful in cases of stomach poisoning. An infusion will induce perspiration and so it has proved very effective in cases of intermittent fever. Like centaury and wormwood, it is a general tonic and stimulant for the whole system. It is also considered good for the blood and an aid to the memory. In small doses a warm infusion of the flowers and leaves can be given to nursing mothers to induce a plentiful supply of milk. Homoeopaths use a tincture from fresh plants to treat hepatitis and arthritis. It is also used externally in the

treatment of shingles. Mességué recommends using the plant in a hip-bath to ease piles and claims success with it for expelling worms and healing cuts and wounds.

The Romans ate all parts of the plant: they boiled the roots, used the young leaves in salads and ate the flower heads like globe artichokes. Nowadays, small amounts of young leaves can be added to spring salads as a tonic or an infusion can either be drunk as a mild laxative or used to clean wounds.

Blessed thistle can either be collected in the wild or easily grown in a herb garden from seed. Plant in ordinary soil in the sun. Gather flower tops in July.

Stemless Carline Thistle *Carlina acaulis* is a monocarpic short-lived perennial, native to central and southern Europe, which is found growing in poor, dry, sandy pastures and chalky banks. Stemless carline thistle has a long, fleshy tap-root and a short stem that, when present, rarely exceeds 50 cm (20 in). The flat, spiky leaves form a tight basal rosette and the flowers are gathered into heads which have a yellowish heart, surrounded by silvery-white, radiating bracts that resemble daisy petals, while the outer bracts are very prickly. The flowers bloom from May to September.

The generic name is derived from the legend of Emperor Charlemagne who had a dream in which an angel appeared to him and told him that his army would be cured of the horrible pestilence that was destroying it, if treated with the plant on which the angel's arrow landed – the carline thistle.

Whether or not his army was cured history has not revealed, but for a long time the plant

Carline Thistle *Carlina vulgaris*

was considered to have properties that countered poisons and snake bites.

Although these claims are unsubstantiated, the stemless carline thistle is definitely used for treating skin disorders as well as being a tonic. However, excessive amounts may induce vomiting. In times past distilled water from the stemless carline thistle was in great demand as an aphrodisiac but nowadays it is mainly used in dried flower arrangements because the heads retain their appearance for a long time. They are also used as a kind of rustic barometer because they expand in dry weather and close when rain is imminent.

Carline Thistle *Carlina vulgaris* is quite common all over Europe on chalk hills.

Deadly Nightshade or Belladonna *Atropa belladonna*

Deadly Nightshade *Atropa belladonna* (flower)

Deadly Nightshade *Atropa belladonna* (fruit)

Deadly Nightshade, Belladonna *Atropa belladonna* is a perennial plant, native to western, central and southern Europe, south-west Asia and North Africa and naturalized in North America. It grows in shady parts of woods and thickets or near old buildings and ruins on chalky soil. Deadly nightshade has a thick, whitish, fleshy root and a stout purplish stem that grows to heights of 60–150 m (2–5 ft). The dark, dull green leaves, 8–25 cm (3–10 in) long, are oval and pointed, generally single lower down the stem and in alternate pairs higher up. The drooping, dark purple, bell-shaped flowers bloom from June to August and the shiny black berries develop from August to November. The whole plant has an unpleasant smell when crushed.

The generic name for the plant is probably derived from the Greek *Atropos*, the one of the three Fates who held the scissors to cut the thread of life – an allusion to the deadly nature of the plant. The specific name probably comes from the Italian *bella donna*, 'beautiful woman', and alludes to the fact that Italian women squeezed belladonna juice into their eyes to make them shine brilliantly and alluringly – one of the attributes of the plant being to dilate the pupil. Another common name, dwale, is thought to derive from the Old Norse *duale*, dead sleep, referring to the plant's narcotic qualities. The other common names, devil's berries, naughty man's cherries, devil's herb and deadly nightshade all refer to the lethal properties of the plant.

Despite its highly poisonous nature, deadly nightshade has been valued as a medicinal plant for centuries and was widely cultivated in medieval gardens. It was reputed to be the plant that poisoned Marcus Antonius's troops during the Parthian wars and that, during the sixteenth century, Macbeth's soldiers used it to poison an invading Danish army during a truce by mixing it into the peace cup. At the beginning of the nineteenth century a young German pharmacist, Friedrich Wilhelm Serturner, extracted white alkaloid crystals from the crude drug opion. He called it opium. Following his techniques, other pharmacists quickly isolated other alkaloids from the medicinal plants that most interested them because of their powerful effect and one of these was atropine from deadly nightshade.

Atropine, contained in the juice of the root and leaves, is much used in modern medicine as a narcotic, sedative and diuretic. It is used for disorders of the nervous centres and as an antispasmodic in conditions of the stomach, intestine and bile duct; also to relieve whooping cough, asthma or fevers. Externally, it is used for gout, neuralgia and rheumatic pains, in the treatment of Parkinson's Disease, and in ophthamology. Hahnemann, the founder of homoeopathy, proved that tiny doses of belladonna tincture offered protection from scarlet fever. Thus Beth, in Louisa M. Alcott's *Little Women*, is told to 'go home and take belladonna right away' when they realize that she has been nursing a baby with scarlet fever. Weiss says that he has found it invaluable in the treatment of ulcers, chronic intestinal disease and spastic constipation, and claims that no synthetic anticholinergic drugs are as effective as belladonna or have fewer side effects.

Deadly nightshade is highly poisonous and should never be taken unless under expert medical supervision. It is inadvisable to grow it anywhere in a garden where children or domestic pets could be tempted by it.

Thornapple or **Jimson Weed** *Datura stramonium*

Datura metel

Thornapple or **Jimson Weed** *Datura stramonium* is an annual plant, of uncertain origin, which can now be found in most parts of the world. It grows wild in waste places, cultivated ground and among old ruins. Thornapple is a stout, erect, dichotomously branched herb that reaches a height of 1 m (40 in). The large, alternate leaves are ovate-triangular and cut into several lobes on the margin. The single, fragrant tubular flowers are white with six prominent ribs, and bloom from July to September. They are succeeded by the spiny, green seed-capsules which look rather like large walnuts.

The common name jimson weed is a corruption of Jamestown in Virginia and arose because soldiers sent there in 1676 to put down Bacon's rebellion ate some cooked young shoots of jimson weed and were said to have behaved very peculiarly for several days as a result. When they finally came to their senses, they couldn't remember anything that had passed.

Numerous Indian tribes throughout North and South America were aware of the intensely narcotic effect of thornapple. The plant was used in initiating rites, for purposes of divination and prophecy, to induce dreams and visions and as an anaesthetic for setting bones or performing surgery. In India, thieves and assassins administered jimson weed to their victims to render them unconscious and it has been suggested that the priests of Apollo at Delphi used this plant to induce prophecies.

Thornapple is related to belladonna, containing the same powerful alkaloids hyoscyamine and atropine which act on the nervous system. Since the nineteenth century the leaves have been used for their narcotic, diuretic, antispasmodic and pain-relieving properties and it was a constituent in medicine used to calm mental patients and induce sleep and amnesia. The leaves were also smoked to relieve asthma, taken in tincture or pill form to allay whooping cough or bladder spasm, and in ointment or plasters to soothe scalds, burns, muscular rheumatism, piles and abscesses. Weiss reports that in modern phytotherapy, thornapple is one of the main constituents of burning powders used to bring relief to asthma patients as a simple self-help remedy that can be used at night. However, thornapple is poisonous and dangerous; many deaths have occurred from overdoses, so it should never be taken except on prescription from a qualified practitioner.

Very easy to grow from seed but probably best avoided as it is so poisonous.

Datura metel is a very poisonous plant, similar to thornapple, but with larger, upward-facing flowers.

Bittersweet or **Woody Nightshade** *Solanum dulcamara* is a perennial shrub or climbing plant native to Europe, Asia and North Africa, which is found naturalized in North America. It commonly grows wild in hedges, woods, stony beaches and waste places. Bittersweet has a cylindrical, fibrous root with a scrambling, light-brown branched stem that reaches lengths of 30–200 cm (12–80 in). The alternate, stalked, glossy leaves are oval to heart-shaped and three-lobed with two smaller, lateral leaflets. The violet flowers grow in loose, drooping clusters and bloom from May to September.

The generic name is derived from the Latin *solamen*, 'a comfort or consolation', and indicates how highly this genus of plants was regarded medicinally. The specific name means 'bitter-sweet' which alludes to the fact that,

Woody Nightshade *Solanum dulcamara*

when first chewed, the leaves and root taste bitter but later have a sweet flavour.

In the past bittersweet was considered an excellent remedy for a range of illnesses. Gerard praised it for those suffering bruises or falls, believing that it dispersed congealed blood. Boerhaave thought it as good as sarsaparilla for use as a restorative tonic and others claimed it cured syphilis, pleurisy, rheumatism and fever.

Weiss reports that bittersweet is considered a powerful and effective drug for the treatment of rheumatism, gout and scrofula because of the combined diuretic, metabolic and narcotic effect of the plant. It is also prescribed for chronic eczema and skin complaints. However, caution is advised when using this plant as it can have toxic side-effects. Only use when prescribed by a medical practitioner.

Chaste Tree or **Hemp Tree** *Vitex agnus-castus*

Chaste Tree or **Hemp Tree** *Vitex agnus-castus*
is a fragrant, deciduous shrub, native to
southern Europe and western Asia and also
found in South and North America. It grows in
dry soil on shores and coastlines. Chaste tree
grows to heights of 1–6 m (3–12 ft) and has
dense branches that divide frequently at the top;
the twigs are covered in a grey, felty down. The
large, dark-green leaves, composed of five to
seven narrow segments, are smooth above and
white and felty below. The fragrant blue or pink
flowers grow in whorls on a long, slender spike
and bloom in September or October, followed
by round, purple-black berries containing four
seeds.

The common name arose from the plant's
ancient reputation for securing chastity and
when Greek women performed their spring-
time rites to Ceres they decked their couches
with chaste tree garlands. In the Middle Ages
the freshly pulped berries were used to relieve
paralysis and pains in the limbs and the
powdered seeds were given to dampen
sexuality. Modern research indicates that the
plant acts on the hormone-producing glands and
stimulates progesterone production so it has also
been successfully used to promote milk-flow in
breast-feeding mothers.

Tinnevelly Senna *Cassia angustifolia* is a tender
shrubby pea plant found from north-east Africa
to India, which grows wild and is cultivated.

Tinnevelly senna has a long history of use as a
purgative and is particularly useful for those
suffering from habitual constipation. The active
principles it contains are anthraquinone
glycosides, which acts on the colon, and
tartrates, which inhibit the absorption of fluid
from the stomach and thus increase the laxative
effect. However, it may cause muscle

contraction in the uterus so it should not be
taken during pregnancy. In small doses it brings
reliable relief for constipation but in larger doses
it is inclined to cause vomiting and griping
pains. The pods are gentler in action than the
leaves but in most commercial preparations it is
generously mixed with syrup and aromatic
herbs such as ginger, cloves or cinnamon to
make it more palatable and to counteract
nausea.

Numerous species of senna exist world-wide
and most are used in a similar way.

Castor Oil Plant *Ricinus communis* is usually
grown as an annual herb but can become a
shrub. Native to India, it is now culivated in
fields and grown for ornament in gardens, and
naturalized in almost all parts of the world.
Castor oil plant is rather variable in growth
depending on habitat but it generally has a tap-
root and an erect, dark-red stem that reaches a
height of 4 m (13 ft). The large, alternate leaves
are palmate with five to nine lance-shaped lobes
with an irregularly toothed margin. The clusters
of reddish flowers form an oblong, terminal
spike, male and female on the same plant, and
bloom from August to October, followed by the
fruit which is generally oval and laterally
compressed. The seeds have a shining, mottled,
leathery, grey-brown outer coat and a thin,
brittle, dark-brown inner coat.

The generic name is derived from a Latin
word *ricinus*, used by Pliny to describe a dog-
tick and referring to the shape and colour of the
seeds, and the name castor comes from Jamaica
where they called the plant *Agnus Castus*
although it does not resemble the real plant of
that name.

The castor oil plant has been known since
earliest times; its seeds have been found in

Egyptian tombs, and both Dioscorides and
Pliny wrote several centuries later of its use as a
medicinal purgative.

In the Middle Ages it was grown in gardens
for ornament and occasionally for medicine
though later it was imported from Jamaica for
that purpose, having fallen into disuse in
Europe. Nowadays, it is widely cultivated for
the oil obtained from the seeds which is
included in fuel mixtures for precision engines
and as a lubricating oil. It is also used as a
drying oil in painting; it is employed in the
manufacture of candles and varnishes and high-
class furniture and car polishes; it is used in the
manufacture of fly papers because it is repellent
to these pests and it is used as a basic ingredient
in cosmetics and soaps.

Medicinally, it is best known as a gentle
laxative, excellent for convalescents, children
and pregnant women. The only problem with
castor oil is its unpleasant taste which can cause
sickness. It is generally disguised by lemon or
sassafras oil or taken with milk or coffee but
capsules are probably the least offensive way to
take it. In the Canary Islands, breast-feeding
mothers use the fresh leaves as a compress to
encourage milk flow. The oil can be used
externally to soothe itch or ringworm.

The most important thing to remember about
the plant is that the seeds, if eaten, can be fatal.
The walls of the seeds and the waste matter left
after expressing the oil contain a highly toxic
substance called ricin which is violently
purgative. Eating three to five seeds can kill a
child so take great care if growing this plant in
the garden.

Ricinus communis 'Gibsonii' is a garden form
with purplish red leaves and stems, often grown
as a large, decorative border plant.

Tinnevelly Senna *Cassia angustifolia*

Prickly Ash *Zanthoxylum americanum* is a small to medium, prickly, aromatic tree, native to central and eastern North America, which grows wild in damp woods and shady areas. Prickly ash has greyish bark covered with sharp, scattered prickles and can reach a height of 7.5 m (25 ft). The alternate, pinnate leaves are comprised of four to five pairs of leaflets and the small, green flowers bloom from March to April, before the foliage. The dark berries encased in a reddish-green capsule grow in clusters at the top of the branches.

The generic name is derived from the Greek words *zanthos* and *xylum*, 'yellow wood', and the common name alludes, of course, to the prickly nature of the tree. Another common name, toothache tree, reflects the popular habit of chewing the bark to relieve toothache.

Prickly ash was a popular medicinal plant among the American Indian tribes. The powdered roots or bark were used for toothache, rheumatism, typhoid, skin diseases and as an emmenagogue. It is also used as a tonic for a weakened stomach or digestion, and a decoction may be prescribed for colic, lethargy and poor blood circulation in hands and feet. Externally, a decoction of the powdered root can be used as a compress on ulcers and wounds. The aromatic leaves and berries have a smell that is reminiscent of oil of lemons, and the berries and bark are hot and acid-tasting – far worse than the pain of the toothache that they cure according to one American writer, Dr Millspaugh!

Spikenard *Aralia racemosa* is a perennial plant, native to eastern North America, west to Missouri, which grows wild in rich woods. Spikenard has a thick, large aromatic root-stock and a numerously branched stem that reaches heights of 90–180 cm (36–72 in). The large, alternate leaves have oval to heart-shaped leaflets with double-toothed margins and the large clusters of small, greenish flowers bloom in July and August, succeeded by the round, reddish-purple fruits.

Spikenard was a popular medicinal plant among some American Indian tribes. The pounded aromatic root was used as a poultice to reduce swellings by the Potawatomi tribe and the Ojibura used it with wild ginger to dress broken bones. The Cherokee drank an infusion of the root to cure backache and it later became popular with the colonists not only for this purpose but also for rheumatism, asthma, coughs, skin problems and pulmonary conditions.

Not commonly grown in herb gardens.

Castor Oil Plant *Ricinus communis*

Bronze Castor Oil Plant *Ricinus communis* 'Gibsonii'

Prickly Ash *Zanthoxylum americanum*

Spikenard *Aralia racemosa*

Old Man's Beard or **Travellers' Joy** *Clematis vitalba*

Old Man's Beard or **Travellers' Joy** *Clematis vitalba*

Old Man's Beard or **Travellers' Joy** *Clematis vitalba* is a perennial, climbing plant, native to Europe, North Africa, the Caucasus and North America, which grows wild in hedgerows, thickets, woodland and rocky, calcareous slopes. Old man's beard is a sub-shrubby plant with thin, trailing stems which can grow as long as 30 m (100 ft). The pinnate, opposite leaves have small, toothed, distant leaflets and the four-petalled, fragrant white flowers grow in panicles and bloom from July to September, followed by woolly plumed fruits which give the plant its common name, old man's beard.

This plant is poisonous and should never be taken internally. Externally it causes inflammation, blisters, and sores, so is used by homoeopaths to produce a sympathetic reaction.

Horse-chestnut *Aesculus hippocastanum*

Blue Passionflower *Passiflora caerulea*

Can be grown from seed but is not so commonly grown as the decorative garden varieties of clematis.

Horse-chestnut *Aesculus hippocastanum* is a large deciduous tree, native to Albania and Greece, which is now widely naturalized throughout western Europe and introduced into North America. It is commonly planted for ornament and often self-sown. Horse-chestnut has a broad crown and reaches a height of about 25 m (82 ft). The trunk has rough, scaly, dark grey-brown bark and the dark-green palmate leaves with five to seven leaflets are obovate with pointed tips and serrated edges. The fragrant pink or white flower clusters bloom in May, followed by the roundish, prickly fruits containing two reddish brown seeds (conkers).

The origin of the generic name is unclear, but both the specific and common names arose from the belief that the plant could cure horses' coughs.

Introduced into Europe in the seventeenth century, horse-chestnut is known to have narcotic, fever-reducing and tonic properties. The bark of the branches was used instead of quinine during Napoleon's reign and a decoction of the outer covering of the fruit is recommended for circulation disorders and venous congestion such as haemorrhoids and varicose veins. In North America, Indian tribes mixed the crushed conkers with lard as a remedy for haemorrhoids. In line with tradition, horse-chestnut fruits are now scientifically recognized as being a valuable remedy for diseases of the venous system. They contain two important principles: aesculin and aescin. Aescin, a saponin, affects capillary permeability and improves the tone in the walls of the vein, making it a useful treatment for varicose veins and thrombophlebitis and for

relief of swelling with bruises and fracture. It is also an effective treatment for painful cramp in the legs at night.

Horse-chestnuts have been used to make a nutritious cattle fodder and at one time they were also used to make soap and in laundering because they contain saponin. An old country remedy for rheumatism and haemorrhoids is to carry two or three chestnuts in the pocket, replacing them when they become hard.

Horse-chestnuts can be found in large gardens and parks and conkers are plentiful in autumn.

American Wild Passionflower *Passiflora incarnata* is a herbaceous perennial, native to southern North America and introduced into Europe and other areas where it flourishes if the climate is suitable. It is also widely cultivated for its beautiful flowers. American wild passionflower has a rhizome from which spring several climbing stems with tendrils, that reach a height of 6 m (20 ft). The leaves are three-lobed and finely serrated, and the sweet-smelling flowers are pale peach or yellowish, ringed with purple. They bloom from July to October and are succeeded by a large, ovoid, many-seeded fruit that is orangey when ripe and greenish-yellow when dried and shrivelled; its yellow pulp is sweet and delicious to eat.

The generic name is derived from the Latin *flos passionis*, 'flower of the passion', alluding to the symbolic similarity of the flowers to the instruments of Christ's Passion: the corolla represents the crown of thorns, the three styles of the pistil are the nails, the stamens the hammer, the pointed leaves the spear and the tendrils the whip.

Although passionflower was used to some extent by native American Indians, it was not

until the late nineteenth century that the flowering and fruiting tops were recognized as having mild sedative and hypnotic properties and used to relieve insomnia and soothe nerves. It is now used in homoeopathic medicine for nervous insomnia and is also prescribed for nervous complaints of the heart or stomach and nervous disorders connected with menstruation and menopause.

To ease these complaints make a mild decoction by putting 30–45 g/1–1½ oz of chopped leaves and flowers into 1 l/1/2 pt of water, heat gently to boiling then leave to infuse for ten minutes. Drink three cupfuls a day.

Blue Passionflower *Passiflora caerulea*, native to South America, is often grown in gardens, but needs a protected position as it is a little tender.

Sassafras *Sassafras albidum* (in autumn colour)

Sassafras *Sassafras albidum* is an aromatic, deciduous shrub or tree, native to eastern North America as far west as Texas, which grows in thickly wooded areas. Sassafras has grey to orange-brown, irregularly ridged bark and grows to heights of 6–15 m (20–50 ft). The green leaves are either oval or have two or three lobes and they turn yellow or reddish in the autumn. The small yellow-green flowers grow in loose clusters and bloom from April to May. The round, dark-blue berries ripen in September.

Sassafras was a very popular plant with American Indian tribes. They used the root and bark to treat a whole range of diseases including fever and measles. Early settlers quickly sent large shipments home to Europe where it gained a reputation for curing syphilis and rheumatism. The roots, flowers and leaves have variously been made into teas to act as a tonic, lower blood pressure and induce perspiration in colds. In Louisiana the leaves are dried and used as a condiment called filé for flavouring stews and sauces – it being the chief spice in the famous Cajun dish 'Gumbo Filé'.

The aromatic oil distilled from the root bark has been used to scent perfume, soap, toothpaste, mouthwashes, chewing gum and beer but taken in large doses internally the oil can produce marked narcotic poisoning so it should only be taken when prescribed by a medical practitioner. It is now thought that sassafras may be carcinogenic so should not be eaten frequently or in large quantities.

An attractive small tree, easily grown in a garden, with interesting leaves that turn a lovely colour in autumn.

New Jersey Tea or **Red Root** *Ceanothus americanus* is a low shrub, native to eastern North America, which grows wild in open woods and along roadsides and is cultivated for ornament. New Jersey tea has large red roots and downy stems that reach a height of 90–120 cm (36–48 in). The pointed, ovate, toothed leaves are downy and the numerous, small, pretty, white flowers grow in oval clusters in the leaf axils and bloom from May to July, followed by triangular seed vessels.

The common name, New Jersey tea, arose from the use of this plant as a substitute for tea during the War of Independence and the name red root refers to its reddish roots which are used in Canada to dye wool a reddish-cinnamon colour.

New Jersey tea was very popular with some Americans but unpopular with others because it contains no caffeine. Medicinally, it was used by American Indians as a lotion for skin cancer and venereal sores. It is said to have sedative properties and has been used for asthma, bronchitis, whooping cough and dysentery. Its astringency makes it useful as a mouthwash and gargle.

Rarely grown in gardens.

Myrtle *Myrtus communis* is an evergreen shrub, native in southern Europe and south-east Asia and extensively cultivated in temperate areas. It sometimes grows wild in scrubland. Myrtle is a tall, aromatic, much-branched plant with reddish bark becoming grey and cracked with age, that grows to heights of 3–5 m (10–16½ ft). The large, ovate leaves are dark, glossy green above, paler below and highly scented when

crushed. The creamy white flowers grow singly or in small clusters in the leaf axils and bloom from May to August succeeded by a purplish-black, fleshy berry containing kidney-shaped seeds.

Myrtle has a history of use since ancient times. The Greeks and Romans considered it sacred to Aphrodite/Venus and it was worn by winners in the Olympic games. In the Middle East it was used as an astringent dusting powder for babies being wrapped in swaddling clothes. The berries were used for dyeing hair and eaten to sweeten the breath. The oil extracted from the plant was used in cosmetics and perfumes and the leaves added to pot-pourris. The Athenians used to eat fresh myrtle berries and, dried, they were used as a spice.

Medicinally, myrtle eases flatulence and is a soothing expectorant when drunk as a tea. Recent research has shown that myrtle contains a substance which has an antibiotic action, thus explaining its usefulness in chest complaints.

To make an infusion, pour ½ l/1 pt of boiling water on to 15 g/½ oz of myrtle leaves and infuse for five to ten minutes. Strain and sweeten with a little honey if necessary.

Myrtle will grow in a sheltered, well-drained position as long as it is protected from cold, drying winds. To propagate, layer in July and when roots have formed, cut and plant out. Keep earth well-watered and well compacted around the plant. Gather leaves and flowers for drying in late spring and store in airtight glass jars for winter use.

Witch (or **Wych**) **Hazel** *Hamamelis virginiana* is a shrub, native to eastern North America, which

New Jersey Tea *Ceanothus americanus*

Myrtle *Myrtus communis*

grows in dry or moist woods. Witch hazel has several crooked, branching trunks with smooth, grey bark emerging from a single root and can reach heights of 3–4.5 m (10–15 ft). The oval leaves with wavy-toothed edges drop off in autumn just as the bright yellow clusters of flowers appear in September to November. The flowers are followed by the black nuts containing edible white seeds which often do not ripen until the following summer when they are violently ejected from their shells.

There is uncertainty about the derivation of the generic name – an ancient Greek word, *hamemelis* meaning 'a pear-shaped fruit' while an American source says that it is derived from two Greek words, *hama*, 'at the same time', and *melis*, 'a fruit', meaning that the flowers appear at the same time that the previous year's fruits are ripening. The specific name refers to the area from which the plant was first collected and introduced to cultivation, the low damp woods of Virginia. The common name arose from the plant's association with witchcraft and the use of its forked branches as a divining rod in the search for water and gold. (Old English *wicé*, 'pliant'.)

Witch hazel has a long history of use among the American Indians. Decoctions and ointments were made from the leaves and twigs and applied to aching muscles and backs, bruises and sprains; they were also used as an eyewash. Witch hazel leaves were soon listed in the National Formulary for relieving inflammations, bruises and cuts and generally noted for their astringent properties.

Witch hazel is used as a tonic and sedative and considered useful for treating piles and diarrhoea, bleeding noses and varicose veins. It will also soothe insect bites, burns and scalds and soothe tired, aching eyes.

To make an infusion take 30–45 g/1–1½ oz of leaves, twigs or bark and add 1 1/2 pt of boiling water. Infuse for ten minutes. Strain and drink freely to ease bowel complaints. For external use make a stronger decoction by doubling the proportion of witch hazel to water.

Witch Hazel *Hamamelis virginiana*

Greater Periwinkle *Vinca major* (above), **Lesser Periwinkle** *Vinca minor* (below)

Madagascar Periwinkle *Catharanthus roseus* synonym *Vinca rosea*

Lesser Periwinkle *Vinca minor* is a perennial, low-lying, rambling shrub, native to central Europe and western Asia and distributed in more northerly parts too, also introduced and now naturalized in North America. It grows in woods, copses and hedges. Lesser periwinkle has trailing, rooting stems that can reach lengths of 30–60 cm (12–24 in) and short, erect, flowering stems. The smooth leaves have very short stalks and are lanceolate-elliptical. The blue-purple, mauve or white flowers appear singly (or occasionally in twos) in the leaf axils and bloom from February to June.

Greater Periwinkle *Vinca major* native to Mediterranean Europe, grows in gardens and is sometimes found as an escape. As its name implies, it is a large, upright plant with big egg-to heart-shaped leaves.

The generic and common names derive from Latin: either *vincire*, 'to bind', alluding to the long, trailing stems that spread over and bind down other plants in its vicinity, or from *vincere*, 'to overcome', alluding to periwinkle's medicinal properties in overcoming various illnesses. The specific names refer to their size.

Periwinkles have a long history of medicinal use and were frequently associated with magic. The 'parwynke' is mentioned in Chaucer, and in Anglo-Saxon herbals as 'pervenze' and one old name, sorcerer's violet, alludes to its use by magicians in making love-potions. It was also believed to ward off wicked spirits.

Both periwinkles were used medicinally for their astringent and tonic properties and recommended for headaches, vertigo and memory difficulties. Ointment or tea made from periwinkles were reputed to allay internal bleeding, excessive menstruation and bleeding piles. It is also recommended as soothing and calming for all kinds of wounds and skin infections. In homoeopathy lesser periwinkle was made into a tincture and prescribed for babies with internal bleeding. Poultices of periwinkle were said to relieve cramps if wound around the affected area and crushed periwinkle leaves inserted into the nostril will reputedly halt a nosebleed.

Weiss reports that research in the 1950s and 1960s on lesser periwinkle identified the alkaloid vincamine as the most important principle in the plant which, it became apparent, has a specific effect on the cerebral flow. Several trials have proved that vincamine has a beneficial effect on patients with cerebral arteriosclerosis, improving memory disorders, lack of concentration, irritability, headaches and vertigo. It has also been found effective in treating tinnitis and hearing defects in old age.

Both greater and lesser periwinkle can readily be grown in the garden. They are propagated by the long trailing stems which root into the soil and quickly extend in every direction to form a dense ground cover, often to the exclusion of other weaker plants.

Madagascar Periwinkle *Catharanthus roseus* synonym *Vinca rosea* is a small undershrub, native to east Africa and now naturalized in many warm or desert areas and cultivated in greenhouses in cooler climates. Madagascar periwinkle has an erect, cylindrical, branched stem that reaches a height of 90 cm (36 in). The stalked leaves are opposite, ovate to elliptical, with a smooth, glossy, veined upper surface and a paler under surface. The crimson, pink, purple or white-petalled flowers with a darker eye grow singly at the top of the stem or from the leaf axils and bloom from May to October.

Heartsease or **Wild Pansy** *Viola tricolor*

Heliotrope *Heliotropium peruvianum*
'Royal Marine'

Madagascar periwinkle has aroused great interest among scientists during the twentieth century. In 1923 it was discovered that the plant could be used as a substitute for insulin and was therefore useful in the treatment of diabetes. The alkaloids vincristine and vinblastine the plant contains show, statistically, significant anti-tumour activity and are now firmly established as cytostatics for cancer therapy, especially in the treatment of acute leukaemia in children, Hodgkin's disease and solid tumours. Unfortunately, non-cancerous cells are also affected and it takes many months for the neurotoxic side effects to wear off.

Madagascar periwinkle is not hardy enough to be grown outdoors in colder climates but it can thrive if cultivated and protected in a greenhouse or conservatory.

Heartsease or **Wild Pansy** *Viola tricolor* is an annual or short-lived perennial herb, native to Europe and western Asia as far as the Himalayas, though common as a weed all over the world. It grows wild in grassland or on waste ground, favouring acid or neutral soil. Heartsease has a rhizome with slender rootlets and a simple or slightly branched stem that creeps a little and then rises erect to reach a height of up to 50 cm (20 in). The leaves are variable but the lower ones are usually oval becoming narrow as they go out, wavy to toothed at the edge. The flowers are borne singly on a long stalk from the leaf axil and they are a combination of violet and white or yellow. They bloom at almost any time during the year.

A favourite herb for growing in gardens for many centuries, heartsease has numerous other common names which testify to its use as a potent love charm – hence, love lies bleeding, cuddle me, kiss-her-in-the-buttery and so on – but it has also been suggested that the name heartsease may have arisen because of its medicinal reputation as a cordial for the heart. It was also sometimes known as the herb of trinity because in each flower there were three colours. It is a mild diuretic and helps to cleanse the system and stimulate the metabolism. It is prescribed for skin diseases and rheumatism but the root and seeds are emetic and purgative. Paediatricians have reported excellent results using heartsease to treat infant eczema, milk crust and chronic skin conditions. It is taken both internally and externally, as a compress. There has been considerable success with adult eczema too.

To make a mild decoction, put 45–60 g/1½–2 oz of dried plant in 1 1/2 pt of cold water. Leave to soak for an hour, then bring to the boil for twenty seconds. Leave to infuse for ten more minutes, then strain. Drink up to 1 1/2 pt a day for rheumatoid arthritis, weak nerves, exhaustion and jaundice. Also make a concentrated decoction (double the quantity of herb to water) and add it to the bath to soothe rheumatic pain; use externally as a skin lotion for skin complaints. A syrup from the flowers is reputed to make a soothing cough medicine.

Heartsease can easily be collected from the wild or grown from seed in a garden. Collect and dry the whole plant from your garden between June and August when it is in peak condition, dry it gently and store in airtight, glass jars for winter use.

Heliotrope *Heliotropium peruvianum* is a sweetly scented plant from Peru, often cultivated in gardens. It has purplish-green leaves.

Its name is derived from the Greek *helios*, 'sun', because when the flowers open they gradually turn to follow the sun. During the night they turn again to be ready for sunrise the next morning. According to Grieve, heliotrope was used in homoeopathy to make a tincture prescribed for 'clergyman's sore throat and uterine displacement'!

Heliotropium peruvianum 'Royal Marine' has darker flowers and leaves than the main species and is much more common in cultivation.

Pheasant's Eye *Adonis annua* is an annual herb, native to southern Europe and south-west Asia, which has been introduced all over the world. It is sometimes found as an arable weed or as a garden escape. Pheasant's eye has a slender tap-root and a generally smooth, branched stem that reaches heights of 10–14 cm (4–6 in). The leaves are finely cut and the small, scarlet flowers with a black basal spot grow at the ends of the stems and branches and bloom from June to August.

The generic name commemorates the god Adonis from whose blood, it is said in Greek legend, this plant sprang. The common name is an apt reference to the similarity of the flowers to a pheasant's eye. Although regarded as having medicinal properties in former times, it is no longer used today.

Spring Pheasant's Eye or **Ox-Eye** *Adonis vernalis* is a poisonous perennial herb, native in central Europe, which is found wild in mountainous pastures and frequently grown in gardens. Spring pheasant's eye has a rhizome with many rootlets and a simple branched stem that reaches heights of 20–25 cm (8–10 in). The leaves are finely cut and the single yellow flowers with many petals bloom from March to April.

Spring pheasant's eye is a medicinal plant with diuretic and cardiotonic properties. It is used as a cardiosedative, bringing relief to functional heart conditions and arterial hypertension. The effects of spring pheasant's eye are temporary and there is no risk of accumulation. However, it should only be taken under medical supervision, since it contains poisonous glycosides related to digitalin.

Easily grown from seed.

Pheasant's Eye *Adonis annua*

Mistletoe *Viscum album*

Holly *Ilex aquifolium*

Mistletoe *Viscum album* is a woody, evergreen, parasitic plant, native to Europe, North Africa and west and central Asia. It grows on the branches of a variety of deciduous trees, particularly apple trees. Mistletoe favours soft-barked trees and has numerously branched stems up to 100 cm (40 in). The yellowish-green, leathery leaves are a sort of elongated egg shape and the greenish flowers grow in threes, blooming from February to April, succeeded by the white berries which appear in October and ripen by December.

The generic name is derived from the Latin for 'sticky' and refers, of course, to the viscous juice found in the white berries; its common name birdlime also refers to this. The Latin specific name, *album*, 'white', describes the colour of the berries. The common name has given rise to a number of interpretations, the most probable being that it arose from the Anglo-Saxon word *Misteltan* – tan meaning 'twig' and *Mistel* either coming from *mist*, 'birdlime' in old Dutch or from *mistl*, 'different', meaning that the twigs are different from the tree on which they grow.

Mistletoe has a long history of symbolism and legend attached to it, differing from country to country. The Druids considered mistletoe a holy herb and had many ceremonies to cut it for their New Year celebrations. If some fell from the tree, that was considered a bad portent. The tradition of decorating the house with mistletoe at Christmas is probably a continuation of that pagan tradition. Grieve gives the following explanation for the custom of kissing under the mistletoe on New Year's Eve: in Scandinavian legend Balder, the god of Peace, was slain with an arrow of mistletoe and he was restored to life at the request of the other gods and goddesses; mistletoe was afterwards given into the keeping of the goddess of Love and it was ordained that everyone who passed under it should receive a

kiss, to show that the branch had become an emblem of love and not of hate.

The mystery and superstition surrounding mistletoe probably arose because of its power to cure or alleviate the suffering of people with epilepsy or mental disorders. The plant has the physiological effect of numbing the central nervous system, causing loss of feeling and slowing down the heart. Taken in small doses it was used to reduce or stop epileptic spasms and other convulsions, but taken in large doses the plant, and especially the berries, is poisonous and can be dangerous, particularly if eaten by children, causing the symptoms that in smaller doses it cures.

When taken under prescription, mistletoe can be helpful for treating high blood pressure, arteriosclerosis, migraine, dizziness, cramps, sluggish digestion and difficult menstruation. Weiss reports that there has been extensive literature in recent times concerning the use of mistletoe in cancer therapy. Claims for its efficacy in bringing relief to cancer patients and arresting the development of tumours have generally been ignored by oncologists but there is empirical evidence to support its use as a follow-up therapy after surgery or radiation treatment. Many cancer sufferers have claimed that it has improved their general condition and overall sense of well-being right up to the terminal stage. It would be interesting if someone undertook an objective assessment of mistletoe therapy for cancer.

Externally, poultices made from leaves and berries boiled for a few minutes in milk or water bring relief to those suffering from rheumatism.

Mistletoe can be readily gathered from the wild in some areas or it is not too difficult to grow in the garden, although it will greatly weaken its host. Put sticky berries into the crevices of the tree or beneath the branches and the seeds inside the berries will soon send roots

penetrating into the tree to establish themselves.

Gather the leafy branches of mistletoe in the autumn before the berries appear. Dry them in the shade and store in an opaque jar or in a dark cupboard.

Holly *Ilex aquifolium* is an evergreen bush or tree, native to western and central Europe southwards to mountainous regions of the Mediterranean. It grows wild in woods, scrub, hedges and among rocks and is commonly cultivated in gardens and woods. Holly forms a bush or tree which can reach heights of 3–15 m (10–50 ft). It has grey bark, numerous green branches and glossy, leathery, dark-green ovate to lanceolate leaves, arranged alternately, with spines on the margin. The small whitish flowers grow in dense clusters in the leaf axils and bloom from May to August, male and female flowers on different trees. The fertilized flowers are succeeded by its characteristic bright red berries.

Holly has a long history of legends and associations dating back to pagan times. The tradition of using holly to decorate churches and houses at Christmas dates back to the Roman custom of sending gifts decorated with holly boughs to friends at the Festival of Saturnalia, and this custom was adopted by Christians for their Christmas celebrations which occur only a week after Saturnalia. The Druids also decorated their huts with evergreens as an abode for sylvan spirits during winter. Like mistletoe, holly is considered a plant of good omen because its bright green leaves and berries symbolize life in the midst of winter.

Another legend states that the holly first sprang up under Christ's footsteps and the thorny leaves and red berries symbolise his suffering and wounds, hence the tree's other common names: Christ's Thorn and Holy Tree.

The wood of holly is very hard and compact

Variegated Holly *Ilex aquifolium* 'Golden King'

Mistletoe *Viscum album*

Ivy *Hedera helix* (growing up a Hawthorn)

Ivy *Hedera helix* (in flower)

and achieves a high polish so it is much prized by cabinet-makers for inlay work, particularly as it can be stained black, red or green. It is sometimes used as a substitute for ebony on teapot handles. The fermented inner bark is sometimes made into birdlime by bird poachers.

Medicinally, holly leaves have diuretic and diaphoretic properties. They were prescribed for coughs, bronchitis, pneumonia, dropsy, rheumatism and fevers. The berries are violently purgative and can cause excessive vomiting so it is wisest not to use them; other gentler and more effective herbs are available.

Holly is a slow-growing tree but it will grow in almost any soil though it attains its largest size in rich, sandy or gravelly loam. Holly is raised from seed: sown green, it may germinate the following year but, sown red, it does not germinate until the second year. The young plants should not be transplanted until they are 45 cm (18 in) high, preferably in autumn, into well-trenched manured ground. It will take the holly at least two years more to recover the setback of transplantation.

Ivy *Hedera helix* is a woody climber, native to Europe, southwards from Norway extending eastwards to Iran and naturalized in North America. It grows wild in woods, hedgerows and on rocks, walls and old ruins and many

cultivated forms are also grown for ornament. Common ivy can carpet the ground or grow up to a height of 30 m (100 ft). The large, woody stem and numerous branches are covered in adhesive, non-parasitical roots. The leathery, glossy leaves, usually five-lobed, are dark green above and paler below, often with pale veins; they are distinctly aromatic. The greenish-yellow flowers usually only develop in the sun and so grow towards the top of its aerial parts, arranged in dense, roundish clusters which bloom from September to November.

In ancient times ivy was thought to be the enemy of the vine and thus able to prevent intoxication, which is why Bacchus, god of the vine, is always depicted wearing an ivy wreath. Writers of old claimed that a decoction of bruised ivy leaves gently boiled in wine removed the effects of alcohol. Ivy was also considered to be a symbol of fidelity and Greek priests presented a wreath of it to newly-weds.

In ancient and medieval times ivy was prescribed for numerous, different ailments. The berries steeped in white wine were recommended for the plague and an infusion of the leaves was drunk as a purgative. Poultices made from the leaves were said to hasten the healing of wounds and sores and Jean Palaiseul says that Italian mothers would plait ivy-leaf caps for babies suffering from impetigo.

Nowadays, ivy is only recommended for external use medicinally, as strong doses taken internally are poisonous. Fresh leaves applied either directly or as poultices or compresses are prescribed for neuralgia, rheumatism, sciatica, swollen legs and cellulitis.

Ivy leaves are an excellent remedy for corns (bandage an ivy leaf that has been soaked in lemon juice for three hours onto the corn; repeat daily until the corn is ready to drop off); and ivy juice applied as a lotion on the forehead and temples may ease headaches and migraines.

Other uses for ivy are as a hair-dye and as a colour restorer to faded black fabric.

Ivy is easy to grow in the garden or around the house. It is very hardy and long-lived and generally uninjured by frost, smoke or pollution. However, beware of it getting too long and taking over everything because once firmly established, it is difficult to eradicate.

Useful Addresses

The Herb Society, PO Box 415, London SW1P 2HE, England
    Telephone: 01-222 3634
Herb Federation of New Zealand, PO Box 007, Christchurch,
    New Zealand
The Herb Society of America, 9019 Kirtland – Chardon Road,
    Mentor, Ohio 44060, USA
The Australian Herb Society Incorporated, PO Box 110,
    Mapleton 4560, Australia
The National Institute of Medical Herbalists, 41 Hatherly Road,
    Winchester, Hants, England
The National Herbalists Association of Australia, Suite 14, 249
    Kingsgrove Road, Kingsgrove, New South Wales 2208, Australia
The Sydney College of Natural Therapies, 21 Harris Street,
    Prymont, New South Wales 2009, Australia

Suppliers and Gardens to Visit

Britain
Abbey Dore Court, Abbey Dore, Herefordshire
Abbey House Museum, Kirkstall, Leeds
American Nurseries, Claverton Manor, Bath BA2 7BD
Barnesley House, Nr Cirencester, Gloucestershire
The Butser Ancient Farm Research Project, Petersfield,
    Hampshire
Cambridge Botanic Garden, University Botanic Garden, Cambridge
The Chelsea Physic Garden, London SW1
Chiltern Country Herbs, Trinity Farm House, 49 Worminghall
    Road, Oakley, Nr Aylesbury, Bucks
Cheshire Herbs, Fourfields, Forest Road, Little Budworth,
    Nr Tarporley, Cheshire CW6 9ES
Churchfield Herbs, 2 High Street, Yardley Gobion, Towcester,
    Northants
Cornish Herbs, Trelow Cottage, Mawgan-in-Meneage,
    Nr Helston, Cornwall
The Cottage Herbery, Mill House, Boraston, Nr Tenbury Wells,
    Worcs
Culpepper Ltd, Hadstock Road, Linton, Cambridge CB1 6NJ
Elidyr Nursery, Coleg Elidyr, Rhandirmwyn, Llandovey, Dyfed
    SA20 0NL
Gerard House, 736 Christchurch Road, Boscombe,
    Bournemouth, Hants
Glasgow Botanic Gardens, Great Western Road, Glasgow,
    Strathclyde
Hatfield House, Hatfield, Hertfordshire
The Herbary Prickwillow, Mile End, Prickwillow, Ely, Cambs
    CB7 4SJ
The Herb Farm, Peppard Road, Sonning Common, Reading
    RG4 9NJ
The Herb Garden, Hall View Cottage, Hardstoft, Pilsley,
    Nr Chesterfield, Derbyshire
Hollington Nurseries Ltd, Woolton Hill, Newbury, Berks
Iden Croft Herbs, Frittenden Road, Stapleton, Kent TN12 0DN
Ledsham Herb Garden, The University of Liverpool Botanic
    Gardens, Ness, Cheshire
Michelham Priory Physic Garden, Upper Docker, Nr Hailsham,
    East Sussex
The Museum of Garden History, St Mary-at-Lambeth, London SE1
D. Napier & Sons Ltd, 17–18 Bristo Place, Edinburgh 1
Neal's Yard Apothecary, 2 Neal's Yard, Covent Garden, London
    WC2
The Roman Palace and Museum, Salthill Road, Fishbourne,
    Chichester, West Sussex
The Royal Botanic Gardens, The Queen's Garden at Kew Palace,
    Kew, Nr Richmond, Surrey
Royal Botanic Gardens Edinburgh, Inverlieth Row, Edinburgh
The Royal Horticultural Society Gardens, Wisley, Nr Guildford,
    Surrey
Salley Gardens, 82 Julian Road, West Bridgford, Nottingham
    NG2 5AN

Samares Herbs A Plenty, Samares Manor, St Clements, Jersey,
    Channel Islands
Selsey Herb and Goat Farm, Water Lane, Selsey, Stroud,
    Gloucestershire
Sissinghurst, Sissinghurst, Nr Cranbrook, Kent
Suffolk Herbs, Sawyers Farm, Little Cornard, Sudbury, Suffolk
Thornby Herbs, Thornby Hall Gardens, Thornby, Northampton
The Tudor Garden Museum, St Michael's Square, Southampton
Izaak Walton Cottage, Shugborough, Nr Stafford

Australia
Australian Botanical, 22 Mount Street, Prahran, Victoria 3181
Brammovale Herb Farm, 293 Pinjarra Road, Pinjarra Heights,
    Queensland 4069
Buranda Herbal Clinic, 15 Faversham Street, Buranda,
    Queensland 4102
Common Scents Herb Cottage, 745 Old Northern Road, Dural,
    NSW 2158
Coora Cottage Herbs, Thompsons Lane, Merricks, Victoria 3916
Deep Creek Herb Nursery, 3 Deep Creek Road, Mitcham, Victoria
    3132
Dural's Colonial Cottage & Gallery, 62 Kenthurst Road, Dural,
    NSW 2158
The Fragrant Garden, Portsmouth Road, Erina, NSW 2250
Hemphill's Herbs & Spices Pty Ltd, 38 Forge Street, Blacktown,
    NSW 2148
Herbalife, 63 Arlington Avenue, South Perth, WA 6151
The House of Herbs, 10 Pioneer Road, Yandina, Queensland 4561
Lilydale Herb Farm, 61 Mangans Road, Lilydale, Victoria 3140
Melbourne Herb Supplies, 57a Kooyong Road, Caulfield,
    Victoria 3162
National Herbalists Assoc. of Australia, Suite 14, 249 Kingsgrove
    Road, Kingsgrove, NSW 2208
Ninn's Herb Garden, King Street, Thornlands, Queensland 4164
Permaganic Growers (Rosemary Herb Farm), Strachan Road,
    Bulls Brook, WA 6084
Sydney College of Natural Therapies, 21 Harris Street, Prymont,
    NSW 2009
Sydney Herb Supply, 55 Mahers Road, Beecroft, NSW 2119

New Zealand
Aero View Garden Centre, Main Road, Thames
Cedenco Foods Ltd (Nursery), Saleyards Road, Gisborne
Clendon Garden Centre, Corner of Roscommon & Weymouth
    Roads, Manurewa, Auckland
Hillside Herbs, Fairysprings Road, Rotorua
Karamea Wines & Herbs, Tuhikaramea Road RD10, Frankton,
    Hamilton
Kings Herbs Ltd, 1660 Great North Road, Avondale, Auckland

United States
ABC Herb Nursery, P.O. Box 313, Lecoma, MO 65540
Bear Meadow Farm, Route 2, Moore Road, Florida, MA 01247
Bittersweet Farm, 6294 Seville Road, Seville, OH 44272
Brooklyn Botanic Garden, 1000 Washington Avenue, Brooklyn,
    New York, N.Y. 11225
Caprillands Herb Farm, 534 Silver Street, Coventry, CT 06238
Catnip Acres Farm, 67 Christian Street, Oxford, CT 06483
The Cloisters, Ft. Tryon Park, New York, N.Y. 10040
Companion Plants, Route 6, Box 88, Athens, OH 45701
Dionysos' Barn, P.O. Box 31, Bodines, PA 17722
Earthstar Herb Gardens, 438 W. Perkinsville Road, Star Route 1,
    Box 82, Chino Valley, AZ 86323
Earthworks Herb Garden Nursery, 923 North Ivy Street,
    Arlington, VA 22201
Fox Hill Farms, 440 West Michigan Avenue, P.O. Box 7, Parma,
    MI 49269
Fragrant Fields, Route 2, Box 199, Dongola, IL 62926
Hartman's Herb Farm, Old Dana Road, Barre, MA 01005
Hemlock Hill Herb Farm, Hemlock Hill Road, Litchfield, CT
    06759-0415
Herbs 'N' Honey Nursery, 16085 Airlie Road, P.O. Box 124,
    Monmouth, OR 97361

Huntington Library & Botanical Gardens, 1151 Oxford Road, San Marino, CA 91108

Jude Herbs, P.O. Box 563, Huntington Station, NY 11746

Longwood Gardens, Kennett Square, PA 19348

Los Angeles State & County Botanical Gardens, 301 N. Baldwin Avenue, Arcadia, CA 91006

Lost Prairie Herb Farm, Star Route, Marion, MT 59925-9998

Merry Gardens, Upper Mechanic Street, P.O. Box 595, Camden, ME 04843

The National Herb Garden at The National Arboretum, 3501 New York Avenue N.E., Washington D.C. 20002

New York Botanical Garden, 200th Street & Southern Boulevard, Bronx, New York, 10458

Rasland Farm, NC 82 at US 13, Godwin, NC 28344

Richters Herbs, Goodwood, Ontario, LoC 1AO

Rutland of Kentucky, Jail Street, P.O. Box 182, Washington, KY 41096-0182

Sandy Mush Herb Nursery, Route 2, Surrett Cove Road, Leicester, NC 28748

Sunnybrook Farms Nursery, 9448 Mayfield Road, P.O. Box 6, Chesterland, OH 44026

Sunnypoint Gardens, 6939 Highway 42, Egg Harbor, WI 54209

Taylor's Herb Garden, 1535 Lone Oak Road, Vista, CA 92083

Triple Oaks Nursery, Route 47, Franklinville, NJ 08322

University of California Botanical Gardens, Centennial Drive, Berkeley, CA 94720

Well-Sweep Herb Farms, 317 Mount Bethel Road, Port Murray, NJ 07865

Western Reserve Herb Garden at Greater Cleveland Garden Center, University Circle, Cleveland, OH 44106

Wyrttun Ward, 18 Beach Street, West Wareham, MA 02576

Bibliography

L. H. Bailey Hortorium, staff of, Cornell University *Hortus Third: A Concise Dictionary of Plants Cultivated in the United States and Canada*, New York, Macmillan, 1976

Julian Barnard, *A Guide to the Bach Flower Remedies*, Saffron Walden, England, The C. W. Daniel Company Ltd, 1979

Nathaniel Lord Britton and Addison Brown, *An Illustrated Flora of the Northern United States and Canada*, 3 vols., New York, Dover Publications Inc., 1970

Roberto Chiej, *The Macdonald Encyclopaedia of Medicinal Plants*, London, Macdonald & Co. Ltd, 1984

A. R. Clapham, T. G. Tutin and E. F. Warburn, *Flora of the British Isles*, Cambridge University Press, 1962

Sarah Cotton, *Guide to the Specialist Nurseries*, East Sussex, Garden Art Press Ltd., 1989

Culpeper's Complete Herbal, London, W. Foulsham and Co. Ltd

Culpepper's Complete Herbal and English Physician, Glenwood, Illinois, Meyerbooks, 1987

Richard Fitter and Alasdair Fitter, *The Wild Flowers of Britain and Northern Europe*, London, Collins, 1974

Gertrude B. Foster, *Herbs for Every Garden*, New York, E. P. Dutton, 1973

Jill Goodwin, *A Dyer's Manual*, London, Pelham Books, 1982

Gray's Manual of Botany expanded and rewritten by Merritt Lyndon Fernal, New York, D. Van Nostrand Company, 1950

Mrs. M. Grieve, *A Modern Herbal*, London, Penguin Books, 1980 and New York, Dover, 1982

Barbara Griggs, *Green Pharmacy*, London, Robert Hale, 1981

Barbara Griggs, *The Home Herbal*, London and Sydney, Pan Books, 1986

Geoffrey Grigson, *The Englishman's Flora*, Great Britain, Paladin, Granada Publishing Limited, 1975

S. G. Harrison, G. B. Masefield, Michael Wallis, *The Oxford Book of Food Plants*, London, Oxford University Press, 1969

Roy Hay and Patrick M. Synge, *The Dictionary of Garden Plants*, London, Ebury Press and Michael Joseph, 1969

Roy Hay and Patrick M. Synge, *The Dictionary of Gardening – Supplement*, New York, Oxford University Press, 1969

Hillier's Manual of Trees and Shrubs, Winchester, England, Hillier and Sons, 1971

Joy Larkcom, *The Salad Garden*, England, Frances Lincoln, Windward, 1984

Claire Loewenfeld and Philippa Back, *The Complete Book of Herbs and Spices*, Newton Abbot, England, David and Charles, 1974

Maurice Mességué, *Health Secrets of Plants and Herbs*, London, Pan Books in association with Collins, 1981

William A. Niering and Nancy C. Olmstead, *The Audubon Society Field Guide to North American Wild Flowers* (eastern region), New York, Alfred A. Knopf, 1979

Jean Palaiseul, *Grandmother's Secrets*, London, Barrie and Jenkins, 1973

Elizabeth and Reginald Peplow, *Herbs and Herb Gardens of Great Britain*, Exeter, England, Webb & Bower Limited, 1984

Chris Philip and Tony Lord, *The Plant Finder*, Great Britain, Headman Ltd., 1987

Roger Phillips, *Wild Food*, Boston, Little, Brown and Company, 1986

Roger Phillips and Martyn Rix, *Bulbs*, London, Pan Books, 1981, 1989

Roger Phillips and Martyn Rix, *The Random House Book of Bulbs*, New York, Random House, 1989

Roger Phillips and Martyn Rix, *Roses*, London, Pan Books Ltd, 1988

Roger Phillips and Martyn Rix, *The Random House Book of Roses*, New York, Random House, 1988

Roger Phillips and Martyn Rix, *Shrubs*, London, Pan Books, 1989

Roger Phillips and Martyn Rix, *The Random House Book of Shrubs*, New York, Random House, 1989

Oleg Polunin, *Flowers of Europe*, London, Oxford University Press, 1969

Oleg Polunin, *Flowers of Greece and the Balkans*, Oxford, Oxford University Press, 1980

Oleg Polunin and Anthony Huxley, *Flowers of the Mediterranean*, London, Chatto and Windus, 1978

Oleg Polunin and B. E. Smythies, *Flowers of South-West Europe*, London, Oxford University Press, 1973

Harold William Rickett, *Wildflowers of the United States*, New York, McGraw-Hill, 1965

Richard Spellenberg, *The Audubon Society Field Guide to North American Wild Flowers* (western region), New York, Alfred A. Knopf, 1979

Dr František Starý and Dr Václav Jirasek, *Herbs*, London, Hamlyn, 1973

William A. R. Thomson MD, *Healing Plants*, London and Basingstoke, Macmillan Limited, 1978

Piers Trehane, *Index Hortensis*, Wimborne, Dorset, Quarterjack Publishing, 1989

T. G. Tutin, V. H. Haywood et al (ed), *Flora Europaea*, 4 vols., Cambridge University Press, 1972

Michael A. Weiner, *Earth Medicine – Earth Food*, London, Collier Macmillan Publishers, 1980

Rudolf Fritz Weiss MD, *Herbal Medicine*, Gothenburg, Sweden, Beaconsfield, London, AB Arcanum, and Beaconsfield Publishers Ltd, 1988

The Herbal Review various volumes, The Herb Society, P.O. Box 415, London SW1P 2HE

Seeds by Post, Suffolk Herbs, Sawyers Farm, Little Cornard, Sudbury, Suffolk

Hollington – culinary, medicinal, aromatic plants, Hollington Nurseries Ltd, Woolton Hill, Newbury, Berkshire

Index

Aaron's Rod 128
Acanthus 172
Acanthus
  mollis 172
  spinosus 172
Achillea
  decolorans 37
  millefolium 160
  ptarmica 148
Acinos arvensis 44
Aconite 111
Aconitum napellus 111
Acorus calamus 108, *109*
Adonis
  annua 183
  vernalis 183
Adzuki Beans *54*, 55
Aesculus hippocastanum 179
Aegopodium podagraria 107
  'Variegatum' *107*
Agastache
  anethiodora 78, 79
  rugosa 78, 79
Agrimonia eupatoria 123
Agrimony
  Common 123
  Hemp 171
Agropyron repens 122, *123*
Ajuga
  reptans 103
    'Atropurpurea' 103
    'Multicolour' 103
Alchemilla
  mollis 110
  vulgaris 110
Alder Buckthorn 120
Alecost 146, *147*
Alexanders 60
  Biennial 60
Alfalfa *54*, 55
All Heal 134, *135*
Alliaria petiolata 18
Allium
  cepa 21
  cepa var. *proliferum* 21
  fistulosum 20, 21
  mortanum 19
  sativum 20
  schoenoprasum 18
  schoenoprasum var. *sibiricum* 19
  triquetrum 18, *19*
  tuberosum 21
  ursinum 19
Aloe, Cape 100
Aloe ferox 100
Aloysia citriodora 116
Alpine Strawberry 65
Althea
  officinalis 152
  rosea 153
Amaranth, Green 55
Amaranthus
  hypochondiachus 55
  retroflexus 55
  tricolor 55
American Ginseng *158*, *159*
American Ipecac 147
American Mandrake 104
American Wild Ginger *86*, 87
American Wild Passionflower 179
American Winter Cress 49
American Wormseed *58*, 59
Amoracia rusticana *56*, 57
Anagallis monellii 118
Andropogon schoenanthus 19
Anemone pulsatilla 90, *91*
Anethum graveolens 36, 37
Angelica 28, *29*
  Wild or Wood 29
Angelica
  archangelica 28, *29*
  sylvestris 29
Anise 17
Anise Hyssop 78, 79
Anise Scented Basil *42*
Antennaria dioica 146, *147*

Anthemis
  nobilis 80, 81
  tinctoria 89
Anthriscus cerefolium 17
Anthyllis vulneraria 133
Apium
  graveolens 53
  graveolens var. *dulce* 53
  graveolens var. *rapaceum* 53
Apothecary's Rose, The 68
Apple Mint *32*, *34*, 35
Aquilegia vulgaris 129
Aralia racemosa 177
Archangelica officinalis 28, *29*
Arctium lappa *122*, *123*
Arctostaphylos uva-ursi 64, 65
Aristolochia clematitis 148, *149*
Armoracia rusticana 57
Arnica 129
Arnica montana 129
Artemisia
  abrotanum 80, *81*
  absinthium 80, *81*
    'Lambrook Silver' *81*
  campestris subsp. *borealis* 81
  dracunculus
    'Inodora' 36
    'Sativa' 36
  pontica 81
  vulgaris 80, *81*
Asarabacca 86
Asarum
  canadense 86, 87
  europaeum 86
Ash, Prickly 177
Asian Mallow 152
Asperula
  odorata 82, *83*
  tinctoria 85
Atriplex
  hortensis 58
  hortensis rubra 58
Atropa belladonna 174
Austrian Foxglove 139
Avena sativa 56, 57
Avens, Wood 126, *127*

Bairnwort 90, *91*
Ballota nigra 156
Balsamita major 146, *147*
  major var. *tomentosum* 75
Baptisia tinctoria 86
Barbarea
  verna 49
  vulgaris 49
Barberry 65
Basil 42
  Anise Scented *42*
  Bush 43
  Green Bush 42
  Lemon *42*, 43
  Purple *42*, 43
  'Purple Ruffles' *42*
  Sacred *42*, 44
  Sweet *42*, *43*
  Wild 44
Basil Thyme 44
Bay 13
Bearberry 64, *65*
Bear's Breech 172
Bear's Garlic 19
Bedstraw, Hedge 85
Bedstraw, Lady's 83
Bedstraw, White 85
Bee Balm 66
Belladonna 174
Bellis perennis 90, *91*
Bennet, Herb 126, *127*
Berberis vulgaris 65
Bergamot 66
  Lemon 66
  Wild 66
Beth Root 90, *91*
Betonica officinalis 162
Betony 162
Biennial Alexanders 60

Bilberry 65
Birthwort 148, *149*
Bisai *54*, 55
Bishopswort 162
Bistort 126, *127*
Biting Stonecrop 52
Bittercress, Hairy 46
Bittersweet 175
Black Cohosh 166
Black Hellebore 90
Black Horehound 156
Black Knapweed 168
Black Lovage 60
Blackberry 63
Blackcurrant 62
Blaeberry 65
Blazing Star, Dense 154
Blessed Thistle 172, *173*
Blue Buttons 163
Blue Lobelia 162
Blue Passionflower 179
Blue Pimpernel 118
Bogbean 98
Boneset, Purple *170*, 171
Borage 29
Borago officinalis 29
Bouncing Bet 144, *145*
Brassica napus *54*, 55
Briar, Wild 68
Bronze Bugle 103
Bronze Fennel 30, *31*
Broom or Scotch Broom 87
  Dyer's *86*, 87
Bruisewort 90, *91*
Bryonia cretica subsp. *dioica* 169
Bryony, White or Red 169
Buckler-leaved Sorrel *22*, 23
Buckbean 98
Buckthorn 121
  Alder 120
  Sea 64
Buckwheat 57
Buffalo Currant 63
Bugle 103
  Bronze 103
  Rainbow 103
Bugleweed 163
Bugloss, Viper's 112, *113*
Bulbous Comfrey 94
Burdock, Great *122*, 123
Burnet, Salad 53
Burnet Saxifrage 113
Bush Basil 43
Butterbur 99

Calamint 70
  Common 70
  Lesser 70
  Wood 70
Calamintha
  ascendens 70, *71*
  grandiflora 70
  nepeta 70, *71*
  officinalis 70, *71*
  sylvatica 70
Calendula officinalis 50, *51*
Calliopsis 89
Calluna vulgaris 165
Caltha palustris 102
Camomile 67
  Dyer's or Yellow 89
  German 67
  Roman or Lawn 80
  Sweet False 67
Camomilla recutita 67
Camphor Plant 75
Canadian Fleabane 165
Cape Aloe 100
Cape Gooseberry 62, *63*
Caper Spurge 132
Capsella bursa-pastoris 47
Caraway 36, 37
Cardamine hirsuta 46
Cardinal Flower 162, *163*
Carduus benedictus 172, *173*
Carlina

acaulis 173
vulgaris 173
Carline Thistle 173
Carnation 76
Carthamus tinctorius 88, 89
Carum carvi 37
Cascara Sagrada 121
Cassia angustifolia 177
Castor Oil Plant 176, *177*
Cat Thyme 161
Catharanthus roseus 182
Catmint
  Garden 70, *71*
  Wild 70, *71*
Catsfoot 146, *147*
Caucasian Comfrey 94, 95
Ceanothus americanus 181
Celandine
  Greater 98, 99
  Lesser *102*, 103
Celery
  Wild or Cutting 53
  Cultivated 53
Centaurea
  cyanus 150
  nigra 169
Centaurium erythraea 141
Centaury 141
Centranthus ruber 59
Chamaemelum nobile 80, 81
Chaste Tree 176
Cheddar Pink 76
Cheiranthus cheiri 110, *111*
Chelidonium majus 98, 99
Chenopodium
  ambrosioides *58*, 59
  bonus-henricus *58*, 59
Chervil 17
Chickweed 46, *47*
Chicory 49
Chinese Lantern 62, *63*
Chives 18
  Giant 19
Choisya ternata 78, 79
Christmas Rose 90
Chrysanthemum
  balsamita 146, *147*
  cinerariifolium 151
  parthenium *142*, *143*
  vulgare 151
Chicorium intybus 49
Cimifuga
  foetida 166
  racemosa 166
Clary Sage 26
Claytonia perfoliata 46, *47*
Cleavers 84, *85*
Clematis vitalba 178
Clinopodium vulgare 44
Clove Pink 76
Cnicus benedictus 172, *173*
Cochlearia officinalis 106, *107*
Cohosh
  Black 166
  Stinking 166
Colchicum
  autummale 168
  speciosum 168
Coltsfoot 92, *93*
Columbine *128*, 129
Comfrey 94, 95
  Bulbous 94, 95
  Caucasian 94, 95
  Tuberous 95
  White 94, 95
Common Agrimony 123
Common Calamint 70
Common Flax 118
Common Fleabane 148, *149*
Common Foxglove 139
Common Horsetail 125
Common Lime 66
Common Mallow 152, *153*
Common Melilot 148
Common Oat 56, *57*
Common Perilla *58*, 59

Common Sorrel 23
Compact Marjoram 42, *43*
Coneflower, Purple 146, *147*
Conium maculatum 127
Consolida
  ambigua 117
  orientalis 117
Convallaria majalis 104, *105*
Conyza canadensis 165
Coolwort *100*, 101
Coreopsis 89
Coreopsis tinctoria 89
Coriander *14*, 15
Coriandrum sativum 14, 15
Cornflower 151
Corsican Mint 35
Costmary 146, *147*
Cotton Lavender 74
Couch Grass 122
Cowslip 96, *97*
Crataegus monogyna 114, *115*
Creeping Jenny 132
  Golden 132
Creeping Savory 45
Creeping Wintergreen 114
Cress
  Curled 54
  Land *or* American Winter 49
  Winter 49
Crocus sativus 44
Cucumber, Squirting 171
Cultivated Celery 53
Cumin 17
Cuminum cyminum 17
Curled Cress *54*, 55
Curled Dock *22*, 23
Curled Parsley 14
Curled Tansy 151
Curly Mint *32, 33*
Currant, Buffalo 63
Curry Plant 73
Cut-leaved Selfheal 136
Cutting Celery 53
Cymbopogon citratus 19
Cynoglossum officinale 112, *113*
Cytisus scoparius 87

Daisy 91
Dalmatian Pyrethrum *or* Pellitory 150
Dame's Violet 50
Dandelion *48, 49*
Datura
  metel 175
  stramonium 175
Deadly Nightshade 174
Deadnettle, White 93
Dense Blazing Star 154, 155
Dianthus
  caesius 77
  caryophyllus 76, 77
  deltoides 77
    'Wisley variety' 76
  gratianopolitanus 76, 77
Digitalis
  ferruginea 138
  lanata 138, *139*
  lutea 138, *139*
  purpurea 138, *139*
    'Alba' 138
Dill 36, *37*
Dipsacus
  fullonum 167
  sativus 167
Dock
  Red-veined *22, 23*
  Curled *22*, 23
Dog Rose 68
Double Feverfew *143*
Dracocephalum ruyschianum 157
Dragonhead 157
Dropwort 150
Drosera rotundifolia 164, *165*
Dryopteris felix-mas 124, 125
Dyer's Broom 86, 87
Dyer's Camomile 89
Dyer's Greenweed 86, *87*
Dyer's Rocket 85
Dyer's Woodruff 85

Eau de Cologne Mint 34, *35*
Ecballium elaterium 171

Echinacea purpurea 146, *147*
Echium vulgare 112, *113*
Eggs and Bacon 140
Eggs and Butter 140
Elder *or* European Elder 60, *61*
Elder, Ground 107
Elderberry 60, *61*
Elecampane 161
Elymus repens 122, 123
English Daisy 91
English Lavender 72
English Mace 37
English Plantain 102
Epazote *58, 59*
Equisetum
  arvense 125
  telmateia 125
Eruca vesicaria subsp. *sativa* 52
Erygium maritimum 172, *173*
Eryngo 172, *173*
Erythrea centaurium 141
Eupatorium
  cannabinum 171
  purpureum 170, 171
Euphorbia lathyrus 132
Euphrasia
  officinalis 140, *141*
  rostkoviana 140, 141
European Elder 60
European Wild Ginger 86
Evening Primrose 154
Eyebright 140, *141*

Fagopyrum esculentum 57
False Hellebore
  Green 105
  White 105
Fat Hen *58*, 59
Fennel 30
  Bronze 30, *31*
  Florence 30, *31*
  Sweet 30
Fenugreek 16, *17, 54, 55*
Fern, Male 124
Feverfew *142*, 143
  Double *143*
  Golden *143*
Field Poppy 118
Field Scabious 163
Figwort 144, *145*
  Variegated 144, *145*
  Water 144, *145*
Filipendula
  ulmaria 82
    'Variegata' 82
  vulgaris 150
Flag
  Sweet 108, *109*
  Yellow 107
Flat Parsley 14
Flax
  Common 118
  Perennial 118
  Purging 118
Fleabane
  Canadian 165
  Common 148, *149*
Florence Fennel 30, 31
Foamflower *100*, 101
Foeniculum
  officinale 30
  vulgare 30
  vulgare var. *dulce* 30, *31*
    'Purpurascens' 30, *31*
Foxglove
  Common *or* Purple 138, *139*
  White 138
  Woolly *or* Austrian 138, *139*
  Yellow 138, *139*
Fragaria vesca 65
  'Alexandria' 65
Frangula alnus 120
French Lavender 73
French Lilac 134
French Marigold 79
French Parsley 15
French Sorrel *22*, 23
French Tarragon 36
Fritillaria pallidiflora 101
Fritillary, Pale-flowered 101
Fuller's Teasel 167

Fumaria officinalis 121
Fumitory 121

Galega officinalis 134
Galium
  aparine 84, *85*
  mollugo 85
  odoratum 82, 83
  verum 83
Garden Catmint 71
Garden Orach 58
Garden Sorrel 33
Garden Thyme 39, *40, 41*
Garlic 20
  Bear's *or* Wood 19
Garlic Chives 21
Garlic Mustard 18
Gaultheria
  procumbens 114
  shallon 114
Gayfeather 154, *155*
Genista tinctoria 86, *87*
Gentian, Yellow 159
Gentiana lutea 159
Gentle Lavender 73
Geranium
  macrorrhizum 106
    'Album' 106
  robertianum 106
German Camomile 67
Germander
  Sage-leaved *160*, 161
  Wall 160, *161*
Geum urbanum 126, *127*
Giant Horsetail 125
Gillenia trifoliata 146, *147*
Ginger, Wild
  American 86
  European 86
Ginger Mint *32, 33*
Ginseng, American 158, *159*
Gipsywort 163
Gladwin 109
Glycyrrhiza glabra 166
Goat's Beard 144, *145*
Goat's Rue 134
Golden Creeping Jenny 132
Golden Feverfew *143*
Golden Hop 130
Golden Lemon Balm 133
Golden Lemon Thyme 39, 41
Golden Marguerite 89
Golden Marjoram 42, *43*
Golden-rod 154, *155*
Good King Henry *58*, 59
Gooseberry, Cape 63
Goosegrass 84, *85*
Goutweed 107
Grace, Herb of 130, *131*
Grass, Couch *122*, 123
Grass, Lemon 19
Grass, Scurvy 107
Gratiola officinalis 78, *79*
Gravelroot 170, *171*
Great Burdock 122, *123*
Great Lobelia 162
Great Mullein 128
Greater Celandine 98, *99*
Greater Periwinkle 182
Green Amaranth 55
Green Bush Basil 42
Green False Hellebore 105
Greenweed, Dyer's 86, *87*
Ground Elder 107
  Variegated 107

Hairy Bittercress 46
Hamamelis virginiana 180, *181*
Hamburg Parsley 15
Hawthorn 114, *115*
Hazelwort 86
Heartsease 193
Heather 165
Hedera helix 185
  'Golden King' 185
Hedge Bedstraw 85
Hedge Hyssop 156
Helianthemum
  chamaecistus 136, *137*
  nummularium 136, *137*
Helianthus annuus 73

Helichrysum
  angustifolium 73
  italicum 73
Heliotrope 183
Heliotropium peruvianum 183
  'Royal Marine' 183
Hellebore, Black 90
Hellebore, False 105
  Green False 105
  White False 105
Helleborus niger 90
Hemlock 126
Hemp Agrimony 171
Hemp Tree 176
Henbane 158
  White 158
Herb Bennet 127
Herb of Grace 130, *131*
Herb Robert 106
Herniaria glabra 141
Hesperis matronalis 50
Hippophae rhamnoides 64
Hoary Plantain *102*, 103
Hogbean 158
Holly 184
  Sea 172, *173*
  Variegated 185
Hollyhock 153
Holy Thistle 172, *173*
Hop 130
  Golden 130
Horebound
  Black 156
  White 156
Horse-chestnut 179
Horseradish 56, *57*
Horsetail
  Common 125
  Giant 125
Horse Mint 35
Hound's Tongue 112, *113*
Humulus lupulus 130
  lupulus var. *aurea* 130
Hyoscyamus
  albus 158
  niger 158
Hypericum perforatum 158
Hyssop 157
  Anise 78
  Hedge 78, *79*
  Rock 157
  White 157
Hyssopus officinalis 157
  'Alba' 157
  subsp. *aristatus* 157

Ilex aquifolium 184
  'Golden King' 185
Indian Physic 146, *147*
Indian Podophyllum 105
Indian Poke 105
Indian Tobacco 163
Indigo 86
  Wild 86
Indigofera tinctoria 86
Inula helenium 161
Ipecac, American 146, *147*
Iris, Stinking 109
Iris
  foetidissima 109
    var. *citrina* 109
  germanica var. *florentina* 108
  pallida 108
  pseudacorus 108
Isatis tinctoria 84, *85*
Ivy 185

Jacob's Ladder 128
Jack-by-the-Hedge 18
Jack-go-to-bed-at-noon 144, *145*
Japanese Perilla *58, 59*
Japanese Radish *54, 55*
Jerusalem Sage 77
Jimson Weed 175
Joe Pye Weed *170*, 171
Joseph's Coat 55
Juniper 62
Juniperis communis 62

Kidney-vetch 133
Kingcup 102

INDEX

Knapweed *or* Lesser *or* Black Knapweed 168
Knautia arvensis 163
Korean Mint 78, 79

Ladies' Fingers 133
Lady's Bedstraw 83
Lady's Mantle 110
Lamium album 93
Land Cress 49
Large Green Lentils 54, 55
Large Selfheal 135
Larkspur 117
Laurus nobilis 13
Lavandula
  angustifolia 72
    'Hidcote' 73
    'Lodden Pink' 72, 73
  officinalis 72
  spica 72
  stoechas 73
  stoechas subsp. *pedunculata* 73
Lavender 72
  Cotton 74
  English 72
  French 72
  Gentle 73
Lawn Camomile 80, 81
Leek, Three-cornered 18, 19
Lemon Balm 133
  Golden 133
  Variegated 133
Lemon Basil 42, 43
Lemon Bergamot 66
Lemon Grass 19
Lemon Thyme 41
  Golden 39
Lemon Verbena 116
Lemon Vervain 116
Lens culinaris 54, 55
Lentils, Large Green *and* Puy 54, 55
Leonurus cardiaca 122, 123
Lepidum sativum 54, 55
Lesser Calamint 70
Lesser Celandine 102, 103
Lesser Knapweed 169
Lesser Periwinkle 182
Lettuce, Miner's 46, 47
Levisticum officinale 30, 31
Liatris spicata 155
Lilac, French 134
Lily of the Valley 104, 105
Lime, Common 66
Linaria vulgaris 140
Linden 66
Ling 165
Linum
  catharticum 118
  perenne 118
  usitatissimum 118
Lippia
  citriodora 116
  triphylla 166
Liquorice 166
Lobelia cardinalis 162, 163
Lobelia, Great *or* Blue 162
  Lobelia inflata 163
  Lobelia siphilitica 162
Loosestrife, Purple 144
Lovage 30, 31
Love-in-a-Mist 137
Lovage 31
  Black 60
Lucerne 54, 55
Lungwort 95
Lupin, Tree 146
Lupinus arborens 146
Lycopus
  europaeus 163
  virginicus 163
Lysimachia nummularia 132
  'Aurea' 132
Lythrum salicaria 144

Mace, English 37
Mad-dog Skullcap 100, 101
Madagascar Periwinkle 182
Maiden Pink 76
Male Fern 124, 125
Mallow
  Asian 152

Common *or* Wild 152, 153
  Marsh 152, 153
  Musk 152
Malva
  moschata 52
  sylvestris 152, 153
  verticillata var. *crispa* 152
Mandragora officinarum 158, 159
Mandrake 158, 159
  American 104, 105
Manna 55
Marguerite, Golden 89
Marigold 50, 51
  Double 51
  French 79
  Marsh 102
  Mexican 79
Marjoram
  Compact 43
  Golden 42, 43
  Pot 42
  Wild 42, 43
Marrubium vulgare 156
Marsh Mallow 153
Marsh Marigold 102
Matricaria recutita 67
May 114, 115
May Blobs 102
Mayapple 104, 105
Mayweed, Scented 67
Meadow Saffron 168
Meadowsweet 82
  Variegated 82
Medicago sativa 54, 55
Melilot, Ribbed *or* Yellow *or* Common 148
Melilotus officinalis 148
Melissa officinalis 133
  'Aurea' 133
  'Variegata' 133
Mentha
  aquatica 34, 35
  × *gentilis* 32
  longifolia 35
  × *piperita* 34
  × *piperita citrata* 34, 35
  pulegium 34, 35
  requienii 35
  rotundifolia 32, 34, 35
  × *Smithiana* 'Rubra' 32, 33
  spicata 32, 33
    'Crispa' 32, 33
  suaveolens 'Variegata' 32, 33
  × *verticillata* 35
  × *villosa* 32, 33
  trifoliata 98
Mercury 58, 59
Mexican Marigold 79
Mexican Orange 78, 79
Milk Thistle 100
Miner's Lettuce 46, 47
Mint
  Apple 32, 34, 35
  Corsican 35
  Curly 32, 33
  Eau de Cologne 34, 35
  Ginger 32, 33
  Horse 35
  Korean 79
  Pineapple 32, 33
  Water 34, 35
Mistletoe 184, 185
Monarda
  citriodora 66
  didyma 66
  fistulosa 66
Moneywort 132
Monkshood 111
Montia perfoliata 46, 47
Motherwort 122, 123
Mountain Balm 70
Mountain Spinach 58
Mugwort 80, 81
Mullein, Great 128
Mung Beans 54, 55
Musk Mallow 152
Mustard 54, 55
  Garlic 54
Myrrhis odorata 16
Myrtle 181
Myrtus communis 181

Nasturtium 50, 51
Nasturtium
  majus 50
    'Empress of India' 50
  officinale 46
Nepeta
  camphorata 70, 71
  cataria 70, 71
  × *faassenii* 71
Nettle
  Roman 93
  Small 92
  Stinging 92
New Jersey Tea 180, 181
Nicotiana tabacum 168
Nigella damascena 137
Nightshade
  Deadly 174
  Woody 175

Oat, Common 56, 57
Ocimum
  basilicum 42, 43
  basilicum var. *purpureum* 42, 43
  citriodorum 42, 43
  minimum 43
  sanctum 42
Oenothera erythrosepala 154
Old Lady 81
Old Man's Beard 178
Old Warrior 81
Onion 21
Ononis spinosa 140
Opium Poppy 119
Orach
  Garden 58
  Red Garden 58
Orange, Mexican 78, 79
Oregano 42, 43
Origanum
  onites 42
  vulgare 42, 43
    'Compactum' 42, 43
    'Curly Gold' 42
    'Golden Tip' 42
Orris 108
Oswego Tea 66
Ox-eye 183
Oxlip 96, 97

Painted Sage 26, 27
Pale-flowered Fritillary 101
Panax quinquefolius 158, 159
Pansy, Wild 183
Papaver
  rhoeas 118, 119
  somniferum 119
Parietaria diffusa 134
Parsley
  Curled 14
  Flat 14
  Hamburg 15
Pasque Flower 90, 91
Passiflora
  caerula 179
  incarnata 179
Passionflower
  American Wild 179
  Blue 179
Pellitory, Dalmation 150
Pellitory-of-the-Wall 134
Pennyroyal 34, 35
Pepper, Water 127
Peppermint 34
Perennial Flax 118
Perilla, Japanese *or* Common 58, 59
Perilla frutescens 58, 59
Periwinkle
  Greater 182
  Lesser 182
  Madagascar 182
Petasites hybridus 99
Petroselinum crispum 14
  'Tuberosum' 14
Phaseolus
  angularis 54, 55
  aureus 54, 55
Pheasant's Eye 183
  Spring 183
Phlomis

fruticosa 77
russeliana 77
samia 77
Physalis alkekengi 62, 63
Physic, Indian 146
Phytolacca
  americana 131
  clavigera 131
Pigweed 55
Pilewort 102
Pimpernel, Blue 118
Pimpinella
  anisum 17
  saxifraga 113
Pineapple Mint 32, 33
Pineapple Sage 26, 27
Pink
  Cheddar 76, 77
  Clove 76, 77
  Maiden 76, 77
Plantago
  lanceolata 102
  major 102
  medica 102, 103
Plantain
  Common *or* Greater 102
  English 102
  Hoary 102, 103
Podophyllum, Indian 105
Podophyllum
  emodi 105
  hexandrum 105
  peltatum 104, 105
Pokeweed 131
Polemonium caeruleum 128, 129
Polygonatum multiflorum 104
Polygonum
  bistorta 126, 127
  fagopyrum 57
  hydropiper 127
Polypodium vulgare 124, 125
Polypody 124, 125
Poppy
  Opium 119
  Red *or* Field 118, 119
Portulaca oleracea 53
Pot Marjoram 42
Potentilla
  anserina 164
  erecta 164
Prickly Ash 177
Prickly Restharrow 140
Primrose 96, 97
  Evening 154
Primula
  elatior 96, 97
  veris 96, 97
  vulgaris 96, 97
Prunella
  grandiflora 136
  lacinata 136
  vulgaris 136
Pulicaria dysenterica 148, 149
Pulmonaria
  angustifolia 95
  longifolia 95
  officinalis 95
  saccharata 95
Pulsatilla vulgaris 90, 91
Purging Flax 118
Purple Basil 41, 42, 43
Purple Boneset 170, 171
Purple Coneflower 146, 147
Purple Foxglove 139
Purple Loosestrife 144
Purple Trillium 90, 91
Purslane 53
Puy Lentils 54, 55
Pyrethrum, Dalmatian 150

Radish, Japanese 54, 55
Rainbow Bugle 103
Ramsons 19
Ranunculus ficaria 102, 103
Rape, Salad 54, 55
Raphanus sativus 54, 55
Raripila, Red 32, 33
Raspberry 62
Red Bryony 169
Red Garden Orach 58
Red Poppy 118, 119

INDEX

Red Raripila *32, 33*
Red Root 180, *181*
Red Valerian 59
Red-veined Dock *22, 23*
Reseda luteola 84, *85*
Restharrow, Prickly 140
Rhamnus
  catharticus 121
  frangula 120
  purshiana 121
Rheum
  palmatum 120
  rhaponticum 120
Rhubarb, Turkey 120
Ribbed Melilot *148*
Ribes
  nigrum 62
  odoratum 63
Ribwort 102
Ricinus communis 176, *177*
  'Gibsonii' 176, *177*
Robert, Herb 106
Rock Hyssop 157
Rock-rose 136, *137*
Rocket 52
  Dyer's 84, *85*
  Sweet 50
  Yellow 49
Roman Camomile 80, *81*
Roman Nettle 92, *93*
Roman Wormwood 81
Rosa
  canina 68
  gallica 'Complicata' 69
    'Officinalis' 68
    'Versicolor' 68
Rose, Christmas 90
Rose
  Dog 68
  The Apothecary's 68
  Wild 68
Rosemary 12
Rosmarinus officinalis 12
  'Fota Blue' 12
  'Tuscan Blue' 12, *13*
  'Sissinghurst' 12
Rubus
  fruticosus 63
  idaeus 62
Rue 130, *131*
  Goat's 134
  Variegated 131
Rumex
  acetosa 23
  acetosella 22, *23*
  crispus 22, *23*
  sanguineus var. *sanguineus* 22, *23*
  scutatus 22, *23*
Rupturewort 141
Russian Tarragon 36
Ruta graveolens 130, *131*
  graveolens 'Variegata' 131

Sacred Basil *42,* 44
Safflower 88, *89*
Saffron, Meadow 168
Saffron Crocus 44
Sage, Common *or* Garden 24, *25*
  Clary 26
  Golden 24, *25*
  Jerusalem 77
  Painted 26, *27*
  Pineapple 26, *27*
  Purple *or* Red 24, *25*
  Spanish 24
  White 24, *25*
Sage-leaved Germander 160, *161*
St John's Plant 80, *81*
St John's Wort 158
Salad Burnet 53
Salad Rape *54, 55*
Salal 114
Salix alba 98
Sallow Thorn 64
Salvia
  grahamii 26, *27*
  glutinosa 26, *27*
  hians 24, 26, *27*
  horminum 26, *27*
  lavandulifolia 24
  mertaurea 26, *27*

neurepia 26, *27*
officinalis 24, *25*
  'Albiflora' 24, *25*
  'Icterina' 24, *25*
  'Purpurascens' 24, *25*
  'Tricolor' 24
patens 26
  'Cambridge Blue' 26
rutilans 27
sclarea 26
verticillata 26, *27*
Salvia 'Bluebeard' 26, *27*
Sambucus nigra 60, *61*
Sanicle 115
Sanicula europea 115
Sanguisorba minor 53
Santolina
  chamaecyparissus 74, *75*
  nana 75
  neapolitana 'Edward Bowles' 75
  serratifolia 75
Saponaria officinalis 144, *145*
Sarothamnus scoparius 87
Sassafras 180
Sassafras albidum 180
Satureja
  hortensis 45
  montana 45
  spicigera 45
Savory
  Creeping 45
  Summer 45
  Winter 45
Saw Wort 89
Saxifrage, Burnet 113
Scabious, Field 163
Scented Mayweed 67
Scotch Broom 87
Scopolia 135
Scopolia carniolica 135
Scrophularia
  auriculata 144, *145*
  nodosa 144, *145*
    'Variegata' 144, *145*
Scurvy Grass 106, *107*
Scutellaria lateriflora 100, *101*
Sea Buckthorn 64
Sea Holly 172, *173*
Sedum acre 52
Sedum album 52
Selfheal 136
  Cut-leaved 136
  Large 136
Senna, Tinnevelly 176, *177*
Serratula tinctoria 89
Shallon 114
Sheep's Sorrel 22
Shepherd's Purse 47
Silverweed 164
Silybum marianum 100
Sinapis alba 54, *55*
Sium sisarum 60, *61*
Skirret 60, *61*
Skullcap, Virginian *or* Mad-dog *100, 101*
Small Nettle 92, *93*
Smartweed 127
Symrnium
  olusatrum 60
  perfoliatum 60
Sneezewort 148
Soapwort 144, *145*
Solanum dulcamara 175
Soldiers and Sailors 95
Solidago
  canadensis 154, *155*
  virgaurea 154, *155*
Solomon's Seal 104
Sorrel
  Common *or* Garden 23
  French *or* Buckler-leaved 22, *23*
  Sheep's 22
Southern Wood 81
Spearmint *32, 33*
Spinach, Mountain 58
Spikenard 177
Spirea
  filipendula 150
  ulmaria 82
Spoonwort 106, *107*
Spring Beauty 46, *47*
Spring Pheasant's Eye 183

Spurge, Caper 132
Squirting Cucumber 171
Stachys officinalis 162
Stellaria media 47, *48*
Stemless Carline Thistle 173
Stinging Nettle 92
Stinking Cohosh 166
Stinking Iris 109
Stonecrop
  Biting 52
  White 52
Strawberry
  Alpine 65
  Wild 65
  Wood 65
Summer Savory 45
Sundew 164, *165*
Sunflower 56
Sweet Basil *42, 43*
Sweet Cicely 16
Sweet False Camomile 67
Sweet Flag 108, *109*
Sweet Laurel 13
Sweet Rocket 50
Sweet Violet 112, *113*
Sweet Woodruff 82, *83*
Symphytum
  bulbosum 94, *95*
  caucasicum 94, *95*
  ibiricum × *uplandicum* 'Hidcote Blue' 94
  officinale 94, *95*
  orientale 94, *95*
  tuberosum 95

Tagetes
  minuta 79
  patula 79
Tampala 55
Tanacetum
  cinerariifolium 151
  parthenium 142, *143*
    'Aurea' *143*
    'Flore Peno' *143*
  vulgare 150, *151*
  var. *crispum* 151
Tansy 150, *151*
  Curled 151
Taraxacum officinale 48, *49*
Tarragon
  French 36
  Russian 36
Tea, New Jersey 181
Tea, Oswego 66
Teasel 167
  Fuller's 167
Teucrium
  chamaedrys 160, *161*
  marum 161
  scorodonia 160, *161*
Thistle
  Blessed *or* Holy 172, *173*
  Carline 173
  Milk 100
  Stemless Carline 173
Thorn, Sallow 64
Thornapple 175
Three-cornered Leek 18, *19*
Thyme
  Basil 44
  Cat 161
  Garden 39, 40, 41
  Golden Lemon 39, 41
  Lemon 41
  Wild 38, *39*
Thymus
  azoricus 38
    'Broad Leaf' 39
  cilicicus 38, 41
  × *citriodorus* 41
    'Aureus' 40
    'Bertram Anderson' *39,* 41
    'Nyewoods' 40
    'Silver Posie' 40
    'Silver Queen' 40, *41*
    'Variegatus' 40, *41*
  comosus 40
  doerfleri 40, *41*
    'Bressingham Pink' 40, *41*
    'Doone Valley' 41

herba-barona 38, 39, 40
hirsutus 38
montanus 41
nitida 'Peter Davis' 40
odoratissimus 40
pallesianus 40
'Porlock' 40, *41*
praecox subsp. *articus 40, 41*
pseudo lanuginosus 38, 41
pulegioides 41
richardii subsp. *nitidus* 40
serpyllum
  'Coccineus Majus' *38, 39*
  'Lemon Curd' *39*
  'Snow Drift' 41
vulgaris 39, 40, 41
Tiarella cordifolia 100, *101*
Tilia europaea 66
Tinnevelly Senna 176, *177*
Toadflax 140
Tobacco 168
  Indian 163
Tormentil 164
Tragopogon pratensis 144, *145*
Traveller's Joy 178
Tree, Hemp 176
Tree Lupin 146
Tree Onion 21
Trigonella foenum-graecum 16, *17, 54, 55*
Trillium, Purple 90, *91*
Trillium erectum 90, *91*
Tropaeolum majus 50, 51
Tuberous Comfrey 94
Turkey Rhubarb 120
Tussilago farfara 92, *93*

Urtica
  dioica 92
  urens 92, *93*
  pilulifera 92, *93*

Vaccinium myrtillus 65
Valerian 134, *135*
  Red 59
Valeriana officinalis 134, *135*
Variegated Figwort 145
Variegated Ground Elder 107
Variegated Holly 185
Variegated Lemon Balm 133
Variegated Meadowsweet 82
Variegated Rue 131
Veratrum
  album 105
  viride 105
Verbascum
  phlomoides 128
  thapsus 128
Verbena
  × *hybrida* 'Silver Anne' 116, *117*
  officinalis 116
  'Sissinghurst' 116, *117*
  triphylla 116
Verbena, Lemon 116
Vervain 116
  Lemon 116
Vinca
  major 182
  minor 182
  rosea 182
Viola
  odorata 112, *113*
  tricolor 183
Violet, Sweet 112, *113*
Viper's Bugloss 112, *113*
Virginian Skullcap 100, *101*
Viscum album 184
Vitex agnus-castus 176

Wall Germander 160, *161*
Wall-pepper 52
Wallflower 110, *111*
Water Figwort 145
Water Mint 34, *35*
Water Pepper 127
Watercress 46
Weld 84, *85*
Welsh Onion 20, *21*
Western Wintergreen 114
White Bedstraw 85
White Bryony 169
White Comfrey 94, *95*

White Deadnettle 93
White False Hellebore 105
White Foxglove 138
White Henbane 158
White Horehound 156
White Hyssop 157
White Stonecrop 52
White Willow 98
Whortleberry 65
Wild *or* Wood Angelica 29
Wild Basil 44
Wild Bergamot 66
Wild Briar 68
Wild Catmint 70, *71*
Wild Celery 53
Wild Ginger

American 86, 87
European 86
Wild Mallow 152, *153*
Wild Marjoram 42, *43*
Wild Indigo 86
Wild Oregano 43
Wild Pansy 183
Wild Rose 68
Wild Strawberry 65
Wild Succory 49
Wild Thyme *38*, 39
Willow, White 98
Winter Cress 49
Winter Savory 45
Wintergreen *or* Creeping Wintergreen 114

Western 114
Witch Hazel 181
Woad 84, *85*
Wood Angelica 28
Wood Avens 126, *127*
Wood Calamint 70
Wood Garlic 19
Wood Strawberry 65
Woodruff
  Dyer's 85
  Sweet 83
Woodsage *160*, 161
Woody Nightshade 175
Woolly Foxglove 139
Wormseed, American *58*, 59

Wormwood *80*, 81
  Roman 81
Wort, Saw 89
Wych Hazel 180, *181*

Yarrow 160
Yellow Camomile 89
Yellow Flag 109
Yellow Foxglove 139
Yellow Gentian 159
Yellow Melilot 148
Yellow Rocket 49
Yellow Weed 84, *85*

Zanthoxylum americanum 177